The Nevada County Chronicles 1845-1851

The Nevada County Chronicles

Gold Diggers and Camp Followers

1845=1851

David Allan Comstock

Comstock Bonanza Press

GRASS VALLEY • CALIFORNIA

PUBLISHED BY COMSTOCK BONANZA PRESS

18919 WILLIAM QUIRK MEMORIAL DRIVE

GRASS VALLEY, CALIFORNIA 95945

MANUFACTURED IN THE UNITED STATES OF AMERICA

FIRST PAPERBACK EDITION 1988

LIBRARY OF CONGRESS CATALOGING IN PUBLICATION DATA

COMSTOCK, DAVID A.

GOLD DIGGERS AND CAMP FOLLOWERS, 1845–1851

(THE NEVADA COUNTY CHRONICLES; 1)

BIBLIOGRAPHY: P. 392.

INCLUDES INDEX.

1. NEVADA COUNTY (CALIF.)—HISTORY.

2. NEVADA COUNTY (CALIF.)—GOLD DISCOVERIES

3. NISENAN INDIANS—HISTORY.

4. FRONTIER AND PIONEER LIFE—CALIFORNIA—NEVADA COUNTY.

I. TITLE.

II. SERIES.

F868.N5C65   1982   979.4'3703   82-8176

ISBN 0-933994-02-8

ISBN 0-933994-08-7 (PBK.)

without

ARDIS HATTEN COMSTOCK

there would have been no book

CONTENTS

LIST OF MAPS

LIST OF ILLUSTRATIONS

ACKNOWLEDGMENTS

*T*HERE IS no best way to say thanks. Acknowledgments are a way of repaying people and institutions with non-negotiable words for services rendered. As Elizabeth Barrett Browning might have asked—but did not—"How do I use thee? Let me count the ways." Fortunately, some are recompensed by an employer for doing what I require—librarians, for instance. For their cheerfulness as well as their excellence and professionalism, I thank Frances Burton and Dorothy Boettner of the Nevada City branch of the Nevada County Library, and Grace Imoto of the California State Library. I also thank the many volunteers who staff the Sacramento library of the Church of Latter Day Saints.

Russell E. Bidlack kindly gave me permission to quote from the letters of David McCollum and Caleb Ormsby which were previously published in his book, *Letters Home: The Story of Ann Arbor's Forty-Niners.* The words of James Wilkins in Chapter 18 are quoted with the permission of the Henry E. Huntington Library and Art Gallery, publisher of *An Artist on the Overland Trail: The 1849 Diary and Sketches of James F. Wilkins.* I am indebted to Frances G. Long, Fred Searls III, and William H. Miller, Jr., for permission to use letters of the Niles and Searls families.

I have made much use of Rolfe family information provided by Catherine J. Webb, both in her books and in her correspondence with me. Phyllis Gernes steered me in the direction of John Steele's memoirs, *In Camp and Cabin,* at an important point in my research. Rebecca and Kevin Dwan read and criticized my earliest efforts, as did Susan Wolbarst, Janet Haseley and Frances Long, all of whom offered much useful advice, resulting in a restructuring of most of what I had written.

Later drafts were read by Archie and Maggie Caldwell, Janet Haseley, Frances Long, Hank Searls, Doris Green Searls and others. The Caldwells convinced me that I was on the right track, an opinion that found enough echoes to encourage me to plunge ahead. Richard Smith read Chapter 1 and was especially helpful with suggestions about *nisenan* customs and language.

My mother has had a greater share of responsibility in this book than the rearing of its author. A few years ago she wrote a biography of General Mariano Vallejo (*Vallejo and the Four Flags;* Comstock Bonanza Press, 1979) which I helped her produce and sell. Her success encouraged me to proceed with my own project, and because the pen and ink drawings which my father created for her book contributed to its success, I felt I could do no better here than to follow the examples set by my parents.

I have saved my editor, Lorna Price Dittmer, until the end because she is bound to have the last word anyway. But there is another and better reason: it was she who put the magic into this mix, announcing that we were about to enjoy every kind of success. She did this so often and so well that all of us began to believe her and so we all worked even harder. Whether or not all the good things happen which she predicts, Lorna is one of the very best things to happen to me. I enjoy sending my work off to her because I know that it will be returned in far better condition than it departed.

As I look over these paragraphs I see that I have included more women than men, which doesn't surprise me. That's how I like it. And for those of you who may ask (as Lorna did), "What about your wife, you clod!?" I repeat the words of dedication: *without Ardis Hatten Comstock there would have been no book.*

D. A. C.
Grass Valley, 1982

NEVADA CITY, CALIFORNIA (1852)

INTRODUCTION

*T*HE STORY of the pioneers and miners who invaded the lands of the *nisenan* Indians between 1845 and 1850 and created a political subdivision known today as Nevada County, California, is an exciting and fascinating part of the mosaic of California history. The politics and culture of California for a long time took their color from events in the gold camps; Nevada County in particular became an important locus for men and women whose concerns and preoccupations eventually helped frame the identity of the emerging State. Traces of the color persist to this day, despite veneers of convention that time has overlaid upon the picturesque, dynamic, and often violent society of those early days.

The sand and quartz of Nevada County were among the lodestones that drew the most sudden westward emigration in the nation's history. Set off by the discovery of gold at Sutter's Mill in 1848, the movement became one of the most potent democratizing agencies Americans had yet experienced. Virtually no stratum of society was unaffected by the call to adventure, opportunity, and hope for undreamed-of wealth. In the matrix of these considerations, and in that of the history of California more particularly, no one has recorded the important roles played by Nevada County pioneers. That they merit their own story is unquestionable; that they have been neglected and forgotten for a hundred years is, to me, unfathomable.

I am a second generation Californian, but until I married Ardis Hatten in 1967 I was ignorant of Nevada County history and its import. From her and others who grew up here, I soon learned enough to pique my curiosity. This interest grew when in 1971 we moved into Ardis's family home near the town of Grass Valley. It is only a short distance from this house to the homestead established by her grandparents in 1898 on Sontag Hill (a current misspelling of the Sonntag family name).

Past this homestead winds the road to the former mining camps of You Bet and Red Dog. The road is paved only as far as the last cluster of mailboxes west of the bridge over Greenhorn Creek. Beyond that point the road is dirt and gravel. If you follow the road a few miles to the vanished site of You Bet you will be rewarded with a breathtaking view of the You Bet hydraulic diggings. This immense scar on an otherwise beautifully wooded mountain landscape stretches grandly north and south between the road on its western rim and the white cliffs of Chalk Bluff on the eastern boundary. Despite Nature's valiant effort to reclaim the rocky basin, it remains a shocking reminder of the environmental havoc created by the removal of millions of tons of earth in the ninety-year-long search for gold.

Above Chalk Bluff the forest begins again, although these trees are new growth, and nothing like the vast, dense forest which once shaded arriving emigrants. From the Chalk Bluff Ridge one can look across Steephollow Canyon to Lowell Hill, where the old California Trail led thousands of newcomers down the ridge to Johnson's Ranch and Sutter's Fort.

When Ardis and I built our house in 1973–74 we chose a site in this rugged and somewhat remote area. We built the house with our own hands, and today we cook and heat with wood cut from our land. We read by the light of oil lamps; kerosene is hauled in with our other supplies over the same unpaved roads used long ago by Ardis's family to haul lumber in wagons from a steam-powered sawmill high in the mountains.

The people who formerly occupied these lands are often in our thoughts, miners as well as members of the nisenan tribes who left behind grinding rocks, tools, and stone flakes to remind us of their tenure. To learn more about these vanished neighbors I consulted books, librarians, and local historians. But the more I learned, the more I desired to know, and I found my sources waning at the very time my curiosity grew most intense. I was beginning to sense the existence of an exciting story. In the spring of 1977 I decided to find and write it.

My first resolution was to write about people rather than historical events. I wanted to tell the story by writing about real people, however, and two persons whose histories intrigued me were Tallman Rolfe and Niles Searls. Each was born approximately a hundred years before me. I found myself relating closely to many of their early experiences, for the time I spent as a soldier in strange lands was similar to that of gold rush sojourners in the recently occupied territory of Alta California. With one important difference: soldiers must obey a strong authority imposed upon them, whereas California adventurers were free of most controls except those created by self-discipline. Because some were unable or unwilling to rule themselves, communities eventually were forced to impose public controls; but for a short time, self-discipline was the most important stabilizing influence in gold camps.

My earliest introduction to Rolfe, Searls, and other pioneers was in the pages of *History of Nevada County, California*, published in 1880 by Thompson and West. This particular volume, full of errors as it is, nevertheless contains more useful information than any other single source. Its worst failing was the absence of an index, so Ardis and I compiled one which had about 7,500 listings and was eighty-five pages long. One day I came across a booklet entitled *Coast to Coast by Railroad: The Journey of Niles Searls, May 1869*. This account of his return to California twenty years after he first crossed the plains on horseback contains letters he wrote to his wife while he was a passenger on the first transcontinental rail trip from New York to California. The book's editor, Mrs. Frances G. Long, granddaughter of Charles Niles and grandniece of Cornelia and Mary Niles (all three cousins of Niles Searls), stated that she possessed "letters and many other family papers."

I wrote to her at once, requesting information. Her reply was friendly and chatty, but not encouraging. "I must tell you," she said, "that I'm working sporadically at editing some things and am in a quandary as to what information to share." I wrote once more, and then we were contacted by a California couple who identified themselves as friends of Mrs. Long. They came to visit us and among the subjects discussed was the New York village of Rensselaerville, where Niles Searls had lived and gone to school before going to California. Mrs. Long, I learned, now lives in the house where Niles studied law in 1848. In many ways this village in the Helderberg Mountains and the town of Nevada in the Sierra Nevada resemble one another. I discovered that much of Nevada County's charm had been transplanted from New York.

In August 1978 Mrs. Long's daughter, Janet Haseley, wrote to me from her home in North Carolina:

You have no idea what a job you have set for us in asking for a look at some of the old family letters. There are hundreds and my grandmother started sorting through some over forty years ago, my mother has dabbled with a few and every summer when I am visiting in New York I get inspired to try to go through some and work on family trees, etc. It is a monumental task, and far more time-consuming than any of us realized. . . . Even though my grandmother had semi-sorted the originals, there still is no way to know what material we have without reading over the letters and neither my mother nor I seem to have found time for this. You understand, of course, that there would be no point in sending you copies of all the letters she has, and some are from entirely different people, such as her grandfather Charles Niles' letters home when he was in the Civil War.

We're sorry to be so slow in replying, and sorry to be of so little assistance right now. We ARE working on it, however.

In a postscript Janet added, "Ran across Niles Searls' ten commandments and rule of conduct written in 1846, and some Cornelia [Niles] wrote for herself when inspired by his . . . Thought you might like to see both, and am enclosing a copy, as they cast a bit of light on their personalities. The more I read of Cornelia's letters, the more I like her sense of humor. Some letters to her from Niles are also light in touch, but she is my favorite." Anxious to read these tantalizing documents, I swiftly riffled through the envelope. Finding nothing, I turned back to the letter and saw a penciled note at the bottom which read: "can't find copy—will send when I get home."

More time passed without further word from Janet or her mother. As 1978 came to a close, we received a copy of *The Haseley Herald*, Janet and Ed's annual letter to friends and relatives, which described the family's rather strenuous activities in 1978. A handwritten note in the margin concluded with this query: "how about a hand-delivery? How far is it and how complicated to reach Grass Valley from San Francisco? We leave here 6 am Jan. 21 and return 8 pm Jan. 28. Might be able to see you one day the 26th or 27th. Or do you ever get to S.F.?" We learned that Ed Haseley would be attending a symposium at San Jose State University, and Janet was coming along with some of the family letters.

We met in San Jose and spent most of one day getting acquainted and looking at old letters. It was an exciting day, and the weeks that followed were equally so. I wrote Janet in February 1979 to describe my pleasure:

After we returned home it began to snow and we were snowed in for about a week, which was all the excuse I needed to entirely neglect all of my other work so that I could work uninterrupted on transcribing the letters into typed form. Not only were the letters delightful, but they managed to tell me almost all the things I wanted to know! Talk about the answer to a biographer's dream—this is it. . . . Of course, now that you have whetted my appetite, I am wanting more.

About twice each year, packages of letters continued to arrive by mail. Amazingly, the quality remained high, the contents astounding, more so than one should reasonably expect; eventually I received more than 400 letters from Mrs. Long. (The equally astonishing postscript to this story is that in October 1981, while the manuscript was being edited by Lorna Price, I received a letter from William H. Miller Jr. of New York, who had heard of my project from Janet. He is a descendant of Emily Niles, youngest sister of Cornelia, Mary, and Charles—and he, too, has hundreds of letters which dovetail with the correspondence owned by Mrs. Long. Since that time he has sent me a number of them, two of which have been incorporated into this book; the rest, which have to do mostly with Cornelia Niles and her future husband, will become an integral part of my second book in this series.)

As for Tallman Rolfe, the other principal character, I am greatly indebted to Catherine J. Webb, who has written two books about her ancestors, including Tallman's brother Ianthus, who came to Nevada City in 1851. In those volumes, *A Family History of California,* and *History Reconstructed: The Story of Tallman, Ianthus, Horace, and Samuel Rolfe,* she has recorded much valuable and interesting material, which has been useful to me. However, because much of her narrative lies outside the time frame of this book, I had to rely on my own sleuthing to fill in many of the blank spots. But thanks to Catherine, who has become a friend as the result of our mutual fascination with the Rolfe family, Tallman will have a great deal more to say for himself in the second book. We were unable to locate any correspondence for the 1845–51 period, but many letters exist for the 1850s and 1860s when Tallman was a newspaper editor in Nevada City, California.

At first I was very unsure of being able to unearth enough accurate material to permit me to write about particular Indians, so I was pleased when Wema, chief of the local nisenan tribe, thrust his way into the picture. Because many miners knew him and were impressed sufficiently to record their encounters, I soon found myself with a third major character to represent the other population present in Nevada County's future borders. Although his name has been spelled in many ways (including "Weimar," also the name of a nearby town in Placer County, and "Weymeh," which appeared on a poster in 1852), I have chosen Wema as the closest approximation to the nisenan name, when pronounced in the Spanish fashion.

Serious problems arise from the lack of written language among California Indians, at least in the sense of European record-keeping. Oral records have disappeared as a result of war, disease, and relocation which destroyed the tribe's identity, and by the insistence of whites that Indian children speak only English. There remain only records kept by outsiders who at best were careless and uninformed, at worst were vicious and hostile. But Wema forced himself into my consciousness and caused me to view these recorded events from a new and larger perspective.

In order to communicate this awareness I have used a technique which is valid in fiction but controversial in a volume of history. Given all the facts known, and what I could glean from modern experts about local nisenan culture, I have tried to imagine what Wema, a man of intelligence and political acumen, would have thought and done. I endeavored to construct an awareness of his thoughts and actions and those of his kinsmen as they struggled to cope with problems of survival completely alien to any they had known before.

I expect some readers will argue strenuously against this approach, and I anticipate, understand, and respect their reasons. Nevertheless, I leave it to other readers to decide whether my method of narration achieves a useful and proper end. To me it seems logical to assume that even if Wema and his friends did not behave exactly as portrayed, what they actually did could not have differed significantly.

In this first volume of *The Nevada County Chronicles* a number of people appear whose ambitions and dreams were altered dramatically by the discovery of gold at Sutter's Mill in 1848. Their lives become more closely intertwined as events move forward, but the whole tale cannot be recounted in one volume. The second will describe life in Nevada County in the 1850s, the marriages of its young men to eastern sweethearts, and the growing political and editorial prowess of Niles and Tallman, as well as that of their new friends, John McConnell, William M. Stewart, Aaron Sargent, and Edward D. Baker. For the time being, however, let us examine what came before their fame and fortune.

PUBLISHER'S NOTE: *Brides of the Gold Rush 1851–1859*, the second volume in this series, was published in 1987 by Comstock Bonanza Press, 18919 William Quirk Memorial Drive, Grass Valley, CA 95945.

NISENAN COUNCIL MEETING

CHAPTER 1

FIRST INVASION

January–February 1845

I

FOR A LONG TIME Jepe stood quietly and watched from his place of concealment. The snow-covered meadow which absorbed his attention lay on the opposite side of a river whose icy waters rumbled swiftly through a boulder-strewn canyon. Beyond the meadow was a forest, and beyond the forest the high peaks of the Sierra Nevada sparkled brightly against a backdrop of cerulean blue sky.

The clear winter sun was so bright that Jepe had cut narrow viewing slits in a thin piece of bark to protect his eyes against the glare. Although it was uncomfortably cool in the shadow of the trees where he hid, he was afraid to stand too long in the sun, where he might have been observed. In the sharp wind he clutched the fur cape more tightly round his body. He realized too well how ridiculously inadequate his garments were for exploring the high country, but under normal circumstances he should not have been there at all.

The *nisenan* tribes spent their winters far below the snow line, where game was plentiful and temperatures mild. There was no reason to endure such discomfort were it not that Jepe had been ordered on a special assignment. He had been selected because he was Chief Wema's favorite runner and reporter. His name, Jepe, meant "winged" in the nisenan language.

When a break occurred in the winter storms in mid-January, Wema had asked Jepe to investigate a strange rumor which had reached the ears of the chief. The report was most disturbing, for it raised serious questions about the future security of his people. It had its beginnings at the fort of Johann Sutter, whom the nisenan called "Sutel."

"Sutel" was one of the *wolesem*, a white foreigner, and like many of his kind on the other side of the great valley, he had purchased slaves from chiefs of nearby villages. Although permitted outside the fort walls during the day in order to labor in the fields, at night they were locked up in small dirty rooms without latrines or bathing facilities. Those who tried to escape were beaten or killed.

It was from these slaves that the free nisenan learned about the white intruders who came to the fort after leaving their wives and children in the mountains. According to the informants, the white men had not gone back for their families as one might suppose, but had joined a war party being formed by Captain Sutter. Now they and many of the whites from the fort had gone south to fight the *panjol* warriors, those who called themselves *Californios*.

Meanwhile, the white women and children were said to be camped somewhere near the headwaters of the river which ran through Wema's territory. It was called *hin-nise,* and only the nisenan lived where it flowed. However, Sutel had called it by a new name, arrogantly and ignorantly labeling it "Juba," after the nisenan village which faced its mouth.

Jepe was satisfied at last that he could learn no more from his examination of the area. The sun had now dropped behind the mountains which lined the Pacific horizon, causing the air to grow colder yet. As he prepared to descend to warmer elevations and home, Jepe's mind was full of the strange sights and sounds from across the hin-nise. Soon the forest was silent except for the crisp rhythm of his snowshoes moving quickly down the hill.

Largest of all the structures in Wema's village was the *kum*. Whereas most private dwellings were steeply conical in shape and no more than fifteen feet in diameter, the kum was a round house nearly forty feet across, covered by a low-pitched roof. Erected over a round pit four feet deep, its roof was a circle of pine saplings whose butt ends rested firmly on the upper edge of the excavation, while their upper ends lay across beams supported by forked oak posts. At the center a gap in the logs provided a smokehole for the fire.

Around the inside of the excavation, a row of short poles had been driven into the ground to line and reinforce the earthen wall. The kum was a comfortable building. The roof was insulated and waterproofed with layers of brush, grass, pine needles and dirt. The floor was thickly carpeted with piles of fresh aromatic pine boughs, which were frequently replaced. Even in the coldest weather one could sleep here without clothing, for in the firepit at the center of the kum a fire burned night and day during the cold weather.

The fire also served as a calendar during the winter, which was considered to be six months long. In each village one old man was assigned the task of recording the passage of time by means of six identically sized pieces of green oak. Each stick measured about three inches long and represented a single month. Every night the old man used one stick to stir the fire three times. When the stick had been reduced to a certain predetermined length the month had ended. On the following night the old man would begin to stir with a new stick.

Although it was used sometimes to accommodate visitors in the winter, the kum was used chiefly as a meeting place. Shortly after Jepe had been dispatched to the mountains, the elders and members of the council had gathered here at Wema's invitation. For two days they had discussed the stories from Sutter's Fort. Now, while they waited for Jepe to return, subchief Walupa prepared the ceremonial pipe for smoking.

He began by taking a few dry leaves of *pan*, the local tobacco, and rubbed them between the palms of his hands until they were finely pulverized. Next, he filled the pipe's soapstone bowl, which had been carved to hold just enough *pan* to go once around the circle. He extracted a small live coal carefully from the fire and placed it on top of the tobacco. After taking two or three puffs, Walupa wiped the foot-long stem clean with his hand and passed it to his neighbor.

Suddenly the village dogs began to bark and the soft hum of voices outside the kum grew louder and more excited. "I think he has returned," Wema calmly announced. Outside, the people stopped their activities to watch Jepe enter the village. Ignoring them, the runner jogged toward the kum, coming at it from the east, for its door faced the rising sun.

Thrusting aside the large slabs of bark which covered the entrance, he stepped inside. His compact body shone with perspiration in the light of the fire. He still breathed quickly and heavily, and the strain of his journey showed in his face. Gradually the rhythmic rise and fall of his chest slowed. Jepe saw that Wema was signaling for him to join the council by the fire.

Not a word had yet been spoken, and even after he sat beside them nothing was said. Despite their great curiosity, heightened by two days of speculation, they were waiting for Jepe to regain his breath and composure. It was Wema who finally broke the silence, and then merely to make polite inquiries about the runner's family. The replies came softly and with equal politeness. Only when he was quite satisfied that Jepe was completely at ease did Wema refer to the great matter.

"You have had a long journey."

"That is true."

"Did you bring it to a successful conclusion?"

"I was able to observe many things. Perhaps they will be of some interest."

"Please tell us of the things you observed."

"First," began Jepe, "I went to the place where the wolesem were seen coming out of the mountains in the month before this. Where there was no snow on the ground I was able to follow their trail. They seemed to prefer the upper ridges, so when I reached the snowline I continued to travel by that route. I was not sure that I had chosen the right trail until I saw smoke from their fires.

"At last I came to a place where I could see their camp. I saw two houses made of logs, in the wolesem fashion. I saw many children—maybe twelve, maybe fifteen. From within the houses I could hear the cries of more than one baby."

Now Wema interrupted:

"Adults—how many adults?"

"I saw a man and a boy cutting wood. I also saw a man who appears to be ill. He cannot move about easily."

"You saw no other men?"

"I saw no other men."

"And women?"

"I saw five women. They came out at different times, never all at once, so it is hard to be certain—but I believe there were five."

"What else did you see?"

Jepe hesitated, as if reluctant to continue. Then, with a sigh, he added, "I also saw five wagons."

"Wagons?" Disbelief rose in Wema's voice. "How can there be wagons in the mountains? Wagons surely cannot travel in such country! What are you saying?"

Jepe shrugged. "I cannot say how they came to be there. I only know that they are there. And that there are no animals to pull them."

Wema and the others exchanged puzzled looks. Jepe's words had introduced a mystery which none could explain.

"Did you see any wolesem weapons?" asked Wema, changing the subject. "Do they have any rifles?"

"I did see two rifles. There may be others inside the houses."

"Is there any more that you wish to say to us?"

"I don't think so. That is what I saw."

With the announcement that he had concluded his report, Jepe's part in the proceedings was finished and the council members clapped and shouted their approval in the customary manner. After he left the building, a new pipeful of pan was prepared and passed, which gave the men time to consider what they had heard.

As they smoked, Wema considered the men he had chosen to meet with. Some had short tempers and must be handled with care. Others had trouble making decisions, either because they were too ready or too slow. Some, he knew, would try to urge the group to unwise moves. He sighed, knowing that only he would be held responsible for the consequences of their words and actions.

Although Wema was a man of middle age, he was younger than several of the council members. No longer so active as in his earlier years, he had gained some weight in the time since he had been chosen chief, or *huk*. Tall by nisenan standards, Wema stood nearly five feet nine in his deerhide shoes. His skin was deeply tanned, his face neatly plucked. His chest was deep, almost barrel shaped, and his shoulders broad.

At one time, before his elevation to chief, Wema had enjoyed participating in contests with other men of the tribe. Now he could not afford to do so, for it was not wise to provide opportunities for challenge to those who were ambitious or opposed his views. If he had to compete, he preferred to choose his own ground, contest and time. There were already too many occasions, such as now, when he was required to deal with problems not of his choosing.

Wema eyed one of the younger members of the council; if anyone were going to create a problem, this was the man. He hoped trouble could be avoided. With a shrug of his shoulders, Wema turned to the oldest member and said, "I'd like to hear your words, uncle."

The old tribesman acknowledged the request with a sideways glance and a slow nod of his head. His voice was high and thin.

"I remember when the wolesem first came to the valley below," he began. "I didn't see them with my own eyes, but I spoke to those who had. At the time, we supposed they were some kind of devil or evil spirit, so we called them *ysim*. First to arrive were the men we now know as *panjol wolesem* who speak the language of *español*. The best that can be said of them is that they chose not to inhabit our regions. Nothing good can be said about the *janki wolesem* who came later. Ysim!" hissed the old man. "Devils they surely are. We can expect much trouble if they invade our territory."

The others listened in silence. A few heads nodded as if to agree with the old man's remarks. Then Wema motioned to the second member of the circle. He was the same age as the chief and he spoke with quiet anger:

"Before the time when I was a man, the wolesem were almost unknown in this part of the world. As children we had heard stories about them, but did not know if they were spirits or real people. When the wolesem Sutel came to the great valley, he caused our cousins to lose their freedom. Although he claims to be a huk, he is a false chief who doesn't listen to the people. The valley people are his slaves, and I fear the wolesem will try to enslave us. Because their weapons are so powerful, they may succeed."

The third speaker was more optimistic. "Perhaps," he suggested, "the wolesem will not wish to stay, for they have always preferred to live in the flat lands. They will probably leave when their men come back from the war in the south." Others spoke when he was finished, often echoing the remarks of previous speakers. Presently it was the turn of the youngest of the council, the man whom Wema regarded with apprehension.

"Everyone agrees that the wolesem are natural enemies of the nisenan. If they come into our territory things will go badly for our people. Since the first step has been taken by them, we must act quickly to make sure it is the last. It is obvious what we must do. Before their warriors return from the battles in the south, we must attack their camp in the mountains. If we delay a single day, we may miss our chance, for we cannot know when they will return. Perhaps some will say that it is no very great deed to kill women and children, but surely it is a wonderful thing to save our own people! If we do not attack while they are weak, we will become their victims when they are strong. *We have no choice!*" He shouted his final words defiantly in Wema's direction and it was evident that his fervor had communicated itself to others in the group.

The atmosphere in the roundhouse had suddenly become so charged that Wema felt the meeting was about to escape his control. But his face remained impassive. Only one more speaker remained before it would be Walupa's turn. To Wema's great relief, the next speaker urged caution and ended by expressing his desire that they would consider all the alternatives carefully before reaching a decision.

"I've listened to your words with interest," began Walupa. "Much of what you say is well spoken. I cannot disagree when you say that the wolesem are dangerous neighbors. Our gray-haired uncle speaks the truth when he calls them devils, for that is what they surely seem to be. That's why we must be cautious."

Wema wondered whether Walupa was merely stalling for time. He appeared to have nothing new to say. Wema listened as the subchief continued:

"If you recall what we have been taught since childhood, you will remember that devils are not the same as ordinary people, for the reason that they are not human. It takes both skill and magic to outwit a devil—powerful magic. With a devil, nothing is what it seems to be, so one must always be suspicious, always on guard. Although there may seem to be times when the devil is weak and vulnerable, we must take care that it is not an illusion. A devil may pretend to be at a disadvantage in order to fool us."

Wema knew at once that Walupa had found the key which would unlock the puzzle. He felt a surge of affection and respect for his friend and ally, who once more had demonstrated his great value. Walupa's words had made an impression on the council and now it was up to Wema to persuade them. Although he had never once betrayed his inner turmoil, the cool presence which the others observed was now matched by the total confidence he sensed within. Wema began to explain to the council how they must act:

"We are dealing with a dangerous opponent who will try to provoke us to haste and carelessness. He'll try to confuse our thinking, to divide us, turn us against one another. He may wear many faces, assume many forms. But we have our own weapons and our own magic. At times like these we must trust our spirit friends to help us. We have in our village the finest magician alive—our *jom* undoubtedly understands the white devil and will advise us how to proceed. I'll consult with him this very night and tomorrow we shall meet again. In the meantime, it's useless for us to talk until we hear his advice."

Although the youngest councilman was not pleased to realize that he had been dismissed, he had no choice but to accept. Much as he disagreed with the proposal, he was not anxious to appear to oppose the jom. No one wished to be at odds with the shaman.

By the time Walupa had found the jom and brought him to the chief's house, Wema's wives were ready to serve them supper. There was plenty of *choja*, the thick, rich soup made from black oak acorns. The soup was cold, but the freshly baked bread was hot to the touch and tantalizingly aromatic. Walupa took his place beside Wema, taking care not to brush against the jom. To touch the shaman, even accidentally, could result in death unless corrective measures were taken to reverse the accident of bad medicine.

With a grunt of pleasure, Walupa reached for a loaf of acorn bread and sniffed its fragrance before thrusting it into his mouth. As he bit into the firm, grainy texture of the baked acorn meal, he felt once more keen good fortune that he had been born nisenan. One should never value too lightly the worth of such simple but priceless pleasures as a tasty meal shared with good companions in a weathertight and comfortable shelter.

The shaman was seasoning his soup with seeds and roasted insects when Walupa suddenly exclaimed:

"Hey, Wema, do you remember when we were boys, how we used to hunt gophers together? Those were really great times! Sometimes I wish that's all we had to do, even today—just go out and have good times."

Wema's face became animated and he nodded his head in vigorous agreement. "I wish I had a gopher to eat right now, but they're too far down in the ground, waiting for the long days to wake them up."

The shaman ignored them, continuing to eat. Suddenly, Wema wished he hadn't asked Walupa to bring him—not yet, at least. He would have preferred to eat alone with Walupa and forget for a time the unpleasant matter which lay ahead. With the jom right here beside them it was impossible to forget. The thought made him frown, which in turn brought a cloud to Walupa's face, and both resumed eating in silence. Finally, Wema set his empty bowl on the floor and turned his thoughts to the shaman.

His mind went back to the time when the jom had been just another youngster, without special powers of any kind. Then one day he said he had dreamt that spirits had come and told him that he was to become a shaman. From that day on his whole life had changed. He had gone to study for several years with an older shaman, and continued to have visions and dreams and visits from the spirit world.

Eventually he began to work alone, establishing his own practice. He knew how to gather herbs, prepare and prescribe medicines, and the proper ways of healing. He also had learned how to kill, for the true work of the jom was life and death. He did not kill in the usual human ways, but in mysterious and magical ones, incomprehensible to laymen. He could cause one person or an entire family to die without ever actually touching them.

The shaman was sometimes hired to get rid of troublemakers, or retained by a family to kill those who had wronged them. However, regardless of whether he was hired to cure or kill, the jom was never paid for his services unless he was successful. But despite enormous power, life was not easy or happy for him. He was denied the privilege of marrying or sleeping with women, because his touch could easily destroy the object of his affection. Nor could he consume meat, salt, or grease, which were like poisons for him. He was not even safe from retaliation, especially if surprised by assassins, for should a victim's family decide to have him killed, no one would come to his aid. The price of being feared is that one is secretly hated. His killers would not be punished.

Wema was aware that much of the jom's magic was no more than tricks performed by sleight-of-hand, but there was much more that could not be explained so easily. His power in some respects rivalled that of the chief, so it was important to maintain a friendly relationship, with each respecting the prerogatives of the other. Nevertheless, Wema always felt uneasy in the presence of the medicine man and never took him fully into his confidence. Because it was difficult to judge how far the shaman could be trusted, it was Wema's practice to reveal to him no more than he needed to know.

"I'm pleased you could spend the evening with us," he said at last. "On a long night it's good to be in the company of the friends of one's youth—such as you and Walupa." He added the last in case the jom had missed his point, for Wema knew that the shaman believed himself not well liked.

"I'm pleased that you should say so," replied the shaman. "Not many people look on my profession with such discernment as Chief Wema reveals. It is the sad truth that most do not see the jom as their friend. I carry a heavy responsibility and there are times when I think I should like to live simply, as others do. But then the spirits remind me that it is not for me to decide, that I have been chosen for my task. I must accept my fate with humility. So it's a comfort to hear you speak of me as your friend." The shaman permitted a small smile to settle briefly on his usually impassive face.

"I've heard it said that shamans are sometimes able to throw poison across hills or mountains. Is this true?"

"I've heard of such feats, but I'm sorry to say that I've yet to witness such an act. Whether it is possible to curve magic over or around obstacles such as hills is hard to know. I, however, have thrown poison for as far as the eye could see."

"You've done it yourself?"

"Indeed I have."

Wema shook his head in wonder. "What about throwing poison over an entire village—can that be done?"

"Oh, definitely. Yes, that's something I witnessed personally during my apprenticeship. The fine old man who was my teacher once destroyed a village just like that!" The shaman clapped his hands with startling percussion. "Not one person survived."

"A whole village? It amazes me what your kind is capable of. Doesn't it amaze you, Walupa?"

"It's pretty frightening, if you ask me."

"I agree, it would be frightening if this power were in the wrong hands. We can thank our good spirits that we have a jom who is responsible as well as clever."

Actually, Wema was rather disturbed by the shaman's replies, despite the fact that nothing had been said much beyond what the chief had expected to hear. Nevertheless, it was unnerving to sit beside one who could speak with such sober assurance about the destruction of entire villages. Wema would have preferred not to talk about such matters, but at present he felt he had no alternative.

"Suppose a jom had never visited a village," he suggested. "Could he work magic on the place without actually being there?"

"No, he would have to visit the place at least once. After that, he could retreat some distance before throwing the poison, but first he must go there."

Although this was not the answer Wema had hoped to hear, it came as no surprise. Complicated magic was required to solve complex problems, he guessed. Well, if the shaman could walk on fire, and that Wema had seen for himself, he supposed that a walk across the snows would be no worse. One more thing might help, however.

"I suppose it's not beyond the jom's powers to become invisible?" he asked, hopefully.

"It has happened on one or two occasions. However, I must warn you that the fees for the acts of magic we have been discussing are very large." The shaman looked directly into Wema's eyes. "I assume this conversation has a purpose."

"Perhaps. How large is *very* large?"

"That depends. How many people might be involved?"

"Let's say twenty-five. Or is that too many?"

"No. Is this village nearby? Would I know the victims?"

"The place is about two days' travel from here. I doubt you would know anyone."

"Excellent. That way is better. It seems to make things harder when you're dealing with persons you've known for years."

"I can well imagine. Well, it's not likely you'd know them, because they're all wolesem."

The shaman's features froze.

"Wolesem?" He said the word softly, scarcely more than a whisper.

Wema watched the color disappear from the jom's face. Never before had he observed the shaman in such an unguarded moment. Wema was careful to conceal his grim satisfaction in having forced the man to share his own discomfort. But he knew that now was no time to exploit this weakness. He could not risk losing the shaman's services either because of fear or humiliation.

"Wolesem?" he repeated. "A wolesem village?"

"Yes, wolesem." Wema arched his eyebrows in mock surprise. "Why, will that make a difference?"

"I—I don't know. I've never heard of nisenan medicine being used on the wolesem. Perhaps it would work, but until now, no one has ever proposed such a thing."

"Well, now Wema has."

"I see." The shaman struggled for composure.

"Now I will tell you exactly what I have in mind. It's not absolutely necessary that the wolesem should die. They could become ill or simply go away."

Wema saw that the shaman's active mind had come alive. Color was returning to his face, and although Wema had relished his knowledge of the other's fear, for the sake of his plan he was reassured by this evidence that the medicine man had not lost heart.

"You said twenty-five?" asked the shaman.

"Right."

"Men?"

"Two men—five women—the rest are children."

"Ah. The object is to cause these women and children—and two men—to leave, is that correct?"

"Yes, that's it. Can you do it?"

"I think so. Yes, I am sure. But it will cost a great deal. A very great deal."

Wema nodded solemnly, then said, "Let's talk about that for a moment. I'm sure you realize that some things in this world are above price, isn't that so?"

"Above price? I'm afraid I don't understand."

"Let me give you an example: don't you agree that to save our people is a thing above price? Wouldn't you be willing to contribute your skill to save the lives of all your people?"

"Is that what I would accomplish?"

"Exactly. If you succeed, every nisenan who ever lives will owe you a debt."

"Please explain further. What kind of debt would they owe me?"

"They would owe you perpetual gratitude. They would remember you with love and affection forever."

"Forever?"

Wema could sense the shaman's fascinated speculation about such a miraculous change of status—he was tempted. But already the chief knew his ploy wasn't going to work. One could not trick a jom so easily. A medicine man could not be successful without knowing a great deal about human nature. Before the jom could speak, Wema said:

"It's late; let's sleep and we'll talk tomorrow."

II

IT TOOK LONGER for Wema to negotiate the fee than to persuade the council to hire the shaman. Strong words had been exchanged in the council house before it was agreed that the shaman would receive a horse if he drove out the intruders. Inasmuch as none of Wema's people owned such an animal, it was understood that one would have to be stolen. This had caused further debate. Many saw in this arrangement the seeds of further conflict with the white intruders, but others argued that it could be done in such a way as to throw blame on another tribe, especially one of those to the north, whom the nisenan disliked.

The argument which carried the day was the unspoken one: most suspected that the shaman would fail and thus forfeit his fee. The decision made, the council adjourned its session, and rain began to fall. With the resumption of the winter storms, Wema decided to hold off for awhile. Because it appeared unlikely that the foreigners would pose a threat as long as it snowed in the mountains, the mission was delayed. Wema, Walupa, and the shaman stayed in their houses, huddling close to warm fires.

It was for this reason that no one was out and about to observe Dennis Martin when he came hiking through the Indian country, hugging the ridges which rise alongside the Bear River. Who would have thought that anyone would climb into the mountains alone at this season—especially a white man?

Martin had come away from Sutter's Fort on the twentieth of February, not long after the volunteer army had quit the field of battle in southern California. On discovering that they were expected to confront fellow Missourians instead of Mexicans, they had refused to fight. Returning to the fort, the prodigal fathers and sons began to make amends for long neglect of their suffering families. Unwilling to wait until the others had arranged for pack animals and supplies, Dennis, whose father was in the snowbound camp, set off for the mountains alone.

Despite the rain, he moved quickly into the foothills. He got along without snowshoes until well above the 4000-foot elevation, and even after putting them on he continued to make good progress, for he had been raised on such footgear in the Canadian wilderness.

Then, to his surprise, he came upon two men clumsily making their way through the snow. One he recognized as James Miller, who had married the sister of Dennis's brother-in-law. The other proved to be Miller's son, accompanying his father on a desperate errand. Two months having elapsed since the departure of the first group of men, it was feared at the camp that they had perished, perhaps at the hands of savages. Although the Millers were unfamiliar with the route, they hoped to find their way to Sutter's Fort and help.

Dennis assured them aid was coming. He also expressed grave alarm that the women and children were now under the sole protection of his father, Patrick, the only man in camp. Quickly dividing Dennis's load between them, the three men hurried on to the campsite. Once there, Dennis told the overjoyed wives about the strange events which had delayed their relatives. He assured them that a pack train could be expected in a very few days.

Martin Murphy's wife introduced Dennis to her newborn child, Elizabeth. She asked him if he had learned the name of the river by which they were camped.

"Captain Sutter says it's the Yuba River," he replied.

"Do you recall how Mrs. Miller named her baby Ellen Independence because it was born alongside Independence Rock? Since little Elizabeth was born here in the mountains beside the Yuba River, I'm going to call her Elizabeth Yuba Murphy."

"That's a fine name," said Dennis. "From what I hear, she must be the first American child to be born in California."

Not all the adults and children had fared as well as Elizabeth Yuba and Ellen Independence. Before leaving for Sutter's Fort, the men had butchered most of the cattle which remained after pulling the wagons over the summit. Left to freeze, the meat was to be used as needed by the camp. However, the food had not been shared equally but was distributed in proportion to previous ownership of the animals, so it was not long before Isabella Patterson and her children, not members of the Murphy-Miller-Martin clan, had been reduced to eating hides. Fortunately, no one had died and no one was seriously ill.

Having satisfied himself that he had done what he could to help those at the camp, Dennis announced that he was going to take advantage of a lull in the storm to attempt a crossing over the summit. His destination was Truckee Lake, where he hoped to find young Moses Schallenberger still alive. Moses, the only member of the overland party who had not crossed the Sierra divide, had agreed to stay behind and guard six wagon-loads of valuable goods. Whether he had been able to survive the winter, no one knew. At Sutter's Fort no one had been optimistic about his chances.

Although the others tried to dissuade Dennis, he shrugged off their warnings, laced on his snowshoes, heaved on his pack and was off. By late afternoon he had crossed the summit and by evening was embracing the forlorn, but still alive, Moses. Dennis improved Schallenberger's snowshoes while they sat and talked inside the primitive cabin in which he had spent the winter. In the morning the two young men climbed to the summit and headed for the snowbound camp on the Yuba.

Someone was shaking Wema, calling softly into his ear, trying to wake the chief without disturbing his wives who slept nearby. It was early morning, not yet light, the sky overcast and starless.

"Wake up, it's me—Walupa," came the insistent voice.

"Why are you here so early?"

"I have news of the wolesem. Men and horses have been seen going into the mountains toward the snowbound camp. They'll reach it by to-morrow or the next day."

Wema sat up, stretched himself and yawned. He rubbed his dark eyes and ran his fingers through the long black hair which hung loose about his shoulders. Many thoughts crossed his mind, and as he made plans he absentmindedly combed the knots from his hair and tied it neatly at the back of his head, letting the ends fall loose, like the tail of a pony. This done, he wrapped a robe of rabbitskins around his shoulders, stood up, and motioned Walupa to follow him outside into the clear, fresh mountain air. Only then did he speak:

"We've got to see what they're up to. Jepe will have to go back up there."

"What about the jom?" reminded Walupa.

"I'm thinking about that." Wema frowned. "Perhaps they mean only to remove the women and children."

"But if their purpose is to fortify the village and stay?"

"That's the other possibility. I don't want to send the shaman if he's going to complicate matters, but on the other hand it might be well to get him up there before he changes his mind—he may not be pleased when he finds the population has increased."

"By wolesem men," added Walupa.

"Yes, that, too. Well, if he can remain invisible I don't suppose he'll create a problem."

Walupa snorted. "He's not sure he can close the eyes of the wolesem."

"I know," said Wema. "That's what worries me. Nisenan magic may be useless against the whites. I'd rather put my trust in nisenan cleverness, which is why I think you'd better go along with Jepe and the jom."

"You're serious, aren't you?"

"I'm always serious when it comes to the wolesem."

The three fur-wrapped figures climbed one at a time until all had reached a position on the backside of a large outcropping of granite which overlooked the white people's camp. They had arrived nearly a day ahead of the pack train. Walupa could see that the women were expecting someone or something because of the way in which they and the children kept looking down river. He guessed that the camp had somehow been informed of the train. Either there had been a pre-arranged plan or someone had slipped undetected through nisenan country. Whichever it was no longer mattered. What mattered was what they intended to do once the train arrived.

"Where will you enter the camp?" he asked the shaman.

"Have you observed the place in the woods where the women go to relieve themselves?"

"Yes."

"I'll go there tonight when they're asleep."

"You mean you'll enter by that path?"

"No, I mean that I will go to the same place where they go. I don't need to go any farther."

The jom said no more, but Walupa now understood his meaning. It had long been suspected that shamans could poison humans by touching the end of a stick to a sample of the victim's urine. For this reason, most were careful not to allow the medicine man to catch them in the act of urinating, for fear he had been hired by some enemy to do them harm.

Walupa approved of the plan, for he preferred to have the medicine man stay away from the cabins. It bothered him not to know where the white men's horses would be corralled; too close to the latrine and it might disturb the animals when the jom approached his chosen spot.

Leaving the shaman to keep an eye on the cabins, Walupa slid quietly down from the rock to overtake Jepe, who had gone before him. The runner waved to Walupa from the base of another great bulge of granite about a hundred yards away, but when the subchief headed in that direction, Jepe dropped suddenly from view.

Puzzled, Walupa hurried to the spot and found a low, wide crevice at the base of the rock wall. A deep cave had been created under a broad overhang which served to keep the entrance free of snow. Crouching low, he entered the cave, which felt warm because the chilling winds could not follow. The room was dry and comfortable.

Jepe, who was inside already, said, "Look what is here."

Walupa stared at the pile of dry wood in the back of the cave.

"I put it there," said Jepe. "When I first came here, the skies were clear and the sun was hot. It's always good to have dry wood and I thought I might have to return."

Walupa nodded to the runner and went back outside, pulling the fur robe tightly to him as the cold wind once more collided with his body. The shaman signalled to him from the rock and when Walupa climbed up beside him, he whispered:

"Do you see?"

Walupa saw men and animals appearing and disappearing among the trees and brush far down the canyon. "They'll be here before dark," he said.

About an hour later, the three tribesmen watched in fascination as the white people embraced. In a scene of happy confusion, children competed with one another and their mothers for the opportunity to hug and be hugged by their bearded fathers and brothers. Frightened by the commotion, the horses grew restless; the men quickly went to the task of unpacking and caring for the pack animals.

Until then, Walupa hadn't known what he hoped or even expected to see. Suddenly everything became clear when he realized that the horses were not fully loaded—such animals were able to carry nearly twice their present burden. There was the clue: the whites did not intend to stay. Only enough provisions had been packed in to feed the party during the trip back to the fort. The extra horses were for riding, as the women and children of these people were notoriously soft and pampered.

About to share this revelation with his companions, Walupa changed his mind and held his tongue. It occurred to him that if the wolesem left of their own volition, not only would the shaman fail, which was of no consequence to Walupa, but, more important, Wema's plan would also fail. If, on the other hand, Wema's plan appeared to succeed, even though he would have to share the credit with the jom, some glory also would accrue to Wema's subchief Walupa.

So Walupa kept his counsel and the shaman crept toward the camp late at night, where he disturbed neither horses nor sleepers. He touched his stick everywhere that the women had been, and came away. For the rest of the night the shaman danced and sang far off in the woods where none could hear or see him. Returning to the cave at dawn, he collapsed beside the dying embers of the fire.

Throughout the morning he slept fitfully, sometimes calling out in his delirium. Finally he relaxed and slept more peacefully. When he awoke in the late afternoon, he was bathed in sweat. He opened his eyes and saw Walupa looking down at him.

"They are gone," Walupa told him. "They have left, all of them, including the animals. Your magic has worked even against the wolesem."

A great smile spread across the shaman's wet face, and as he lay on the floor of the cave, he pictured himself riding from village to village on a magnificent horse of his own.

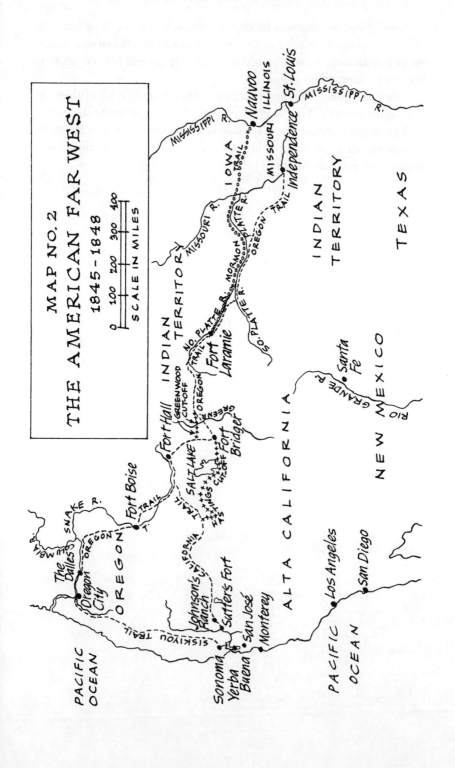

CHAPTER 2
MORMON PRINTER
March 1845–February 1846

1

*D*O YOU KNOW HOW to drive an ox team?"

"No, sir—but I learn fast," replied the eager youth.

"Maybe so, maybe not," the older farmer shook his head. "Taking care of a team and keeping a wagon repaired ain't the sort of work you've been doing. It's hard, dirty work, and it has to be done regular. No matter how mean the weather or how poorly you feel, the animals come first."

"I know that, sir."

"I know your family and I hear you're a dependable lad, but I still wonder, can you handle the job?"

"I know I can, Brother Stevens. I'm plenty strong and I'm not afraid of hard work. I won't let you down, I promise."

Stevens had frowned while the boy was speaking. He laid a hand on Tallman Rolfe's shoulder and said:

"That's another thing. If you *should* come, I'd want to hear no more talk of Brother or Sister. We're leaving all that behind us, do you understand? My family has suffered enough from bad treatment at the hands of the gentiles. It wasn't so bad when we still trusted the Prophet and the High Council—it seemed worth the abuse, because we were right and the others were wrong. But that's all behind us. I don't want any more trouble."

"Yes, sir. That's just fine with me."

Stevens eyed Rolfe intently. Although he would have liked to ask some other questions of the younger man, he decided to leave matters as they stood. The less said, the better, at least until they were clear of Nauvoo. The important thing was that he must have a driver soon. It was March 1845 and other emigrants were about to leave. The trouble was that Tallman Rolfe was not the sort of fellow he had wanted to hire. Stevens was looking for a farmer or teamster—not a printer and would-be lawyer.

Tallman Hathaway Rolfe was one of eleven children of Samuel and Elizabeth Hathaway Rolfe. The first Rolfe had emigrated to America from England in the early seventeenth century. For several generations they had lived in Massachusetts, but in the late eighteenth century Benjamin Rolfe took his wife, Mary Sweet, to New Hampshire. Samuel Jones Rolfe was born in Concord on August 26, 1793 or 1794, and on March 4, 1818, he married Elizabeth Hathaway in a part of Massachusetts soon to become the state of Maine. Tallman and seven of his brothers and sisters were born in Rumford, but in the fall of 1834 the Rolfes left Maine forever. A Mormon missionary had converted them to the faith of the Church of Latter Day Saints. With their eight children, the youngest of whom was Horace, aged ten months, Sam and Elizabeth traveled to Kirtland, Ohio, to take up a new kind of life.

Thomas Campbell, a former Presbyterian minister, and his son Alexander were evangelists whose determined efforts to bring about Christian unity had an unfortunate tendency to produce the opposite effect. A series of alliances with the Presbyterian and Baptist churches provoked controversies which soon led to disassociation. Sidney Rigdon, an associate of the Campbells, was a sensational revivalist who had created a communistic colony at Kirtland in 1830. Among those he had converted to Campbellism was Parley Pratt, who later became a Mormon.

In 1832 the Campbells joined Barton Stone's Kentucky Christians to form a new sect, the Disciples of Christ. Rigdon broke with the Campbells and was persuaded by Parley Pratt to join with Joseph Smith, founder of the Church of Latter Day Saints. Rigdon's colony converted en masse, and became a Mormon stronghold and Smith's headquarters.

Tallman's brother Samuel, named for his father, was born at Kirtland on January 3, 1836. In March the Kirtland Temple was finished and dedicated, but within two years Kirtland itself was finished as a Mormon center. Much stress had taxed the community, not the least factor being a nationwide collapse of banks of credit. During a temporary absence of Joseph Smith in the summer of 1837 the Mormons split into two bitterly feuding groups. The dissenters set up their own church, instigated lawsuits against the elders, and forced many, including Brigham Young, to leave town to escape arrest.

Smith tried to heal the split when he returned, but after much unpleasantness, he left for Missouri, where the western headquarters of the Mormon Church had been established. He was followed by 600 of the faithful, including the Rolfe family. It was not a good time to be arriving in Caldwell County, Missouri. The first Mormon colony had been located near Independence, in Jackson County. But as the colony's population increased, so did friction between Saints and non-Mormons. Eventually Smith's followers were forcibly expelled across the Missouri River into Clay County. From there they had been driven north into Caldwell County, created by the legislature expressly as a refuge or reservation for the Mormons.

By 1838, when the Rolfes appeared in Missouri, open warfare had erupted between Mormons and "gentiles," even in Caldwell County. Governor Lillburn Boggs angrily ordered the Saints out of his state, offering annihilation as the only alternative. Joseph Smith, undaunted, selected Nauvoo, a spot on the east bank of the Mississippi River in the state of Illinois, as the new Zion. The Mormons began moving across the river in 1839. William Jasper Rolfe was born to Elizabeth on December 8, 1839, just before she left Missouri soil.

Tallman's father was a carpenter and joiner. His two older brothers, Gilbert and Benjamin, were plasterers. When Joseph Smith called for men to work on the great Temple at Nauvoo, all three volunteered their services. Tallman was apprenticed at the age of fifteen to learn the printing trade at *Times and Seasons*, the Mormon newspaper. Ianthus, two years younger, became a cabin boy on a riverboat. In the winter of 1841–42 Gilbert Rolfe married Eliza Jane Bates, a seventeen-year-old Mormon from England.

When he was eighteen, Tallman began reading law with Chauncey L. Higbee, a general in the Nauvoo Legion. Though technically a branch of the state militia, the Legion was in fact Joseph Smith's private army. Chauncey's brother Elias, also a lawyer, had gone with Smith to Washington City to ask Congress for help in collecting for the Mormons two million dollars from the state of Missouri for property destroyed and confiscated. They had failed, and when Smith appealed to President Van Buren he was told: "Sir, your cause is just—but I can do nothing for you."

Elias and Chauncey's third brother, Francis, was also a church elder. Francis and Chauncey had figured prominently in the series of scandals which eventually destroyed Smith and his brother. Tallman observed much of what ensued from a privileged position: the first scandal erupted during his apprenticeship at the newspaper, the second while reading law with Chauncey. Both arose over the practice of plural marriage, or "spiritual wives." For years non-Mormons circulated and published stories about alleged sexual practices of the Saints' church, charges routinely denied.

But in the spring of 1842, Nancy Rigdon, the pretty nineteen-year-old daughter of Sidney, showed her father a letter sent her by the Prophet. Smith had tried to seduce her in a private meeting, she claimed, and she had been allowed to leave only after she threatened to scream. The letter, which had come on the following day, cautiously suggested that God would not disapprove if Nancy agreed to a liaison.

Sydney Rigdon angrily confronted the Prophet, who claimed he only wished to test Nancy's virtue. The letter was given by Nancy to Francis Higbee, who then gave it to John C. Bennett, formerly Smith's closest advisor. For a year Bennett and Smith had been feuding quietly after Smith discovered his assistant engaged in using the Prophet's authority to seduce women. When Bennett protested that he was doing nothing that Smith hadn't already done, the Prophet expressed his displeasure because Bennett had not married his partners. To make matters worse, one woman swore that Bennett promised to perform abortions on those who became pregnant by him.

It was John Bennett who had first forewarned Nancy Rigdon about Smith's intentions; now, with the letter in his hands, he hoped to force Smith to give up some of his power. The Prophet countered by bringing charges against Bennett and the Higbee brothers. When the High Council questioned Francis and Chauncey, they admitted they too had practiced adultery. Soon all of Nauvoo was buzzing with rumors.

On June 23, 1842, Bennett was excommunicated. His response was to begin submitting a series of letters to the *Sangamo Journal* at Springfield, Illinois. In them he exposed the alleged sexual and political wrongdoings of Joseph Smith. The letters were widely read and eventually published in book form.

Meanwhile, the Higbee brothers somehow avoided an open break and stayed within the hierarchy of the church. William Law became Smith's top advisor, replacing Bennett, and Tallman Rolfe went to work in Chauncey Higbee's office.

One day, William Law discovered that his wife had been approached by Joseph Smith. He demanded that Smith go before the High Council and confess his sins; Smith refused. On another occasion, Dr. Robert Foster came home early from a business trip and found Smith dining with his wife. She confessed that the Prophet had tried to convert her to the "spiritual-wife" doctrine. Chauncey advised both Foster and Law this was nothing; some of the leading elders had as many as ten or twelve wives apiece.

Such talk made its way quickly through the community of Nauvoo. It also reached the ears of Joseph Smith, who surprised everyone by printing the charges without comment in the *Times and Seasons* and the *Nauvoo Neighbor*. At the same time, he ordered Foster brought to trial before the High Council on a charge of slander. When he learned Foster planned to introduce forty-one witnesses who would attest to the facts, the trial was hastily cancelled, but Foster was excommunicated, along with William, Jane, and Wilson Law.

Francis Higbee then sued Joseph Smith for slander. Dr. Foster, William Law, and Joseph Jackson testified before the Carthage Grand Jury, and the jury brought indictments against Smith for false swearing, adultery and polygamy.

By way of response, Smith countercharged Francis Higbee with perjury, seduction, and adultery. The *Times and Seasons* declined to print all the details of his charges, claiming they "were too delicate for the public eye and ear." Two of Smith's witnesses (one was Brigham Young), swore that Higbee consorted with prostitutes and that he had contracted venereal disease from a Frenchwoman. Even Chauncey was attacked. Affidavits from the two-year-old Bennett scandal were dusted off and introduced again to show that Chauncey Higbee had seduced three women.

At the height of these charges and accusations, Smith's opponents published the first and last edition of the Nauvoo *Expositer*. When it hit the streets, its impact was so profound (at least in Smith's mind) that the Nauvoo Legion was ordered to wreck the *Expositer* print shop and destroy its equipment. The predictable result of this mayhem was that Joseph and Hyrum Smith were arrested and taken to jail at Carthage, Illinois. Even Smith was not surprised when a lynch mob comprised of militiamen from Carthage and Warsaw executed him and his brother on June 27, 1844.

The subsequent martyrdom of the Smith brothers and reactions on both sides produced so much hostility in western Illinois that it was evident the Mormons would have to leave Nauvoo. To many, Tallman Rolfe in particular, future prospects for Mormons looked bleak and unappealing.

Because of the unique opportunity he had had to view events at close hand, at the newspaper office and in Chauncey Higbee's office, Tallman's faith had been shaken severely. The claims of the church to moral superiority were just that: claims—at best unsubstantiated, at worst demolished.

Pondering his own future, Tallman Rolfe realized he was not willing to be identified with the hierarchy of his parents' church. Because Joseph Smith was also its founder, Tallman wondered if the church itself had validity. With the exception of Benjamin, two years older than he, there was no one in the family with whom he could discuss his doubts. His father was close to Brigham Young and would brook no dissent in his household, but Ben was talking of leaving the church in order to seek employment in the state of Missouri.

Ever since the assassination of the Smith brothers, the economy of Nauvoo had been collapsing. Never far from poverty, Mormon families now were hard pressed to make ends meet. Some were emigrating to other regions, and the direction most chose was to the west. To those who lived on the frontier the course westward seemed the only natural one; when Governor Boggs had earlier forced the Mormons to retreat eastward to Nauvoo, in Illinois, Joseph Smith had seen it as a temporary solution at best. Before his death he was discussing plans for a new westward migration beyond the Missouri River.

In order to relieve their family's poverty, Samuel Rolfe's four eldest sons decided in 1845 to leave home. Gilbert, the oldest brother, was taking his wife and son to Iowa. Eliza Jane was expecting a second child in a few months so they could not delay. Ianthus was being sent east to Massachusetts where relatives could put him to work. Ben had his own plan. While it was dangerous for a Mormon to again set foot in Boggs's territory, repentant ex-Mormons were received with open arms. If the Rolfe family was to travel with the Saints across the open plains, they would need equipment and supplies. Why not finance the move with gentile money? At least this was how Ben, who did not consider himself a Mormon, explained his intention to work for wages in Missouri to the family.

Tallman Rolfe, in the midst of the change around him and the uncertainties within him, waited for some sign that would help him decide on a course of action. His own doubts, and his authoritarian upbringing, made this difficult. But when he heard that Brother Stevens was taking his family to Oregon and would need a driver, Tallman decided to act. He hurried out to the Stevens farm to apply for the position. Now he stood impatiently beside the middle-aged farmer and anxiously awaited his decision.

Stevens examined the young man thoughtfully and weighed his options. The Rolfe boy might not have been what he'd hoped for, but he was a whole lot smarter than anyone else who had applied. A smart lad, if he wasn't lazy, might be worth more in the long run than a foolish one with experience. "Come on back to the barn and I'll show you how to hitch and drive a team. You can drive them 'round the farm for awhile and see if you get the hang of it."

"Yes, sir! Thank you, sir!"

"Now, don't you go thanking me yet—I haven't said I'd take you— just show me what you can do."

II

FOUR MONTHS LATER, in July 1845, Tallman watched with amusement as young Bill Swasey argued with another emigrant over a bull. They were at Fort Hall, in Oregon Territory, and Swasey had found the animal, a fine Durham, wandering loose beside a stream 150 miles back on the trail from Fort Laramie. His opponent, a man named Stewart, claimed the bull was his. Among the group of onlookers who had gathered at the entrance to the corral were friends of both men.

The others did not seem to be amused. Swasey stood before the gate, legs apart, holding a rifle in front of his body. His companions, also armed and ready, had ranged themselves on either side.

"I'll shoot anyone who tries to lay a hand on the bull," Swasey angrily declared. "If that was your bull, you left it back there to die. I rescued it and brought it here, so now it's mine to do with as I please!"

"The devil you say!" swore Stewart, equally furious. He then advanced in a manner so menacing that Swasey's friends aimed their weapons at Stewart's chest and warned him back. This slowed his forward progress, but not his tongue. "I bought and fed and raised that bull, and I drove him all the way from the States."

"So why did you abandon him in Indian country?"

"Because he wandered off. I wanted to look for him but the company refused to wait. I meant to go back or send for that bull soon as we got here. Since you saved me the trouble I'm willing to pay you something, but the bull belongs to me!"

"Well, that's a nice story, Stewart, but I don't believe you. You see, I've talked with people from your own outfit, and they heard you say you hoped to God the wolves would eat him! I found him footsore on the main trail, so my opinion is you couldn't be bothered to wait while he rested."

"Don't call me a liar!" shouted Stewart. "Where I come from, we hang people for stealing livestock. I'll be damned if I'll let a cattle thief call me a liar!"

The situation no longer seemed humorous to Rolfe, so he moved to a position less likely to be in the line of possible fire. As he did so, he noticed a group of older men, bearded and long-haired trappers, who were on their way to the corral from the trading post. In the lead was Captain Grant, the Hudson's Bay Company factor who ran Fort Hall.

"All right, lads, what seems to be the problem?" he called. Grant was nearly six feet three inches tall and amply proportioned. His round, red face bore a cheerful expression, and his voice was calm and polite. Stewart, obviously pleased by Grant's arrival, confidently explained his grievance. Grant listened carefully, then said:

"I've already heard Swasey's version. In fact, it appears that I'm somewhat involved, for I agreed to trade him 600 pounds of flour for the bull, on the assumption that it was his."

Stewart was shocked, and he roared his disapproval: "He's got no right to the animal—the bull is mine! I demand that you return my bull at once, Captain Grant!"

Grant stared coldly at Stewart.

"Let's get something straight, Stewart: You and your companions are my guests as a matter of necessity, but I did not invite you to come here. In fact, I'd rather that none of you would continue your journeys, but would go back to wherever you came from. You'd be better off and so would I. But that's something over which I have little or no control, and as you have come, as a gentleman and representative of the Hudson's Bay Company, I intend to treat you in as friendly and civil a fashion as I can muster. I would appreciate a similar effort on your part."

Grant paused to let the remarks take effect. Then he continued, "Before you interrupted, I was about to say that I had assumed Mr. Swasey was the bull's owner, but as this assumption has been disputed by yourself, it will be necessary to settle the question in a proper manner."

One of the trappers limped over to Stewart. Tallman guessed he was Peg-Leg Smith, the hardy mountaineer who was famous for having amputated his own limb.

"Look here, stranger," Peg-Leg drawled, "never you worry. We'll get to the right of the thing."

Before Stewart could reply, Captain Grant said, "Thank you, Mr. Smith. Now let's proceed with the case. I suppose each of you has witnesses who will testify to the facts?"

Stewart and Swasey indicated that their companions were ready to do so.

"Fine. Let's hear the facts then, and later we'll see how the facts fit the law. We have certain laws of our own out here."

As the witnesses presented their statements for or against various allegations, Tallman watched and listened with fascination. This was a new form of justice, he thought—new to him, at any rate. He wondered about the mysterious wilderness statutes to which Grant had alluded. So far the general shape of the hearing was not unlike that of a regular court, but he noted that there had been no swearing-in and there was no jury that he could see. Perhaps Grant had the power to act as judge and jury at this post.

When no new information could be elicited, Grant called a halt to the testimony and quickly summarized what had been said. When Tallman saw that he was addressing his remarks to the trappers, he suddenly realized that these mountaineers were going to be the jury.

One ancient specimen, identified earlier to Tallman as "Old Greenwood," declared he didn't believe Stewart had meant to go back for the bull. In fact, said Caleb Greenwood, "I misdoubt any man would go a hunert and fifty miles to find a bull that's likely to be dead. It don't make sense to me."

"It appears to me," said Peg-Leg, pointing to Stewart, "this fellow lost interest in that bull a long ways back. When he found out that someone else had got him and fetched him to Fort Hall, then he got re-interested. Can't say as I blame him, though—it's a fine animal."

When the others expressed similar opinions, Grant asked, "If, as you think, the animal was abandoned and later found by someone else, who is the rightful owner? Mr. Smith, what's the law in these parts?"

Peg-Leg drew himself up as nearly erect as possible and delivered his decision in the same manner of exaggerated sincerity and sobriety which characterized all of his tales: "The law in these parts says if a man comes across a bull that's been left to care for itself, he's free to claim it for his own. Especially if he gets it out of the hands of wild animals and rascally Indians."

"Well, there you are, gentlemen. You've heard the law. My verdict is that the bull now belongs to Mr. Swasey," announced Captain Grant.

In a gesture of conciliation, Swasey turned to Stewart with an offer. "I'll tell you what I'll do. Captain Grant was going to trade me 600 pounds of flour, which our company needs to get to California. You said you'd be willing to pay me something for bringing the bull to the fort, so if you'll give me 400 pounds of flour, I'll give you the bull. What do you say?"

"I say to hell with you!" snarled Stewart. "The devil take you, the whole lot of you!"

As Stewart and his comrades turned and angrily departed in the direction of their wagons, Grant and the trappers headed back to the trading post. Tallman went over to the corral. He noticed that Swasey and his companions were about the same age as himself.

"Is it true you're going to California?" he asked.

"That's right. There's twelve of us going on horseback. Why? Did you want to join us?"

Tallman was still unaccustomed to being treated in so friendly a fashion by total strangers. He wondered if Swasey would act differently if he knew Tallman had come from Nauvoo.

"I'd like to, but I can't," he replied. "I've promised to drive a wagon to Oregon for another man."

"Too bad—but perhaps you can talk him into going to California instead. Lots of others are, you know."

"I know. Old Greenwood has been trying to persuade our outfit to take the California road, but Mr. Stevens doesn't think it's possible to take our wagons over the mountains. The Oregon guides say it can't be done."

"Greenwood says he took wagons to Sutter's Fort last winter."

"That's what I heard. He claims most of the women and children wintered in the mountains—even says one of the women had a baby while they were snowbound!"

"I hadn't heard that story. I wonder how they got the wagons over the summit? Greenwood seems to have been the first to solve the problem, he and his sons. Did you know his sons were part Indian?"

"Wasn't Greenwood married to a Crow woman?"

"That's right. He lived with the Crows for awhile. He says he's eighty-two years old! Claims he was at St. Louis in 1787 when it was still a Spanish possession."

"That would make him more than forty years old at the time of the Louisiana Purchase—do you think it's true?"

"It sounds like a whopper, I know, but so far I've heard no one dispute his word about his age. All the trappers at the fort say he was an old codger when they met up with him. Of course, you can't always trust what they say, either."

"I wonder if it's true what he says about Sutter. According to him, Captain Sutter plans to meet the California emigrants with supplies and help them over the mountains. And that's not all—he says Sutter will give six sections of rich bottom land to the head of every family that settles near his fort."

"Well, it might be true, but I wouldn't put too much store by it. But I think your folks will be sorry if they don't come to California. I hear the climate's not nearly so good in Oregon."

"That's what Greenwood keeps saying. And he claims it's dangerous on account of Indians."

"Captain Grant would agree, but you have to keep in mind that the Hudson's Bay Company wants to keep us out of Oregon, even though it's supposed to be held jointly by England and America. They're afraid we'll take it over if many more settlers move into the country. Grant is trying to discourage people from going north."

"What's he think about California?"

"He hasn't much to say in favor of going there, either. But that's because he doesn't know too much about it and doesn't want to encourage folks to take chances. I don't think he really cares. He tried to talk us out of going when we first arrived. He said our party was too small and we were too young. But we were determined to go and when Old Greenwood's son, John offered to take us, Grant said it was our necks and he guessed Greenwood knew as much as anybody, having been twice over the trail in the past year."

"Well, I wish I was going with you, but it looks like I'll have to visit Oregon first. Don't be surprised if you see me some day soon in California, though!"

"I hope I will. If that happens, what name shall I know you by? I'm Bill Swasey."

"Glad to meet you—the name is Tallman Rolfe. Good luck to you and your friends."

"And to you!"

III

"You say the toughest part is still ahead? I can't believe that—how can anything be worse than what we've just come through?" Tallman Rolfe stared at Frank Martin in open-faced wonder. It was now September 1845, and they had been observing the scores of wagon trains now gathering at The Dalles, on the southern bank of the Columbia.

"That's what I'm told. It seems we'll have to build our own boats and rafts in order to go down the river to Oregon City. This has become the largest emigration in history and there are none to be had at any price. And we'll have to get rid of the animals. It's impossible to bring them down the river."

"How far do we have to go?" asked Tallman.

"About sixty miles, and it must be the meanest and roughest water in the world, to hear the locals tell it. I don't know if they're trying to throw a scare into us or if they're telling the truth, but I must admit the Columbia is some river. By the way, can you swim?"

"Some. I sure wouldn't like to try swimming out there if I could help it."

"That's the way I feel."

"We should have taken the other trail, maybe—that new shortcut from Fort Boise. That bunch who did will be laughing at us for sticking to the old route."

"I doubt it. From what I picked up at the trading post, I'd guess they were in real trouble. Some say they're starving to death and a rescue party is being raised to go to their aid."

"So that's what's up. I saw them loading pack animals down at the corral, but thought it was some trappers about to go off on a hunting trip."

"You're right—they're going hunting for people. The guides apparently lost their way on the new route—it wasn't marked very well—and the wagons are stuck somewhere near the headwaters of the Deschutes River."

"Isn't that the river we just crossed?"

"That's it. If the other train can be located, they'll try to bring them down the river to The Dalles."

"So they'll have to travel down the Columbia same as us! I'm glad now we stuck to the old trail."

"I thought you might be—say, there seems to be some kind of trouble down there. It looks like Stevens and Barlow are having words. Let's go see what it's all about."

A crowd was forming near the two older men and as Rolfe and Martin approached they heard Sam Barlow say:

"Look, Stevens, I don't know about you, but I didn't bring my outfit halfway round the world just so I could abandon my animals sixty miles short of my destination. Even if I wanted to sell them, I can't get a fair price here, where every one is doing the same."

"I know that, Sam. But we're all in the same boat, don't you see? We'd all like to keep our animals, but there's no way to do it."

"Who says? I need those animals—I can't farm without 'em."

"Naturally, we'd all like to take our livestock with us, but how in blazes do you figure to do what no one else has done? There's no way to get your wagons over those blasted mountains!"

"I'll build my own road if I have to! It won't be the first and it won't be the last. I'm not going to quit now—not after coming this far. Maybe you can afford to take the loss and buy new stock, but I can't."

"By God, Sam, have you completely lost your reason? You heard what happened to those wagons that left the road at Fort Boise. They weren't satisfied to stick to the old trail, so now they're starving somewhere in the mountains. And those blamed fools who listened to Greenwood and went to California are most likely in the same fix!"

Stevens had figured Barlow for a clever and sensible person until now. It angered him that anyone could be ignorant and stubborn enough to risk the lives of his family in order to hang onto a few dumb animals, and for this reason he made one last desperate effort to dissuade the man:

"You know nothing of the country, Barlow. Think of your family, if you won't think of yourself. Don't their lives mean anything to you?"

Barlow was stung and his face reddened. "They mean everything to me, as much as yours to you. That's why I'm not going down that river. D'you call that a safe trip? Think again. Lots of folks have drowned out there before they ever came in sight of Fort Vancouver. If you want to chance the lives of *your* kin on the river, why go ahead and be welcome. I'll take my chances on the land."

Stevens snorted and shook his head. Then, seeing Tallman and Frank among the onlookers, he called out, "Come on, lads. No use trying to talk sense to this fellow. We'd better step lively and build some rafts if we hope to reach the Willamette before Thanksgiving!"

As the three men walked away, Tallman began to chuckle to himself and Frank asked what was on his mind.

"I was thinking about that fellow Stewart, who lost his bull to Swasey back at Fort Hall. He's probably glad now that he didn't have to drive it all the way to Oregon—he would have lost it again, anyway!"

IV

"SEEN OUR NEW PAPER?" asked the Oregon City storekeeper. "Brand new: The *Oregon Spectator*," he announced proudly.

Tallman examined the four pages with a professional eye. Each page measured about eleven by fifteen inches. It was a neat looking sheet and he saw it had been made up with care. The so-called "Organic Laws" of Oregon, approved by an unofficial legislature in 1845, had been published on the front page of the newspaper.

"How often does it come out?" he asked.

"Editor says twice a month. Makes you stop and think when you realize you're staring at the first copy of the first paper on the coast!"

"That's something to think about, I'll grant you." Tallman considered mentioning his years on the paper in Nauvoo, but thought better of it. Instead, he asked about something which had bothered him for several months. It was now February 1846 and ever since September he had wondered about Sam Barlow.

"Do you happen to know anything about a man named Barlow who was going to try and make his way over the mountain from The Dalles?"

"Barlow? Sure. He made it through all right. Says he's going to open up a road this year and charge folks to come over it. Mighty clever fellow, that Barlow."

Well, now he knew. Somehow it pleased Tallman, and he hoped that fellow, Bill Swasey, and his friends had made it through to California as well. While the proprietor was totaling his purchases, Tallman said:

"I hear some folks hereabouts are looking for a school teacher. Know who they might be?"

"Must be the folks south of town, some eight or nine miles from here. They've got a pack of younguns between 'em and they talked about starting a school last time they was here. Whyn't you ask the sheriff? Joe Meek knows where everybody's at and what they're up to."

"Thanks, I will. Do you happen to know where I'd find him this time of day?"

"Try the tavern across the road. He's usually there, unless he's out collecting taxes. But this ain't too fine a day for tax collecting." It had been raining all morning, something Tallman had come to expect in western Oregon. He wondered if the sun ever shone on this end of the continent.

"Comes to three and a half dollars, assuming you want the paper," announced the shopkeeper.

"The sheriff collects taxes?" Tallman laid the coins on the counter. "Doesn't the tax collector take care of that?"

"Don't need one, especially when Meek's the only man can make 'em pay. Besides, it's the only way he can make his salary. Unless he picks up the taxes, there's no money to pay him."

"It makes sense, I guess. I never thought of it that way. Well, thanks for your help!" Tallman stepped outside and peered through the rain. Oregon City had been created years before by Methodist missionaries and retired trappers. Now it boasted four general stores, two taverns, three tailor shops, one hatter, two blacksmiths, two cabinetmakers, two silversmiths, one cooper, two gristmills, two sawmills, a tannery, and a brickyard. There were also one doctor, three lawyers, a Methodist church and a Catholic chapel. Rough as it was, Tallman had seen no larger community since leaving home.

He crossed the muddy road to the tavern, wiped most of the mud from his boots onto the board walk and went inside. When he asked for Sheriff Meek, he was told that Meek was present but the sheriff was not.

"I don't understand," said Rolfe. "I thought they were one and the same."

"So they was," answered a voice from the end of the bar, "so they was, but Joe Meek has quit as of today! I've got me a new job, selling subscriptions to the newspaper."

Tallman walked over to the tall bearded man dressed in buckskins. "Are you Mr. Meek?" he inquired.

"Nope; I'm *Joe* Meek." The ex-sheriff looked Tallman up and down and asked, "Who might you be?"

"I'm Tallman Rolfe and I was told you knew where everyone lived. The storekeeper said you might know the folks who are looking for someone to teach school."

"Are you fixin' to teach school or go to one?" asked Meek. This drew an easy laugh from the bystanders and Meek eyed them with mock indignation. "T'ain't funny. I asked the lad a serious question. He don't look too old to go to school."

The others snickered, but Meek remained serious. Tallman was annoyed and stiffly answered, "I was planning to apply for the position, if it pays well enough."

"I'll tell you what, young feller, if it pays well enough, I'll go for the job myself!" The gallery shouted its approval. "Let me give you some valuable advice, Tallman. It's no trick to find yourself a position, but collecting the pay is plumb discouraging. That's why I quit the sheriff business. When I was sheriff, them other fellows took their shares first and I got what was left. Now that I'm working for the newspaper, I take my money first, and the editor gets what's left."

"I'm not sure I see the connection with school teaching."

"Why, it's easy: you'll get to collect the money for your scholars and then they'll use it to pay the rent on the schoolhouse, like as not."

"I see." Tallman grinned and waited. Seeing that the young man would not be put off, Meek said:

"Yeah, I think I know what folks you mean. Come on outside and I'll point the way."

Outside, the rain splashed noisily and steadily, pouring like a waterfall from the wooden awning under which Tallman and Meek stood. The ex-sheriff pointed in a southerly direction and said: "See that barn at the bottom of that long hill with the row of pines along its top? Head for the barn and when when you get to it you'll find a wagon road heading out into the woods. Follow the road about eight miles till you come to a big meadow with half a dozen cows in it. You'll see a cabin and a shed alongside, and a mean dog with black and white spots will come out and try to gnaw your leg. Got all that?"

"Yes sir. That's the place?"

"No sir, that ain't the place. *Next* place is the one you want, except there ain't no good way to tell you how to find it unless I tell you this way, understand? Place you want is Smith's place, but that's not much help because nearly everybody in those parts is named Smith. Think you can find it?"

"I think so. Thanks for your help."

"You're welcome, son—don't get wet," and with that parting advice Meek strode back into the tavern. Tallman pulled the collar of his coat up around his neck, turned the brim of his hat down over his ears and stepped out into the downpour.

As he hiked south through the muddy ruts, Tallman thought how different this country was from Missouri and Illinois. In some ways it was better and in some ways poorer. Most settlers were grateful for the absence of fever and ague. Along the Missouri and Mississippi rivers the illness was so common during the summer and fall as to depopulate entire neighborhoods. Recently it had been ravaging communities in the winter months as well. Even those not stricken fatally were apt to be subject to recurring bouts for many years. In Oregon no new cases had appeared and many who had suffered previously claimed their health was much improved.

On the other hand, one of the great disappointments was the scarcity of wild game. What game there was could be found only at such a distance from the settlers' farms as to give them little opportunity to hunt except in winter, and then the weather was wet and miserable.

They also complained of being unable to find such wild foods as honey, grapes, nuts and plums, which they were accustomed to have in abundance back home. The exceptions were hazelnuts and berries: blackberries, raspberries, strawberries, blueberries, and cranberries grew wild in great profusion. The lack of wild foods with which they were familiar caused hard times for newcomers, but those who had been in Oregon for a while soon raised crops which gave them plenty to eat and and store.

The greatest problem was to replace wornout clothing. Oregon suffered from an acute shortage of raw materials from which to produce cloth. Wool, cotton, and flax were not to be had locally, so cloth had to be imported. Prices were high and money almost nonexistent. Its absence created many problems, as Tallman was fast discovering. There could be no hotels in a country without money, and those who most needed accommodations were the very persons least able to produce cash.

When new arrivals such as Tallman were forced to travel in search of employment or unoccupied land, they had no choice but to accept whatever charity older settlers were willing and able to extend. The log cabins in which most people lived were so small that they barely contained the families who had built them. Bedding, like clothing, was scarce, so travelers were expected to carry their own blankets and sleep on the floor. Often it was a severe hardship for the settlers to share their small quarters and hard-won provisions.

Already Tallman had heard the story of one man who finally grew tired of being host to every stranger who passed his farm. He felled a tree, split out a slab and sawed it into a board about one by two feet in size. After shaving it smooth with a drawknife, he used a piece of charcoal from his fire to print the single word "Entertainment" on the board. As soon as he had hung this traditional hotel advertisement from a pole in front of his house, most travelers ceased to knock on his door.

The sign worked so well that for three months not a single passerby stopped long enough to pass the time of day. Finally, because he lived by himself, the settler became so lonely that he removed the sign from the pole and put it away, to be saved until he once more wished to be left alone.

Tallman was chuckling at the recollection of this tale when a farm wagon came bouncing and splashing down the road and overtook him. Tallman jumped out of the way and the driver reined his animals to a stop.

"How far you going?" he called out. "Can I give you a lift?"

Tallman explained his destination and purpose. The driver nodded and smiled. "Good thing I came along," he said. "I can save you a long, wet walk."

Rolfe took this for an invitation to ride and began to climb into the wagon, but the driver quickly held up his hand.

"Wait," he said. "That's not my meaning. It's true, I'm going where you're headed, but what I meant to say was there's no need for you to continue. There won't be any school this year. I'm sorry to say we can't afford to pay a teacher. Some of us are ready, but it looks like not enough can contribute their share at this time."

"That's bad news."

"Bad for both of us. I'm sorry because I'd like my oldest pair to get some schooling, but I guess they'll have to learn at home for a while longer. I'm afraid if we can't find enough neighbors next year who can help out, we'll have to to move on. I can't wait until my children are grown, just because times are hard."

"Well, good luck. Thanks for the information and for saving me the walk. I think I'll forget about teaching school for the time being and try farming. I know a fellow who'd like to share a claim with me. Maybe you know him—his name is Stump."

"Stump? No, can't say as I do. But it's probably a good idea to go in with someone if you've never farmed before. Got a family?"

"No, I'm not married. I'd like to see more of the west before I settle down. I guess there's plenty of time for that later on. I just turned twenty-one when I reached Oregon," replied Tallman.

"Plenty of time, you're right about that," agreed the other, "though it's easier to run a farm with a few extra hands. Well, I've got to git—nice talking to you—good luck!"

Tallman waved and the wagon eased forward through the ruts. The rain had not quit for a moment and it showed every sign of continuing for a week. Rolfe shrugged his shoulders and headed back to town.

CHAPTER 3

GREENWOOD'S TRAIL

September 1845–November 1846

I

I CAN'T FIGURE what Mr. Ide aims to do," said the pretty but sunburned and dust-streaked young woman. She stared up at the high granite cliff overlooking Moses Schallenberger's abandoned cabin at the edge of Truckee Lake. A dozen or more men were hard at work cutting brush and prying boulders and rocks from the narrow ledge on which they stood. On the floor of the valley where she stood, wagons were being emptied and their contents stacked in carefully segregated piles.

"First thing he wants to do is clear a pass over the mountain," replied her stocky husband as he helped her unload the wagon. "Once that's done they'll take some of the oxen up to that first shelf."

"You mean that one just below where the men are working?"

"That's it. They'll put several yoke of oxen on the ledge and hitch 'em to an empty wagon with long ropes. When the team has moved as far as it can along the ledge, the wagon wheels will be blocked to keep it from slipping while they untie the hitch, back up the oxen, and take up the slack. Then they'll pull the wagon a little higher up the trail until the team runs out of ledge once more. They'll do that over and over until the wagon's finally up there on the ledge with the oxen."

"Gracious, what a lot of work! But what happens then?"

"The oxen will be moved up to the next higher ledge and the wagon will be hauled up again the same way. Meanwhile, another team will be taken to the first level to lift the second wagon. We'll do that till all the teams and all the wagons are on top."

"That could take forever!"

"Not quite; but it's the only way."

"But the wagons will be empty—how will we get our belongings up there—what we've been unloading here on the ground?"

"Only one way."

"Are you saying we're supposed to carry all our food and belongings to the top of that mountain? I'm no pack mule!" declared the young woman.

"Well, you've got a choice," retorted her husband.

"What's that?"

"Leave it all here."

"It's going to take weeks!"

"Greenwood and Bill Ide figure no more than two days if everyone pitches in and works from sunup to sundown."

Their own wagon was almost empty now. Like most others in the train, it was small and lightweight, but strong. These were ordinary farm wagons, much smaller than the Conestoga freight wagons used in Pennsylvania and Ohio. Each wagon bed had low sides and was no more than four feet wide by ten or twelve feet long. The wagons were made out of hardwoods—even the axles and wheels, although these were reinforced with just enough iron to increase strength without adding too much weight.

Each wagon usually was pulled by six oxen yoked in pairs. The driver walked beside them and controlled the team by shouting, swearing, and cracking his whip. No reins were used and the driver never rode on the wagon. For that matter, unless families had mules or horses, everyone except infants and invalids walked, because the springless wagons jolted unmercifully. Besides, most wagons were so overloaded that teams were unable to haul any extra weight.

"But suppose it's the same on the other side?" asked the young woman. "What if we've got to lower the wagons down the back side of the mountain?"

"In time we will have to, but not right away. Old Greenwood says we'll have to drop the wagons down some cliffs at Bear Valley, but that's twenty or thirty miles past the summit."

"I'll be so glad to get to Sutter's Fort! If I'd known how awful this trip was going to be, nobody could've talked me into leaving—not even you!" said his wife.

"Never you mind—you'll forget it all once we're in California. Can you believe how good it will be to own six whole sections of our very own land?"

"I just hope it's true. I swear I don't believe a thing strangers tell me any more. And I know I'll never make it back home again—we'll never see our kinfolk till we die." Tears began to fill the corners of her soft brown eyes, but when she saw the distressed look on her husband's face, she quickly brushed them away.

"Come on," she said, taking her husband by the arm and hugging him to her side. "Let's go help Mrs. Ide and Sarah—they've got three wagons to unload while Mr. Ide is busy up there."

II

JOHNSON'S RANCH, partly flat-lying fields and partly rolling hills, lay north of Sutter's Fort and the Bear River. A wide, shallow place along the river known as Johnson's Crossing was the most convenient ford for emigrants. The ranch was part of a Mexican land grant obtained by Pablo Gutiérrez. William Johnson and Sebastian Keyser purchased the land in 1845 after Gutiérrez was hanged by rebel *Californios* when they caught him spying for Sutter's raggle-taggle army.

Keyser had been a friend of Sutter's in their pre-California days, and Bill Johnson had been a sailor on the California to Sandwich Islands run. The two men divided the ranch in half; Johnson lived on his part with Tom Fallon and the McFaddens. One day toward the end of September 1845, Tom was fashioning a California-style saddle tree when the sound of approaching horses caused him to look up from his work.

"Great God! Where did you drop from?" he asked the group of hot and dusty riders who quickly surrounded him.

"From the States!" laughed Bill Swasey. "We've just come over the mountains from Fort Hall."

"Pretty fast traveling, if that's so. You're the first ones through this season. How was the trip?"

"Not bad. But we're starved for decent food—for the past two or three days we've had nothing to eat but pine nuts, acorns and coffee!"

"That's not bad grub, once you're used to it," grinned Fallon. "At least, so the Indians say! This your entire company?"

"Yes, but there's more coming behind us. Their wagons are slow."

"Wagons? Well, I'll be! Folks last winter had wagons, but they had to leave them behind. Wait until Sutter hears about this. I guess he'll dance a jig!"

Next day, after the long caravan of wagons crept into the small settlement at Johnson's Ranch, the new arrivals were treated to noon rations of boiled beef, fresh potatoes and real bread. During the afternoon, while the animals grazed in the tall grass, dusty emigrants gathered at the river to wash themselves and their clothing.

Five-year-old Ben Bonney splashed about in the water until he came up with a handful of odd-looking pebbles. Doctor W. B. Gildea, a dentist from Saint Louis watched as Ben and his friends exclaimed over his find. Finally, his curiosity aroused, Gildea called out:

"What's that you've got, Ben?"

"I dunno. It looks like wheat, sort of, but it's prettier and it's heavy."

"May I have a look?"

"All right—will you give it back?"

"Of course, Ben." Gildea examined the light-colored particles carefully. "Did you see any more like this where you found it?"

"There's lots more." Ben stared at his find, then looked at the dentist. "Why? Doctor, what did I find?"

"I think it's gold, Ben. It looks to me like you've found gold."

Ben waved his hat wildly to attract his father's attention. "Hey, Pa, I found gold! Come and see!"

Jarvis Bonney came over and took the pea-sized nugget from his son's hand. After a brief and cursory examination, he handed it back to the boy.

"Might be, then again, might not. Hard to say."

"That's gold, Mr. Bonney, believe me. Don't forget, I use it in my work. But if I were you, I'd keep this kind of quiet. Later, once we've settled and located our land, it might do to come back and try our luck at mining. If it's as the lad says, we could make our fortunes!"

"*If* it's as he says, and *if* it's gold—those are mighty big 'ifs,' Doctor! I'm not saying you don't know your business, but mine's coopering and carpentering, not mining. A man's more apt to prosper by sticking to what he knows."

"Be that as it may be, I don't suppose you'd object to Ben and me doing a little prospecting in the morning?" asked the dentist with a smile.

"Of course not, if you've got time for that sort of thing. I'll be much too busy, but I'd be obliged if you kept an eye on him. The river's not much along here, but the lad can't swim a stroke."

Throughout the next day, Gildea and the boy explored the rocks and crevices along the shores of the river, and, to their surprise and pleasure, found much to collect. Before the sun had set, they had filled a one ounce bottle from the doctor's medicine kit. They were much too busy to notice the naked *nisenan* scouts who watched from the bushes on the river bank.

III

GENERAL MARIANO G. VALLEJO wanted to stop the emigration before it was too late. In December 1845, Mexican President José Herrera received a letter from the *Californio*. As usual, it was a plea for funds:

The emigration of *norte americanos* to California today forms an unbroken line of wagons from the United States clear to this department, and how can they be turned back without forces and resources? It is necessary, sir, it is indispensable that the Supreme Government should send us both. This has been for some years my incessant supplication. Troops and money!

Only by uniting both can they save us from the imminent danger that surrounds us. It would be very desirable to close that door of communication between the United States and this country, even at some sacrifice. Castro having made propositions to Sutter for the purchase of his establishment, he said that he would cede it to the government for one hundred thousand dollars.

I grant that this is a very high price to pay for a few pieces of cannon, a not very scientifically constructed bastion, some moats, ten or twelve adobe houses, and corrals of the same material; but the security of the country is what is to be paid for, and that is priceless.

President Herrera knew where he could get the money Vallejo wanted. U.S. President James K. Polk had sent John Slidell to Mexico City with the offer of seven million dollars to help Herrera solve his economic problems. In exchange, Polk wanted the Mexicans to use two million dollars of the money to settle overdue claims to American citizens and abandon its own claims to the land north of the Rio Grande.

Herrera and the Mexicans found the offer outrageous and unacceptable. And because Mexico already had severed relations with the United States shortly after Polk's election, the Mexican president refused to speak directly to Slidell. But before Herrera could act on either request, in the unlikely event he wished to, matters were taken out of his hands.

On December 31, 1845, a military junta overthrew his government and installed General Mariano Paredes y Arrillaga in his place. The new government had no intention of negotiating with Polk's representative,

Slidell. Neither did it wish to send money or supplies to Alta California, where *Californios* often had rebelled against the central government. The Mexican Army was ready to fight the Americans, but not in General Vallejo's department.

Meanwhile, in Washington, President Polk offered a new interpretation of the Monroe Doctrine on December 2, 1845. He warned European nations not to interfere with the territorial expansion of his country. England and France had tried to prevent Texas from becoming a state, and England was challenging the United States on the Pacific Coast, particularly in the Oregon Territory. Polk said to Congress:

> The British proposition of compromise, which would ... leave on the British side two-thirds of the whole Oregon territory, including the free navigation of the Columbia and all the valuable harbors on the Pacific, can never for a moment be entertained by the United States ... the people of this continent alone have the right to decide their own destiny. Should any portion of them, constituting an independent state, propose to unite themselves with our confederacy, this will be a question for them and us to determine without any foreign interposition.

Not all Americans agreed. Robert C. Winthrop, a Massachusetts congressman argued in favor of continuing joint occupancy of the Oregon Territory with England. Said Winthrop, "As to land, we have millions of acres of better land still unoccupied on this side of the mountains."

IV

WAR WITH MEXICO! The nation plunged happily into the fray when President Polk declared in May 1846 that General Taylor's American forces had been attacked by Mexican troops on American soil. So popular was Polk's campaign for territorial expansion that his call for volunteers paralyzed the recruiting apparatus. So many rushed to serve that lots had to be drawn to determine which fortunate lads would be permitted to become heroes. Only in New England was there any organized opposition to the war, where anti-slavery sentiment was strong and growing, and there was bitter resentment over the recent admission of Texas as a slave state.

At Fort Leavenworth General Stephen W. Kearny was told to raise an army of one thousand Missouri volunteers and leave at once for New Mexico and California. But before Kearny's troops could begin their trek, the annual migration to Oregon and California had begun.

Among those traveling beside the Platte River in the summer of 1846 were the families of Lillburn Boggs, James Reed, and George Donner. In

1838, while governor of Missouri, Boggs had driven the followers of Joseph Smith from his state, declaring: "The Mormons must be treated as enemies and must be exterminated or driven from the State if necessary for the public peace—their outrages are beyond description."

Now, eight years later, Boggs and his own family were being forced to leave Missouri "for reasons of health." Although he cited the growing incidence of ague and fever in his state, Boggs had a more personal problem: In 1842 the former governor came within an eyelash of being murdered when an unknown (but widely suspected) assailant fired buckshot through a window and wounded Boggs in the head and neck. Miraculously he survived, despite one shot lodged near his brain. The attempted murder was thought to be the work of the notorious Mormon secret organization, Sons of Dan.

Also on the emigrant trail, but moving east, were some Americans who had wintered at Sutter's Fort. In this party were such seasoned guides as Jim Clyman, Jim Hudspeth and Caleb Greenwood, the latter now eighty-three. Another member of the party was an ambitious lawyer and self-styled guide, Lansford Hastings, who was promoting a new route across the Utah desert.

Hastings had never seen the new trail, but John C. Frémont, who had traveled part of the way, told him about the so-called southern "shortcut" while at Sutter's Fort. When the men from California reached the spot where Frémont's tracks parted from the old trail, Hastings insisted that they follow the new road. After all, he was anxious to see for himself the trail which he had described in such glowing terms in his recently published guidebook.

His companions, less enthusiastic, nevertheless were equally curious, with the notable exception of Old Greenwood and his sons, who refused to leave the main trail. The company parted and later reunited at the Green River, both groups getting through without mishap, but when Jim Clyman went on ahead to meet the emigrants at Fort Laramie, he advised everyone against taking the new "Hastings Cutoff."

Among those he advised were Boggs, Reed, and Donner, but only Boggs listened. At the Green River he went north, following the trail of Caleb Greenwood, whose ten-year-old son "Governor Boggs," was his namesake.

V

CHARLES T. STANTON and his companion, Bill McCutchen, reached Sutter's Fort early in October 1846. Within days Stanton was back on the trail, retracing his steps, heading east. McCutchen was too ill to travel, and Stanton dared not wait a single day before going back into the mountains with two of Sutter's nisenan herdsmen and seven mules packed with provisions. Somewhere in the great Utah desert McCutchen's family and others in the company were desperately in need of food.

In mid-October Stanton arrived at the headwaters of the Bear River just as Lansford Hastings' westbound company lowered the last of its wagons into Bear Valley. As men and animals of both parties rested, two men staggered into the camp, seemingly more dead than alive. At first Stanton assumed they were strangers, but on closer inspection he was shocked to recognize Jim Reed and Walter Herron, both members of the company he hoped to aid. Astonished to find them in California when he had supposed they were still in the desert, Stanton exclaimed:

"Jim! Walt! Are you all right? You look terrible!"

"Stanton—thank God!" Reed's voice was scarcely more than a dry whisper. "Food—we need food. Haven't had a thing but roots and beans—*four* beans!"

"Of course—can you make it over here to my camp? I've got plenty of food. I was bringing it to the company. But where are they?"

"Far side of the mountains—on the desert."

"I don't understand," said Stanton. "Where's your family—your wagons? How did you get separated?"

"Long story," replied Reed, now busily engaged in eating biscuits and coffee. He sighed before going on. Finally he said, "Snyder, blast his hide—tried to kill me."

Stanton couldn't trust his ears. "What? Snyder tried to kill you? I can't believe it!" John Snyder was one of the best liked young men in the entire company. The words didn't ring true.

"It's true. He hit me—hit my wife, too. I fought back, trying to save my own life. Believe me, he tried to kill me!"

"What did you do?"

"Killed him—had no choice. I didn't want to, but it was him or me."

Stanton listened in shocked silence. He found it hard to imagine either Snyder or Reed creating a disturbance, let alone a fight to the death. Everything was insane—it didn't seem possible for matters to have taken such a hideous turn in the short time since he had left the train.

"Are you saying you killed Snyder and ran off from the train?"

"No! No, of course not!" exclaimed Reed, angrily. "They forced me to go. I wanted—tried to stay—but some said they'd lynch me! The few friends I have insisted I go—said they'd look after my family."

"Good Lord, I can hardly credit it," said Stanton, shaking his head in wonder. "But what about you, Walt? Surely you weren't in on this fight, too?"

"No, I wasn't. In fact, we and the Donners were miles ahead. We didn't know a thing about it till Mr. Reed came along and told us."

"I don't understand why you left the train, Walt." Walter Herron was one of Reed's three teamsters. It seemed to Stanton that Herron shouldn't be here—he ought to be helping Reed's family.

"I figured Mr. Reed couldn't make it alone, what with the Indians and everything. And I thought the two of us might do better at finding game, though that wasn't the case. Anyway, I just couldn't stand to see him go off alone that way."

"Did you get the supplies?" Reed abruptly asked Stanton.

"Yes, I did. I've got seven pack mules and a pair of Indians to help me."

"I'm glad to hear it. My family's just about out of food by now and so are most of the others."

"In that case, I'd better get moving," replied Stanton.

"Do me a favor, Charley?" asked Reed. "Make sure my family is taken care of, will you? I'm worried sick. Outside of the Donners, there's hardly a soul I can trust. Some are just plain mean. I'm scared of what they might do while I'm away." Reed had a wife and four children, the youngest aged three. George and Jacob Donner, both in their sixties, were close friends of the Reeds.

The Donners and Reed had been prosperous businessmen back in Springfield, Illinois. Reed's arrogant and haughty manner sometimes inclined others to resent him. He liked to flaunt his wealth, and on earlier occasions had snubbed Stanton, whose Chicago business had failed. Now Reed was forced to swallow his pride and ask for Stanton's aid.

"I'll look after them the same as if they were my own," Stanton promised. "But what will you do? What shall I tell your folks? Where'll you meet them?"

"I'm coming right back soon as Walt and I can get some more provisions from Sutter. Tell Margaret I'll get back to her just as fast as I can."

"All right." Stanton turned to his nisenan companions. "Come on, you vaqueros—let's pack out."

Several nourishing meals shared with members of Hastings' party enabled Reed and Herron to recover their health while descending to the valley of the Sacramento. At Johnson's Ranch, in stark contrast to the desperate situation across the mountains, emigrants were celebrating a festive event. One of the newly arrived emigrants, Reverend James G. T. Dunleavy was marrying Sebastian Keyser, owner of the other half of Johnson's Ranch, to Miss Elizabeth Rhodes, formerly of Roy County, Missouri. Reed and Herron paused just long enough to toast the bride's health before going on to Sutter's Fort in the company of Lillburn Boggs.

Sutter agreed to furnish more food and pack animals for the beleaguered company, but as Reed was making his arrangements, Lieutenant Colonel Frémont (promoted from Captain only hours before by California's naval commander), sent an urgent message to the fort. Frémont was raising an army of volunteers to go to Los Angeles and fight rebellious *Californios*. Short of horses, arms, and provisions, the new colonel was requesting that those emigrants who had just arrived across the plains join him and outfit themselves for the long march south!

Despite the predicament of those still in the mountains, Herron and Reed promptly enlisted. Reed, however, conditioned his service upon first arranging for his family's safe arrival. He turned down an offer of a captaincy and left Sutter's Fort with Bill McCutchen, now recovered from his illness. They went back to Johnson's Ranch, gathered more supplies and left that place on November 3, 1846, with thirty horses, one mule, a few hundred pounds of flour and a hindquarter of beef. With them went two nisenan slaves borrowed from Sutter.

It rained and then the rain turned to sleet and finally snow. At the end of the first day they camped in a foot and a half of snow at the lower end of Bear Valley. Sleet extinguished their fire, so they went to bed hungry. In the morning they crossed the valley and were surprised to find a couple, Mr. and Mrs. Jotham Curtis, living in a makeshift shelter.

Curtis explained his presence by saying the meadow had looked so inviting in October that the couple had decided to winter there. Now two feet of snow covered the grass and their cattle had strayed and become lost. Their provisions were nearly gone and hunger had reduced them to killing their dog.

Reed and McCutchen at once offered some of their flour and beef, but the dog was nearly baked in Mrs. Curtis's dutch oven. While she made bread, the others sampled the pet, McCutchen pronouncing it "very good dog."

It was decided to leave one of the Indians at the Curtis camp, along with several horses and some food. After promising to take Mr. and Mrs. Curtis with them on their return trip, Reed, McCutchen, and the second vaquero took off. Climbing the 600-foot wall with two dozen animals was slow and hard, but at last they reached the top. After struggling for three more miles through powder snow up to their stirrups, the men called a halt and made camp.

During the night, while Reed and McCutchen slept, the vaquero slipped away with three horses, unwilling to continue on the risky mission. When McCutchen awoke and found him gone, he saddled another horse and followed as far as the Curtis camp. He was told that both vaqueros had fled in the direction of Sutter's Fort.

Disgusted and tired, McCutchen again climbed with his horse to the top of the cliff, found his camp and stumbled into bed. Next day, the pair went higher into the mountains, expecting at any moment to meet the Reed-Donner train on its way down. The farther they went, the more it snowed. When the drifts became too deep for the horses, they lay down and refused to move.

For a while the men continued on foot, unwilling to give up. Finally they were forced to admit defeat. Without snowshoes it was impossible to travel in the deep, soft snow, but neither man possessed or knew how to make them. Nothing in their past experience prepared them for this moment.

Reed and McCutchen silently dug out the horses and retraced their hard-won steps. At Bear Valley they gathered up the remaining horses and the Curtis family. Later, down at Sutter's Fort, Johann Sutter assured the men that the stranded emigrants should have no trouble if they rationed their cattle.

Not for three months, February at the earliest, would it be possible to send another relief party into the mountains. In the Sierra Nevada it continued to snow, harder and earlier than any year in Sutter's memory.

NEWSPAPER PRINTSHOP

CHAPTER 4

FOURTH ESTATE

Spring 1845–January 1847

I

GEORGE L. CURRY, editor of the *Oregon Spectator,* was going through the pile of mail and newspapers which had just come from the post office when a brand new masthead caught his eye.

"Looks like we've got a new rival on the coast, John."

"Oh? Who might that be?" John Fleming, his printer, looked up from the type case.

"New weekly down at Yerba Buena. *California Star,* it says. Fellow named Brannan is the publisher—Samuel Brannan. E. P. Jones is the editor. Ever hear of 'em?"

"Nope."

"Nor I."

Curry went back to his reading and Fleming continued putting type in his composing stick. In a few minutes Curry spoke again:

"Here's something kind of interesting in the *Californian*—they claim Brannan is leader of the Mormons. Listen: 'Published and owned by S. Brannan, the leader of the Mormons, who was brought up by Joe Smith himself, and is consequently well qualified to unfold and impress the tenets of his sect.' Hmmm. He must be part of that bunch that came around the Horn last year. Remember? There was a story about them in the Honolulu paper."

"I wouldn't think there'd be much demand for a Mormon paper in California," commented Fleming.

"Well, that's the strange thing—according to the *Californian* the *Star* is a Mormon paper, but the *Star* says it's not! Sounds like we might be in for some lively correspondence! I must say, the *Star*'s a lot better looking than the *Californian*. Almost has the look of a New York paper."

"Not bad," said Fleming, looking at the paper over Curry's shoulder. "Not bad, indeed! Look at that heading—seven levels of display! That's pretty professional—why don't you ever do anything like that, John?"

"You buy me the type and I will. It's a wonder we look as good as we do with the stuff we've got to work with. Maybe I ought to go down to San Francisco Bay and go to work for this Mormon fellow!"

"You know I'm only jesting! What would you and I do with such a fancy set-up, anyway? We couldn't sell any more papers. Besides, our readers don't care how it looks, just so we publish half-way on time and spell the names right."

"Most of our readers don't know the right way to spell their own names," joked Fleming. "But I agree—this new paper sure beats that Monterey sheet. Take a look at this, Tallman—look like what you used to do, back in the States?"

Tallman Rolfe, Fleming's assistant, wiped the ink from his hands and came over to the desk. He was trying to remember where he had heard Sam Brannan's name before. It had a familiar ring. Had Brannan been in Nauvoo?

Rolfe had been working in the *Spectator* office throughout the winter in order to support the farm he and Stump had taken up in the spring of 1846. Under the Oregon Land Laws each could claim up to six hundred and forty acres of public land without paying anything but the recording fee. But to gain clear title, they had to live on the land and make permanent improvements in the first six months.

The two young men had worked long hours during the spring and summer, clearing and fencing fields and building a cabin for the winter—but they couldn't produce crops that first year. Because they would need money to buy provisions and seed for the coming year, Tallman proposed that he look for a job. Stump could remain on the farm to keep squatters off and to keep from having to pay the five dollar penalty levied by the local government for temporary absence from the land.

Tallman went first to the newspaper office, where he was rewarded with a position as Fleming's assistant. When he applied for the job, Tallman told his new boss about his apprenticeship on the Nauvoo *Times and Seasons*. To his relief, Fleming appeared unconcerned. The printer had known Mormons back in Ohio, and thought them a little strange, but so were most people in the printing trade. He agreed with Tallman, however, that it was best to say nothing about the matter to anyone else, for Oregon City was full of Missourians with strong prejudices against the self-styled Saints.

The news about Sam Brannan stirred many emotions. Later, when Curry left the office and Fleming asked Rolfe if he had known Brannan, Tallman replied: "I've been asking myself the same question. The name is familiar and I'm beginning to think I may have seen him once at the *Times and Seasons* office."

"Did he work with you?"

"No, it was after I'd left to study law, and I don't think he ever worked there, either. You see, sometimes I used to come by the newspaper office after work. I still had friends on the paper and we'd walk home together. One day I got there a little early or else they worked a little late that evening. While I waited for them to clean up, Joseph Smith came in with a younger man who he said was going to start a new church paper in the East."

"You think the man was Brannan?"

"It was a name like that. It's so long ago, it's hard to be sure. Anyway, Joseph Smith had brought him to the office to show how we did things at Nauvoo. He was supposed to learn everything he could before going on to New York."

"To New York?"

"I'm sure that's where he was going—to New York City."

"Might be the same fellow, all right," said Fleming. "New York is where those Mormons came from last summer. Was he a printer?"

"Yes. In fact, he owned a press. I think that's why Smith was sending him east. Smith was willing to pay to get his press out of storage, where it had been while he was doing missionary work for the church. That would save the expense of buying new equipment."

"Sounds like it could be the same man. Funny. I could almost swear I knew a fellow by that name, but I don't recall his being a printer. But I've never been to Nauvoo or New York. Lived most of my life in Ohio."

"That's interesting. I lived there for a time as a boy. My family was at Kirtland until my twelfth birthday," said Tallman.

"That so? It really is a small world we live in! Well, have you finished with the proofing? Next page is about ready to go."

Nothing more was said that day about the *California Star* and its mysterious publisher, but thoughts of Nauvoo and the Rolfe family continued to occupy Tallman's mind. Ever since that day in March nearly two years ago, when he had said his last goodbyes, concern for his family's safety had been the greatest of his private worries. Only once during that time had he heard from them. His brother Ianthus was living with relatives in Brighton, Massachusetts, and the rest of the family was preparing to join the great western exodus to Zion. Last year's arrivals in Oregon said that thousands of Mormon emigrants were spread across the whole of Iowa, and a battalion of Mormon volunteers was reported to be marching alongside General Kearny's Missourians on the Santa Fe Trail. Supposedly, they were on their way to New Mexico and Lower California to fight the Mexicans, but it seemed more likely they'd be fighting one another before they ever got to Santa Fe.

II

IN 1844 JOSEPH SMITH discovered that one of his missionaries in the western settlements owned a printing press and knew how to use it. Smith called Samuel Brannan back to Nauvoo and told him he was to take his press to New York and begin publishing a missionary paper. Sam could hardly wait.

As a boy, he had spent five years as a printer's apprentice in Ohio. Later, while employed as a printer in New Orleans, Sam bought one of Hoe's Washington hand presses on which to print a literary journal. When that venture failed, he went to Indianapolis and put out an abolitionist paper. That, too, had failed and so he had gone home to Ohio and put his press in storage.

In Ohio he had been converted to the teachings of Joseph Smith and soon was doing missionary work for the Church of Latter Day Saints. Although he didn't mind spreading the new gospel by word of mouth, Brannan was delighted when Joseph Smith asked him to do it with type in America's greatest city.

When he got to New York, Brannan advertised for helpers. Edward Kemble, sixteen-year-old son of a newspaper editor in Troy, applied for the job of printer's devil. Kemble had worked for his father and Sam decided this experience outweighed the fact that Kemble was not yet a Mormon. He balanced the scales by hiring a Mormon lad, John Eager, who knew nothing about type or presses. Sam hoped each would learn something from the other.

Shortly after *The Prophet* began to be circulated on New York streets, Joseph Smith was killed by assassins, and Sam Brannan made one of his first serious errors. Instead of waiting to see which way the wind blew, he took sides in the dispute over who should succeed as leader of the Mormons. He joined those who backed Smith's son and was rewarded by being "disfellowshipped" by Brigham Young and the Apostles. Brannan was not ready to break with the church, so he made a quick trip to Nauvoo, went before the Apostles and freely admitted his error. His confession was accepted and Brannan was reinstated as publisher and editor of the *Prophet*.

In the summer of 1845, Elder Orson Pratt thought the paper's name ought to be changed to *The Messenger*. By removing obvious Mormon connotations from the masthead he hoped to increase the paper's circulation and influence in New York City. The change was made, but the public was not impressed. The paper continued to limp along under its new title.

Then, in November a startling thing happened. Sam Brannan received an exciting directive from Parley P. Pratt, brother of Orson. Elder Pratt said:

Our Apostles assembled in meeting have debated the best method of getting all our people into the far west with the least possible hardship. ... I enclose to you a letter of instructions from the Apostles, authorizing you to lead the group of Saints in its exodus from New York City and the Atlantic seaboard.

Brother Brigham is, this day, sending a letter to my brother Orson directing him to call a conference of all Saints in your mission to lay before them the plan to emigrate by water from New York.

The sailing ship *Brooklyn* left New York harbor on February 4, 1846, carrying 230 passengers, fifty pigs, two cows, farm and mechanics' tools, books, luggage, and a newspaper office, complete with press and type. Most, but not all, of the passengers were members of the Mormon Church. The *Brooklyn* was going first to Honolulu to deliver a cargo of freight for the Sandwich Islands. Then the *Brooklyn* would sail for San Francisco Bay to deliver her human cargo to the Mexican port.

Brannan's company arrived in the Sandwich Islands in July, and the Honolulu *Friend* printed a very friendly article concerning the Mormon emigration:

THE MORMONS. *Their present Condition and Prospective plans.*—As has been already stated, they estimate their numbers by hundreds of thousands, very many of whom have come off from other denominations. This is true of the company on board the "Brooklyn."

Some have come from the Baptists, others from the Methodists, a few from the Presbyterians, while almost every denomination has its representative among them.

So far as we are able to learn, California is now to be their grand central rendezvous, while the beautiful region around San Francisco Bay is the chosen spot where the latter-day saints propose to settle. Abating much from the highly colored descriptions which we have always heard respecting that region, it must still be regarded as a most enchanting spot, and the most desirable location for a colony to found upon the long line of the North and South American sea coast.

The natural facilities of the country and bay conspire to render it certain that many years cannot elapse before flourishing cities and villages will diversify the scene. The watchword of the Mormons now is "California." The few score of emigrants on board the "Brooklyn" are but a fraction of the immense numbers already on their way thither.

The *Brooklyn* sailed into San Francisco Bay on the last day of July 1846. When Brannan looked toward the lonely village of Yerba Buena, he was surprised to see the familiar Stars and Stripes being whipped about by brisk ocean winds. San Francisco, he discovered, was no longer a Mexican port.

Since July 7, 1846, the American flag had been displayed here and at Monterey, while at Sonoma American adventurers had concocted a flag of their own, the symbol of the independent state of California. This had been raised for a short time after the arrest of General Mariano Vallejo and his brother. The Vallejos had been taken to Sutter's Fort and imprisoned by order of Frémont.

After determining that Commodore Stockton, who had established martial law in California, was desperately in need of a printer, Sam Brannan ordered his printing press brought ashore. Kemble and Eager soon were busily producing documents and proclamations for the Navy. Brannan wisely chose to let the newspaper business languish while he took advantage of this rare opportunity to let the federal government subsidize the Mormon missionary effort. He did not know that the Mormon Battalion, now on its way to California, was part of a similar arrangement whereby the wages of Mormon volunteers were being used by Brigham Young to finance the emigration to Zion.

Meanwhile at Monterey, a Navy man and a civilian started their own newspaper. On August 15, 1846, Dr. Robert B. Semple and Rev. Walter Colton launched *The Californian*, first paper in the state and second on the Pacific Coast. In order to interest new and old residents of California, it was published in English and Spanish, both versions appearing side by side.

The Californian was smaller than the *Oregon Spectator*. Its four pages, each about 8½ by 12½ inches, were printed two at a time on a wooden Ramage press which the Mexicans had purchased from a Boston firm in 1833. Governor José María Echeandía and his successors had used it for government documents. The new owners, who had appropriated the equipment, said:

> We are not fond of making apologies, but at present we beg leave to inform our readers that the materials on which the Californian is printed, was found in the public buildings here, and have been used for the Spanish language, and in deed has been much injured by neglect. Many of the letters have been wasted or mislaid, and the whole very much out of order, so that, in fact, we have made our first number almost from chaos.

Reverend Colton was chaplain on board Commodore Stockton's ship, the *Congress,* which arrived at Monterey a month earlier. He had been a Congregational minister, professor of moral philosophy (with degrees from Yale and Andover Theological Seminary), editor of newspapers at Philadelphia and Washington City, and the author of two books about his naval voyages. Andrew Jackson had appointed him to his chaplaincy in 1831 despite Colton's vigorous efforts to prevent Jackson from forcing the Cherokee Nation out of Georgia. Now he was *alcalde* of Monterey.

The partnership was almost incongruous: Semple, a rough-hewn giant who stood six feet eight inches tall, was the son of a former Virginia physician and legislator who had moved west to Kentucky. At Frankfort, on the *Western Argus,* young Bob Semple learned the printer's trade. Later he studied and practiced dentistry, medicine, and the law.

Restless, and finding little satisfaction in any of these pursuits, he came west to California with Hastings in 1845. A year later, he was part of the band of settlers who arrested the Vallejos at Sonoma, and was chosen secretary of the Bear Flag Republic. Tiring of this role, too, he went to Monterey and joined Captain Daingerfield Fauntleroy's dragoons. He met Colton at Monterey, and when they decided to publish *The Californian,* Semple resigned from the dragoons.

In the first issue of the paper, the editors urged Californians, new and old, to unite and form a colonial government. A legislature could be elected and a delegate sent to Congress to ask for formal recognition for the new territory.

At Yerba Buena Sam Brannan read his copy of *The Californian* with a great deal of interest, fascinated by the possibilities it raised. Events were moving fast and Sam realized he might have to modify his plans. For one thing, until now he had thought of his proposed publication only as a means of serving the Mormon church. Now, viewing the poorly printed Monterey paper with amused contempt, he saw a new vision.

California, it appeared, was going to be a very lively place, but Monterey was not where the future lay. Why, then, should he limit his horizons by issuing a narrowly defined missionary paper? Brannan was convinced that he and Ed Kemble could produce a weekly of professional quality. Joseph Smith and Brigham Young hadn't elevated themselves by setting modest goals. Think big—that was the way!

III

ED KEMBLE MISSED out on the big moment. When Sam Brannan decided to launch the *California Star* at Yerba Buena, Sergeant Kemble was at the Mission of San Buenaventura with Colonel Frémont. Three days after the first issue was printed on January 9, 1847, the *Californios* surrendered to the Americans and the war in California came to an end.

With Kemble gone, Brannan chose Elbert P. Jones to edit the new paper. Jones, a Kentucky lawyer who had just arrived in California, was not a printer, so Sam had to help John Eager set the type and run the press.

Before the second issue was ready, Lieutenant Washington A. Bartlett USN, Yerba Buena's *alcalde,* came into the *Star* office with a stranger at his side. A month earlier on December 10 Bartlett and some friends were caught in the act of requisitioning cattle from a Santa Clara rancho and taken prisoner by Francisco Sanchez and his vaqueros.

News of the capture traveled to San José and Yerba Buena, where a rescue mission was put together hastily. Two companies of United States Marines, a dozen or so Yerba Buena horsemen, and a company of volunteers from San José fought a one-hour battle with Sanchez at Santa Clara and forced him to relinquish his prisoners and sign a treaty of peace.

Bartlett introduced his companion to Sam as James Reed, an acting lieutenant in Captain C. M. Weber's San José company, who had aided in his rescue. Bartlett wanted Sam to hear the story of Reed's family, stranded in the Sierras. On January 16, 1847, the *Star* reported Reed's tale to its subscribers:

EMIGRANTS IN THE MOUNTAINS

It is probably not generally known to the people that there is now in the California mountains, in a most distressing situation, a party of emigrants from the United States, who were prevented from crossing the mountains by an early fall of snow.

The party consists of about sixty persons, men, women and children.

They were almost entirely out of provisions when they reached the foot of the mountain, and but for the timely succor afforded them by Capt. J. A. Sutter, one of the most humane and liberal men in California, they must have all perished in a few days. Captain Sutter, as soon as he ascertained their situation, sent five mules loaded with provisions to them.

A second party was dispatched with provisions for them, but they found the mountain impassable in consequence of the snow. We hope that our citizens will do something for the relief of these unfortunate people.

Near the end of January, Rev. James G. T. Dunleavy came into the *Star* office with a notice which Bartlett wanted published. It was a new ordinance:

WHEREAS, the local name of Yerba Buena, as applied to the settlement or town of San Francisco, is unknown beyond the district, and has been applied from the local name of the cove, on which the town is built;

Therefore, to prevent confusion and mistakes in public documents, and that the town may have the advantage of the name given on the public map,

IT IS HEREBY ORDAINED, that the name SAN FRANCISCO shall hereafter be used in all official communications and public documents, or records appertaining to the town.

> Wash^n A. Bartlett
> Chief Magistrate.

Published by order,
J. G. T. Dunleavy, Municipal Clerk.

"Why change the name?" asked Brannan. "I think Yerba Buena's kind of pretty."

"It has something to do with the new city that Vallejo and Semple are promoting across the bay. They say it's called Francisca because that's the name of General Vallejo's wife, but some of the local people think it's confusing."

"You mean Bartlett and his friends might have trouble selling their own lots here at Yerba Buena if people start settling at Francisca?"

"Something like that. But I must say it's true that Yerba Buena isn't well known. I never heard of it before coming to California last year."

"Well, I'll print your notice, but I think I'll leave Yerba Buena on my masthead. I don't really think Bartlett has the authority to make a change like that."

"Suit yourself," replied the Methodist minister, preparing to leave.

"Watch your step, Reverend," called Sam, as he carried the notice over to the type case. "It's pretty slippery out there. We had a quarter-inch of ice on the street a few days ago!"

"I know. Old timers say it's the coldest winter in memory. No one can remember seeing ice alongside San Francisco Bay before."

Sam was already lost in thought. That fellow Semple was a clever rascal, despite the obviously inferior quality of his newspaper. Sam wondered what kind of deal his competitor had made with the general since Vallejo's release from Sutter's Fort. His suspicions were not unfounded. On January 4, 1847, his journalistic rival had written a letter to a nephew in Illinois in which he boasted of his recent successes:

I did not write to you last Spring, not for want of a disposition, but for want of time and paper. Permit me now to remind you that California is under the United States Government, and that everything has changed much since I left St. Louis.

I arrived in California the twenty-second day of December, 1845, little more than one year ago with *one little horse,* no money, and no clothes but a suit of leather. What a change one little year can make. Without a friend to urge me forward, I went to work at carpentering; then I took half of a farm and sowed wheat.

On the ninth day of June, last, I joined a party of revolutionists. On the tenth we took about two hundred horses and eighteen prisoners. The prisoners were released. On the fourteenth we took the fortified town of Sonoma, with thirty-three men.

I continued in the service until the fifteenth of August; got a printing press and commenced publishing the "Californian," and within the last few days purchased and paid for a site for a city on the Bay of San Francisco (five miles); one-half in partnership with General Vallejo, the wealthiest and best educated man in California; and have about four hundred dollars in cash left, and owe no man anything but good will.

I have the confidence of all in power except one or two, and I have got them afraid of me, with my industry and knowledge of business. My property is worth two hundred thousand dollars, and popularity enough to get into any office in the gift of the people.

Now, my dear boy, if you have finished your studies and can get to this country, with a small library and your knowledge of the Spanish language, and my influence, you can make ten thousand dollars a year at the practice of law.

I will take much pleasure in forwarding your interests.

Still your uncle,
Rob't Semple

FOOD PREPARATION IN A NISENAN VILLAGE

CHAPTER 5

SECOND INVASION

Fall 1846–May 1847

I

*I*N LITTLE MORE than a year the *nisenan* people had grown accustomed to the annual *wolesem* migrations. Because Greenwood's Trail skirted the far edge of Wema's territory and arriving travelers were too tired and hungry to bother the nisenan, there had been little conflict. No new villages had appeared in the mountains and the *jom*, proudly riding a fine Spanish horse, took full credit for getting rid of the intruders.

Occasionally, while collecting nuts and acorns, the natives found themselves being watched by curious newcomers. At first they had fled from the white travelers, but in time they learned to ignore those who came along. Once in awhile they became very bold and mocked the whites by imitating the sounds of their language. It was great fun and everyone laughed when this happened, even the wolesem. Such naiveté on the part of those who were being ridiculed caused the nisenan harvesters to laugh some more and was one of the reasons why Wema's people came to think of the wolesem as children.

Except for a certain degree of skill at hunting game, it seemed the pink-skinned people knew very little about the gathering of food—at least in a natural and sensible way. They always made things harder than was necessary, insisting that their slaves work in the hot sun for long hours every day just so that their plants would grow in long, straight rows in open fields. Even more ridiculous was their insistence on planting seeds to grow grass. The white people seemed not to realize what a waste of time and energy this was. After all, acorns, nuts, berries, grains, mushrooms, and vegetables grew themselves. Only harvesting and preserving were necessary.

The newcomers were inefficient in other ways, too. The tribesmen had watched them expend much labor moving heavily loaded wagons over very steep and rocky terrain—but if the animals died or lacked the strength to go on, everything might be abandoned alongside the trail. Wiser planning could have prevented such wasteful practices. The nisenan would have taken only the most important items and used the most practical form of transportation, thus assuring that everything would reach the final destination.

On the other hand, the wolesem could be very clever at times. That valuable metal, iron, was an example. The nisenan called it *hijélu*, after the *panjol* word, *hierro*. It was marvelous what white men could do with it and how it would behave in their skilled hands. They could fashion many excellent tools and weapons. They also created some things out of wood that were attractive but unnecessary. Beds, chairs, and tables were nothing but artificial substitutes for things which already existed in nature: rocks, logs, pine needles, or the ground itself.

Sometimes they overlooked the simplest and most obvious devices; for instance, a ladder for climbing trees to collect nuts and acorns. Most nisenan children knew how to make one by cutting or breaking the branches from a pine sapling in such a way that one long stub was left at one end to be used to hook it over a tree limb, and several short stubs could be used for footholds while climbing. Despite its utter simplicity, it never failed to fascinate the foreigners, who enjoyed examining and exclaiming over each pine ladder.

As they spent more time observing the wolesem, Wema's people noticed that the customs of the *janki* or *melikan* often differed from the panjol wolesem. Johnson's Ranch, or Chansen Lanjo, became a favorite location for studying the pink-skins. In this particular year, during the acorn harvest, several of the nisenan were given a rare opportunity to witness a wolesem ritual.

Most agreed afterward that it must have been a wedding ceremony, for when it was over, the young woman who took part became the newest wife of Sebastian Keyser. Keyser was known to the valley tribes as the occupant of the ranch west of Chansen Lanjo, and he was the second participant in the ritual. Also present was a wolesem shaman, who chanted and waved his hands to drive away demons.

When it was over, the observers returned to their villages, and remembered and faithfully retold every detail of the ceremony. What they and their listeners found most fascinating was the moment when Keyser and the guests came and pressed their faces, one at a time, against that of the bride. Prior to this, they had noticed that wolesem adults seldom touched one another with gentleness, so this behavior at the wedding was surprising. Obviously it was part of the traditional ceremonies, but this did not take away from the fact that the foreigners had exhibited human emotions in a public setting. In some ways they were, after all, like real people.

II

"WHY WOULD YOU do such a thing? Especially without first asking me?" Although Walupa was angry with his daughter, he was careful not to raise his voice. It would have been undignified.

"They are very sick, Father. Would you have us leave them out in the storm to die? Even the wolesem are human."

Walupa ignored her last remark. He had his own opinion, but to state it would have taken a long time, and now was not the time. Instead, he asked, "Where are they?"

"At my sister's house. She is feeding them."

"How many?"

"Seven. Five are women. They're all in poor condition."

"How poor?"

"I think they could die."

"And if they die here, we'll be blamed."

"It won't be our fault."

"Will the whites think so? No. They'll say we killed them."

"How? By starvation?"

"Why not? They'll say we refused them food."

"But we didn't."

"You don't understand. These intruders will believe any bad thing about us. They're savages! We'll have to move them out of here."

"They can hardly walk."

"Let them crawl—I don't care!"

"But if they die before they're gone from our lands, how is that different from dying in the village? Won't we be blamed anyway?"

Walupa was silent. His daughter was speaking the truth. At length he said, "Find your brother. Tell him to come to me."

Walupa would have his son present the problem to Wema, who was in the adjoining village. Let the chief solve the affair.

" 'The wolesem are to leave your village in the morning. If you don't think they can travel alone, send an escort with them. Get them to Chansen Lanjo as fast as you can.' " Walupa's son was repeating the chief's words to his father.

"What else did he say?"

" 'Travel from village to village as much as possible. That way they can be sheltered and fed and kept alive more easily. If they cannot travel the full distance in one day, provide temporary cover for them until they reach the nearest village. I'll tell the villages to expect you.' "

"Is that all?"

"Just one more thing. Wema says 'I don't expect Walupa to go with the wolesem, but I hold him responsible for keeping them alive until they are safe at Chansen Lanjo,' " his son replied.

In the morning, four nisenan youths left with the seven exhausted travelers. For the next six days the mixed party moved slowly from one village to the next, climbing hills and descending ravines. They forded swollen streams, climbed over slippery rocks, and waded through acres of damp brush. On the seventh day the white people refused to move. Only one, a man, could stand or walk. The feet of all of them were torn, bleeding, and frost-bitten.

After much discussion in both languages, plus many signs and signals, it was agreed that two of the Indians would go on with the one white man who could stand. Johnson's Ranch now was not far; the other members of the party would wait beside the trail until help came.

The Ritchie family, new emigrants who had built a small cabin on Johnson's Ranch, were the nearest settlers. As the trio approached the Ritchie house, a woman emerged from the cabin and gave a little cry of terror. Then, seeing that the man being supported by a pair of Indians was one of her own kind, she came forward and helped him walk into the cabin. The escorts waited outside and listened nervously to the sound of wolesem voices on the other side of the wall.

Suddenly another woman ran from the cabin and hurried off in the direction of buildings farther down the river. Despite their apprehension,

Walupa's men did not move. When the woman returned, four men with packs came with her and showed by signs that they knew about the others waiting by the trail.

They set out in the dark, and when the rescuers reached the exhausted party, it was nearly midnight. Before anyone could stop them, the four Indians melted into the shadows and disappeared.

III

EVER SINCE THE FAILURE of his attempt to cross the mountains with McCutchen, James Reed had been trying to organize a relief expedition for the stranded emigrants. He went to San José in November 1846, but Frémont had taken most of the available manpower to Los Angeles. Captain Weber was recruiting volunteers in mid-December to rescue Lieutenant Bartlett from Francisco Sanchez, so Reed chose this opportunity to make his way to Yerba Buena, where he had been told to appeal to the naval authorities for help. Weber had appointed him acting lieutenant of the company and they had marched to Santa Clara.

After the successful confrontation on January 2, Bartlett was released and Reed accompanied the *alcalde* to Yerba Buena. There he received encouragement but no assistance from the military, who advised him to go directly to the local business community. Bartlett called a public meeting for February 3. Most of the community were present, including many officers of the fleet stationed at San Francisco. When Reed was introduced he begged permission for Reverend Dunleavy to speak for him. Reed had first met the Methodist Episcopal minister while crossing the plains the previous summer. They met a second time the day Reed and Herron arrived at Johnson's Ranch as the preacher was marrying Sebastian Keyser and Miss Rhodes. During his stay at Yerba Buena, Reed observed that the minister had proved to be a talented speaker. Dunleavy was also popular with the naval officers, who appreciated his ability to hold his liquor while carrying on a lively conversation.

Selecting the clergyman as his spokesman was a good move. After Dunleavy's impassioned plea, about $700 was raised on the spot, with offers of more to come. Reed for the first time began to feel hope, especially when money and offers of assistance continued to pour in. But on February 6 chilling news reached San Francisco. A letter from Sutter's Fort reported the arrival at Johnson's Ranch of seven persons who claimed to be the only survivors of a party of nineteen that had tried to escape from the mountains. The letter read, in part:

... After wandering about a number of days bewildered in snow, their provisions gave out, and long hunger made it necessary to resort to that horrid resource, casting lots to see who should give up life, that their bodies might be used for food for the remainder.

But at this time the weaker began to die ... and as they died the company went into camp and made meat of the dead bodies of their companions. ... all the females that started, 5 women, came in safe ...

Nine of the men died, and seven of them were eaten by their companions. The first person that died was Mr. C. S. Stanton, the young man who so generously returned to the company with Capt. Sutter's baqueros and provisions; his body was left in the snow. The last two that died was Capt. Sutter's two Indian baqueros and their bodies were used as food by the seven that came in.

Many others were still in the mountains, trapped at Truckee Lake. A relief party had gone out from Sutter's Fort on February 5, among their number William Eddy, the only member of the party of seven survivors who could still walk. The second relief, organized at San Francisco, started from that place on February 7. The *Star* reported:

A company of twenty men left here on Sunday last for the California mountains with provisions, clothing &c for the suffering emigrants now there. The citizens of this place subscribed about fifteen hundred dollars for their relief, which was expended for such articles as the emigrants would be most likely to need.

Mr. Greenwood, an old mountaineer, went with the company as pilot. If it is possible to cross the mountains they will get to the emigrants in time to save them.

Also with Caleb Greenwood (now in his eighty-fifth year), was James Reed, still hoping to find his family alive. McCutchen's wife was among those who had found their way to Johnson's Ranch. According to a letter dated February 13 at New Helvetia, the women were recovering quickly from their ordeal. Addressed to editor Jones of the *Star*, it reported that

Capt. E. M. Kern, commander of this district, returned from Johnson's settlement on the 11th inst. On his arrival at that settlement he found the five women and two men that had succeeded in getting in from the unfortunate company now on the mountains, in much better health than could have been expected; in fact they were suffering merely from their feet being slightly injured by the frost. They are living with the families of Messrs. Keyser and Sicard, and will come down to the Fort for protection as soon as they can walk. ...

Captain J. B. Hull put Selim E. Woodworth in charge of the overall rescue effort. Woodworth was a born adventurer; at the age of twelve he had run away from his New York City home to cross the plains to California. His family caught up with the boy after he had traveled 300 miles and persuaded him to wait a few years before venturing forth again. At nineteen he joined an expedition to the South Seas and China. Although meant to last only three years, shipwreck made it four when Woodworth and the crew had to spend months living with natives on the island of Madagascar.

Upon receiving an appointment as midshipman in the Navy, Woodworth was supposed to accompany Wilkes on the first United States scientific exploration of the Pacific, but was left behind by mistake. From 1838 to 1846 he had sailed on the Mediterranean and Caribbean seas. In the spring of 1846 he asked for and was given unlimited leave of absence to accomplish his boyhood dream of crossing the continent to California. He came to San Francisco by way of Oregon, getting to California shortly before snows trapped the emigrants.

On February 28 Lieutenant Woodworth sent a message to sheriff George McKinstry at Sutter's Fort. The letter was carried by Aquila Glover, part of the first rescue party, who had been called back because of his wife's serious illness and a death in his family. Glover had been keeping a diary of his activities, which he turned over to McKinstry with the letter.

McKinstry prepared a report for Captain Hull on March 5, which was then passed on to the newspapers by Hull:

Mr. Glover, who was put in charge of this little brave band of men, returns to me his Journal, from which I extract as follows:

"—on the 13th of February, 1847, our party arrived at the Bear River valley—14th remained in camp preparing packs and provisions, 15th, left Bear River valley, and travelled three miles and stopped to make snow shoes; 17th travelled five miles and camped on Yuba river, snow fifteen feet deep, dry and soft; 18th travelled eight miles and encamped on the head of Yuba river; 19th travelled nine miles, crossed the summit of the California mountains and reached part of the suffering company about sun down, in camp near Trucke'y Lake."

Mr. Glover informs me that he found them in a most deplorable condition, entirely beyond description. Ten of their number had already died from starvation; and he thinks several others will die in camp, as they are too low to resusitate. The whole party had been living on bullock hides four weeks.

On the morning of the 20th, the party went down to the camp of Geo. Donner eight miles below the first camp, and found them with but one hide. They had come to the conclusion that when that was consumed to dig up the bodies of those who had died from starvation and use them as food.

When the party arrived at the camp, they were obliged to guard the little stock of provision that they had carried over the mountains on their backs on foot for the relief of the poor beings, as they were in such a starving condition that they would have immediately used up the small store. They even stole the buckskin strings from their snow shoes and eat them.

This little brave band of men, immediately left with twenty-one persons, principally women and children for the settlements. They left all the food they could spare for those (twenty nine in number) that they were obliged to leave behind; and promised them that they would immediately return to their assistance.

They were successful in bringing all safe over the mountains. Four of the children they were obliged to carry on their backs, the balance walked. On their arrival at the Bear River valley, they met a small party with provisions, that Capt. Kerns of this fort had sent for their relief.

That same day they met Mr. Reed, with fifteen men on foot, packed with provisions, who, ere this, have reached the sufferers. Mr. Woodworth was going ahead with a full force and will himself visit them in their mountain camp, and see that every person is brought out.

Mr. Greenwood was three days behind Mr. Reed with the horses. Capt. Kern will remain in camp with the Indian soldiers to guard the provisions and horses and will send the sufferers down to this post as soon as possible, where they will be received by Capt. J.A. Sutter with all the hospitality for which he is so celebrated. . . .

Mr. Glover informed me that the waggons belonging to the emigrants are buried some fifteen feet under the snow.

On April 1, 1847, Selim Woodworth was back in San Francisco, where he provided this summary of events for the editor of *California Star:*

Sir—I have but this moment arrived in Capt. Sutter's launch from fort Sacramento, after a passage of 2½ days, and learning that your paper is about going to press, I hasten to drop you a few lines.

Mr. McKinstry has already informed you of the result of the last expedition, in which I brought in 17 of the sufferers.

In my last report from the mountains, I said that one of my men, by the name of Clark (left at the cabins by Mr. Reed), was lost in the snow storm in which Mr. Reed and party suffered so severely.

I am happy to say that he was rescued by the last party of five men that I sent; he had succeeded in killing a bear, and had subsisted on the meat until the day before the timely aid arrived, and has come in safely as also five others from the cabins;

likewise all of the 14 persons left by Mr. Reed on the road, viz: Mr. Brinn, wife and five children; 3 children of Mr. Graves, one of which was an infant at the breast, and Mary Donner, a girl about 11 years of age; three of the latter children being packed on the backs of Oakley, Stark and Stone;

the other five were, 3 children of Mr. Geo. Donner, between the ages of 1 and 4 years, girls; John Baptiste, a Spanish boy in the employment of Mr. Donner, and Simon Murphy, a boy of 6 years of age.

The persons left on the road by Mr. Reed were Brinn, wife and 5 children, Mrs. Graves and 4 children, Mary and Isaac Donner.

The day Mr. Reed left them the boy Isaac Donner died, and the same night Mrs. Graves and one of her children died; the remaining sufferers continued two days without food, but on the third day were obliged to resort to the only alternative, that of eating the dead: they commenced on the two children, and when my party reached them, which was on the fifth day, they were eating Mrs. Graves, and had already eaten the breast, heart, liver and lungs, when a timely supply of food and assistance reached them.

The night previous Mary Donner fell into the fire, and burned her foot so severely that amputation will be necessary in order to save her life. I have hastened down here with some of the sufferers who required immediate medical attendance. Among them are two of my men, Henry Dan and Charles Cady, with feet badly frozen.

I have brought Mary Donner and her brother down that they may obtain medical aid; the Spanish boy and Howard Oakley came down with them as nurses.

When I left the mountains there were still remaining at the cabins Mr. Kiesburg and George Donner, the only two men, Mrs. Geo. Donner, one child and Mrs. Murphy; Mrs. Murphy, Mr. Donner and the child could not survive many days when left, but Mr. Kiesburg and Mrs. Donner could subsist upon the remaining bodies yet some ten days.

The snow at the cabins was going off rapidly, but in Bear Valley and on the Juba River it was yet twenty feet deep on the level.

On the day after his paper published the above story, Sam Brannan and three companions left San Francisco to look for Brigham Young and the Mormon emigration. At Fort Hall Sam took time to write a letter to a New York friend in which he described his trip:

I left Capt. Sutter's post in California on the 26th day of April . . . We crossed the Sierra Nevada of California, a distance of forty miles, with 11 head of horses and mules, in one day and two hours, a thing which has never been done before in less than three days.

We travelled on foot and drove our animals before us, the snow from twenty to one hundred feet deep. When we arrived through, not one of us could scarcely stand on our feet. The people of California told us we could not cross under two months, there being more snow on the mountains than had ever been known before, but God knows best and was kind enough to prepare the way for us.

We passed the cabins of those people that perished in the mountains, which by this time you have heard of. It was a heart rending picture, and what is still worse it was the fruit of idleness, covetousness, ugliness, and low mindedness, that brought them to such a fate. Men must reap the fruit of their folly and own labours. Some of the particulars you will find published in the *Star.*

While Brannan was gone, Jones, Kemble and Eager put out the paper until Jones resigned as editor after a particularly angry dispute with Kemble. Not long after his departure, the *Star* office was visited by a young man dressed in rough frontier garb.

"Can I do something for you?" asked John Eager, who was alone in the shop, washing the press after a run.

"I'd like to speak to Mr. Brannan."

"He's not here. In fact, he's not in California right now."

This information seemed to upset the stranger, who then pulled a folded, dog-eared copy of the *Star* from his coat pocket. After examining it for a moment, he asked, "Can I see Mr. Jones?"

"Mr. Jones is no longer associated with this paper—would you like to speak to Mr. Kemble? He's the editor since Mr. Jones left."

"In that case I'd better talk to him, I guess."

Eager walked to the door of the office and went outside. Several men stood there, talking and enjoying a rare bit of San Francisco sunshine.

"Excuse me, Ed," Eager said to one of the group. "Fellow wants to see you inside."

Ed Kemble stepped briskly into the small shack which served as pressroom and editorial office and extended his hand in greeting. "Good morning! John says you want to see me."

The stranger tried to mask his surprise, but it was evident that he considered Kemble scarcely more than a boy. "I really wanted to see Mr. Brannan, but I understand he's away."

"That's right. Are you a friend of his?"

"Not really; but we may have met in Nauvoo a few years back."

Now it was Kemble's turn to be surprised. This frontiersman didn't fit his picture of someone from Nauvoo—at least, not one who would have known Sam Brannan. Kemble's knowledge of Mormons was limited entirely to those he had met in New York and San Francisco.

"Was your business personal or professional? Perhaps I could help you."

"The fact is, it's a little of both. My name is Tallman Rolfe and I've just come from Oregon, where I was a printer on the *Spectator*. I've been reading the *Star* since January. It seemed to me that Mr. Brannan might know something of my family's whereabouts, so I came down to California with a party of emigrants to see him."

"I see. Then Mr. Brannan knew your family."

"I don't know. But they're members of the Church of Latter Day Saints. When last I heard, they expected to leave Nauvoo and go west. Since Mr. Brannan is an elder and was such a good friend of Joseph Smith, I thought he might know where they'd gone."

"That's odd, because that's the very reason Sam went east. He's gone to meet Brigham Young and find out what he can about the Mormon emigration."

"I've heard rumors they are coming to California," said Tallman.

"Some are here already. In addition to the colony Sam has established, a battalion of Mormon soldiers came to San Diego with General Kearny last winter. They're still there, but once the peace treaty is signed and they're discharged, I expect they'll head north to San Francisco."

"What about the others—those who were in Iowa last summer, according to what I heard from last year's emigrants?"

"That's what Sam is finding out. You'll have to wait until he returns."

"When is that?"

"Late summer or early fall. Will you be around that long?"

"I don't know. I'll need employment if I stay in California. That's the other thing I wanted to discuss with him."

"In other words, work at the *Star*? You say you're a printer—where have you worked besides Oregon?"

"I apprenticed at *Times and Seasons* in Nauvoo. That's a church paper—but you knew that, of course."

"I'm familiar with it. We received copies at New York when Mr. Brannan and I were publishing *The Prophet* and *The Messenger*."

"Pardon me for being forward, but you seem to have entered this business quite early!"

"I went to work for Mr. Brannan when I was sixteen—that was three years ago. Before that I worked for my father on *The Budget* in Troy, New York."

"I guess you weren't much younger than me. I went to work at fourteen, but the difference is that I'm twenty-two now and still not an editor!"

Kemble laughed. "It helped that Jones decided to quit the position while the owner was away! But the fact is, we are short-handed now. A few printers came to California with Colonel Stevenson's New York Volunteers, but they're kept pretty busy these days and we can't count on them."

"Then you might have an opening?"

"Absolutely. Here, I'd like you to meet our longtime printer, John Eager. The pair of you have much in common—his family belongs to the church, too."

Tallman took a moment to grasp Kemble's meaning. "But doesn't everyone at the *Star* belong to the church?"

"Not so," replied Kemble. "I've never been a Mormon and don't intend to become one. How about it—can you start working today?"

Tallman had been anxiously weighing the comparative advantage of being once more gainfully employed versus the disadvantage of identifying openly with San Francisco's Mormon colony. Now Kemble's revelation settled the matter, for his status could remain ambiguous for the time being. "Where do you want me to hang my coat?" he asked with a grin.

Later, Tallman reflected on what he had learned both from Kemble and from his observations around town. How did it come about that gentiles could be employed by a Mormon newspaper? Why did Sam Brannan trust his affairs to non-Mormon editors?

In San Francisco the Mormons and gentiles seemed to live in close proximity without engaging in the mutual abuse and hostility he had learned to expect elsewhere in the west. Was it merely temporary, a truce? Would concealed animosity one day surface in California, or was this place going to be different? For the present, Tallman Rolfe decided to keep his eyes and ears open while saying as little as possible about himself to the other residents of the bay city.

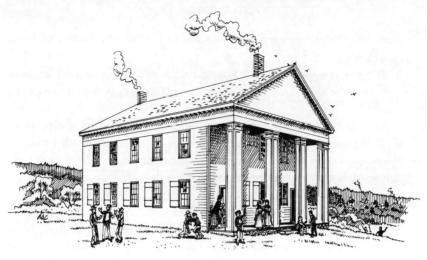

RENSSELAERVILLE ACADEMY

CHAPTER 6
COUNTRY SCHOOLS
Summer 1845–Summer 1846

I

𝒴OU HAVE TAKEN me prisoner with all my warriors. I am much grieved, for I expected, if I did not defeat you, to hold out much longer, and give you more trouble before I surrendered. I tried hard to bring you into ambush, but your last general understands Indian fighting. I determined to rush on you, and fight you face to face; I fought hard. But your guns were well aimed. The bullets flew like birds in the air, and whizzed by our ears like the wind through the trees in winter. My warriors fell around me; it began to look dismal. I saw my evil day at hand."

His silent listeners were enthralled by the stirring words of Chief Black Hawk. But the speaker was a nineteen-year-old student in the village of Rensselaerville, New York. It was Friday afternoon in the summer of 1845, and once again the students were demonstrating the elocution skills they had acquired in preceding weeks. Niles Searls was reciting the speech delivered on the occasion of the famous chief's surrender on August 27, 1832:

The sun rose dim on us in the morning, and at night it sank in a dark cloud, and looked like a ball of fire. That was the last sun that shone on

70

Black Hawk. His heart is dead, and no longer beats quick in his bosom. He is now a prisoner to the white men; they will do with him as they wish. But he can stand torture, and is not afraid of death. He is no coward. Black Hawk is an Indian. He has done nothing for which an Indian ought to be ashamed. He has fought for his countrymen, against white men who came, year after year, to cheat them and take away their lands. You know the cause of our making war. It is known to all white men.

They ought to be ashamed of it. The white men despise the Indians and drive them from their homes. But the Indians are not deceitful. The white men speak bad of the Indian, and look at him spitefully. But the Indian does not tell lies; Indians do not steal.

An Indian who is as bad as the white men could not live in our nation; he would be put to death and be eaten up by wolves. The white men are bad schoolmasters; they carry false looks and deal in false actions; they smile in the face of the poor Indian to cheat him; they shake him by the hand to gain his confidence, to make him drunk, and to deceive him.

We told them to let us alone, and keep away from us; but they followed on and beset our paths, and they coiled themselves among us, like the snake. They poisoned us by their touch. We were not safe. We lived in danger. We were becoming like them, hypocrites and liars—all talkers and no workers.

Mary Niles, fifteen years old, tiny and dark haired, leaned forward in her seat and smiled at her sister. Cornelia smiled back, sharing her pride in their cousin, who was doing so well, articulating every syllable and varying his emphasis skillfully, just as he had been taught to do by Mr. Gallup. It was a masterly performance, each thought.

Black Hawk is a true Indian, and disdains to cry like a woman. He feels for his wife, his children, and his friends. But he does not care for himself. He cares for the nation and the Indians. They will suffer. He laments their fate.

The white men do not *scalp* the *heads,* but they do worse—they *poison* the *heart;* it is not pure with them. His countrymen will not be scalped, but they will, in a few years, become like the white men, so that you cannot trust them; and there must be, as in the white settlements, nearly as many officers as men to take care of them and keep them in order.

Farewell, my nation! Black Hawk tried to save you and avenge your wrongs. He drank the blood of some of the whites. He has been taken prisoner and his plans are stopped. He can do no more. He is near his end. His sun is setting and he will rise no more. *Farewell to Black Hawk!*

A round of enthusiastic applause broke out at the conclusion of this stirring address. Niles bowed and soberly resumed his place on the boys' bench. Then he looked over at his cousins, winked one eye and grinned. Tears filled the eyes of most of the girls, and one or two boys swallowed hard and tried not to show how envious they were.

After school, as Niles and his cousins walked through the village streets with Charles Mulford and the Wickes girls, Deborah and Delight, their conversation centered on Indians and the far west.

"You know," declared Niles, "when I read Cooper and Catlin it makes me want to pack my bags and go as far from civilization as I can travel. Imagine being able to stand on top of a Missouri bluff and look for hundreds of miles in all directions! Catlin says it's so quiet you can't hear a sparrow or a cricket!"

"Come now," protested Charles. "That's a bit of exaggeration, I'd say. It may be quiet out there, but where there's life there has to be sound!"

"I suppose so, but I was just repeating Catlin's words. How much noise can a rabbit make?"

"I've heard rabbits make noise—it's a very sweet sound, I think!" said Deborah.

"Would you really want to go out where there are wild Indians, Niles?" asked Mary. "I feel sorry for what's been done to them, but Black Hawk did say he drank the blood of whites! I'd be scared to go."

"Of course I'd go, but I wouldn't go unarmed—I'm not foolish! I can't think of anything I'd rather do, unless it was go to China."

"Well, not me, thank you," said Cornelia primly. "I'll stay where it's civilized and pleasant, if you please."

"What if you had a husband who wanted to go away on business?" asked Delight.

"Why, I'd let him, of course!" laughed Cornelia. "But I'll not marry someone like that."

"What kind will you marry, Nellie?"

"None of your business, Charles Mulford!"

The young people, whose ages ranged from Mary's fifteen to Niles's nineteen years, parted company when they came to the Mulford store on Main Street. After saying goodbye to Charley, who went in to help his brother after school, the others continued as far as Dr. Platt Wickes's house, where Deb and Delight took their leave. Niles and his girl cousins turned left at the next corner, walked past the Frisbie house and came at last to the home of Judge John Niles.

In the summertime Niles Searls boarded with his Uncle John and Aunt Polly while attending Rensselaerville Academy, but every winter since his

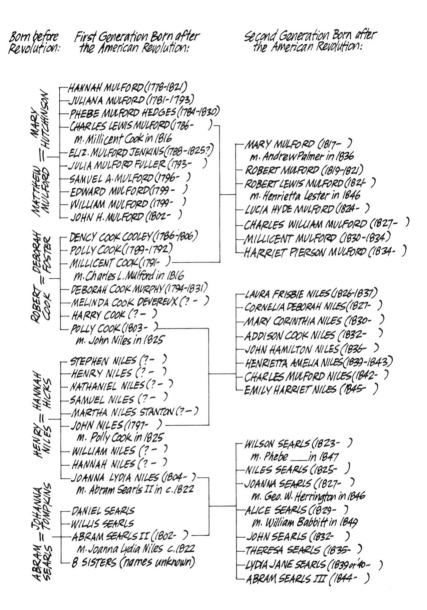

Born before Revolution:	First Generation Born after the American Revolution:	Second Generation Born after the American Revolution:

MATTHEW MULFORD = MARY HUTCHINSON
- HANNAH MULFORD (1778-1821)
- JULIANA MULFORD (1781-1793)
- PHEBE MULFORD HEDGES (1784-1830)
- CHARLES LEWIS MULFORD (1786-)
  m. Millicent Cook in 1816
- ELIZ. MULFORD JENKINS (1788-1825?)
- JULIA MULFORD FULLER (1793-)
- SAMUEL A. MULFORD (1796-)
- EDWARD MULFORD (1799-)
- WILLIAM MULFORD (1799-)
- JOHN H. MULFORD (1802-)

- MARY MULFORD (1817-)
  m. Andrew Palmer in 1836
- ROBERT MULFORD (1819-1821)
- ROBERT LEWIS MULFORD (1821-)
  m. Henrietta Lester in 1846
- LUCIA HYDE MULFORD (1824-)
- CHARLES WILLIAM MULFORD (1827-)
- MILLICENT MULFORD (1830-1834)
- HARRIET PIERSON MULFORD (1834-)

ROBERT COOK = DEBORAH FOSTER
- DENCY COOK COOLEY (1786-1806)
- POLLY COOK (1789-1792)
- MILLICENT COOK (1791-)
  m. Charles L. Mulford in 1816
- DEBORAH COOK MURPHY (1794-1831)
- MELINDA COOK DEVEREUX (? -)
- HARRY COOK (? -)
- POLLY COOK (1803-)
  m. John Niles in 1825

- LAURA FRISBIE NILES (1826-1837)
- CORNELIA DEBORAH NILES (1827-)
- MARY CORINTHIA NILES (1830-)
- ADDISON COOK NILES (1832-)
- JOHN HAMILTON NILES (1836-)
- HENRIETTA AMELIA NILES (1839-1843)
- CHARLES MULFORD NILES (1842-)
- EMILY HARRIET NILES (1845-)

HENRY NILES = HANNAH HICKS
- STEPHEN NILES (? -)
- HENRY NILES (? -)
- NATHANIEL NILES (? -)
- SAMUEL NILES (? -)
- MARTHA NILES STANTON (? -)
- JOHN NILES (1797-)
  m. Polly Cook in 1825
- WILLIAM NILES (? -)
- HANNAH NILES (? -)
- JOANNA LYDIA NILES (1804-)
  m. Abram Searls II in c.1822

ABRAM SEARLS = JOHANNA TOMPKINS
- DANIEL SEARLS
- WILLIS SEARLS
- ABRAM SEARLS II (1802-)
  m. Joanna Lydia Niles c.1822
- 8 SISTERS (names unknown)

- WILSON SEARLS (1823-)
  m. Phebe ____ in 1847
- NILES SEARLS (1825-)
- JOANNA SEARLS (1827-)
  m. Geo. W. Herrington in 1846
- ALICE SEARLS (1829-)
  m. William Babbitt in 1849
- JOHN SEARLS (1832-)
- THERESA SEARLS (1835-)
- LYDIA JANE SEARLS (1839 or '40-)
- ABRAM SEARLS III (1844-)

Interrelationships of the Searls, Niles, Cook and Mulford families, showing status of individuals as of 1851.

sixteenth birthday he had taught school at Bloomfield, Ontario, a few miles from his father's farm at Wellington.

The first Searls to come to America had been an English Army officer, sent over to collect the Stamp Tax in 1766. Seeing how fiercely the colonists resented the tax, Captain Searls asked to be relieved from his unpleasant assignment. His request denied, the soldier resigned his commission and settled among the rebels of Westchester County, New York.

He married a local woman, they had a son, Abram, and Abram grew up and went farther into the wilderness, near the landing of Coeymans on the Hudson River. Here he met and married Johanna Tompkins and raised a family. Another young couple, Henry and Hannah Hicks Niles, lived nearby, and among their six children were John, born in 1797, and Joanna Lydia, born about 1804.

Sometime during the war which began in 1812, John Niles left Coeymans to go to a place called Rensselaerville. There he apprenticed himself to Daniel Conkling, who taught him the tanner's trade. John opened a leather and shoe store in the growing village of Rensselaerville. Before long, Colonel John Niles was commander of the local regiment of the state militia, and in 1820 he married Laura Frisbie, daughter of a prominent citizen.

Two years later, back in Coeymans, his sister Joanna Lydia (known to her friends as Lydia) married Abram Searls II, son of Abram and Johanna. Her first child, a son called Wilson, was born in 1823, the same year that her brother's wife died. In 1825 Lydia had a second son, Niles, and John's second wife gave birth to a daughter, who was given the same name as the first wife, Laura Frisbie Niles.

When the great depression of 1837 hit New York State, Abram and Lydia moved with their children across Lake Ontario into Canada. Here they settled in Prince Edward County, Ontario, on the north shore of the lake. There were four boys and four girls in the Searls family by 1845.

Polly Cook Niles also had produced eight children during the same span of years, but two had died, one of them little Laura Frisbie, who followed her namesake to an early grave. By the summer of 1845 John Niles was forty-eight years old and had become a lawyer and judge. He no longer ran the leather business, but leased his tannery and shop to another man. He had been in and out of the foundry business, the casting of small parts from iron. He lived in a handsome big two-story house on land he had purchased from Doctor Reuben Frisbie, father of his first wife.

The village of Rensselaerville was small and would forever remain so. It lay within the boundaries of Rensselaerville township, Albany County, which, in common with the adjoining county of Rensselaer, was within the manor, or "wyck" of the Van Rensselaer family.

In 1630 a wealthy Dutch pearl merchant had sent colonists to New Netherlands to found Rensselaerwyck. The representatives of Kiliaen Van Rensselaer made several purchases of land from the Mohawk Indians between 1630 and 1649. When the boundaries finally were defined by English authorities in the following century, the manor of Rensselaer extended twenty-four miles in each direction from the Hudson River, east and west. Its southern boundary was at Barren Island and the Cohoes Falls marked its northern limits. It encompassed the entire counties of Albany and Rensselaer and a part of Columbia County.

Until Stephen Van Rensselaer III came of age in 1785, most of this vast domain was wilderness. The new proprietor, or "patroon," offered to lease his lands on what seemed to be reasonable terms. Any family that signed the lease could move onto the property, usually about one hundred and sixty acres, without paying a cent. Although the tenant was free to farm the land and make improvements, certain privileges were reserved to the landlord.

To the Van Rensselaer family belonged rights to all mines and minerals, all creeks, "kills," streams, and runs of water; the right to erect mills, dams, and buildings for the working of mines and mills; all lands covered by the waters impounded by dams, and all firewood and timber which might be necessary for building, repairing or running the mills and mines.

At first this seemed a reasonable exchange, but later, when farmers discovered how poor was the soil on the ridge of rocks and boulders left by ancient glaciers, it was seen that the waterpower of the Helderberg range was the only resource worth owning. The Van Rensselaers were willing to negotiate for these rights, but that came later and was a more costly proposition.

The terms of the lease which all tenants signed varied slightly from time to time and from place to place, but generally all had these features in common: an annual rent of from ten to twenty-eight bushels of wheat, four fat fowl, and one day's service—or the monetary equivalent. To many veterans of the American Revolution it did not seem too much to ask. Between 1790 and 1830 many families settled on the Van Rensselaer lands. By 1838 from sixty to one hundred thousand farmers were paying annual rents, said to have totaled more than forty million dollars in the lifetime of Stephen Van Rensselaer III.

In his later years the patroon grew so rich that when a farmer suffered reverses or had a poor year, the rent was allowed to go into temporary

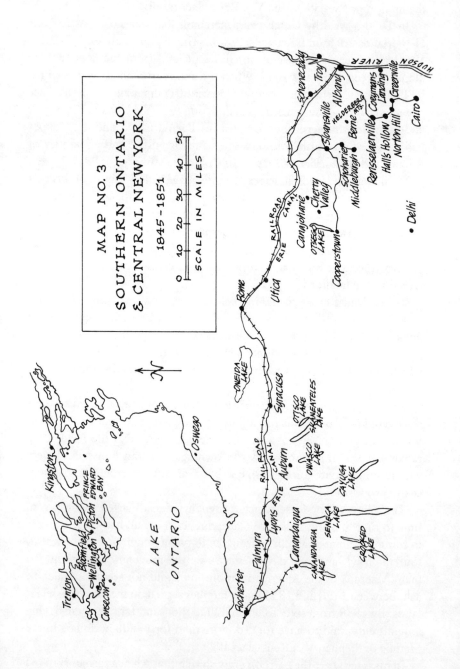

MAP NO. 3

SOUTHERN ONTARIO
& CENTRAL NEW YORK

1845-1851

0 10 20 30 40 50

SCALE IN MILES

HUDSON RIVER

Schenectady
Troy
Albany
Coeymans Landing
Greenville
Cairo
Sloansville
HELDERBERG MTS.
Berne
Rensselaerville
Hall's Hollow
Norton Hill
Schoharie
Middleburgh
Delhi
Canajoharie
Cherry Valley
OTSEGO LAKE
Cooperstown
Rome
Utica
ERIE CANAL
RAILROAD

ONEIDA LAKE

Syracuse
OTISCO LAKE
SKANEATELES LAKE
OWASCO LAKE
Auburn
CAYUGA LAKE
CANAL
RAILROAD
Lyons Erie
Palmyra
Canandaigua
CANANDAIGUA LAKE
SENECA LAKE
CROOKED LAKE

Rochester

Oswego

LAKE
ONTARIO

Kingston
Trenton
Bloomfield
Wellington
Picton
PRINCE EDWARD BAY
Consecon

N

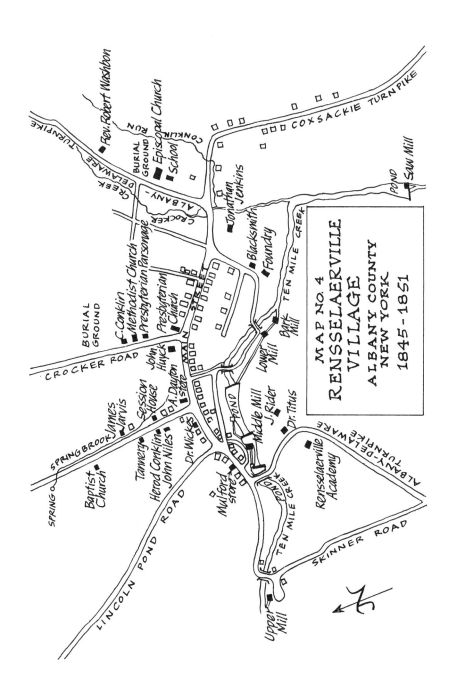

MAP No. 4
RENSSELAERVILLE
VILLAGE
ALBANY COUNTY
NEW YORK
1845-1851

COXSACKIE TURNPIKE

Rev. Robert Washbon

DELAWARE TURNPIKE

CONKLIN RUN

Episcopal Church

School

BURIAL GROUND

ALBANY-DELAWARE CREEK

CROCKER

Jonathan Jenkins

Blacksmith

Foundry

POND

SAW MILL

TEN MILE CREEK

Bark Mill

Lower Mill

J. Rider

Dr. Titus

C. Conklin

Methodist Church

Presbyterian Parsonage

Presbyterian Church

MAIN STREET

BURIAL GROUND

CROCKER ROAD

John Huyck

Session House

A. Dayton Store

POND

Middle Mill

Dr. Wickes

James Jarvis

SPRINGBROOK

Tannery

Herod Conklin

John Niles

SPRING

Baptist Church

LINCOLN POND ROAD

Mulford Store

TEN MILE POND

Rensselaerville Academy

ALBANY-DELAWARE TURNPIKE

SKINNER ROAD

TEN MILE CREEK

Upper Mill

arrears. Bad times and the landlord's liberality resulted in fewer tenants being able or willing to comply with the original agreement. It was even thought by some that the payment no longer was expected. Thus, the landlord gained the title of the "Good Patroon."

When he died in January 1839, his tenants discovered that the rents had not been forgotten or forgiven. To insure their collection, the Good Patroon inserted a proviso in his will that unless his heirs produced the back rents, they would have to pay four hundred thousand dollars worth of his debts out of their own pockets.

The new patroon, Stephen Van Rensselaer IV, told a delegation of tenants that he would not discuss any adjustment in the rents or the terms until all back rents were paid. An angry meeting of farmers endorsed a new declaration of independence at Berne on July 4, 1839. When an Albany County undersheriff tried to serve Isaac Hungerford with a writ of ejectment, he was shown a long knife and ordered off the premises.

The sheriff left, but did not stop serving writs. While he slept at an inn in the village of Rensselaerville, persons unknown destroyed his wagon and harness, and cut off his horse's mane and tail. A second sheriff, Daniel Leonard, was sent to the Helderbergs. He was puzzled when tin dinner horns sounded wherever he went. Then he realized that the horns signalled his approach, and the alarm was being repeated in every direction. Said Leonard:

> I went to the home of James Leggett and met him by the house. I told him I had a paper for him and offered it to him. . . . He then ordered me off his land. I threw the declaration down by him and was going off when he said to me if I wanted to get off alive I must pick up the paper and clear out with it. I told him I was not going to take it up.
>
> He then told his son to get in the house and bring out *that.* I suppose he meant the gun. After some time I picked up the paper and came off with it. Leggett and his son and another person followed me, and Leggett threatened to kill me if I served any more papers.

While waiting for the Albany stage with eleven unserved writs still in his pocket, the sheriff was surrounded by farmers on foot and on horseback. They prevented him from boarding the stage, forced him to burn the writs, then required him to buy drinks for the crowd. When his money was gone, he was turned loose to walk the long road back to Albany.

In October 1839 the Albany County sheriff and three deputies started into the hills with the re-issued writs. Suddenly they heard a chorus of tin horns and were met by a mob of angry farmers, who blocked the narrow mountain road. The officers gave up and went back to the city, where at length the New York State Militia was called out. Citizen-soldiers armed themselves and headed into the Helderbergs, but on the eve of battle, Governor Seward negotiated a temporary armistice.

The militia occupied the village of Rensselaerville for several days in December, three uniformed companies finding scant space for shelter during that period of hot tempers and cold snowstorms. The home of Judge John Niles was taken over by officers of the militia, and for weeks thereafter Addison and Hamilton Niles played war games, to the annoyance of their mother and sisters.

John Niles went to Albany with the militia on unspecified business, and on the third day before Christmas, Polly wrote to her absent husband:

I received your letter last evening, just as I had seated myself to spend a lonely evening, the little girls at singing school, the boys in bed and the babe in my arms, as usual.

When night draws her sable curtains about me, I feel in your absence a loneliness which nothing can supply, but a letter from you is certainly the most welcome visitor—and to hear that you are well and pleasantly situated always gives to our fireside enjoyments additional relish. . . .

It has been extremely cold and blustery, the roads in every direction filled with drifts, of course. All still—considering our village was so late a seat of war, the contrast is the more striking. . . .

As for presents, I hardly know what to say. I think, however, for the boys I would not get war implements; I think Hamilton is as skilled a general I shall ever wish to see him, and I believe Addison begins to grow tired of the employment—he says he shall try to be a very good boy until Pa returns.

Perhaps some new books will be as useful as anything.

The Rensselaerville Academy was started in May 1844 after John and Polly Niles and twenty-six other local families agreed to contribute funds to transform the old Presbyterian Church on the hill into a school. It was to be a place where their children and those of the surrounding countryside should study advanced reading, writing, orthography, elocution, arithmetic, mental algebra and geography. From time to time, other courses such as French and music also were taught.

It was an ambitious project for a village numbering fewer than six hundred souls, but its leading families were smarting from the recent criticism leveled against their township by Albany County's superintendent of common schools. Said he:

Coeymans, Watervliet, Bethlehem, New Scotland, Guilderland and Westerlo [townships] have manifested more interest in securing good education for their children than Rensselaerville, Berne and Knox [townships], and less money is wasted in their schools.

Speaking of the county as a whole, he added: "of no appendages are the schoolhouses so destitute as they are of privies. Of the 176 visited, 148 are wholly without."

Although the parents considered the school in their village to be a step above others in the township, they were determined to provide a quality education if possible, so that students wouldn't have to go away to boarding schools.

When the Academy opened in June, the old church had been remodeled inside and out; four square wooden pillars at the entrance gave it a kind of Grecian look. Mr. Henry Gallup was hired to be the principal and Miss Jane Ann Harris was his assistant.

During that first summer, three cousins from Canada had come to stay with the Niles family and attend the new school. From Wellington came Niles Searls, and from London, Canada West, came Henry and Nancy Niles, children of the eldest brother of John Niles and Lydia Searls. All had enjoyed themselves and after going home to Canada in October 1844, Niles wrote Cornelia:

... the days which I spent in your Village will never be forgotten, and the invariable kindness with which I was treated has made too deep an impression on my mind to be speedily eradicated. ... David Young ... is sorry that he could not arrange his business so as to come to your part of the world and see the pretty girls of whom I have so often spoken in glowing terms since my arrival home, and be it remembered that when I speak of a young ladys being the finest I ever saw, it is with the exception of those residing in Rensselaerville (no flattery intended) and its vicinity. ... I can almost see you and Mary going up the hill to the Academy, perhaps with Deborah, Delight or some of the rest of the girls, and when you get there, there stands Miss Harris, smiling as usual to meet you.

David Young, a close friend, was teaching Niles's sisters Joanna and Alice at the Wellington school. In March 1845, near the end of his teaching engagement at Bloomfield, Niles wrote to his Aunt Polly. This year, Niles explained, Abram Searls was not so willing as before to have his son leave Canada for the summer:

I am now sorry that I did not choose to go to school this winter, as it was the choice of my father that I should continue at school; but now it is otherwise. He has but a few days since bought a farm of one hundred and fifty acres of land, and Wilson thinks of going on it to work this summer, which will be leaving Father almost entirely alone; but still he says I can act at my own pleasure . . .

When I consider my age and the poor progress I have already made, it really discourages me, and I am disposed to say I will go to school no more. On the other hand, I would like well to know as much as other folks, to learn which, it would take me, I suppose, longer than this mundane system will stand.

Nevertheless, Niles had gone once more to Rensselaerville for the summer and was making fair progress until, soon after the successful recitation of Black Hawk's address, his eyes began to trouble him. Often he was unable to study by candlelight. He went back to Canada, unable to complete the term. Once again he was persuaded to teach school instead of continuing with his studies. He told Cornelia on September 11:

My eyes on my arrival home were so much better that I hoped soon to be able to resume my studies, but my prospect for doing so at present is not as good as it was at the time of my return. . . . I have already had a number of offers of schools to teach, and tell them all to bring on their children and I'll teach em.

II

ON DECEMBER 28, 1845, a week after his twentieth birthday, Niles Searls was alone at his desk in the Bloomfield schoolhouse. Outside, it was far below freezing and he was content to stay close to the stove. His breath frosted the glass whenever he left the fire to peer out the window to see if anyone had yet arrived at the Friends' meetinghouse across the street.

He was writing a short letter to his Cousin Mary, and had just told her about the trouble he continued to have with his eyes:

My health has not been good since my return from RVille. The healthful atmosphere of Canada has failed to have as beneficial an effect as I hoped it might have. My eyes still bother me very much every time I take cold, but still I think they will ultimately recover, as it is nothing but weakness that causes them to bother me now. I can read little or none by candle light as yet, which annoys me very much.

The term for which I have absolutely engaged this School will expire in about two weeks and when I commenced here it was with the settled determination to remain no longer than this term, providing my eyes would permit me to study, and now, under existing circumstances, I hardly know what to determine upon. I wish I had some of your sage advice just at present . . .

His teaching job was not disagreeable. He enjoyed living in Bloomfield, and he liked the people, most of whom were Quakers. To his friend David Young he joked that his own biggest problem was that the boys had grown so accustomed to wearing hats in their meetinghouse that it wasn't easy to persuade them to go bareheaded in the schoolroom.

Joanna Searls no longer attended David's school at Wellington now that she was eighteen and married to George Herrington. The Herringtons lived with George's father, Moses. John and Alice were going to the Wellington school, and Wilson had worked so hard and so well on his father's farm throughout the summer and fall that he had been granted a holiday excursion to New York just before Christmas. About this, Niles wrote:

Wilson returned safe home on the 21st, well pleased with his journey. Of course, I asked him more than a hundred questions concerning you all, some of which he could answer, and some he could not. I should think from his conversation that he got as well acquainted with you as I did the first time I saw you.

He says Addison sent a letter by him for me, which he unfortunately left at Halls Hollow by accident. I gave him a scolding for leaving it, but he told me not to make a fuss and he would write one for me that would do just as well in the place of it.

My respects to Addison, and thanks also for his letter, but I would like it better if he had not chosen so careless a messenger. So you are all going to school again, are you, this Winter? That's right, be good children and improve as fast as possible.

I wonder if I shall ever attend school again!

Going again to the window, Niles saw that the meeting was about to begin. Quickly, he wiped his pen, capped the ink, and pulled on his coat and hat. Then he stepped outside into the icy blast and made his way carefully across the road to the Friends' Sunday meeting.

Afterward, Niles told Mary that "the Friends have shook hands and let us all out again, glad enough to get free, at least I am. The preacher, an old Yankee (would that he had always staid in the States), spoke about an hour and said precious little after all; his theme was the *Free Agency* of man, and I should judge from his remarks that he had been brought up a Presbyterian and then either turned out of that church or kicked out, and I can't tell which from his sarcastic remarks."

Niles didn't get around to mailing the letter for several days, and in the meantime wrote out a list of resolutions for the coming year. After rewriting what he called his "commandments," he slipped the first rough draft with its corrections into Mary's letter. It read as follows:

Ten commandments which I, this 1st day of January, 1846, form to be the rule and guide of my future conduct.

1st I will never remain in idleness, but always employ my time in some honest and honorable employment.

2nd I will use every means in my power to gain every kind of information, not derogatory to my character.

3rd I will never abandon a friend, or cease to defend his character until I am convinced that he has lost all those qualities which first caused me to esteem him as a friend.

               betray
4th I will never ~~disclose~~ a secret, or speak disparageingly of others ~~in the presence of strangers, or~~ to any except my most intimate friends.

5th I will shun, rather than court the society, except for information, and never associate with those who consider themselves my betters.

6th I will not form opinions hastily, nor change them when formed, except upon strong testimony.

7th I will not believe anything I do not understand, excepting the book of God.

8th I will guard against sudden outbreaks of passion and never speak hastily, take any decided stand or form firm resolutions while
               enraged
  ~~under the influence of excitement.~~

9th I will be even with my enemies, so long as they wish to continue such, but be always ready to forget and forgive when due acknowledgement is made.

10th I will reverence age, be kind to the poor, haughty to the proud, and as independent of all others as possible.

III

NEITHER NILES NOR Mary nor Cornelia attended school during the summer of 1846. Niles stayed in Canada, where he traveled a bit and visited the falls at Niagara. Cornelia also saw the falls, but during an unplanned excursion taken while visiting relatives in western New York State, so she and her cousin had no opportunity to make their journeys coincide. But Addison Niles, Cornelia's fourteen-year-old brother, was attending the Academy and he wrote to his sister on July 2 to keep her abreast of Rensselaerville doings:

We get along very well at school now, except Mr. Gallup has now and then some slight difficulty with the scholars, though none of any consequence since the affair with Powell. . . . We have had one new scholar lately from Mississippi, a relation of the Daytons.

RensselaerVille has been in as great a state of excitement for about a week past as ever I knew it to be before for any similar cause. There has been four lectures delivered here on the subject of animal magnetism and clarvoyance, by three different lecturers.

The first evening there was, together with a lecture on Mesmerism, a lecture on Phrenology, *by a lady!!* with some experience on mesmerism. Our neighbor Herod [Conklin] had his head examined by the lady and by the description she gave of him one would think he was some great man. He was completely convinced of the truth of her doctrines.

The next evening we had experiments in clarvoyance, that is, a lady was introduced who, when in the mesmeric state, could read the heading of newspapers, tell the time by watches, as well with her eyes bandaged as with them open. Which she performed to the satisfaction of a great part of the audience; however, Dr Wicks insisted afterwards upon putting on another bandage and she failed entirely on account (as the Professor said) of her energies being exhausted &c. &c.

The next day, Dr. Gibson being blindfolded in the same manner that the girl was, read much easier and better than she did. The next in order was 2 persons pretending to cure diseases, one putting the other to sleep and while in that state examining patients, prescribing for them &c. &c.

The next night we had another lecture on mesmerism, clarvoyance by a different lecturer, but bringing with him the same girl who gave us experiments on seeing without eyes before, but being better blindfolded than before, read but very little of what was presented to her, and yet the majority of the audience thought the experiments "perfectly satisfactory." It has been the town talk for a week, although I presume all this is not interesting to you. . . .

Tomorrow is composition day and I have not got my composition quite finished either (the old tune). I think when you read this, if you manage to read it at all, you will think that my Rhetorick does not do me much good; which is a very correct conclusion.

On September 20, 1846, Niles wrote to Mary from Rochester, New York, where he had gone on business for his father:

With pleasure I seize the few spare moments which I now enjoy and devote them to writing a few lines to you, but hang it, how to commence and continue a letter under present circumstances, I hardly know, for I have many difficulties to contend with in the attempt.

In the first place, there is but one chair in this apology for a room, and a second chair is absolutely necessary for me to elevate my feet in, in order to write anything intelligible and meaning[ful]. In the second place, I crossed the lake during the night and had the roughest time I ever was out in, which has left my ideas in a state that can be compared to nothing.

The Pilgrim Fathers were not more overjoyed at the first discovery of the long looked for land than were the seasick passengers of the steamer this morning on beholding the harbor afforded by the mouth of the river. To attempt a description of the scene on board during the night would be useless. Suffice it to say, we were all night in crossing from Coburg to this place. Our tea milk was all turned to butter, and one gentleman affirmed that the *Boat rolled over five times.*

I left home yesterday morning, came to Coburg with my own conveyance, visited the college in that place, found a number of my old friends there and spent a few hours agreeably with them, &c &c. I came over on business and shall return tomorrow. . . .

You informed me in your letter (which contained a great store of information) that from words which Rufus had dropped, you rather expected me to visit Rensselaerville this fall. If my memory serves me right, he at that time thought he might resume his studies again this winter, and I told him that in the event of his doing so, I would return to R'Ville also if there was any prospect of my being able to study.

As to coming for a visit, I shall deny myself that pleasure for a time, in order to see if some of you will not first come to Canada. I made preparations for going to Wisconsin about the 1st of Sept. in company with a son of Dr. Corys of Wellington. He resides with his uncle at the West and I expected to accompany him West with the determination of making a complete tour of the Western World, but it all turned out just like Niles's luck.

We anticipated starting on Monday [August 31], but on Saturday previous I was taken so unwell that our people, who from the first were rather averse to my going, would not consent to it at all, so the subject was dropped.

I have visited the Falls this summer, together with various other places of note in Canada. There is now a project on foot to go on a hunting expedition to the north in the course of a week or two. Whether we go or not is quite uncertain, but if I can get just one good companion

I am off. The place to which we anticipate going is about a hundred miles due north from Wellington, of which distance seventy-five miles is uninhabited wilderness. . . .

Before closing this I would briefly say with respect to the future, I shall not be able to study this winter as my eyes are not improving much, if any, and I shall probably teach again, in preference to doing nothing. . . . I have to hurry home in order to attend a Temperance Soiree which comes off this week, as Niles has an engagement with one on that occasion whom to know is to LOVE, Ahem!

STAGE STOP IN RURAL NEW YORK

CHAPTER 7

LAW SCHOOL

May–November 1847

I

*W*ITH REGARD TO the somewhat sudden resolution which I formed relative to commencing the study of the law, my father appears very well pleased, though he thinks that I ought to attend school a year or two longer at least; of course I am of the same opinion and expect other people are also, still I cannot but think that it is time that I attempt something else."

So wrote Niles Searls to Cornelia on May 21, 1847. He had astonished everyone by going to Rensselaerville for the spring term at the Academy and then coming straight home at its conclusion, instead of staying for the summer session, as planned. But his plans had changed. Niles's decision to study law came after long hours of discussion with Judge Niles and Orvil Chittenden, the other Rensselaerville attorney.

Their advice to Niles had been to spend his summer in hard study to prepare for the entrance examinations he would have to take in the fall.

On May 14, 1847, he said farewell to his cousins and their parents and left for Canada. Four days later he arrived home to find that he had upset some carefully laid plans. To Cornelia he explained:

In perfect keeping with all the rest of my luck, I left R Ville just the wrong time, as Pa and Alice were expecting to leave home for to see me on Thursday next. They will still go, I think, though Alice now talks very doubtful about it. I have tried to persuade her to wait till my return and then to accompany me and attend school, but our people seem to think that they cannot spare her from home so long, therefore I am inclined to believe she will come in company with Pa, but I declare it is mean beyond endurance that I can't be there when any of our people come. . . .

Perhaps you would like to know whether or not I am about to study in as great earnest as was anticipated before I came home. If you could but catch one glimpse of me now, seated as I am at my table with great stacks of books before me, methinks you would come to the irrevocable conclusion that "Niles is the most studious mortal in the world," but it would be a *false conclusion.*

I assure you still, I am studying some and I expect to during my stay at home.

One month later he brought Mary up to date on his activities:

Mr. Gallup frequently says that letters of friendship are usually esteemed according to their length, according to which principle your letter is the better [than Cornelia's] by a very few inches (long measure), and should be answered first, but when he gives us that as the method of judging letters, I always want to enquire of him if he is any connexion to the *"Dutch Justice"* who, in order to settle the accounts of two disputants, weighed their respective acct-books and decided accordingly.

The intelligence that your letter is received will, of course, also inform you that its bearer, Alice, has arrived home—they came last Sunday morning, accompanied by Lewis Tompkins, and William; had a rough time in crossing the lake, and were all more or less seasick. . . . If to have the ague so as to shake the buttons off from one's coat entitles a person to the credit of being unwell, Wilson is also sick, for he has the ague and fever in the real old fashion natural style and no mistake.

Yesterday, Lewis, William, and I went to pay George and Joanna a visit, where I sprained my ankle so that I cannot walk a single step, and last night it was so painful that I could not sleep a wink; . . . as to the manner in which the accident happened, I tell the folks (in fun of course) that it was probably caused by cracking hickory nuts, for I was thus employed just before I felt that it was lame, and I will tell you the same, and won't tell you anything else, because you would say "it's just right for you" (which would be a fact), "now learn to behave better," but just keep cool, now, Mary, for it ain't anybody's business but my own if I do get hurt in wrestling with George and William; still it makes me feel plaguey mean.

There is to be a county temperance soiree at Consecon the day after tomorrow at which a great assemblage of the youth, and beauty, of the surrounding country may be expected; said company to be addressed by a number of young men, among which, and first on the list is *N S* of Wellington, at least so the newspaper hath it ...

My eyes have pretty near recovered their wanted strength. Studying at home is not what it is cracked up to be; there is this visit to make, and that ride, or party to call off the attention of the mind, so that I have about decided to take up my departure rather sooner than I had expected. I still tell people that I am either going to the States or to Toronto, and I do not know which, and still intend to come to RVille in order that you may have an opportunity of satisfying your malicious disposition by fulfilling your threat of legal proceedings against me. ...

Alice says she had an excellent visit with you all and, what affords me no small pleasure, can now talk about Cornelia and Mary with me. Remember me to Deb and Harriet and say to Harriet that I have given up telling wrong stories.

II

HAVING PASSED HIS examinations and been accepted for the winter term at Fowler's Law School, Niles proceeded by way of Rensselaerville to Cherry Valley, New York. He reached the village on Saturday evening, October 23, 1847. His first act was to call upon Mr. John Fowler, a well-known and respected member of the New York bar.

Mr. Fowler's school was new and was being observed with interest by educators and lawyers alike. All were curious to see what results would be achieved by his somewhat novel teaching methods. Niles recorded his first impressions of the man in charge in a letter to Mary on October 25:

In appearance, Mr. Fowler is one of the most majestic looking fellows that I have ever seen; whether a further acquaintance will exhibit him as possessed of mental attractions equal or superior to his personal ones remains to be hereafter determined.

With regard to his students, I can as yet say but little, having seen but three or four of them, the rest being absent, enjoying a vacation which is now occurring in his Law School. The term will commence again the last of this week, and in the interval I am busily employed with preparing to enter with the class upon the studies of next term.

Those of the students that I have seen appear to be intelligent young men, all desirous of prosecuting their studies with vigor, that they may speedily arrive at that distinction which almost every Law Student in the vividness of his fancy expects at some future day to enjoy, but alas, how oft are these anticipations doomed to meet with bitter disappointment ...With regard to my boarding place, of course, Mary, you must know something about *that* as well as sundry other things. At the request of Mr. Fowler, I went to the same place to board where the most of his students board when in the place, and am still stopping there, though it is uncertain whether I shall do so or not for any great length of time.

The house is kept by Miss Smith, a maiden lady of about forty-five, and a magnificent specimen of antiquity she is, too. So fascinating in her appearance—so kind to her boarders—and always so smiling—though I hope I may be forgiven for having taken her smile for ague chills during the first day of my sojourn in her domicil. I'll tell you what I think of doing, viz, to purchase the old specimen and open a kind of Museum (not of fine arts, by jingoes) to be filled up with a collection of relics to illustrate the manners, customs &c of the 17th century.

Her house would, from its age and locality, be in my opinion a fit spot, also, for this interesting exhibition. Could its unpainted walls reflect all that has ever passed before them, what wonders would we see; or had it a tongue half as voluble as that of its owner, how would we listen *spell bound* to tales of those times when, at the gloomy hour of midnight, Ghosts and Hobgoblins stalked the earth. Let him who would feast his soul by a survey of the crumbling monuments of man's hands come here and enjoy what many have sought beyond the briny deep ...

My reasons for thinking that I shall not remain long in my present quarters are simply these: the upper part of her house is divided into two large rooms (without any chance for fire in either) in which all her boarders room and sleep, and from what I can learn, they have but *two* rules for the regulation of their conduct, the first of which is that "the fellow that goes to bed first gets the best bed and the most blankets," and the second is, in principle, very much the same; it runs thus: "He who gets up first wears the best boots all day."

Now, I have no objection to the maxim of "First come, first served," but this extension of it so far as to make them not only first, but also best served, though it may be perfectly right, does not accord with my bachelor ideas of propriety. I have therefore informed her that if she can let me have a certain little room by myself, I will remain under her motherly protection; otherwise I shall be doomed to go elsewhere when the rest of the boarders return.

I was somewhat disappointed in the appearance of this place, as it is not as large as I had supposed; still I think it must be a very pleasant place in the summer time, as the streets are level and pretty well shaded with trees.... I attended Presbyterian Church on Sabbath A.M., but it was so rainy P.M. that I did not go at all, though I had thought to go to the Episcopalian....

Mr. Matchin, another of our students, arrived this morning. He appears to be a first rate fellow, and pretty smart, too. We have just been down street to an auction, where we had some rare sport; or *they,* rather, for as I am a stranger, it would not *do* for me to be anyways wild on the start. Of course, they have one poor fellow to run their jigs upon, and judging from their talk, they do it up strong. His name is Hartzen, and he is now absent from the place.

Within a short time, Niles became a good friend of both Tim Machin and the "poor fellow," Chancellor Hartson. In mid-November Niles wrote to Cornelia on a quiet Sunday evening:

Tim (don't you know Timothy Machen), who was sitting quietly at the other table, up and stopped me right in the middle of a very interesting train of thought by proposing to go to church, but I concluded not to go this evening and am therefore left alone, to employ myself as I choose for the next two hours ...

The plan aimed at in Mr. Fowler's course of instruction I believe to be one of the best that could be well imagined. True, it is as yet but a new thing, and his arrangements are not carried out in some respects as successfully as they will be if he continues on for another year.

The greatest inconvenience at present arises from his not having a proper place for us to study. He has a partner, a Mr. Colman, and five of us study in the office with him, and the rest at other Law Offices in the village. We then have another office for reciting, speaking, and court room.

Mr. Fowler intends to build a large building in the spring for the accommodation of his school, and for the present he makes arrangements for his students to study in the various offices of the place in order that they may have constant access to good libraries &c. The office is emphatically our *home,* and here we stay all the time [except] only when we are at our meals.

Miss Smith has eight boarders all the time, and sometimes ten; five of Fowler's boys, two small boys, and one little girl; besides she has had two other female boarders most of the time since I came. We live in regular boarding house style, which, by the way, I never knew anything about before I came here. I am not going to give you a description of our bill of fare, because it is not anything that you have any business to know about.

One thing, tho, is certain; when we come to the table, what our hands find to do, we do with all our might, and then [we] clear. Miss Smith has taught school thirty-four years and has educated almost all of the ladies, both old and young, in Cherry Valley, and appears to be very much esteemed by those that know her. She gives us all good advice, which, of course, out of respect to her, if nothing else, we adhere to.

Whether I shall continue for any length of time to board with her or not is yet quite uncertain. I like the place well enough with the exception of having no place for keeping clothing or for lodging, except all being stacked together in glorious confusion. I should not have staid until this time, but it appears difficult to get board elsewhere except at the public houses, and I prefer not going to any of them if I can help it, tho it appears to be the place at which most of the boarders in the place go.

You know, Cornelia, when a fellow first goes to college, he always gets a few just to try him on the start. Well, it's pretty much the same here, and I am going to tell you a little about my fun for the first week. When I first came there was a vacation, but as soon as the boys came in, they concluded to try the Canadian.

So after I got to bed (I slept above, then), one of the fellows came and wanted me to lend him a blanket. I told him I would see him in the morning, but that did not answer, and he unceremoniously began to strip the bed, but you better believe it was not many minutes before he and I, as the lawyers say, had joined issue.

The first pitch, he went with his head through the window, smack up to his shoulders, and next turn he landed at the foot of the stairs, nearer dead than alive. The next morning, he (not doubting but that I was very angry) came to ask my pardon. I told him briefly that I never entertained any ill will for such trifles, and added that any time when he wanted more such treatment, I should be happy to wait on him, but Niles don't have any trouble since that.

When the quarter commenced, they all pitched upon me to conduct the first suit. I at first determined not to, but by accident I heard a couple of them talking that if they could get me in on the first trial, they would use me as rough as possible and have some fun. I then consented at once, to gratify the dear souls by giving them a chance for fun. This was on Saturday and the trial was to come off on Monday evening. We pitched upon a subject for trial that evening and joined issue thereon.

Mr. Rockwell (my opponent) then went to hunting up the law upon the case, but I studied on as usual. The next day, he staid in the office and did the same as on the preceding night, while I went to church. Towards night they began to advise me to go to preparing the case. Still I went home and to bed at eight o'clock and waited till they all came down and got to sleep.

Then I got up and went to the office and went into it good and strong, and by three o'clock in the morning I had looked out all the points of law that I wanted and had written out and committed a plea for the jury. I then went home and slept till breakfast time and paid no more attention to the case till night.

During that day they all enjoyed their sly jokes at my expense, but I was too dull or too busy to comprehend anything of what they meant. Night came, and with it the trial, and if I ever enjoyed revenge it was that night in whipping out my opponent, and since that moment I have been well used and on good terms with all of the fellows.

Perhaps you are ready to ask how it is that I can now study evenings so much more than I could use to. All the answer that I can make is that I go right into it without any thought but to get my lessons, and therefore experience no inconvenience, and in this respect I think that I am a little different from most folks.

I can, when excited, endure more labor of any kind than many strong men, but the moment I begin to work mechanically, then it's soon all up with me, and I guess upon second thought it is pretty much the same with everyone. The fact is, we can do, or *become,* pretty much what we resolve to in this world, providing we only think so, and put forth a corresponding effort.

Yesterday afternoon Mr. Hartzen (one of the boys) and I went out to take some exercise by a long walk. We went about three miles, called on a Baptist deacon with whom he was some acquainted, and got a lot of good apples, and then traveled around in a circuit back to this place; during this route purchased a large flock of *sheep,* some *sheepskins,* partially engaged a school, and procured four subscribers to the Dollar Newspaper, an old copy of which I happened to have in my pocket through the kindness of Mary, who sent a couple of them to me.

The folks were all Dutch, and Sam Conkling's ox trade was nothing in comparison. Perhaps you think that this is rather dangerous business, but just hold on till I finish the story, if you please. You see, our lesson in the forenoon had been on the subject of contracts, and we had learned how to make void contracts, which, of course, we did in every case, by slipping in something in such a way that our bargains would not bind us in the least (Don't be green enough to tell of that because I have).

Cornelia wrote Niles to say she was thinking of going away in the summer to teach school. She was uncertain of whether to do so and asked his opinion. He offered it on November 21, 1847:

I at first thought that I would express no opinion on the subject any way. Again, the thought struck me that were my sister to ask my advice or opinion upon any subject, I should certainly give it without hesitation, and why not to Cornelia? Have not she and Mary been as sisters to me for years past? Most certainly—

I have only then to say, Cornelia, that were I in RVille I should oppose your going—I would, positively, with all my might—but as it is, I can't see you if you stay at home—therefore, I say if you feel at all disposed to go to Catskill, do so by all means. I know you will succeed first rate.

I'll warrant you, too, for three cents, so just expell all thoughts as to your success as a teacher (I'll be responsible for that) and conclude whether, other things considered, you would like to go or not. . . .

Rockwell . . . says if you are a good looking girl, he will send as much affection as you could put in a handle basket. Tim, too, says, by gosh, Searls, if you will say a good word to that girl, you may hug my sister.

By the same mail he sent a letter to Mary in which he divulged the news that he had become an uncle for the first time:

Joanna is the mother of [a] hopeful little responsibility in the shape of a young *son.* Of this I received intelligence just before leaving RVille [in October]; I then wrote back and gave strict orders for having the villain named Niles, and thought I would wait till they attached that name to him before I told you anything about it, but instead of complying with my express directions, George's father says the *bohoy* must be named after him, i.e. *Moses.*

"By Moses," if I was there I would show the old chap who would have their way about it. Joanna is still anxious to name him after me, and I know if I was there I could carry the day, but as it is, I spose *Grand Pa* will succeed.

Mary had written telling him about the marriage of their cousin, William Henry Niles Jr., of Canada. His sister, Nancy, had described the new bride in a message to Mary's mother:

You will know by the enclosed card that my Brother is married to a young Lady by the name of Amanda Melissa Tiffany. She is called the best looking girl in Canada West, but rather too delicate for a good wife.

Sister says she is good for nothing but a ballroom butterfly; she is very young, but little past seventeen, and has spent most of her time in school or in traveling. She knows but little of the ups and downs of life; notwithstanding all this, she is called a person of good mind, good Education, and possessing a kind disposition—but you know it is very easy for a person that has never been tried to pass as such.

Once before, at Rensselaerville, Henry had been in love with another young lady named Amanda, and Niles said:

You know, it is an old saying that "one of the name is as good as the same;" if so, Henry had done as well as tho he and his former darling Amanda had consummated their mushroom engagement. . . .

We have ten students at present and are getting along finely. I have never been satisfied with my progress in studying till now. I think I came here just at the right time. I have got a good start, have no difficulty in getting my lessons as well as the rest, a thing that I never did in school.

My eyes are better than for years past and I am full of hope that they will remain so. The Academy here has been undergoing repairs; they have it fitted up very finely, and school begins tomorrow. We are going to use the first department evenings for a court room.

I like Mr. Fowler very much; he is a sociable, intelligent man. He and I took a walk of four miles last evening, by moonlight. He boards with us now at Miss Smiths, but does not room there. I am still staying there and have made no change in any way.

PRESIDIO

Battery

✝ Burial Ground

N

Wharf

Antonio Ortega

Wharf

JACKSON ST.

Californian Office

Saloon

STOCKTON ST.

Lagoon

WASHINGTON ST.

Custom House

Fitch & McKurley

YERBA

Sam Brannan

Casa Grande

Jail

PLAZA

Wm. Hinckley

BUENA

CLAY

School

ST.

Wm. Davis Store

COVE

Brown's (City) Hotel

E.P. Jones

MONTGOMERY ST.

Portsmouth House Ravine

Mellus & Howard Warehouse

SACRAMENTO

Jesus Noe

Leidesdorff Warehouse

MISSION DOLORES

W.A. Leidesdorff

Russ

MAP NO. 5
SAN FRANCISCO
(YERBA BUENA)
1846-1848

YERBA BUENA, ALTA CALIFORNIA (1847)

CHAPTER 8

ALTERED CIRCUMSTANCES

September 1847–March 1848

I

I'D LIKE YOU TO meet Captain Swasey, Tallman," said the editor of the *California Star*. "We met in the California Battalion, and he's just come back from San Pedro."

"I think we may have met already," said Kemble's companion. "How have you been, Tallman Rolfe? Good to see you here in California!"

"Well, I'll be—aren't you the fellow I met up with on the Oregon Trail—the one with the bull at Fort Hall?"

"One and the same!"

"Did I hear Ed say 'Captain' Swasey? I seem to recall you were just plain Bill Swasey a couple of years ago."

"A lot has happened since then. Kemble and I both fought under Frémont last winter. I was Assistant Commissary."

"Well, it's good to see you. I've often wondered how you made out. Do you live at San Pedro?"

"No, but it's a long story. What it boils down to is Colonel Frémont ordered me to seize a Mexican ship down there to transport some of our troops back home after the fight. He told me I must be sure to return it to the owners at San Pedro as soon as we were done, but I've had the devil's own time doing it—no end of things happened. First it was the Navy, and then Larkin, and then General Kearny, and then Larkin again. Every one of 'em tried to get the ship away from me, but I finally managed to give 'em the slip and take it back. But it took most of the summer to manage the trick and make my way back to San Francisco."

"It sounds like some of Frémont's bad luck passed off to you."

"Don't it, though? Isn't that rotten what Kearny's done to him? I can't believe the pettiness of the man, just because he's jealous of Frémont's success and popularity. He'll do anything to wreck the Colonel's career."

"I don't know the right or wrong of it," replied Tallman, "but it would appear that someone's going to have some explaining to do. It seems like a poor way to behave in front of the Mexicans, marching Frémont back to the States in disgrace right after he's just won the war."

"It's not Frémont's disgrace—it's Kearny's, and he'll find it's so, once they're back in Washington!" declared Swasey.

"What are your plans, Bill? Are you going to stay here in California now that the war's over?"

"I'm thinking of going into business here in San Francisco, though I haven't decided just what kind yet."

"That's good news. I'd like to talk to you sometime about your adventures in the mountains with Old Greenwood."

"And I'd like to hear about your trip to Oregon. We'll see each other a lot this winter, I'm sure. I'm certainly glad we both got here at the same time!"

It wasn't more than a week until Ed Kemble again introduced Tallman to someone whose face was vaguely familiar. This time it was Sam Brannan, publisher of the *Star,* who had returned from the Great Salt Lake, where he'd met the vanguard of the Mormon emigration.

"Tallman Rolfe?" exclaimed Brannan. "If that doesn't beat everything! I was asked to look for you, but never thought to find you in my own office."

"Who asked after me?" Tallman exclaimed. "One of my family?"

"Indeed—your brother Ben! He was with Brigham Young and I spent about a month with him, traveling from the Green River to the Great Salt Lake."

Sam went on to tell how he and Charley Smith had arrived at the river on the last day of June to find the advance company of Mormons already there, building rafts to get across. The emigrants, exhausted from the mysterious illness that wracked their bodies with fever and pain, found it hard going.

When Sam tried to tell Brigham Young about California and its wonders, the Mormon leader listened with growing impatience and scorn. He distrusted Brannan and made little effort to conceal his dislike of the man who once supported his rival for leadership of the church. Finally Young told him to quit arguing and go back to California, gather his colony and bring it to Salt Lake. The decision had been made.

But when the Mormons began to follow in the year-old tracks of the Reed-Donner party, Brannan again incurred the wrath of the patriarch by warning that it was this very section of Hastings' Cutoff that had worn out men and animals of that ill-fated group. According to Young it was not the fault of the route but Divine Judgement falling on the innocent and guilty alike because of Mrs. Murphy. He claimed that she had broken with the church in Nauvoo and this was her punishment for joining a train of anti-Mormons.

A member of John S. Higbee's company heard of Sam Brannan's arguments with Brigham and made a point of seeking him out one evening after a grueling day of dragging oxen and animals through ravines and over steep ridges. He introduced himself as Benjamin Rolfe and said he had a younger brother who had gone to Oregon a couple of years earlier. Ben thought it was possible that Tallman Rolfe might have wandered south to California after the Americans took over. Knowing that Brannan had been living in California, Ben wondered if he might have run into his brother.

Sam had explained that California was a pretty large place and even if Tallman had left Oregon, there was no reason to suppose they would cross paths. But he promised to make inquiries upon his return. One day he heard Brigham compliment Ben and was surprised when the Mormon leader urged Rolfe to join the church.

"What's this I hear," he asked the young man later, "about you and the church? Why are you here if you're a gentile?"

Ben told him that he'd been raised in a church family, but had not been convinced it was the way for him. In 1845 he had gone to Missouri to work. On hearing that his father had been selected to be a member of the pioneer vanguard that was to break trail across the plains, Ben hurried back to Nauvoo. Because he was convinced the task would exceed his fifty-two-year-old father's strength, Ben had persuaded the authorities to send him instead. The lead group had contained 143 men and boys, two small children, and three women, the wives of Brigham Young, Lorenzo Young, and Heber Kimball.

Behind them was the larger emigration of Mormon families, among them Tallman's father and mother, Samuel and Elizabeth, their children, and Gilbert Rolfe's wife and children. Sam Rolfe was captain of eighteen wagons, responsible for the transportation of forty-two persons to Zion. All had spent the winter on the plains before continuing to the Great Salt Lake in June 1847. Brigham Young, Sam Brannan, and Ben Rolfe came to the valley in late July. About 250 members of the Mormon Battalion arrived several days later from Pueblo, on the Arkansas River, along with other Mormons from Mississippi. The rest of the Rolfe family was expected in September, but by then Sam Brannan was long gone, having returned to San Francisco.

"What is it like at the Salt Lake?" asked Tallman.

"I can think of only one point in its favor as a Mormon colony," replied Sam. "I doubt that anyone will care to run them out of it."

Tallman's heart sank. "It's that bad?"

Sam nodded his head. "No power on earth could persuade me to leave California for that desolate valley."

Strangely, when Sam's report of his travels appeared in the *Star* on September 18, 1847, it didn't exactly present the information he'd given to his staff. For reasons of his own, Sam continued to foster the myth about Mormons and California. According to the paper:

Mr. S. Brannan, publisher of this paper, after an absence of nearly six months, arrived at this place on Friday morning last, 28 days from Fort Hall.

By him we learn that the emigration to this country, this year will not exceed ninety wagons. An advance company of about twenty-five wagons is supposed to be now on Truckey's Lake, while the most tardiye are in all probability at least 150 miles from the sink of Mary's River. . . .

Mr. Brannan informs us that the emigration to Oregon was still "rolling on;" that up to the 18th day of Aug., seven hundred and seventy wagons had passed Fort Hall, and before the expiration of the month, many more were expected.

Of the "Mormon emigration," there had arrived at the great Salt Lake, up to August 7th, 480 souls. This body, for the most part males, is but an advance of an extensive additional caravan, consisting of four or five hundred wagons.

Here they have laid off and commenced a town, planted large crops, which are described as being forward and flourishing, and have at hand eighteen months' provisions to be used in the event of a failure of crops.

They contemplate opening an entire new road through to this coun-

TALLMAN HATHAWAY ROLFE

try, in connection with the present rendezvous, and which completed, they move *en masse* to the valleys of California.

The "Mormon Battalion," of about 200 men, had been met in the mountains of California, many of whom were returning to winter here. Of this Battalion, 150 whom sickness detained at Santa Fé, had joined the emigration at Salt Lake, their term of enlistment having expired; Col. Cook had been sent by Gen. Kearney to discharge them.

Mr. Brannan gives the general health of the emigration good, few deaths having occurred throughout the travel.

Not all of the Mormon Battalion had left California; in particular, eighty men had been hired by Johann Sutter to help build his flour mill near New Helvetia (as he called his fort) and his new sawmill in the mountains. James Marshall was in charge of the work on the sawmill. Sam Brannan had stopped at the fort long enough to make an agreement with Sutter whereby Sam and Charley Smith were about to open a store in one of the old adobe buildings.

"A store? At Sutter's Fort? Whatever for?" asked Kemble.

"When emigrants arrive overland, they always come to the fort, sooner or later. It's the best known place in the West. But Sutter is no businessman. Either he gives supplies away or he sells on credit, and then he fails to collect. I'd hate to calculate how much money he's lost in recent years. It just slips through his fingers."

"I don't see what that has to do with your store."

"Sutter didn't at first, either, but it didn't take long to persuade him. All he really wants to do is sit back and be the lord of the manor—he doesn't know the first thing about running a business. But with my store, I'll make the deals and he can send everyone to me and won't lose a cent. I'll pay him for anything I sell for him at the store and he'll be way ahead."

"Can you run a store up there and still carry on the paper down here?"

"Sure. Charley Smith is going to tend store at the fort, you fellows will take care of the paper, and I'll take care of the buying. Henry Mellus and Bill Howard said they'd supply me with goods from their warehouse."

"Well, I guess it might work out," admitted Kemble, "but I doubt you'll get rich from it."

"Don't be too sure, son. That valley is going to prosper. You just mark my words."

*

Life hadn't prospered for Sebastian Keyser. His bride of less than a year had run off already. Someone told him he'd better print a notice in the paper so she didn't put him into debt. He and whoever advised him got together and wrote an announcement for the *Star,* which was printed on September 4, 1847:

NOTICE

My wife, Elizabeth Keyser having left my bed and board, the subscriber would inform the public that he will not be accountable for any debts of her contracting after this date.

Sebastian Keyser.

Bear Creek, Aug. 20th, 1847.

Keyser was used to having *nisenan* or Kanaka wives. The kind of treatment he was used to offering those who shared his quarters was not up to the quality expected by Elizabeth Rhodes, so she had left him. Meanwhile, on the adjoining ranch, William Johnson persuaded little fourteen-year-old Mary Murphy to be his wife. She had been a member of the Reed-Donner party, and old Bill Johnson, the grizzled ex-sailor, was one of those who helped rescue her in February. Other survivors who found husbands in the summer of 1847 were Elitha Donner, also fourteen, and Mary Graves, twenty-one.

San Francisco had a new *alcalde,* George Hyde; Lieutenant Bartlett had been returned to sea duty. Also gone were Commodore Stockton, who had returned to the East by the land route, following one month behind General Kearny and his prisoner, Lt. Col. John C. Frémont. California had a new military governor, Colonel Richard B. Mason. Mason was at Monterey, and *The Californian,* like the *Star,* was now at San Francisco.

II

TWO MEN ON HORSEBACK approached the old adobe barracks at Monterey. The building was two stories high. At the front, and on the outside of the structure, was a wide stairway leading from the ground to a covered porch on the upper level.

"Is this it?"

"I guess so. Ask that soldier over there by the corral."

"Hey, soldier, is this the governor's place?"

"You mean Colonel Mason? That's his office. He's upstairs."

"Can we get our horses fed and watered?"

"Bring 'em over here and I'll have 'em taken care of."

Thanking the soldier, the men dismounted and left their horses. Before going upstairs, they stretched and flexed their legs, getting used to the feel of solid earth after the long ride. They stared up at what formerly had been the Monterey barracks for the Mexican Army. When General Kearny turned over his command, Colonel Mason had moved out of Thomas Larkin's house and into the top floor of the old barracks. The outside stairs had been added by Mason, who also instructed his carpenters to cut a large door through the thick adobe wall from the porch into the large outer office shared by a soldier-clerk, a civilian interpreter, and the governor's aide, Lieutenant William Tecumseh Sherman.

The men climbed the new stairway, its wooden treads still green and rough, although sea air and winter rains were beginning to soften their raw color from gold to grey. One man opened the large wooden door and both passed inside. They sniffed the freshly whitewashed walls and looked awkwardly about the room. A young red-haired officer asked them their business.

"We're here to see the governor."

"I'm afraid he's pretty busy just now. Perhaps I could see to your business."

"No sir. The Captain said not to talk to any but the governor. He was certain on that."

"The captain? Which captain was that?"

"Captain Sutter."

"Oh, yes—*that* Captain. Well, if you'll give my your names, I'll tell the governor you're here, though I can't promise he'll have time to see you today."

"I'm Charles Bennett," said the more aggressive of the two, not bothering to identify his companion. "It's pretty important business."

The lieutenant knocked on the heavy oak panels of the door leading to the governor's office and a muffled voice said something which Sherman interpreted as a command to enter. Once inside, he pulled the door shut behind him.

Bennett and his friend could hear nothing but a low murmur from the far side of the adobe partition. Then Sherman came out and told them to go in.

The door was closed again and the lieutenant resumed his seat in the outer office. He was engrossed in his work once more when, after about twenty minutes, Colonel Mason came out of his office and said, "Come in here for a minute, Sherman."

Sherman followed the governor, who picked up some pieces of colored gravel from his table. He held them in the palm of his hand for his aide to see.

"What do you think of these? Do they look like gold to you?"

Sherman eyed them for a moment, then took up the larger piece and examined it carefully. He bit it and then said, "The only gold I've seen in its natural state was at Georgia, about four years ago, and that was a lot finer than this. Otherwise it looks much the same."

"Is there any way to test it, without making an assay?"

"I know a pretty crude test, but it's fairly accurate. It won't tell us much about purity, of course."

"What's that?"

"I'll need an axe and a hatchet, sir. Just a minute and I'll have Sergeant Baden get them," Sherman said, stepping to the door to the outer office. When the clerk had brought the needed tools, the lieutenant laid the nugget on the side of the axe blade and began beating it with the back of the hatchet. The yellow metal flattened and spread until Sherman announced:

"I'd say it's gold, sir."

"All right. That's all I wanted to know. Now, read this." Mason handed his aide several documents. The first was a letter from Sutter:

New Helvetia Feby 22d 1848

Sir:

By the bearer of this Mr. Charles Bennett, I have taken the liberty of sending for your approval articles of agreement made by Mr. Marshall and myself with the Yalesumney tribe of Indians. Should it meet with your approbation you would confer a special favour by sanctioning it. Mr. Bennett can give a full description of location &c, &c. We have been at great expense in building and settling the place and would like to be protected in our title or claim for the term expressed in the Lease.

The settlement will be of great benefit to the Indians by protecting them against the wild tribes above them, furnishing them with food, clothing &c and teach them habits of industry. It will also be the means of settling the lands at the base of the California mountains which are of a very superior quality by protecting the settlers against the Indians.

I have the honour to be very Respectfully your

Obt Servt. J. A. Sutter

The other papers purported to be the articles of agreement with four Indian chiefs identified as Pulpuli, Gesu, Colule, and Sole. Charles Bennett and William Scott had witnessed the document and Sutter had approved it in his role as Indian Sub Agent; General Kearny had placed him in charge of all Indians on or near the Sacramento and San Joaquin Rivers before turning the government over to Mason.

This indenture, made the first Day of January, in the year of our Lord One thousand Eight hundred and fourty eight, between Pulpuli and Gesu, Chiefs, Colule and Sole, Alcaldes of the Yalesumney tribe on the part of said tribe of the Territory of Upper California of the one part, and John A. Sutter and James W. Marshall of the Territory of Upper California, Sacramento District of the the other part.

Witnesseth. That the said Pulpuli, Gesu, and Colule & Sole for and in consideration of the yearly rents and covenants hereinafter mentioned and reserved on the part and behalf of the said Pulpuli, Gesu, Colule & Sole as agents for the Yalesumney tribe, their heirs, executors and administrators, doth rent and lease unto Sutter and Marshall the following described [tract] of Land for the term of twenty years: beginning at the mouth of a small creek known by the Indian name of Pumpumul, where said creek empties into the south branch of the American fork, a tributary of the Sacramento River, thence north one mile, thence up said fork on the north side at the distance of one mile from said stream to a point three miles above a saw mill building by said Sutter and Marshall, thence in a south east direction until it strikes crossing the south branch the said Pumpumel Creek, thence down the same to the point of beginning, and likewise grant to the said Sutter and Marshall the right and privilege of cutting Lumber at any point on or near the said south fork, and to float the same down the said stream and the privilege of making a road from said mill to New Helvetia, the same grant being made for the following purposes and conditions,

viz. the said Sutter and Marshall to have the right to erect a saw mill and what other machinery necessary for their purpose and to cultivate such land as they may think proper, and likewise open such mines and work the same as the said aforesaid tract of land may contain, the said tribe reserving to themselves the individual residence of said tract of land, excepting such as may be enclosed by said Sutter and Marshall.

The said Sutter & Marshall doth bind themselves to erect one pair of mill stones and to grind the grain for said tribe taking one bushel in eight, and to pay on the first day of January each year one hundred and fifty dollars to Pulpuli, Gesu, Colule & Sole, their heirs and assigns, for the use of said Yalesumney tribe during the term aforesaid, said payment to be made in clothing and farming utensils for the common use and benefit of said tribe at the fair market value;

and the said Sutter and Marshall of the second part at the expiration of said term agree and bind themselves, their heirs and assigns, to give quiet and peaceable possession of the aforesaid premises unto the said Pulpuli, Gesu, Colule and Sole, their heirs and assigns, they paying the said Sutter and Marshall a reasonable price for the mill and buildings that may be put on the said premises by them.

In witness thereof the said parties of the first and second part set their names and seals. Done this the fourth day of February in the year of our Lord one thousand Eight hundred and fourty eight.

"Are you going to approve it?" asked Sherman.

"I can't. I'd like you to write a letter to Captain Sutter telling him why. First, I want you to explain to him that because California no longer is a Mexican province, the old laws no longer apply. Second, because there has been no treaty of peace thus far, the American laws do not yet apply. Even after a treaty has been signed, there will have to be a public survey before the usual land laws or preemption laws can be valid. He can make all the agreements he wants, but I can't promise him title to the land, at least not at the present time."

"What about the gold? Who does that belong to?"

"I don't know. There may not be enough to worry about. In a sense, it belongs to nobody, since no government has clear title to California at the moment. After it is officially in the hands of the United States, the courts and Congress will have to decide. By then, you and I will be gone from this place and it will be none of our concern."

"But if the gold mines prove rich, won't others dispute Sutter's exclusive right to be there?"

"Of course, because he has no such exclusive right. But I don't think he has very much to worry about. After all, there are no settlements within forty miles of his mill, if what these gentlemen say is true. I doubt he'll be troubled by trespassers, so long as he doesn't advertise his find."

After Sherman wrote the letter, Mason read and signed it. As they watched the men from Sutter's Mill ride off, Mason said:

"Honestly, Sherman—how much of that legal jargon do you suppose those savages really understood?"

"Not much, I would think, sir. I don't suppose it matters any longer. The document is null and void."

"Aha! You're assuming the parties of the second part will inform the parties of the first part that the agreement is worthless—and if you think that's about to happen, you're as naive as the Indians, I fear."

III

IT WAS COLD AND WINDY in San Francisco when John Bidwell stopped by the office of the *California Star* one day in March.

"Hello there, Sergeant Kemble! It's good to see your bright and shining face again."

"Well, Major Bidwell! What brings you down from the country?"

"I had to pick up some young trees and vines from over at San Rafael, so I thought I'd visit my friends around the bay before heading home."

"Glad you did. Things are pretty quiet these days—not like during the war. Do you ever miss the army life at San Diego?"

"Not a bit. Soldiering isn't near so satisfying as farming. By the way, maybe things won't stay so quiet. Captain Sutter says his men have found gold near his mill."

"That so? Which mill—his gristmill?"

"No, the sawmill. I don't know if you heard about the one Jim Marshall and those Mormons have been building all winter. It's in the mountains on the American River. Couple of months ago they turned up some gold in the tailrace!"

"What a lucky stroke! Find very much?"

"I don't suppose so, leastways they're not making a very big occasion out of it, but it's enough to keep everyone wide awake looking for more."

Just then, Sam Brannan walked into the office, spied Bidwell, and greeted him warmly. "You'll be interested in this news, Major," he said. "I've just got a letter from Charley Smith up at my store at Sutter's Fort. He's telling me the wildest story; you'll never guess in a hundred years!"

"Something to do with gold?"

Brannan's face fell. "You've heard! Who told you?"

"Sutter did, just a day or two ago."

"So it's true. Who else have you told?"

"About the gold? Well, on my way down from the fort I stopped to see General Vallejo and we talked about it a little."

"Anybody here in town?"

"Before I got here? Well, I told Ben Buckelew at the office of the *Californian*."

"Damn!"

Bidwell was startled. "Why, what's the matter? I told you, too. I didn't want to play favorites."

"Sure, I understand that. But with their press date earlier than ours, they'll be in print three days before we come out—it'll be stale news by Saturday!"

"It'll be stale by tomorrow, Sam," said Kemble. "The whole town will know by nightfall, and next week no one will care."

"I guess you're right, Ed. No harm done, Major!"

"I'm glad to hear that—I wouldn't want to injure a friend. Well, I've got to be on my way. The trees and grapevines I ordered at San Rafael ought to be ready to pick up by now, and I'd like to get them home and into the ground. It's already getting late in the season to plant. Say, if any of you are ever up in our neck of the woods, stop and see me. Anyone can give you directions, even the Indians."

"We'll do that very thing, Major!"

After Bidwell was gone, Tallman Rolfe asked Kemble what he knew about the rancher. The editor explained that John Bidwell had come to California in 1841 and worked for John Sutter during most of the intervening years. Now he was living on the Arroyo Chico land grant, where he was engaged in planting, surveying, and building cabins and outbuildings.

On Wednesday, March 15, 1848, the rival *Californian,* now published and edited in San Francisco by Benjamin R. Buckelew, contained the following item:

GOLD MINE FOUND—In the newly-made race-way of the saw-mill recently erected by Captain Sutter, on the American Fork, gold has been found in considerable quantities. One person brought thirty dollars' worth to New Helvetia, gathered there in a short time. California, no doubt, is rich in mineral wealth; great chances here for scientific capitalists. Gold has been found in almost every part of the country.

Buckelew, a jeweler and watchmaker by trade, had acquired *The Californian* from Semple and Colton in the summer of 1847, and one of his first acts had been to drop "The" from its name. For awhile Robert Gordon had taken over the editing and then the publishing of the paper, but now it was back in the jeweler's hands.

Having been beaten to the story, Ed Kemble made no effort to play up the news. On March 18 the *Star* stated only that gold had been found "about forty miles above Sutter's Fort." But one week later, the *Star* reported further developments: "So great is the quantity of gold taken from the new mines . . . that it has become an article of traffic in that vicinity."

In the meantime, Sam Brannan had arranged for Dr. Victor J. Fourgeaud to act as the special editor for the April 1 edition of the paper, which was to be a promotional or "booster" issue. Brannan was making arrangements for two thousand copies to be carried back to Independence, Missouri, by a special messenger. This issue was to contain many glowing descriptions of California's attractions, real and imagined. Brannan and Sutter hoped it would increase the 1848 emigration.

Included in Dr. Fourgeaud's report was this information about the gold discoveries:

[California] has a mine of gold, and a probable estimate of its magnitude cannot be derived from information we have received. It was discovered in December last, on the south branch of the American Fork, in a low range of low hills forming the base of the Sierra Nevada, distant thirty miles from New Helvetia.

It is found at a depth of three feet below the surface, and in a strata of soft sand rock. Explorations made southward, the distance of twelve miles, and to the north five miles, report the continuance of this strata and the mineral equally abundant. The vein is from twelve to eighteen feet in thickness.

Most advantageously to this new mine, a stream of water flows in its immediate neighborhood, and the washing will be attended with comparative ease. . . . We saw, a few days ago, a beautiful specimen of gold from the mine newly discovered on the American fork.

From all accounts the mine is immensely rich, and already we learn the gold from it, collected at random and without any trouble, has become an article of trade at the upper settlements. This precious metal abounds in this country. We have heard of several other newly-discovered mines of gold, but as these reports are not yet authenticated, we shall pass over them.

Before Brannan left San Francisco to take the special edition up the Sacramento River to Sutter's Fort and hand it over to the courier, he had a long talk with Ed Kemble and Tallman Rolfe.

"Tallman, I'd like you to take charge here for awhile. I'm not going to be around much during the next month and I'd like Ed to go up to Sutter's Mill and see for himself what's going on."

"All right, Mr. Brannan. Even with Eager gone, I think Yates and I and the new pressman ought to be able to keep things going."

John D. Yates, who worked part-time at the *Star,* was a soldier at the Presidio. He had worked as a printer in Albany, New York, until his friend Ed Gilbert, associate editor of the Albany *Argus,* talked him into enlisting in Company H of Colonel Jonathan D. Stevenson's New York Volunteers in the summer of 1846. Now both were stationed at San Francisco, waiting for the treaty with Mexico to be signed so they could be discharged. John Eager no longer worked on the paper, having moved to Monterey with his mother a few weeks earlier.

"I may be gone before you get back, Ed, but I'll see you as soon as I can," said Brannan. "As soon as I return from Sutter's Fort, I'm to pick up enough supplies from Mellus and Howard to take care of my two new stores, and I'll want to get them moving up the river right away."

"Two *new* stores? What are you talking about?" asked Kemble.

Sam grinned. "I'm going to open one at Sutter's Mill and another on the river, about midway between the mill and the fort."

"Whatever for?"

"You'll see when you get there, Ed. All those Mormons from the battalion who were working for Sutter are out looking for gold—everyone has gone crazy over gold! It's the darnedest thing you ever saw. Since they all have to fetch supplies from the fort, I thought I'd simplify things by bringing the stores to them."

"But surely there aren't enough miners to warrant two stores in addition to the one at the fort?"

"Just wait'll you get there. There are so many Saints at one camp, it's known as Mormon Island!"

"Sounds crazy to me," Kemble said dubiously.

"It is—but maybe we'll all make a little money from it before it's over."

As Sam started out the door, Tallman held out a letter and said, "Do you suppose the courier would take this with him?"

"What's that? A letter to your folks?"

"Yes. Even if he doesn't go by way of the Great Salt Lake, there may be someone going from Fort Hall who could deliver it."

"Don't worry—we'll get it there somehow, Tallman," replied Sam with a broad grin. "When they hear about California they'll want to come and join you!"

PLACER GOLD MINING

CHAPTER 9

FIRST RUSH

April–May 1848

I

*J*OHN BIDWELL TOLD ME he could see no reason why gold should
only be found along the American River," said Major Reading.
"In fact, he mentioned a trip he took on the Bear River four years ago
with a fellow named Gutiérrez. I guess you fellows never knew Pablo
Gutiérrez, did you? Before your time."

Pierson B. Reading was speaking to Edward Kemble and George Mc-
Kinstry, his fellow passengers aboard the launch *Rainbow*, bound for
Sutter's Sacramento embarcadero. Reading, who had a ranch near
Mount Shasta, was thirty-one and had worked at Sutter's Fort under
Bidwell after coming to California in 1843. He had obtained his rank of
major while serving as paymaster for Frémont in 1846 and 1847. McKin-
stry had been sheriff at Sutter's Fort during the rescue of the Reed-
Donner party.

"Well," Reading continued, "Gutiérrez used to do some work for
Sutter from time to time and used to own the Johnson and Keyser

ranches—they were all one at that time. Anyway, Pablo told Bidwell there was gold along Bear Creek or River, whatever you want to call it. He said it was farther up in the hills than where his house was. Bidwell was interested and so they went off on a little prospecting trip together."

"Did they find any gold?" asked Kemble.

"No, but Gutiérrez showed him where it was. He didn't have anything to pan it in—kept saying he needed a *batea* to get at the gold. That was before Bidwell learned how to speak Spanish very well—nowadays he can speak it as well as a native Californian, but then he was just learning. So he thought a batea was some kind of special mining device and when Gutiérrez told him he'd have to send to Mexico to get one, he kind of lost interest."

"But a batea is nothing more than a flat, wooden bowl—every Mexican family has one or two!" exclaimed Kemble.

"Sure, you and I know it now, and so does Bidwell, but Gutiérrez didn't own one—he wasn't married—and by the time Bidwell found out what it was, it was too late. Pablo was dead."

"What happened to him?" asked McKinstry.

"The poor fool let Sutter talk him into carrying secret dispatches for him during the revolution in the winter of '44–'45. The rebel Californians caught him and hanged him for a spy, down by Gilroy's ranch."

"Did Bidwell ever go back by himself?"

"No. Things got too lively after that and he joined up with Frémont. Now he's busy with his own ranch and he says he nearly forgot all about it until the other day when he took a look at the American River mines."

"I wonder if anyone has prospected on Bear Creek."

"Funny you should say that—the year after Bidwell was up there, a dentist from Saint Louis came overland with Major Snyder and Captain Swasey. You know Jake Snyder and Bill Swasey don't you, Ed? I thought so. Well this dentist—Gildea, I think his name was, it started with a "G" just like Gutiérrez, I remember that—well, Gildea did some prospecting on the Bear just above Johnson's Ranch, and claimed he found quite a bit of gold. In fact, he showed us some after he got to Sutter's Fort in the fall of '45."

"You saw it?"

"Yes. I was working for Sutter then and Gildea wanted me to go with him in the spring. He wanted to organize a company to go shares on what we found."

"And did you?"

"No. This fellow died in January of '46—just one year after the Mexican. Kind of strange . . . almost like the place had a curse on it!"

"That's quite a story!" exclaimed Kemble.

"Getting back to Bidwell—you were saying that he thought there might be gold on the Feather River," said McKinstry. "What makes him think so?"

"He says he washed a few pans of dirt last month and found some gold. Not much, but enough to get him excited. He's talking about putting together an expedition of Indians and other ranchers up where he lives. He wants to prospect the Feather from one end to the other, if necessary."

"What about you? Haven't you got a ranch up there somewhere yourself?"

"I'm a lot farther up, but I'm thinking of taking a look at the Trinity River—that's what I call it, anyway. I think Bidwell's got a good idea, especially about bringing in Indians to do the heavy work."

"I suppose that makes sense," said Kemble, "assuming the Indians cooperate. But can you trust them? What if they decide to take your scalp and the gold, too?"

"Not much danger of that," replied Reading with a chuckle. "They're too ignorant to understand the value of gold. They have their own forms of exchange and they're not much impressed with ours, thank the Lord. As long as you supply them with enough food and trade goods, they're content. It's true, there are a few troublemakers among them, but they're not hard to spot. It's just a matter of getting rid of them."

"How do you mean, 'get rid of them'?" asked Kemble.

"Oh, not what you're thinking," laughed Reading. "No need for anything drastic. We just run them off—tell them to get on their way if they won't behave. They've learned to respect the authority of a Colt's revolver. But most are content to take what we offer, because it's so much better than what they're accustomed to."

Seven days later, the *Rainbow* tied up at the Sacramento embarcadero, where one of Sutter's Indian servants was quickly dispatched to the fort to tell of their arrival. Within a short time several Indian vaqueros arrived with a saddle horse for each guest. After a supper of beef and frijoles at the fort, Sutter informed them he would escort any who wished to visit the mines in the morning. At sunrise the party, which included Kemble, Reading, McKinstry, Sutter, some vaqueros, and a pack mule started for the mountains.

Later, when Kemble was back in San Francisco, the young editor described his host to Tallman Rolfe:

"He looks to be in his mid or late forties, and his hair is quite gray, but he stands very erect. He has a kind of ruddy complexion, and kindly blue eyes. But you should have seen him on his mule—it's a sight I'll never forget!" Kemble laughed at the memory.

"We were moving along at a pretty good clip, because we were anxious to get to the mines, but Sutter was a mite cautious whenever it came time to ford a stream. There he was, seated on that mule; he had a great broad-brimmed hat on his head and a gold-headed cane under his arm, and when his mule stumbled, he would talk to it in a quiet voice and say: 'Gott bless me, Katy! Now den, child, de oder foot. So!'"

"How long did it take to get there?"

"We arrived at the mill early in the afternoon. It's pretty far from the settlements. We saw only one house during the entire journey. The mill is located in a beautiful spot, completely surrounded by marvelous groves of pine trees. When we got there, no one was working, because the spring runoff has flooded the millrace and the bar where they were mining."

"No one was mining?"

"No—apparently the water was too high. In fact, no one seemed very anxious to tell us anything about the mines. Sutter introduced us to Marshall, who's in charge at the mill, and he wouldn't volunteer a thing. I received the distinct impression he would have preferred it if Sutter hadn't brought us around. The Captain tried to explain that we were friends, but Marshall never did open up."

"Did you find out anything at all?" asked Tallman.

"Not much. I finally asked Marshall where the gold was, and he answered, 'Everywhere! You'll find it anywhere you've a mind to dig for it,' and he waved his arm in the general direction of the river. We decided it was useless trying to get any information out of him, so we decided to experiment for ourselves."

"How did you wash the dirt?"

"Someone offered us the use of an Indian basket—whether that will actually do the job, I don't know. We didn't really know how to proceed, although Major Reading did find a small bit of color before we left. I never found a thing but rocks and sand."

"It sounds as if you didn't make any great discovery!"

"You're right. Down at the fort I was told there had been a lot of activity just before the thaw began in the mountains and before the river rose. I just don't know. It may be all humbug."

"You said Bidwell and Reading were thinking about working Indians. Do you know if anyone is doing that along the American River?" asked Tallman.

"I can't say for certain, but I rather doubt it."

"Why is that?"

"One night we were sitting around the fire after supper when a very strange thing happened. Indians began to appear, first from one direction, then from another. They didn't all come at once, but would come in bunches of two or three. It was eerie, and a little bit frightening."

"I guess it would be!"

"Every few minutes there were more and more of them, and it seemed as if there were fewer of us! But Sutter and the others knew them and didn't appear to be alarmed, so I began to relax a little. Later, I found out they were mostly local chiefs and warriors who often come to sit around the fire when Sutter visits the place. They trade with him or sell him slaves."

"Do they do that?"

"Oh yes, at least these foothill ones do—they're a rascally sort, even with their own people! Well, after they'd been there for awhile, one of the chiefs got up and began to deliver a long speech or sermon to us. Of course, we couldn't understand a word of it, but one of Sutter's Indians interpreted for us. What he had to say came down to this, more or less: his ancestors knew all about gold, but they considered it 'bad medicine.' They said that all the gold throughout the mountains belonged to a powerful demon who would destroy whoever searched for it. This demon is supposed to inhabit a lake in the mountains, and its shores are lined with gold. Anyone who meddles with gold has to pay a dreadful price to the demon of the gold lake.

"As he spoke, the other chiefs nodded their heads in agreement, and I couldn't help thinking the old fellow might be right."

"Surely you don't believe there is a demon inhabiting a gold lake?" asked Tallman, amused.

"Well, no; not necessarily that. But I can't get it out of my head about those two fellows who each claimed to have discovered gold on the Bear River."

"Gutiérrez and the dentist, what's-his-name?"

"Gildea. Yes. There's something peculiar about the fact that each died—suddenly and unexpectedly—not long after discovering the gold, and exactly one year apart. Almost like an omen. You can say it's ridiculous, and perhaps it is, but on the other hand, we both know how many people have died through the ages searching for gold. There's no reason to believe it will be any different in the future. My personal opinion is that it's foolish to chase rainbows. It's better sense to stick to the business you know."

"I suppose you're right. But it's hard not to think of what one could do with a fortune!" said Tallman with a sigh.

In the *Star* of May 6, 1848, Kemble had little to say about his trip to the mines: "Great country, fine climate; visit this great valley, we would advise all who have not yet done so. See it now. Full-flowing streams, mighty timber, large crops, luxuriant clover, fragrant flowers, gold and silver."

To his astonishment, many San Franciscans seemingly took his advice. One week later the editor of the *Star* lamented:

The Town is now completely quiet. A fleet of launches left this place on Sunday and Monday last, bound "up the Sacramento river," close stowed with human beings led by the love of "filthy lucre" to the perennial yielding Gold Mines of the North, where any man can find upwards of two ounces a day, and two thousand men can find their hands full—of work! Was there ever anything so superlatively silly? Honestly, though, we are inclined to believe the reported wealth of that section of country "thirty miles in extent" all sham—a superb take in, as was ever got up to "guzzle the gullible."

But it is not improbable that this mine, or properly, placera of gold can be traced as far south as the City of Los Angeles, where the precious metal has been found for a number of years in the bed of a stream issuing from the mountains, said to be but a continuation of this Gold Chain, which courses southward, forming the base of the Snowy Mountains.

The magnitude of the mine, as it is called, is not yet ascertained, but our best information respecting the metal, and the quantities in which it is gathered, vary much from many reports current, yet place it beyond a question that no richer mines of gold have ever been discovered upon the face of the continent.

Should there be no paper forthcoming on Saturday next, our readers may assure themselves it will not be the fault of *us* individually. To make the matter public, already our "divil" has rebelled, our pressman, (poor fellow!) last seen of him was in search of a pickaxe, and we feel, with Mr. Hamlet, we shall ne'er again look upon the likes of him.

Then, too, our compositors have in defiance, swore terribly out against "type-sticking" as vulgar and unfashionable—and insidiously whisper "where are *our* patrons?" Hope has not yet fled us, but really, in the phraseology of the day "things is getting curious!"

II

"HAVE YOU SEEN the latest *Californian*?" Tallman asked Private Yates.

"What do you mean—the *latest*? It's not yet Wednesday, or has my calendar gone crazy?"

"Your calendar is all right, but this week they published a special issue on Monday. Here, read it and you'll see why."

TO OUR READERS: With this slip ceases for the present the publication of the Californian.... The reasons which have led to this step are many and cogent.... The majority of our subscribers and many of our advertizing patrons have closed their doors and places of business and left town, and we have received one order after another conveying the pleasant request that "the printer will please stop my paper" or "my advertize-ment," as "I am about to leave for Sacramento."... We really do not believe that for the last ten days, anything in the shape of a newspaper received five minutes attention from any one of our citizens.... The whole country from San Francisco to Los Angeles and from the sea shore to the base of the Sierra Nevada resound with the sordid cry of "gold!, gold, GOLD!", while the field is left half planted, the house half built, and everything neglected but the manufacture of shovels and pick axes and the means of transportation.

"What do you suppose Brannan and Kemble will do?" asked Yates, when he had finished reading the single sheet.

"I don't know, but I plan to find out. It won't do us much good to have no competition, when there aren't enough subscribers or advertisers left to keep even one paper alive."

Later, when Kemble returned to the *Star* office, Rolfe confronted him with the sheet.

"I know, I know. I've already seen it," he replied.

"What's going to happen? Are you going to shut down the *Star* as well?"

"I'd rather not," said the young editor. "This is our chance to estab-lish ourselves as the only newspaper with good sense, and an interest in the city's future."

"*What* future? Everyone's leaving town and going to the mines!"

"Not everyone—and the others will return, once they discover that gold isn't lining all the river banks. And we'll be here waiting when they get back."

"But how can you afford to go on publishing when we have no adver-tisers?" asked Tallman. "What about the bills? And who's going to pay our wages?"

"We'll find a way," Kemble assured him. "Have you ever failed to get your pay yet?"

"No—but there's always a first time," Yates reminded the editor. "I don't see why you don't close so we can go to the gold fields, too. I wouldn't mind picking up a bit of gold!"

"What about you, Tallman?" asked Kemble. "Surely you haven't succumbed to this fever?"

"I guess I have. I agree with John. What's the sense in struggling to keep the paper alive when there's no one in the city to read it?"

"But it won't last, Tallman," appealed Kemble.

"All the more reason why we should go now, before it's too late."

Ed Kemble gazed bleakly at his printers. "Does everyone else in the office feel as you two do?" he asked quietly.

"Everyone? Have you been too busy to notice that we're about all that remains of the staff? The devil you hired to replace our last one is gone already—he left as soon as he collected his wages. I tell you, everyone but us has left San Francisco."

"Well, you at least have to stay," said Kemble, addressing Yates. "You're a soldier, so you must stay here with your company at the Presidio."

"Not really. Men are deserting every single day. Not that I have to resort to that—Lieutenant Gilbert is an old friend of mine, and he's told me that if I want to go he'll give me leave. You see, because he's second-in-command, he's obliged to stay, but he's willing to help me go if I'll share the profits with him."

"Why should he want to do that? He could get into serious trouble."

"Not Lieutenant Gilbert. He and Captain Frisbie are thick as thieves. That's why they organized Company H. Captain Frisbie is going out with a party next week to catch deserters from Company F, but I'll have a pass to go where I like!"

"It's your neck, I guess. But, how in the world am I going to get along without the two of you?"

"You don't have to—just come along with us!"

"Are you serious? You expect me to go along on this crazy expedition?"

"Why not?" asked Tallman. "We could have a great lark if you'd come, too. What if we don't find any gold? Who cares? We'll have a fine outing!"

"Come on, Ed," urged Yates. "Forget the paper—everyone else has."

Kemble felt himself weakening, but he tried one last appeal. "I'll tell you what: If the pair of you will stay on for two more weeks, and you still feel the same at the end of that period, I'll shut the paper down and we'll all go to the mines. Is it a deal?"

John and Tallman looked at one another. Yates frowned slightly, but Tallman answered, "Why not? That'll make it the middle of June. By then the rains should have stopped. I'm willing. What about it, John?"

Yates broke into a grin. "I'll tell Lieutenant Gilbert."

HOUSE OF JUDGE JOHN NILES, RENSSELAERVILLE

CHAPTER 10

MUDDY ROADS

January–May 1848

I

*W*E'RE ALMOST THERE," announced Addison Niles. "I can just make out the church spires above the trees."

"I hope I haven't missed the stage," replied Niles Searls. "I've lost all sense of time."

"I don't think we've been gone more than two hours of the three we allowed."

Niles was on his way back to law school after spending the holidays with his cousins at Rensselaerville. Addison had come along as far as Schoharie in order to bring Niles's horse back to the village. From Schoharie Niles was to take the stage to Sloansville, transferring there to the Cherry Valley stage.

The mountain roads had disintegrated into muddy, rutted trails. Each wheel track or footprint was filled with water, and in places where overflowing creeks and ponds flooded it, the road vanished entirely. The day was cold, wet, and disagreeable in the extreme, and it was the first day of 1848.

As they rode along, the cousins tried to cheer themselves by talking about the good times of the past several days. But, like the holidays themselves, eventually the gay mood became somber. After toasting the New Year on the previous evening, Niles had proposed that they all agree to celebrate each coming New Year together, in spirit if not in person.

"I wonder if we'll ever share our holidays again in one place," Cornelia had mused.

"What a gloomy thought!" came Mary's brisk response. "I expect we'll have lots more good times together."

"Perhaps," Niles had said, "but I'm inclined to go along with Cornelia. I'm not sure where I'll be in a year's time." One day, of course, Niles hoped to find someplace he could truly call his home. Between his parent's place in Canada and his uncle's house in Rensselaerville he felt conflicting tugs, and at this point in his life neither seemed more than a temporary resting place. But until he could see more of the world, he knew that he wouldn't know where he belonged.

At the stage stop in Schoharie Niles and Addison discovered they had time to spare. In the face of the worsening storm, Addison was anxious to get home, so they parted early. As he rode off, Niles urged him to give the horses a "good lot of oats" to make up for the nasty trip.

When the stage arrived, Niles took a seat opposite an older gentleman who introduced himself as the editor of the Prattsville weekly. Hackstaff was his name and he knew the Niles family in London, Ontario, including Nancy and the new bridegroom, Henry. More interesting to Niles, however, were the tales Hackstaff related about his early years in Texas, especially his part in the assault on the town of Mier.

After the Texans were defeated at the Alamo in 1836, both there and at Goliad General Santa Ana committed such great atrocities against the Americans that the infuriated Texans were equally ruthless at San Jacinto. The hatred created on both sides led to sporadic border fights throughout the 1840s.

After one such raid on San Antonio by Mexican General Woll in 1842, a group of Texans, including Hackstaff, retaliated by attacking the Mexican town of Mier on Christmas Day of the same year. After a hard and bloody battle with the soldiers of General Pedro Ampudia, the Texans finally were beaten. They surrendered and were taken prisoner. But Hackstaff avoided capture by hiding in a haystack until dark, after which he took "leg bail," as he put it.

The other prisoners were not so lucky. When some tried to escape and were caught, General Santa Ana sentenced them all to death. Later he relented and reduced the sentence to one man out of each ten. The victims were chosen by lot, blindfolded, and shot.

As Hackstaff came to the end of his story the stage rolled into Sloans-ville, too late to meet the last stage for Cherry Valley. It was Saturday night and as none would be leaving before Monday, Niles had to think about lodging. Just as it occurred to him that Tim Machin and his family lived nearby, he saw a familiar face. It belonged to Seneca Gallup, brother of the principal of the Academy at Rensselaerville.

"Hello, Mr. Gallup!" he called. "Are you stranded, too?"

"Why, hello, Niles! Yes, I am. where are you staying?"

"I was about to look up a friend who lives here in Sloansville. Would you like to come along?"

"Do you think I'd be welcome? Who is your friend?"

"He's a fellow law student at Cherry Valley. I'm sure the Machins won't mind, not when I tell them about your illustrious family! Even if we sleep on the floor, it's a lot better than going to the public house—and we'll be among good company!"

"Then I'm with you!"

II

CORNELIA SETTLED HERSELF in the big rocking chair by the fire, set her letterbox on the table by her side, and placed some pillows and a large book in her lap. Then she took a sheet of writing paper from her box, placed it on the book, and began to write to cousin Niles. It was January 18, 1848, and no one had heard from him since New Year's Day.

It is now four days since I last set any foot upon "terra firma," and today is the first day in that time that I have felt anything like being com-fortable, but this afternoon . . . I think I can contrive to pass away the time very well in writing to you (or rather trying to write, for my hand I find is not as steady as it might be).

You must know that, having taken some cold, a very fanciful swelling commences under my upper lip, which really made me quite sick for a time, and I find has taken away some of my strength.

My face—I wish you could have seen it. We thought some of advertis-ing [a] shilling a sight—children and fools half price—and so make a little out of the affair.

Your *Chubby* is *emphatically* appropriate just now, for my face is natural now, to what it was yesterday, yet one lip seems to have dis-solved all partnership with the other, and is protruding itself something less than an inch beyond my nose. . . .

I feel thankful for the visit you made us during the holidays. It seemed rather more lonesome for a few days after you left, but then it was like settling up all old accounts and starting new in the world again, and everything has seemed more cheerful and pleasant for the last two weeks than it had for many weeks before. I forget how to feel gloomy in visiting with you. . . .

We have wished very much to hear when and how you reached Cherry Valley—whether your journey back did not make you sick . . . and I am indulging a little the hope that Mary will bring home with her a letter tonight answering all these questions. . . . The scarlet fever is very prevalent—Addison was quite sick with it on Sunday, but is well now, had but a slight attack. If you are well, I hope you will be very careful and not expose yourself on these damp cold days. . . .

We all commenced as we anticipated on Monday, and since then have been very busy in studying. I find Geometry somewhat difficult. . . . That, with French, is all I have taken, as I do not wish to be overtasked this winter. . . . Mr. Gallup has been unusually pleasant to me, and has requested me to take charge of one or two classes, if it will not interfere too much with my studies. As I would like to review some studies, I think I will do so. . . .

Perhaps you think two studies are hardly worth going to school for, but we have three different lessons in French, so that my time is well occupied, I can assure you. . . . (4 o'clock P.M.) Mary has come and brought a letter, too. Now all my wishes have been realized. I see it's a long one, for it takes her a long time to read it. She says, though, that you are well, so all my fears were useless.

Mary looked up from her letter and, seeing that Cornelia was watching her, said, "would you like me to read it aloud?"

"If you wouldn't mind too much, that would be nice."

"All right. I won't start again at the beginning. You can read that to yourself later. I'll just tell you that he missed the stage at Sloansville and had to stay over with Tim."

"Oh, that's nice! About Tim, I mean, not the stage."

Mary began reading aloud where she had left off:

. . . had a first rate time, and took the stage on Monday evening, just dark, for this place, came through in an open wagon, and if I recollect right it was real muddy; at all events a man offered me fifty dollars an acre for the earth that was on my coat when I arrived here, but I preferred to keep it until spring, when I intend to plant potatoes in the pockets and shall probably raise enough for our family's use during the ensuing year.

I boarded with Miss Smith two or three days after my return and then left, and am now boarding at the public house. Two others of the students (Ely and Austin) board at the same house, as it is a public house of the best stamp (not a groggery) of those found in country villages.

We have everything that we can wish for, with the exception of regularity in the time of our meals. They frequently wait for the arrival of the stages rather longer than is pleasant to a hungry man.

You know, Mary, I told you I should leave Miss Smith if she had sent Green off; well, she did not send him away for the simple reason that she could not prevail on him to go. Perhaps then you would like to know what was the cause of my leaving and that is just what Miss Smith wanted to know, but could not find out for the life of her.

The only reason that I gave her was that she had breakfast too early (½ past 6) and when she offered to change the hour, I had made an engagement with Mr. Wilkins, and could not consistently break it, however much I might prefer to remain under the hospitable roof of the aged maiden. True, it was hard to break the cords of harmony that bound us together, yet I summoned all my resolution, and have now pretty much overcome all my sorrow at leaving.

You better believe now, Mary, that the old Lady is a fine, good hearted woman, and keeps a very good boarding house. True, some of the boys say they have taken cold by drinking of her coffee, but then I always remind them that wood is scarce and the sleighing poor.

The bread, too, likewise the extract of cow (some call it butter) were not infrequently the subjects of their wanton calumny here, though I did not often interpose, as those articles were usually old enough to take their own part.

I intend now to board on the itinerant plan, until I go around at all the boarding houses in town and find where they live best. Mr. Colman (Fowler's partner) proposed to board me if I choose to go with him rather than remain where I am. I shall do so the middle of this week. I have no doubt that I should like it with him, as he is a wide awake little fellow, and his wife appears to be a very fine woman . . .

It took me the whole of the first week after my return to get my mind on my books again and to get regulated, but last week I studied more, I think than I ever did before in the same length of time. Indeed, I feel now as though I had reduced the thing to something like the outline of a system.

My division of time is something like this:

In the morning I study chancery practice from ½ past six till breakfast time (about ½ past 8); from 9 to 10, Cowen's treatise; 10 to 11, recite; 11 to 1 pm, Cowen's treatise for next day; 1 to 2, dinner; 2 to 5, Phillips' Evidence; 5 to 6, prepare my cases for trial or read the news; 6 to ½ past,

Tea; ½ [past] 6 to about 9, attend trial, and from that till bed time I read History, look out any points of law that have come up on trial, or talk or write or, in fact, almost anything, till bed time comes round.

On Sabbath I read from the best of all books a little, and have taken up Abercrombie on the Intellectual Powers, which I intend to look over. . . . They have the small pox at Cooperstown, also at Canajoharie, but we have agreed to have nothing to do with it here, if we can prevent it. . . . Have those extra [church] meetings all ceased to impart consolation to the hearts of mourning sinners—i.e. are you all properly converted, or are you given up as hopeless, abandoned outcasts, to whom no ray of gospel light is ever destined to awaken to a sense of duty?

Polly Niles's voice interrupted the reading. "Come on, girls, it's time for supper. Help me get the table ready before your pa comes in. You can get back to your letters after supper."

When supper was over and Niles's letter read again for all the family, Cornelia picked up the sheet on which she was writing and resumed her letter to her cousin:

That letter certainly came very apropos—it has reminded me of twenty things which I had intended you should be informed of, but which I have hardly strength enough to put upon paper now, for I find my head begins to feel rather weak in the upper story (anything new?).

While hearing some parts of your letter, I was under the necessity of holding my lip with both hands, for fear I might extend into something like a smile; the consequences might have been fatal. If I had disfigured myself for life, who would have been the cause of it? . . .

They have continued the evening [revival] meetings in the session house, but as the Methodists have been getting up rather more smoke and noise, the attendance has been small. I have been [going] very regularly, about twice a week, and intend to, so long as they may continue. . . . 13 joined the church last Sabbath, and 4 the Sabbath before. . . .

Did you know Addison studied [French]? He seems to take to it as naturally as a fish to the water, and already begins to say some very pretty things in Français to the girls in the class. We have almost resolved to speak in French entirely. We have sport, I can assure you. Mr. Gallup hardly speaks to us in English, and he laughs not a little at our half English and half French. . . .

Charley Mulford came down last night to know if you was still alive. So you have really left Miss Smith. I guess it is well for her peace that you have, but I fear your health will suffer for want of exercise, now that fun cannot form part of the daily routine. . . . I don't believe I have said *all* I know yet, at least I hope not, but you are heartily welcome to it, such as it is, and don't let it be long before I shall see one from you.

> Your afft
> Chubby.

Three weeks later Niles answered Cornelia's letter. Although he had commenced boarding "on the itinerant plan," he was not moving about as much or as soon as expected:

Whether the delay is caused by the superior qualities of the ginger-bread &c, with which I am provided, or by the fascinating company of [Charles Colman's] lovely wife (than whom there is no finer), I am at a loss to determine. One thing is certain, we have good times. Butler also makes it his headquarters there. . . .

We have sixteen students at present. One new one came in yesterday. His name is Landon and he comes from Vermont.

Niles teased Cornelia about her admonitions to be careful of his health, assuring her that he was following her instructions with the greatest care. As an example, he said:

. . . the night this snow came I recollected that the gate was left open, and went out and closed it after I had coat, vest, boots, and stockings all off, through fear that I might take cold if it was left open till morning—yet, after all my care and obedience, I have taken a slight cold and have been troubled with my eyes for the last week a considerable, not having been able to study more than half of the time . . . My eyes are now much better, and will be entirely well in a day or two. . . .

I should have written before, but have been for the last three weeks very busy in deciphering a letter which Filkins wrote me. Don't tell him, for then he would know how to punish me . . . Ed's letter is just like the Bible. I find something new every time I read it, from the fact that I translate differently some part of it every time.

On February 27, 1848, Niles told Mary:

I have become so far depraved as to decide upon remaining home from church this afternoon . . . . The fact is, one mind requires a whole day to comprehend and apply such a sermon as that was. If I had some person to assist in the work, it would perhaps be a shorter task, but somehow I have no one to assist me in the least. Our boys are ready to lend a helping hand in ordinary difficulties, but when a religious subject is broached, the reply is "that's further than we got."

MARY CORINTHIA NILES

Don't think now, Mary, that we are a lot of graceless young scamps that never go to church, or read our Bibles; oh no, don't think so. Could you see us march up to Bible-class every Wednesday evening at 8 o'clock, some 9 or 10 strong, you would think were all theologians, instead of law students. . . .

I can now account satisfactorily for the manners of the college student being harsh, and for the uncouth appearance presented by graduates who, when they entered college, were genteel and refined in their manners. Living together as we do here, and associating with none but our fellow students, we are fast becoming a saucy, degenerate, uncivilized, outrageous, ridiculous, pugnacious, rebellious, scandalous lot of loafers, wholly unfit for anything in all creation except *Lawyers.*

III

EXCEPT FOR THE FACT that she wanted to write about it while the experience was still fresh in her mind, Cornelia would have gone straight to bed, for all that it was only seven o'clock. She, Mary, and Addison were completely worn out, having just returned from Uncle Stanton's farm. Their journey had been an exhausting experience, physically and mentally. But she wanted to tell Niles about it before retiring for the night. She began by telling the cause of the trip:

Luther Stanton is dead and buried. The last attention that we can ever pay to him has been paid, and he is laid in the cold grave. . . . Uncle Samuel came up Monday afternoon to inform us, and Tuesday morning at 7 o'clock we started for Norton Hill, intending to meet the funeral procession there, as Uncle said the sleighing was so bad we could not get to Uncle's the other way by 10 o'clock; but finding it passable that way, and getting there early, we rode on to Uncle Stanton's, and then returned with the procession to the old Methodist Church this side of Greenville, where the funeral was held.

The services were very impressive and well conducted, and from the church we went to the grave; and then, finding our horse nearly tired out, it being by that time nearly all bare ground, we rode back to Uncle Stanton's and staid all night.

All the friends from Coeymans and other places were there at the funeral, beside a *very* large congregation from all the neighboring places. . . . There was a procession more than half a mile in length from the house, and of course, all the trouble usual in a large concourse of people; yet everything seemed to go in a quiet, orderly manner, with respect to the ceremonies.

He selected a pleasant spot for his grave. Uncle had bought a lot in that yard, at Luther's request, and he pointed out the spot in which he should be laid.

There were none of the friends returned to Uncle's but us, and I think we never went where I felt that our company was so much enjoyed by young and old, as there ... even this morning it seemed hard for us to leave ... We left Uncle's this morning at nine, and as the snow was all gone there, George brought Mary and I about 4½ miles in his waggon, and thought we would find snow the rest of the way, but with two of us walking nearly all of the way, we got to Hall's Hollow and staid to dinner—and being most afraid of a waggon to go through the drifts, we did not get one there, as we intended, but came on the best way we could to Moses Smith's.

There was not two rods of snow, so far, and you would have laughed to have seen us coming; Addison walking all of the time, and most of the time Mary or I, and sometimes when I got so tired I could not stay in the sleigh, I would walk beside the horse with Mary, and Addison perhaps behind, out of sight.

We could not get a waggon at Moses Smith's, but there was a man there with a two horse waggon and only *three women,* and he said we must ride on the *back seat* in his waggon, and so Addison trotted on, and we arrived safe at home after a time, but Oh! how tired.

After being all day on the road, to finish off with riding 4 miles in a lumber waggon over the roughest kind of roads was enough to have killed common folks, but through it all, we preserved the best kind of spirits and had some fun, such as laughing at people riding in waggons when it was so muddy, as sleighs were so much more easy.

But we are home once more, and by tomorrow shall feel well as ever. Ma came out a while ago and said that we must go to bed, for there sits Mary with her head against the wall, nearer asleep than awake ...

On the next evening, March 9, 1848, she had another matter to discuss with Niles—teaching:

My class in Algebra finished the book yesterday and are now preparing for examination, when I expect they will reflect much honor upon their teacher. I am often asked if I do not intend to teach next summer, as Rose, Caroline, and even Deborah are talking of it, but I answer, "I guess not," though I don't believe but I intend to, as much as the rest.

Now, if you hear of anyone that wants anything like me next summer, you may let me know, though you need not put yourself out of the way at all, as it is *barely possible* that I may choose next spring to take comfort at home through the summer. ...

Mr. Gallup has just been [here] for an hour or so . . . His health is better than it was, but he intends to procure an assistant next summer to teach half of the time, which will make it easier for him. I do not know whether Miss King will stay or not, or who he will get to supply her place should she leave; it will be difficult to find another equal to her. . . .

Lucia heard from Polly Cook at Brooklyn the other day, and she made particular inquiries about you, and wished to know if that "young pickle" was in a thrifty condition, and if there was a chance for a crop.

IV

"WHATS HE HINTING AT?" asked Mary.

"Who?"

"Niles. I was just rereading one of his old letters and comparing it to what he said in the latest one to you. There's something mysterious going on, and I'd like to know what it's all about."

"What do you mean?" asked her sister.

"Well, listen to this:

I have been much more busy than usual for the past fortnight . . . I have been laying out all the work which I expect to do before leaving Cherry Valley, and the sooner it is accomplished, the sooner I shall go.

It may be done by the first of June, and possibly by the first of May, that is, if health and eyes remain good. Then I think of leaving, and whether I shall return or not depends upon a contingency which may or may not happen. What it is, you shall know in good time.

"Yes, I see what you mean. I remember that letter now, but I'd forgotten what he said. But what did you mean about comparing it with my latest letter from Niles?"

"Do you have it handy?"

"It's here in my letterbox—under the seals. Here it is." Cornelia handed the folded sheet to Mary, who began reading from it aloud:

April 20 '48

I am going to write about ten lines just to say that I am well and have a severe headache;

that we have a vacation, but I am still studying;

that I should have left here before now, but there is still one or two places where I have not yet boarded;

that I shall expect to leave here next week Thursday for a ramble, but may not;

that if I do, I shall come to Rville, but not under a week after starting;

that sister Joanna has been very sick, but is now nearly well;

that I have joined the *Odd Fellows*, but am not sorry as yet;

that I shall not write of a great many things which I would like to, but hope soon to see you, face to face

Yours in friendship, love and truth

N Searls

"Now," said Mary, "If he left Cherry Valley when he said he might, that would have been yesterday, Thursday, the twenty-seventh."

"Yes, but he said he might not start then, and if he did, he wouldn't arrive here in less than a week."

"Which means either we'll see him next week—or we won't!"

"You're beginning to sound like Niles," laughed Cornelia. "But if he's coming at all, it had better be soon, because I'll have to leave Rensselaerville by next Friday at the latest, if I'm to be on time for my teaching job at Fishkill Landing. I must say I hadn't paid much attention to Niles's hints about a 'contingency' that we'd 'know about in good time.' I just thought it was more of his joking, but maybe you're right. Maybe he was serious. Oh dear, I couldn't bear to go away without knowing!"

One week later, Polly Niles heard a knock at her back door. Before she could answer it, a voice cried out: "Anyone to home? I've buttons and laces to sell—will anyone buy?"

"Niles, you silly boy! How good to see you!" and Aunt Polly hurried across the back hall to embrace her nephew. After holding him tightly to her for a full minute she released him at last and backed away to look him up and down. Just then, her six-year-old, Charley, came in from the hall to investigate the commotion, and Polly told him:

"Be a good boy and find your sisters, quickly—tell them Niles is here!" Then, seeing little Emily just behind Charley, she said, "Look Emmie, look who's here—it's your big cousin Niles! You remember him, don't you?"

Three-year-old Emily nodded her head and stared up at the young man, who then bent down and lifted her onto his shoulder.

"My how you've grown, Emmie—now you're the tallest one of all!" Emily grinned shyly back at Niles, who turned his head sideways in order to peer into her tiny face.

"Hello, Niles," greeted Cornelia warmly, as Charles led his sisters into the kitchen. She took her cousin's hand and kissed his cheek.

"Hello, Niles," echoed Mary, kissing him on the other cheek.

"Where's Addison?" asked Niles, in surprise. "I haven't missed him, have I?"

"He's upstairs in bed and can't come down, but he wants terribly to see you," answered Cornelia. "Come on up before you do anything else."

"He's not well?"

"That's right, Niles," replied Polly. "He's been quite sick until today, but seems improved this morning. Neither Doctor Wickes nor Doctor Lay knows what is troubling him, but both say to give him lots of rest and keep him comfortable."

"Well, let's be off to see the invalid at once," declared Niles, leading the way.

Later, when they were downstairs again, Niles said, "You say he's improved? He certainly looks awfully weak and pale."

"If you'd seen him last week you'd realize how much better he is today. We're in hopes the weather will improve and his spirits and health along with it," said Cornelia.

"It will do him so much good to have you here to talk to. He's been low-spirited lately. We haven't had much time to spend with him while we got Cornelia ready for her school."

"What's that? Cornelia's got a school?"

"They've hired me to teach at Fishkill Landing for the summer," said his cousin.

"Capital! I'm delighted to hear it!"

Aunt Polly interrupted at this point to call everyone to the table. "Everyone come and sit down. I've put out cake and fresh milk for us all, but especially for Niles. He's starved, I imagine."

"He may be starved," said Mary, "but I'm dying of curiosity! Out with it, Niles—what's your secret? Confess!"

Niles looked blank. He continued eating his cake while he looked innocently around the table. "What secret?"

Mary's eyes blazed. "You know what I mean, Niles Searls! What's the big mystery you've been keeping from us—you've hinted at it, you know you have!"

"Oh, that. I suppose this must be what you have reference to," he said as he took a piece of paper from his waistcoat pocket and slowly unfolded it. "But there's no mystery about it, none at all. It's a most public affair."

Mary took the sheet from him, read the first few words and said, "Oh my! I never imagined!" She looked at him in shocked wonderment. "Why didn't you tell us?"

"I couldn't be sure."

"What is it?" "What are you talking about?" cried Cornelia and her mother at the same time. Mary passed the paper to them and Cornelia began reading it aloud:

132

IN SUPREME COURT

May 3d 1848

David C. Beattie, Barnabas B. Eldridge, Niles Searles, James C. Spencer, Edward S. Shumway, George W. Thorn, Philander Butler, Thomas Wright, Jr. & Rufus T. Baldwin, having applied for admission at this present term and it appearing to the Court that they are respectively of the age of twenty one years and upward and of good moral character;

And it appearing also by an examination in open Court that they possess the requisite qualifications of learning and ability;

It is ordered that they be respectively admitted to practice in all the Courts of this State as Attorneys, Solicitors, and Counsellors.

By the Court

H Shipherd *Clerk*

I certify the foregoing to be a true copy of an order entered in the minutes of said Court

Witness my hand and official seal this
3d day of May AD 1848

H Shipherd *Clerk*

When Cornelia finished reading, the women looked at one another and then at Niles with confused and happy expressions.

"How wonderful!" said Aunt Polly. "Good for you!"

"Congratulations, Niles," said Cornelia. "But how? I don't understand. You've only gone to Mr. Fowler's school for six months—isn't it unusual to pass the bar so soon?"

"I guess you could say it's not the regular thing. But I imagine it's been done before. It was Philander Butler's idea, not mine. He was going to take the May examination himself, so he talked me into tagging along."

"But hasn't Butler been studying longer than you?"

"Yes, but he noticed that I was about on a level with him at school, so he thought I might have as good a chance as he, if I studied extra hard beforehand. That's what I've been doing during the spring vacation."

"So you're a real lawyer now!"

"Certified by the State of New York. Of course, I've still got lots to learn, and I'll have to go back to Cherry Valley or read law in someone's office if I really want to practice properly."

"I just don't know what to say," said Mary.

"Try saying 'Counsellor Searls;' I'd like to hear how it sounds."

"Yes, Counsellor Searls. How's that?"

"I like it. I had a feeling I might!"

RENSSELAERVILLE, NEW YORK (1848)

CHAPTER 11

NEW DIRECTIONS

May–June 1848

I

*N*ow that you've passed the bar, what are your plans, Niles?"

"I'd like to spend a few days here at Rensselaerville—then I'm going down to Coeymans to visit before leaving for home."

"Fine," said Aunt Polly. "We're about to start our spring house-cleaning. We could use a strong back!"

"I thought Cornelia took care of that," replied Niles with a laugh.

"Didn't we tell you? Cornelia's going to Fishkill Landing in the morning to start teaching school."

"So soon? But that's splendid news! I just wish you didn't have to leave right away, Cornelia. I haven't seen you to talk to since New Year's."

"I know," agreed his cousin. "It's been terribly long—and now I won't be home till August! There were so many things I wanted to talk over with you. Drat!"

"Well, let's not waste time crying," said Mary. "Deborah and Charley are coming over shortly to say goodbye to Cornelia. Now we can have a party to celebrate Niles's good news as well!"

"Capital! I suppose Charley's the same old sixpence?"

"He certainly is. He's working in Robert's store on Main Street. Now that his brother put him in charge of sorting the mail, we call him the assistant postmaster!"

"That reminds me," said Mary. "I promised Charley I'd mend the post office flag if he'd bring it by some evening. Perhaps I should ask him to carry it with him tonight."

"Not tonight," said Niles. "Not unless you're planning to do charades and personate Betsy Ross—or was this to be a quilting bee?"

"All right," laughed Mary, "but I'll remind him, anyway. I can sew it after Cornelia's gone."

"I wish I didn't have to go," said Cornelia. "Mr. Rankin could just as well have waited another week to begin the school. Then I should have had time to visit with Niles and see the caravan."

"A caravan? Here in the village? What a lark!"

"Yes, Niles. Didn't you see the posters? Raymond and Rogers have combined their traveling shows. They'll be performing on the lot across from the Crocker house next Wednesday."

"I don't suppose it would do for Cornelia to let on to the folks at Fishkill that she prefers wild animals to scholars!" joked Niles.

"She wouldn't be the first schoolteacher to reach that conclusion," remarked Polly.

II

"THE COUNTRY'S BEAUTIFUL this time of the year," declared Niles, "and my family would like to have you come, I know." He spoke formally, choosing his words carefully. "Would you consider coming to Wellington with me for a visit, Mary, when I return from Coeymans?"

Mary seemed intrigued, but doubtful. "I'd love to, Niles, but I don't think Ma can spare me. We've got to clean house for the summer season and Cornelia won't be here to help. Ma can't possibly do it all alone."

"Then we won't go till you've finished. I'm willing to wait."

"Would you really? That might satisfy Ma. But then there's Pa. He couldn't stand the expense, not after getting Cornelia ready and all the other unusual things that have come up this spring. I'm afraid it's out of the question."

"It doesn't cost much to go from here to Wellington—and once there, it won't cost you a shilling."

"Oh, Niles, you just don't know! You have no idea what it costs to go away. I don't have a thing to wear."

"That's silly—of course you do!"

"Not summer things. I have a few winter outfits, but they won't do for this time of year."

"What would you need?"

"Not much, but you'd be surprised how the little things add up. For instance, I need a bonnet and shawl and shoes. I'll need dresses—of course, I was going to get those anyway, but they're not made."

"Is that all?"

"I shouldn't need a trunk, I suppose, for I can get along with Pa's trunk and his carpet bag. It would be nice if I could get a new satchel. But the dresses are the real problem. I need white dresses and they'd take time to make up. I'm afraid it's just a wild project!"

"Maybe so, but do try, won't you? This might be your last and only opportunity to see the glories of Canada—at least in my company," Niles urged.

"Why do you say that? I thought you'd made up your mind to stay in this area. You're not thinking of going west, still, are you?"

"I haven't made up my mind to anything—except to take you home with me! But I do intend to visit Mr. Chittenden tomorrow, and I'm going to talk to your Pa when he comes back from Albany."

"About working with one of them?"

"Perhaps. Mostly, though, I'd like their advice. I've been thinking I might be better off in the west. With all the competition here, it could take years to become established and begin to earn a respectable living."

"Hasn't that always been the case? Doesn't everyone have to work his way up and prove his ability?"

"Of course—only now there are more and more persons studying the law, while the opportunities for them are not growing as fast—at least not here in the east."

"Are you suggesting someplace like western New York?"

"I'm thinking of places even farther away—perhaps in the southwest. I think the treaty with Mexico will be ratified soon. When that happens, business and trade will expand rapidly in Texas. The population already is growing by leaps and bounds."

"But Texas is so far away!"

"Not so terribly far—remember that transportation is improving and the world is shrinking! I'd like very much to see Texas, even if I didn't choose to stay. And I'd like to visit the other western states, as well."

"How long do you think you'd want to stay—forever? Or would you someday come back to New York?"

"Oh, I don't suppose I'd want to stay forever. I'd probably want to come back here to raise a family, when I was ready. From what I've read of frontier life, it seems rather coarse and unrefined, not at all the place to raise children."

"I'm certainly glad to hear you say that! For a minute I thought you might be considering life in a log shanty with a swept dirt floor! I can still remember hearing Aunt Dency tell about her first visit to cousin Tom Cooley's house in Attica. Dency was so shocked! She said, 'His wife and children were *dirty!*' I had visions of your poor wife cooking dinner in a great iron kettle hung over an open fire!"

Niles laughed. "I don't guess you'd favor taking up that kind of housekeeping, would you?"

"You'd better believe I wouldn't! I've no intention of going back to the way my grandparents lived: homespun clothes, homemade soap and candles, cooking over an open fire! It may be good enough for some, but not for me. I want to live with all the modern comforts of the nineteenth century!"

Mary spoke with such vehemence that Niles looked at her with surprise. There was a long pause before he spoke. "I think you're absolutely right," he said, before changing the subject.

III

THE CARAVAN ARRIVED on May 10, 1848. The streets already were lined with townspeople who had seen posters tacked to every barn, store, or crossroad post for miles around. The gaily decorated chariots turned off Main Street and made their way slowly up Crocker Road past the burying ground. At the training lot they halted. While the horses were being unhitched from the wagons, roustabouts started putting up the main tent. The crowd drew close to admire the animals as they were being fed and watered.

When Mary arose in the morning, it was raining and the sky was full of dark clouds. During breakfast, the rain stopped and small patches of blue sky appeared in the distance. By the time she and Niles left the house with Harriet Rider, who had come by on her way to the show, the sun was shining brightly, so the girls decided to leave their India rubber rain gear at the Niles house.

They arrived at the training lot just as the crowd was being herded into the great tent. Inside, they found seats along one side of the canvas-covered arena; on the other side were long rows of cages containing the animals who would perform for them. "Look!" cried Mary. "They've arranged the animals on *both* sides—the wild beasts on one side and the multitude on the other!" Her friends laughed, but Mr. Gideon Cornell, the foundryman, scowled.

The band began playing and out came the famous elephant, "Columbus," drawing a great round of applause. Then there was the monkey act, with clowns cavorting as crazily as their ancestral cousins. The crowd shrieked with laughter, applauding, calling and whistling as each act was paraded before their astonished eyes.

And then, without warning, calamity struck. Mary wrote to her sister after it was over:

We were having fine sport with the *country* folks around us, and the monkey ride had just commenced when there came a heavy shower of rain, hail, and a tremendous wind, which in a very few seconds tore the posts of the tent from the earth and sent the whole mass of canvas, with chains, poles, ropes, &c fluttering about the people's heads, and after surging back and forth awhile, dashed them to the ground.

Such a sight you never saw, nor can you imagine it in the least. Such screaming and fainting, hollering and swearing, and breaking, and rushing, and crushing. It rained in perfect torrents, and hailed stones larger than peas; the wind blew a perfect hurricane, and the mud was over shoe.

Everyone looked out for number one, and for that reason, I think, all had the good fortune to escape uninjured. Harriet Rider and I sat together about the middle of the tier of seats. We sat still until the canvas and posts had gone over our heads and then crawled through the seats and ran with all our might as far as Mr. Chittenden's, went in there, and, finding the doors locked, went into the barn and waited til [the house] was unfastened and then went in.

By that time Harriet was about gone. Mr. Chittenden's house was full, some in hysterics, some fainting, some making ginger tea, some making fires, and drying dresses and shawls, &c. Wetter rats you never saw. We were not out two minutes scarcely, and our dresses, shawls, gloves, bonnets, *everything* was literally *wringing wet*. I got Harriet undressed and got her to bed, and then went around to see the fun. I should say there must have been nearly a thousand people there, and yet, strange to say, not one was hurt more than a little bruise or scratch. The tent went up like a balloon almost, and sailed over the people's heads, leaving them in their seats without shelter or protection. I wish I could describe to you the crowd that passed in a continual stream as we stood in the door. White dresses, silks, mulls, all served alike.

Niles found us after awhile and went home, harnessed the horse and took Harriet and I home, and then went back to see the rest of the cattle show, for they cleared away the ruins and went right on in the open field, wind and rain to the contrary notwithstanding. I guess there was few enough on the whole to pay cost.

IV

NILES WROTE TO CORNELIA from Cherry Valley on his way home to Canada on the twenty-sixth of May:

... you have probably heard that Mary thought some at one time of going home with me, but sure enough, she did not. 'Twas my fault, tho, for I wanted very much to have her company home—yet upon the whole, they thought it was not best under present circumstances.

I went from R Ville to Coeymans, saw the friends—staid in Uncle's store for a few days, where I measured calicoes, weighed snuff, tobaccos, candles, &c &c, then came on to Canajoharie night before last to take the stage yesterday morning for this place. . . . Saw the boys, shook hands all round, and was honored with the title of counsellor.

After returning to Wellington he wrote again, this time to Mary, to tell her of his activities and plans for the future, which still were far from settled in his mind:

I am comfortable seated by a good fire which I have just kindled to keep off the chilliness occasioned by a cold northwester with which we are being favored.

Alice is sitting on the sofa, sewing, and Mother has been lecturing me for getting poor, miserable, mean, worthless, rotten thread for them to sew with. I plead guilty to the charge and tried to get a dissertation on the peculiar properties and features of the genuine article and the traits by which it may be distinguished at a furtive glance from the spurious samples that are thus palmed off on an unsuspecting community.

Father and Wilson are busy drawing flour from the mill to Wellington, and I, like any other boy, have been riding back and forward during part of the forenoon, but quit long enough before dinner to have a sail on the lake. Had a fine time—got my feet wet &c. . . .

Joanna is much better than I expected to find her, and little Niles is decidedly one of the greatest boys ever produced in America. With such a name, how could it well be otherwise? We think of taking him to school very soon. . . . I have promised already to make just 99 visits before I leave home. I know I shall not fulfill the one half of them, but then, how can I get rid of promising? They all say, "Why, certainly you will not be in a hurry about returning. Have you so far forgotten Canada as to wish to leave it again so soon?" . . .

I have not yet determined when I shall leave, or where I shall go next. The propriety of my spending a season in New York, if opportunity offers, is now being discussed. My own private, individual notion, if explained, would read something like this: In case I do not go to New York, I think of returning to Cherry Valley and remaining there till fall, say about October, then of going, or rather wandering, off to the west and southwest to remain during the winter, by the expiration of which time I can probably form some opinion with regard to the advantages and disadvantages of N. York State and the western world that will lead me to a final decision in the matter of location.

I have laid the matter before Father and Mother, who profess to treat it as a boyish idea, tho I know they believe me in earnest. I shall leave early in July, as there is no objection in particular to keep me longer, and I may as well go at one time as another. . . . Mother says she supposes you will never come to Canada, now. Do you suppose she is anywhere near correct?

Two weeks later, on June 27, 1848, he wrote to Cornelia, teasing her about a swelling on her lip which she had mentioned:

What a beautiful appearance you must have presented as you stepped around among your promising pupils, imparting a word of advice here, of caution there, complimenting this young lady upon the happy effort which she has been making for advancement in her more difficult studies, or quieting that brainless young imp and exciting him to study by informing him very quietly that he is a perfect facsimile of Gen. Washington in his schoolboy days, with the single exception that the former was rather more given to study and less inclined to whisper—and all this, too, in your usual, effective way, heightened by the peculiar aspect of your *phiz.*

Well, Cornelia, accidents are liable to overtake us all, yet upon a little reflection, I am not wholly certain but that the calamity of which you speak may be the natural consequence inevitably attending the gratification of your most prominent phrenologic development. . . .

I will not trouble you with a long disquisition of the causes assigned by anatomists for the increase of any given member of the human frame, for in the end, it all amounts to this:

Action produces a determination of blood to the part exercised, by which it is increased in size, wherefore I infer the lips and tongue of a great talker will be affected in the same way with the hands of a sailor or the right arm of a blacksmith. I make these assertions in a friendly way, without much investigation, and with the sole object of freeing you from solicitude in case of another attack. . . .

It would be hard for me to describe to you the manner in which I spend my time. It is occupied, however, in sailing, hunting, fishing, visiting, rambling, and riding. Seldom a day passes without my taking a ride somewhere or other, or without my going to Wellington, where I usually take the old arm chair in the Post Office, which is a very quiet room adjoining the store, where I chat with David Young, when he is at liberty, or read the news &c &c. . . . Alice goes with me a great deal, of course, but just at present she and Elmira (of course you know Elmira) are very busy in making collars and all that sort of thing for me.

I expect to leave again somewhere about the 10th of next month, perhaps a little before that time, but where I shall be stationed for the next year is quite uncertain. It may be in Oswego, in C. Valley, RVille, N. York, Kentucky, Texas, or some other place not yet thought of by me. It is now necessary for me to determine in what part of the world I expect to practice, with a view to completing my studies in such place. Therefore, I have a strong notion of spending the winter somewhere at the south, providing I do not go to N. York—and this will be determined in a few days.

If I go to New York I shall certainly call and see you, but if not, I can form no idea when, where, or under what circumstances we may meet again. It may be in a few weeks, and I cannot but indulge the unpleasant thought that it may be possibly a long while first, in the event of which I suppose should we again meet, our friendship would be so far effaced by time as to leave little of that fervor which now I believe to be its characteristic, at least on my part. Yet, notwithstanding all this, I suppose you and I are much like other people, and the little that I have learned, partly by observation and partly by experience, teaches me that the poet is pretty near correct when he says,

> School friendships are not always found,
> Tho fair in promise, permanent and sound;
> The most disint'rested and virtuous minds,
> In early years connected, time unbinds;
> New situations give a different cast
> Of habit, inclination, temper, taste;
> And he that seems your counterpart at first,
> Soon shows the strong similitude reversed.
> Young heads are giddy and young hearts are warm,
> And make mistakes for manhood to reform.

I have grown nearly half an inch taller since the first of May, all owing, no doubt, to my having been admitted to the degree of counsellor &c. Really, you were very unkind to forbid my using any more law terms.

What shall I do now? When you were elevated to the dignity of a school teacher, I supposed, of course, that our acquaintance must cease unless by some means I could also advance to an equality with your station. But after having toiled diligently for many months until I was enabled to pass the fiery ordeal and, as I thought, to take a station that would entitle me to your friendship, I am to be told not to use any more law terms . . . and you yourself know that I never used only just enough law phrases to sustain my dignity.

That's the way big folks try to keep down those who are ambitious of rising. Very well, "I don't care." I am willing to remain simple.

Niles Searls.

P. S. I have not heard from any of your folks since I left there, but am rather expecting a letter from Mary, as I wrote to her some time since; but I suppose you monopolize the letter business. . . .

CORNELIA DEBORAH NILES

CHAPTER 12

BREAKING TIES

July–September 1848

I

*D*ID YOU EVER consider working with plants instead of clerking at the store?"

Charley didn't answer Mary's question at once, for he was struggling to squeeze his small frame past a thorny rose bush without getting caught. He was putting together a bouquet of flowers for his sister-in-law, making use of blooms from the Niles garden. Mary had gone down to Mulford's store to mail a letter and while there had invited Charley to come and pluck what flowers he wanted.

"Yes, of course," he replied, when the elusive blossom he sought was safely in his basket. "Do you remember a time about four years ago when I was in Toledo, working for my brother-in-law, Mr. Palmer? I wrote and asked Cornelia to send me some flower seeds, because I was dying to work in the garden again!"

"I remember that—you sent a whole long list of flowers you wanted!

You were in such a hurry that you wouldn't wait for Mr. Palmer to come back from New York to bring them, but insisted that we slip them in with the newspapers being mailed to you!"

"That's right—I *couldn't* wait. It had been so long since I'd seen a proper flower garden that I couldn't wait to start one of my own. You sent me asters and dahlias and foxgloves and canterbury bells and I don't know what all. I certainly appreciated what you and Cornelia did to get those seeds to me!"

"You asked for chrysanthemums, too, but you couldn't spell the word! We knew what you meant."

"I still can't spell it—can you?"

"Heavens, no, not without help! You also wanted violets and Sweet Williams and border pinks."

"That's so, I remember that."

Mary, watching with admiration as Charley arranged the blooms and decided what more to add, remembered an earlier conversation with Cornelia about Charley's botanical bent.

"Charley," Cornelia had said, "is well on his way to becoming an ordinary shopkeeper."

"Of course," Mary had replied. "Most Mulfords are shopkeepers or merchants of one kind or another."

"Well, it's a shame, because Charley should be doing something he really cares about."

"Such as?"

"Such as working with plants and flowers and growing things."

"Well, he does, doesn't he? He's always helping people with their gardens, and he knows the names of every plant, bush, tree, or flower in the village."

"That's just what I mean—he ought to be spending his time doing that—all of his time, not just his leisure time."

"Do you mean he should be a farmer or a gardener on some big estate? I don't think he'd like that."

"That wasn't what I had in mind. But there are botanists, for instance, people who discover ways to improve plants. Anyway, I think a man should work at whatever interests him and allows him to make full use of his God-given talents."

"Have you ever discussed this with Charley?"

"No, I haven't. I guess the opportunity never arose."

Recalling Cornelia's words, Mary now pressed Charley to continue. "You know," she said, "I can't imagine any other young man in Rensselaerville who would ask me to send flower seeds to him."

"That's what everyone says. I suppose that's one reason I gave up any thought of making it more than a hobby. But I hope you aren't feeling sorry for me on that account, because I enjoy business, too."

"Even keeping books and sweeping floors and things like that?"

"Even things like that, for that's part of learning how to run a proper business. Some day I'll hire other people to do those jobs, but I'll know what to expect from them when I do."

"Then you're not just working in the store because of family tradition?"

"Did you ever stop to think that the tradition came about because so many of us like being merchants? I think that's the case with most of us—with me it is. Well, I'd better hurry back to the store. I've got all the flowers I need—thanks a lot, Mary, and Henrietta will thank you, too, when she sees her bouquet!"

As Charley turned to go, he recognized a familiar figure walking toward them. "Will you look who's back," he cried. "It's Niles himself!"

"So it is," replied Niles. "Hello, Charley and Mary! I just chanced to be in the neighborhood and thought I'd stroll by."

"Chanced to be in the neighborhood! I thought you'd gone to Texas!" said Mary.

"And I thought you'd broken both arms or dropped off the face of the earth!"

"Why would you think any such thing?"

"Because I haven't received one word from here since I left."

"What do you mean? I wrote to you twice."

"The only letter I received was from Cornelia at Fishkill."

"I think I know what happened," interrupted Charley. "There's been some kind of trouble with the postmasters all along the U.S.-Canadian border. The mail probably was held up."

"I did hear something to that effect, but I couldn't wait around any longer to find out. I decided to come down and see for myself what has been going on in Rensselaerville."

II

AT SUPPER THAT NIGHT, Niles told his cousins and their parents about his plans for the summer. "I've decided to read law with Mr. Chittenden for a few months, and while I'm here I think I'll share rooms with Ed Filkins so as not to interfere with your summer visitors."

"Filkins has left town for the summer," commented Mary. "You'll have to do better than that."

"Really? Every time I come to Rensselaerville he leaves—I'm beginning to think he's running away from me! Well, I'll find lodgings somewhere else. I just wanted you to know that I wasn't planning to disturb your arrangements."

"You know you're always welcome here, my boy," said Judge Niles. "We're always glad to have you."

"I know that, uncle, but I also know that this isn't the time of year when you'd be likely to seek boarders. I appreciate your generosity and I don't intend to abuse it."

"Well, you're welcome to stay here till you find something," said his aunt. "We won't be having any guests this week, for sure."

"Thank you, Aunt Polly. Say, I've been meaning to ask someone about the burned fields all around here—and the burned buildings in the Doctor's yard. When did that happen?"

"Didn't Mary write you about our fire?" asked Judge Niles.

"I did, Pa, but the mails have been held up at the border. Niles didn't get either of my letters."

"It was just about a month ago—the thirteenth of June, I guess. The fire began in the Wickes's barn. It's a wonder we have any village left at all. If everyone hadn't pitched in with a will, it would have wiped out the whole place."

"That bad? I wish I'd been here!"

"We could have used you, that's sure! You should have seen your Aunt Polly—she was carrying water and pumping through the whole affair. Mary, too."

"You ought to have seen Maria Jarvis and her mother carrying whole tubs of water," added Mary, "and even Miss Betsy King was bringing pails of water."

"Mrs. Frisbee had told Miss King to stop bringing water and go upstairs and save her own belongings first," said Polly. "Deb Wickes told us Miss King started to go after her things, then stopped and thought how selfish she was being, and dropped her clothes right there in her room and came downstairs and went back to hauling water!"

"Isn't that just like Miss King, Niles?" asked Mary.

"That sounds like her, all right," he agreed. "What time of day was this?"

"About 9:30 in the morning," replied the Judge. "The wind was blowing a regular gale at the time, and when the Doctor's barn caught fire, burning hay and straw flew in all directions. It set fire to buildings all over the village. We had people on every roof working to smother the flames and sparks before they could take hold.

"At one time or another about eight or ten buildings were on fire, and most of them caught fire more than once. Doctor Wickes's house caught fire several times. Let's see; there was Mr. Frisbee's house and store, Mr.

Dayton's store, Mr. Huyck's store, Mr. Dwight's store and our store—you know, the one occupied by Gurdon Conkling. Even Mr. Shufelt's house over by the mill, and Jonathan Jenkins's barn caught fire, so you can see how far the burning debris was carried."

"What a frightening experience! Did your house escape entirely?"

"Miraculously, yes, but it was close. Our leather store was on fire three or four times—it was damaged some, but not too badly. What really worried me was the Conklin house next door, where Robert Mulford lives. Burning material kept landing on its roof. If it had caught and burned, I doubt we could have saved our place. I still find it hard to believe we saved so much. Only the Doctor's barn, carriage house and sheds were lost!"

"That is truly amazing—especially so when you're all so close and with a wind blowing!"

"It was blowing, all right! Well, as I said, we couldn't have done it without help—many, many people from outside the village came here to lend a hand. And we were fortunate to have the use of two steam engines from Mr. Cornell's foundry. He'd just built them, and they were in first-class working order. We couldn't have pumped enough water without them."

"Do you know how the fire started?"

The sudden silence caused Niles to look round the table in puzzlement. Finally Polly spoke:

"No one knows for sure, but they suspect it was little Eliza who lived with the Wickes family. It's a sore point now among the villagers, so I'd be careful what I said, but maybe Deb wouldn't mind telling you about it when you see her."

Nothing more was said that evening about the fire, but several days later, when Niles and Mary spent an evening with Deb and Charley, Mary raised the question.

"I'm not sensitive any longer," said Deborah, "though I was at the time, I guess. A lot of hard things were being said and we were pretty upset. But that's all water over the dam, now."

"Did Eliza really set it, then?" asked Niles.

"No one knows for sure. I can tell you what happened and you can judge for yourself. Let's see; the fire was on Tuesday, but it wasn't till about Friday or Saturday that anyone began to voice their suspicions. When they did, it seemed everyone was pointing a finger at little Eliza. Especially when she suddenly told us she wasn't going to stay with us any longer."

"She hadn't mentioned leaving before?"

"No. Well, first it was Mosely who suspected her. Then it was all of

Mr. Hasey's folks. Next it was Mr. and Mrs. Rivenburgh, and finally even Ma admitted she'd suspected her from the first, but kept still 'cause it seemed wicked even to think of Eliza."

"But why Eliza?"

"It just seemed every circumstance pointed right to her. No one else had been in the barn that morning except Rufus and Pa. Neither of them had pipes and, obviously, they wouldn't set it on purpose. It couldn't have been a spark from someone's chimney, because the fire started inside. I must confess, though, I could hardly believe it, even when everyone else was convinced."

"What did you do? Was she arrested?"

"Well, Pa talked to her for awhile, but she denied it. Finally, Pa told her father he could take her home if he'd promise to give her a hard talk and punish her severely. But then, after they'd left, we began to hear of so many things she'd said that seemed to point to her guilt. The last straw was when Pa discovered her father had taken a jug of our best rum with him! That made Pa think how bad it would be if she went unpunished, so he called for the constable and sent him out to find her."

"Constable Harry Cook?"

"Yes, Mary and Cornelia's uncle. And he caught up with Eliza and her father just before they reached home and he brought her back to our house Saturday evening. Rufus and Ma talked with her for a long time before she finally confessed. But she didn't act sorry for what she'd done, so they took her to Judge Niles's office. Then she went into a real hysterical fit and no one could do a thing with her!"

"Pa said she should return to the Wickes family," said Mary, speaking for the first time. "She was to stay with them over Sunday."

"Arson is a serious charge," declared Niles. "Was anyone present to look out for her own interest?"

"No," answered Deborah, "and that created a whole new problem. Stories began to circulate that she was really innocent but had been whipped and made to confess. You can just guess what excitement Rensselaerville was in!"

"I can indeed."

"Rufus was told to take charge of her, but, never supposing any of us would let her go, he made no effort to watch her, especially as Ma was with her all the time. Ma spent most of Sunday with her in the front chamber. She began to think it all over, how Eliza was just a little girl, and how Ma had taken her from her own mother with a promise to exercise a motherly care over her. So when the stories reached her about our forcing Eliza to confess, Ma realized she couldn't have any part in delivering Eliza up to justice without her own mother knowing a thing about it and without having seen her in so long."

"Do you mean to say your mother let her escape?"

"That's right. Without telling the rest of us, she sent Eliza home to her family with my sister Helen."

"What happened Monday morning? There must have been a hue and cry when they found the prisoner gone!" said Niles with a grin.

"You'd better believe there was!" Deb grinned back at him. "I'm smiling now, but I surely wasn't when it happened. You should have heard the desperate threats that were made—some were wanting to arrest Ma for committing an offense in the eye of the law, while others were about to go in search of Eliza. Ma was so upset that she went to bed sick, and my face was so sore from wiping away the tears that I could hardly touch it."

"And did they go and get Eliza?"

"No, they didn't. By that time, no one who'd been damaged by the fire was willing to sign a complaint. We decided it was best to forget about it. If Eliza was responsible, I think she's had scare enough to last a lifetime."

III

Cornelia arrived home in August at the end of the first quarter term, tired but still full of enthusiasm for her school. As far back as June, her father had shown concern, feeling on the one hand that her school might prove too small to pay her adequately, and on the other that it might prove too much of a task for her strength.

"When you have taught long enough to cool your fever for teaching," he had written, "we shall be very glad to have your company at home, and if at the close of the first quarter you feel as though you would rather be at home, don't hesitate on any account to close your school and return."

Cornelia's fever for teaching had not abated. "They're all such fine children," she said proudly, "and their parents are so concerned that they work hard and learn well. You should see the letters they have sent to me. Wait, I'll go upstairs and find them for you."

When she left the room, Polly said to her husband, "Well, I see no reason why she shouldn't go back for another three months, but I hope she hasn't formed the idea of teaching during the winter."

"Surely not. Winter is no time for a young lady to be teaching school," replied the Judge. "It's one thing to handle a small group of young children in the summer, when the older and rougher boys are working in the fields, but winter term is a task for young men. Schoolmaster in the winter, schoolmistress in the summer and fall. Besides, her health is much too delicate for her to be out in winter storms."

Cornelia returned with a handful of letters and gave them to her father.

My dear Madam.

I wish to send my little boy to you as a scholar for the present at any rate. I am not able to ride down with him myself not being very well. I feel that the Teacher & Mother should be friends and shall hope to become better acquainted in the future. Sam has only been taught a little by myself—he can spell words of three letters, but has never been taught to learn a spelling lesson by himself and would require some aid in pronouncing the words.

I thought I would write these few explanations to save you the trouble of finding out these little things as he is rather backward perhaps for his age and in expressing himself to strangers—he has written a little on the slate merely the easy letters, and he also has been in the habit of drawing on a sheet of paper—making mugs and various small figures horses also he is very fond of drawing such as they are—If you are willing I should like him to continue to do so as I wish him to learn drawing. I send a drawing book he has used a little—If you have any reading or spelling book you prefer and think good will you supply him.

As he has had scarcely any boy play mates I believe he has not learnt any bad language and I wish very much of course to guard against it although it is very difficult to prevent boys I suppose. Excuse the freedom of my remarks [and credit] them only to the natural desire of a mother for an only [child]. I will not waste more of your time—but hoping to make you a visit when stronger

I am yours truly
J. Van Wagenen

Sam will come home with his Aunt if you please—and terms I just now remember will you make as moderate as you think just to yourself as my husband and myself must needs class ourselves with the poor of the land—

J.V.W.

*   *   *   *   *

Mrs Whittemore will be obliged to Miss Niles if she will let her know by her sister, her terms for these two little ones. Mrs W. only wishes them taught to read and write and the little girl will occasionally bring her sewing. They will remain no longer than 1 o'clock—
Wednesday. July 5th [1848]

Miss Niles

I send my little boy to your school this morning. He has been taught reading and spelling. He reads pretty well without being able to spell as well.

Will Miss Niles watch him in his intercourse with other boys during the hours of recreation. If he does not obey please send me word. I have a broken limb or I would call and see you. His studies I of course leave to your judgement. His name is Henry—

Mrs James Freeland

*   *   *   *   *

Will Miss Niles please excuse Henrys absence last week. He had the rheumatism. Please not allow him to sit by the open window nor in a draft. I would rather that he did not play out in the wet today. He says he was disobedient once last week. Miss Niles will please enforce strict obedience from him. I think obedience the first lesson to be learned in every child. If he is not obedient I wish to know it.

yours with respect

Mrs James Freeland

Judge Niles read quickly through the notes and passed them on to his wife without comment.

"What about the fees?" he asked Cornelia. "It always seemed to me that Mr. Rankin and the school board were asking too much. Here in Rensselaerville township no one has ever asked more than three dollars a term per pupil, and even that's not an easy sum for many families to afford."

"I think perhaps there is a little more income in that part of the country, Pa, although that's not true of all of the folks down there. But I didn't think it was my place to say anything."

"Well, you're probably right. Then you're bound to go back for another term?"

"Oh, yes, Pa! I couldn't think of leaving now, when I've just begun. The boys and girls are just beginning to show some real progress and I just couldn't abandon them now."

"And you're content with your boarding place, Cornelia?" asked Polly.

"Very much, Ma. If I were not, then I might be more willing to come home, and if I had a school such as Caroline King has, I don't think I should like it a bit. I couldn't endure to be boarding around among strangers, a week here and a week there. But Mr. and Mrs. Brett are so nice that living with them is nearly as pleasant as if I were at home."

"Then I suppose your father and I are agreed that you may go back for another three months. In the meantime, however, we are overjoyed at the prospect of having you home for a full month! By the way, have you noticed that we're going to have sidewalks before winter?"

"Yes, I did. It will be a pleasure, not having to traipse through mud any longer."

"They were supposed to have been done in a couple of weeks, but there have been all sorts of delays," said Judge Niles. "I doubt we'll be using them before October, but they'll be ready when you return."

When Cornelia's vacation neared its end, Niles Searls mentioned that he was planning to visit a New York City lawyer and might not be back in time to see her off.

"Why not wait another week—do you suppose you could?" she asked. "Then we could go down the river together—wouldn't that be fun?"

"What a fine idea! I'll drop a line to Mr. Ridwell and tell him I'm delaying my arrival. September is the ideal time for a cruise down the Hudson."

And so it was that on the first day of September, Niles and Cornelia said farewell to their friends in Rensselaerville and boarded the stage for Albany. In the morning they stepped onto the deck of the steamer *Confidence,* along with a group of cadets bound for West Point. Cornelia was amused by their efforts to attract attention, and remarked to Niles that these military men behaved not much differently from her Fishkill students.

"What will you do in New York?" she asked Niles. "Will you have time to visit any of your relatives?"

"Perhaps. First I'm going straight to Mr. Ridwell's office to see about my prospects for employment."

"If you were to move there, I might see more of you than I can while you're at Rensselaerville. After all, Fishkill Landing isn't far from New York."

"That's true, although I may be kept busier in a big city office than in Chittenden's practice."

"Suppose Mr. Ridwell doesn't have an opening. Will you remain in Rensselaerville for the winter?"

Niles hesitated before answering. "I doubt it. One thing I intend to do in the city is gather information about transportation to Texas."

Cornelia's face clouded. "Then you haven't abandoned your plans to go west."

"Far from it. If anything, the frontier pulls me harder with every passing day."

When the *Confidence* approached the dock at Newburgh, where Cornelia would disembark, she took hold of Niles's hands.

"Whatever you do, please keep me informed," she pleaded. "Will you promise to write often?"

"Of course. And you must do the same."

Reluctantly, Cornelia released his hands and left the boat. Two weeks passed before she heard from him. He was back in Rensselaerville when he wrote:

I am going to commence just where I left you, viz at Newburgh. The remainder of the voyage to New York was rather barren of incidents, tho I made some discoveries, such as the fact that each of those stools contained a tin life preserver attached to the underside of the seat—that some of the cadets at West Point are full as green as anybody's boys—that for the want of "Mother" to look after them, some trunks were landed at the wrong place &c.

Arrived in N York about 4, went to Ridwell's office, but he was absent from the city for a week—passed on to the Galveston packet office, 72 South Street—found the packet brig *Mary* ready to sail on the following Tuesday—went on board, found the Capt. a very kind, obliging man, more so than common—resolved at once to come up the river that night, take a horse and waggon at Albany next morning, come to R Ville, pack up and return in time for said packet—went to the pier and found the Albany boats had all left—was compelled therefore to stay in N York till Sunday night, which rendered it out of the question for me to think of going that trip—remained in N York til Monday morning, during which time I found that the ship *Gen. Lamar* will sail for Galveston in about 20 days, but could not learn the exact day, indeed it was not yet determined—left word for the Capt. (who was absent from the city) to write as soon as they determined on the day—could go by New Orleans any week, but don't like to be caught there at this season of the year.

Now, Cornelia, perhaps you are ready to ask, "Are you not sorry that you were detained so as to miss of going on at once?" I reply, no, tho I was at first a little, yet now I am glad of it. To have gone then would have taken me away in a too great a hurry, while by waiting till the next packet goes, which is a better vessel, I shall have time to be fully prepared to go, or upon mature deliberation to abandon the project altogether, which last I am quite likely to do. All things will come right in the end . . . .

On the twentieth of September, Cornelia replied:

School duties are through for the day, and I have from now until tea-time to employ in any manner I choose, and unless some unforeseen event occurs, I shall probably spend it in writing my last "will and testament" to you, before your departure to an unknown land. . . .

As I read your account of your trip to New York and found that I proved to be, from beginning to end, a perfect drawback to all of your plans, I was not a little out of humor with myself, but you seemed to anticipate all of my regret and put me into good humor again by your conclusion "All things will come right in the end."—and so they will, Niles. . . . Mary said you had reason to think the vessel you would like to have gone in was wrecked, and the thought of the danger you might have been in is enough to make me glad enough now that I was the means of detaining you.

And I shrink from the idea now of your going there. If I thought it was to benefit you in anyway, you know I would not hesitate a moment in saying "go," however much more pleasant it might be for you to be nearer to us. . . . but I have misgivings which I cannot do away with. . . . Perhaps before this time you have decided to take your departure in some other direction than Texas, but if not, you will, I suppose, go down soon; are you not going to call and see me? Perhaps if you should, I should be able in some way to prevent your being ready to take passage, and thus save you from impending evil—who knows.

A few days later, Cornelia received a letter from Deb Wickes in which she mentioned that Mrs. Chittenden had given birth to a son, that Euphrasia and Mr. Laughpaugh were to be married and that the sidewalks were progressing very slowly. She reported that Maria Amelia Tompkins would be teaching at the session-house school across the street from the Niles house, and she mentioned an evening party at the Mulford house and an afternoon tea party at the Wickes residence, but not a word did she have to say about Niles Searls.

STEAM LOCOMOTIVE AND CARS

CHAPTER 13

MOVING WEST

October 1848–February 1849

I

*I*T WAS A BANNER MONTH for travel. On October 4, 1848, Mrs. Harry Cook and Mrs. Samuel Hasey left Rensselaerville to shop and visit with New York City relatives and friends. On October 7 Deborah Wickes and Augustus Cornell went over to South Westerlo to call on Susan Morse, the young lady of whom he was enamored. Susan agreed to make a return visit during the winter, and she especially hoped to meet Cornelia Niles, whose appearance she thought was "very prepossessing."

When Rose King heard that she could go down the Hudson for a shilling, off she went to New York, where Phebe Cook found her darting about the streets, "head flying from one window to another as fast as she could turn it!" Rose said she had been to the Fair and to Barnum's Museum, and she was about to have her daguerreotype taken.

During the following week, while Rose still was marveling at the sights, Maria Jarvis arrived, along with Euphrasia and her new husband, Mr. Laughpaugh. And on the weekend, even Cornelia found time to slip away from Fishkill Landing and go to the city. Big as it was, New York was not so large that it kept Rensselaerville people from running into one another at all the popular places.

Nevertheless, not till Cornelia returned to Fishkill did she learn that

Niles Searls had come down the river with her Aunt Phebe Cook and Mrs. Hasey. In mid-October she had the news from three different sources. First was the letter from Niles himself; second, Mary wrote to tell of his leaving Rensselaerville on October 3 and of the letter he had sent from Pittsburgh; third was the note from Charley Mulford, which stated:

Our new sidewalks begin to add greatly to the appearance of our streets. You of course know Coz Niles Searls has left us. He is now upon the broad world a wanderer, and the last news from him left him searching for a place large enough to hold his shingle—a large place, that.

I hope Niles may find a good place where there are plenty of girls and "no bigger chaps;" in a way a *"ne plus ultra"* place that would be. Ah!

Niles explained that he expected originally to remain in New York for a day or two and would return to Fishkill to say goodbye to Cornelia,

. . . but next morning I began to feel homesick and came right on, through fear that I might give it up altogether if I tarried longer. I wanted very much to go to Texas, but have about given up the long cherished idea.

Finding no vessel ready to leave for that state, he bought a railroad ticket and took the cars, first to Philadelphia and then to Baltimore. From Baltimore he continued by rail to Cumberland, Maryland, and went from there by stage to the Monongahela River and boarded a steamboat bound for Pittsburgh. There he penned a quick note to Mary before going on the steamboat *Consul,* which was going down the Ohio River to Cincinnati. Mary told Cornelia about an adventure Niles had while on his way to Pittsburgh:

He said there was a blind young man in the stage part of the way who had been to Philadelphia to be doctored and had spent all he had, and the agent would not let him go any further by the stage without paying. He was on his way home and had not a single penny (he lived in Kentucky).

His mother was *dead,* and his father a drunkard. Niles became so much interested in him that he took up a collection for him among the passengers, and then procured a free passage for him to Pittsburgh, and thought he should be able to, also, down the Ohio.

Such adventures as that are just the kind [Niles] loves to meet with, and I hope he will find enough to take up his attention till he gets settled himself. He told many other things about his journey, but I presume he will write you soon himself, and he can tell you much better than I . . .

He does not seem to be in very good spirits. He did not say so, but I know by his letter that he feels as if he had *now* left his *second* home, and was more alone than ever before.

Writing from Cincinnati, Niles described to Cornelia the next leg of his trip:

We left Pittsburg on Monday, and were consequently four days in coming down here—a distance of five hundred miles, being detained every night by fogs. Ours is doubtless the last boat that will ever descend the Ohio—in fact, we have, in my opinion, destroyed the river altogether, having scraped the bottom all out of it, so that it cannot for the future hold any water.

We were aground for five hours once in coming; twice on snags; ran down one flat boat, drowned an Irishman, and committed sundry other depredations during the passage. I should like well to give you a full account of my travels, but have not time or space.

Cincinnati, "Queen of the West," with its ten thousand beauties (I don't mean beautiful women), this morning for the first time opened to my view. Though yet but in its infancy, it contains between one and two hundred thousand inhabitants, and is decidedly the finest city in the world—at least of those I have ever seen. If you hear anybody speak of handsome cities, please present my compliments and say *Cincinnati* exceeds them all. . . .

I arrived last evening, having traveled over eleven hundred miles. I need not add that my route has been intensely interesting—I have been up early and late—endeavoring to gain all the information in my power relative to the different places through which I have passed. . . .

The wonders of the western world are before me. Perhaps you would like to know where I am going; answer, going West. How far? answer—don't know. My passage is paid to St. Louis, Mo., and we start in an hour or less; indeed, the steam is up and I am afraid I shall not have time to go with this to the [Post] Office before starting . . .

For many weeks they heard no more from Niles, but life went on at a busy pace in New York State. Deb Wickes informed Cornelia of the arrival of Miss Slocum, Libby Conkling's house guest. "She appears to be a real pleasant, pretty girl. I do hope she will stay, for it is most dreadfully dull and she looks as if she was not afraid to laugh once in awhile."

Cornelia's mother agreed that Miss Slocum was quite pretty and reminded her of Nancy Niles.

"We are to have a couple of weddings this month if Bill Watson don't cut his throat again and Jim Mackey don't sicken of his bargain," wrote

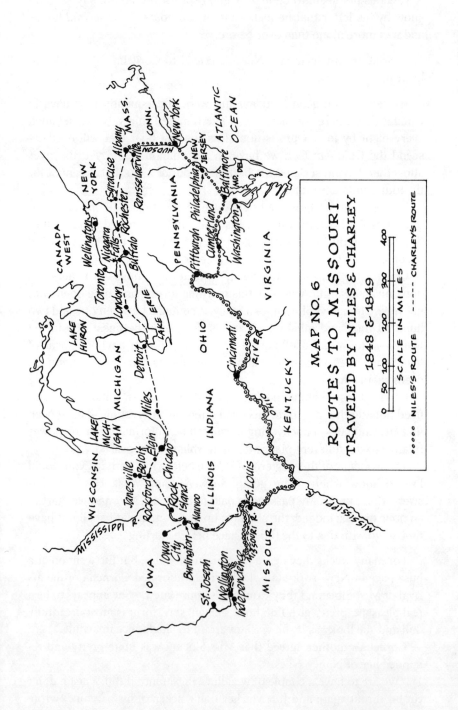

MAP NO. 6
ROUTES TO MISSOURI
TRAVELED BY NILES & CHARLEY
1848 & 1849

SCALE IN MILES
0 50 100   200   300   400

ooooo NILES'S ROUTE   ----- CHARLEY'S ROUTE

Deb. "You have heard probably of Amanda's marriage—she is at Greenville now, happy as love and Mr. Miller can make her."

A young minister came to the Presbyterian pulpit to preach for two Sundays on a trial basis. Mr. Smith, in order to quiet the dissension which broke out within the congregation over whether he should be replaced, resigned his post early in the summer and moved to Durham. The new man, whose name was W. P. Doe, was the latest in a series of trial ministers. He preached twice in October, and between times officiated at the marriage of Lib Watson to Jim Mackey. Said Mary:

We have got a young minister who is engaged to spend two weeks here, and will doubtless stay longer, if it is the wish of the society; and in case that he should do so, I think there will be considerable efforts made in *certain quarters* to furnish him with a wife. I heard a great deal said about him at a quilting at Mr. Tompkins' (to which I had the honor of being invited), and the conclusion on all sides seemed to be that he was worth *setting caps* for.

For my part, I think him a good natured young man of no more than ordinary talents which, however, are sufficiently appreciated by himself. . . . I have seen Deborah a good many times this week. . . . She is very lively and sociable nowadays, and I am very sure she is either *positively engaged,* or else has given it up *entirely.* I have had no chance yet to determine which, but have little doubt it is the former. I am half sorry if it is so, for I think she is too smart for [Lloyd]. I understand that he is not at all liked in Delhi. Mr. Filkins says that the young men make a great deal of sport of [Lloyd's] self conceit, and wonder how the girls can live without him in R Ville, if they think as much of him as *he* pretends.

Addison now was interested in teaching school. He and Augustus Cornell went to Windham and Cairo, New York, looking for positions. Augustus found the school vacant at Cairo and engaged it for the winter. Rufus Stanton talked of giving up his school and going over to Windham, so it seemed that Addison could have Rufus's old school.

Caroline King closed her school for the winter, but Rose still was teaching and so was Betsy. Maria Amelia was teaching now in the Rensselaerville session house, and Deb Wickes was horrified when she learned that Cornelia was talking of spending the winter teaching at Fishkill. She wrote her friend in dismay:

I did not know that you had the faintest idea of spending the winter at Fishkill. I hate to have you think of it, but Mary says she should not be surprised if you did. It will seem dull when you come home again to stay, I know, for Rens Ville is a real out of the way place . . .

Polly Niles wrote to her daughter about the same matter:

Were I to follow the dictates of a mother's heart, I should say, "come home," for it would be pleasant indeed to see all my dear ones around the family board. For myself, I would be glad were it never to be broken, but *well* I know this *will not* be.

It is a satisfaction [to me] that you cannot realize[,] that you can all remain at home if you choose; that you have a good, a pleasant home. With this thought from me, I can talk with you about leaving it for a season without a feeling of sadness, which different circumstances would cause.

I believe you have been frank on your statement for and against staying, and I think I can see them as you do, partly, and yet I cannot balance them as you can. You remarked in one of your letters that when you was home you wished you was in Fishkill, and when you was in Fishkill, you wished you was *home.*

Now, this is the world as *it is,* and so you will find it through life. In no one spot are all the pleasant things of life centered. In no individual will you find everything agreeable. One reason is, *our own* taste is incorrect, and the same can be said of all.

Now, the great difficulty is to choose. First, Rensselaerville at this season has few attractions. As to the young society, you know them *all*—the only addition I know is a Miss Slocum, boarding at [Gurdon Conkling's house]. . . . Our friends from a distance have all made their visits, and we shall be obliged to lean upon our own resources for enjoyment. *You would add much to ours,* but will you be contented to employ yourself through the winter in domestic affairs?

If so, we can find enough to do, if you have not enough of your own. I think we will live much as we did last winter, though we think we shall not keep fire in the bedroom. Addison studies at the office, and Hamilton has so much head ache that he does not study evenings. I fear Pa's health will not be as good as it has been. . . . [Your brother] Charley employs himself sometimes in playing and sometimes in drawing. Emma is Emma, yet a little tamed since the cold weather has shut her in the house. Grandma must be indulged in any things she wishes; this I consider a privilege as well as duty. She has borne with my follies; why should I not bear with her weakness? . . .

But no more about our lives. Now it will be late in the season when your school closes. Could you come home and return before the river closes? Can you get along with a school in the winter, if you should have sufficient encouragement to stay? These things, and a hundred others, you must judge of yourself. . . . Your school is now better than Miss King's. There seems to be a good deal of dissatisfaction with her. Many would be glad to have you return and take her place, but she will not leave this winter.

Deb Wickes also made note of the problems of Betsy King, Mr. Gallup's assistant at the Academy:

Miss King don't get along very smoothly in her school. She has had a good deal of trouble lately with Mary Brewerton and some other scholars, and I don't think she will stay a great while longer.

Mr. Gallup is the same old sixpence, and what do you think, Cornelia, he is actually on the point of buying a piano for the academy—we are to have a teacher of music, and I suppose he expects to make some *great* speculation out of it, but I *hardly doubt* it.

Mary's reactions to the new music teacher were mixed. She told Addison that she was eighteen years old and, as nearly as she could judge, was "a first rate player and a poor singer; that is, she sings the *notes correctly,* but has a poor voice and little taste."

On November 7, 1848, Charley Mulford received a letter from Niles Searls. It was postmarked in Jefferson City, Missouri, and Charley told Cornelia that:

[Niles will] probably stop at Independence in the employ of a gentleman [who is] purchasing land warrants of returned soldiers, but he did not direct us where to write, and spoke of his remaining there in such an uncertain manner that we dare not write until further information.

Quite an adventure he had on board the steamer while ascending the Missouri. A sawyer passed through the boat's bottom and deck and tore up a stateroom within four feet of him, the occupants of which lost their trunks but escaped themselves, although sleeping in their room at the time.

Cornelia, unsure of what was meant in this instance by a "sawyer," looked it up in the school copy of Webster's *American Dictionary,* which said: ". . . a tree which, being undermined by a current of water, and falling into the stream, lies with its branches above water, which are continually raised and depressed by the force of the current, from which circumstance the name is derived. The *sawyers* in the Mississippi render the navigation dangerous, and frequently sink boats which run against them." She shuddered as she placed the dictionary back on its stand.

II

CORNELIA WAS COMING HOME! Not only that, but she would be arriving a week earlier than expected, thanks to a miscalculation she had made in her first letters about the school closing.

In October, Mary wrote to ask if her sister planned to make a winter hat and cloak before or after her return. Mary also wanted a matching hat and cloak and thought Cornelia might like to purchase fabrics in New York for both of them.

"You know, I never did such a thing as to buy a hat or cloak or anything else much, and know precious little about it, anyway," Mary wrote. "Ma is going up to sit with Aunt Patty Conkling tonight, and we are going to have a seamstress tomorrow. Ma says she wants me to sew with her this week."

Polly also wrote to say, "If you should go [to New York] before we hear from you and purchase, you could send us a sample and the price and place, and we can send by our merchants when they go."

A week before she was to return, Cornelia replied:

I have not yet bought your dress, and from your directions shall do so now. Our hats I shall see about tomorrow, and will try to find some trimming for Ma, though it is doubtful whether I can. I have no trimming on my own dress yet, except some plain buttons to answer to go to New York.

Those hoods will be very nice, and I think *you* had better have one, but I guess I will wear my straw for a second best, as it is already trimmed and lined—and will save expense and trouble. . . .

They all seem very sorry to have me leave, and I am sure I shall feel badly enough to part with many of them. Yet I am quite tired and will be glad of rest.

Now that Addison was teaching at Cairo, Mary tried to give him some pointers on writing letters to the folks at home:

Ma says you must write home oftener than you have . . . I presume you cannot think of anything that seems worth writing, but do as Cornelia does—tell what you have to eat and drink; what your scholars study, how old they are, and how ugly, and everything that happens from morning till night. Anything will be interesting to us who stay at home here, shut up alone, and depending almost entirely upon *letters* for our society.

Addison replied with a hurried and anxious plea:

You will no doubt be surprised to receive another letter from me so soon, and perhaps still more surprised when you see what it is written for. Last Saturday, there came a dancing master into this place, to try to raise a school. All of the young fellows in Cairo with whom I am acquainted are going to engage in it. I have been pressed by many to join the school, and of course declined giving them any answer, but thought I would write home and see what our folks would think of the plan.

Rufus wants me to go into it with him, and wanted me to write home and see if Pa and Ma would like it. Those who will compose the school are the most respectable young men in the place, some of my age, some older and younger. I have felt very awkward several times in company because all danced but me, except when Rufus or Augustus happened to be there.

But now Rufus is going to learn and we shall be left all alone. If I do not attend the school, I shall in effect be excluded from the society, for as the school is once a week, and all, both boys and girls, will be there, they will in effect constitute the whole young society.

And I can see very plainly that if I want to go in company at all, I must join the school. And it will certainly be *very* dull without I do. Besides all this, it is an accomplishment which will be almost necessary anywhere but in RensVille. I am sure anything that would render my movements more graceful would not be lost on me.

I want you to talk with our folks about it and let me know immediately, for the school commences the latter part of the week and I must give an answer. The terms are 60 dollars for 13 lessons. There will probably be about 16 couples, $3.15cts apiece. This I shall, of course, expect to pay with my own funds when I get them. Write immediately.

All to no avail. The answer, as he feared, was negative. When Cornelia came home and learned of Addison's request and the denial, she sat down to explain the reasons behind the refusal:

I am rather sorry that you could not learn to dance, as I understand from *experience* that you will sometimes feel awkward and unpleasant, yet it is perhaps best that you should not; and, after all, Addison, you are yet too young to go into society much.

You have more character and *manners* than most boys of your age, yet it is not customary for gentlemen to go into society very much, especially to *dancing parties,* until they are older than you are. . . . I cannot say that I like Rufus' manners, principles, or influence very much, and hope you will keep your eyes wide open when with him and not allow him to lead you into any of his oddities and rudeness. . . .

Perhaps you will think I am ignorant of how things are in Cairo and imagine them very rude, and fear you will be *spoilt*. Now, that isn't so. I think your trip to Cairo will be of no harm to you, and will show you some of the world. Yet, after all, I do not like Cairo customs, and *know* that you would not if you should see better society, and I would do or say anything to preserve your natural good principles, refinement, and delicacy from being turned into such a course as Rufus's.

His sisters were full of advice for Addison. Mary wrote a warning to the sixteen-year-old schoolmaster:

I hope you will not have to undertake to whip any of the larger boys, for you know you are not *very large* yourself, and you may be the one to *get whipped.*

Mary, however, did not dwell on the subject. Instead, she brought him up to date on local news and gossip:

I do not think it would be worth while for me to take [piano] lessons now. I should have no instrument to practice on. I thought at first I would claim the offer Mr. Conkling (Albert) made me of the use of his, but Mr. Doe boards there and it would not answer to go there, you know.

By the way, I like him better than I did at first. I think he improves. He is engaged, I suppose, for a year. I expect some of the good people here would be glad to have him for an "engagement for *life.*" . . .

Have I told you about our reading society? I cannot remember what I have told. We girls have met twice, and spent the evening partly in reading and partly in talking and eating apples, and have enjoyed ourselves very much, probably more than we shall again, as Sarah has taken the liberty of inviting in some who care more for fun than reading . . .

I visited Maria Amelia's school yesterday and observed two faults in her teaching. One was, she talked to me *about* the scholars, *before them;* and the other, she did not explain things so they *comprehended* them.
. . . Mr. Chittenden had a letter from Niles last week, saying that he was at Wellington, about 60 miles from Independence, Mo., staying with a planter owning 20 slaves. He had been buying soldiers' rights [to acquire public lands] and I believe had made considerable by it. Thought some of going out with his host the next day to *hunt buffaloes.* Could not tell us yet where he should be by the time a letter could reach him.

III

PRESIDENT JAMES K. POLK delivered his annual report on the State of the Nation on December 5, 1848. One paragraph among many captured national attention, for it confirmed rumors which had appeared in newspapers for several months:

It was known that mines of the precious metals existed to a considerable extent in California at the time of its acquisition. Recent discoveries render it probable that these mines are more extensive and valuable than was anticipated. The accounts of the abundance of gold in that territory are of such an extraordinary character as would scarcely command belief were they not corroborated by the authentic reports of officers in the public service, who have visited the mineral district, and derived the facts which they detail from personal observation.

The people of Rensselaerville read about the great gold fever which had seized the country and wondered if their countrymen all had gone mad. Two months elapsed before it showed signs of breaking out of the larger cities and into the New York countryside. On February 5, 1849, Addison said in a letter to Cornelia:

A company is about organizing here to start about the first of March. It is no humbug, either, for the leaders *are men* who won't flinch from anything they undertake. The company is limited to twenty and they go for two years. They have regular officers and a constitution and by-laws.

They have held one meeting, and meet again Tuesday to sign their names to the Constitution. Drinking, gambling and swearing are prohibited. If I were a little *older,* I should give up my school to come, and talk with our folks to get leave to go for a fortune. But I am too young, and *I can't help it.*

"Thank goodness for that," sighed Cornelia. "But Niles is not too young, and I worry that he may already have gone to California."

After a few days, Mary answered Addison, saying:

The gold fever does not rage here at all; they laughed at me when I tell how it rages in Cairo. They know nothing about it, for there are none of the sort of folks here that would go.

We hear nothing from Niles yet. Cornelia wrote to Alice [Searls] last week, and Pa has written to Mr. Lauderdale, the man he was with when he wrote last. I have made up my mind he is sick or gone to California. *I* think it is the latter, but either one is bad. I hardly know which to hope it is *not,* but I try to hope it is *neither.*

In reply to Cornelia's inquiry, twenty-year-old Alice Searls wrote a letter from the school she was attending at Picton, twelve miles from her home in Wellington, Ontario:

As you are so very anxious to know something respecting our dear brother Niles, I will relate all I know from him. We received a letter from him November 18th. It was six weeks coming, therefore we cannot hear from him very often.

When he wrote, he was stopping with a Colonel Lauderdale and expected to stay until spring. He writes that he likes the country exceedingly well, that it is the finest country he ever saw, and that the people are very kind. They have plenty of negroes, and that it is very handy to have one to black his boots and make fires.

He thinks of staying there until spring and then either coming back to New York state or commencing law practice there, but I think that he will hardly stay there, or at least I hope not, for it seems much worse to have him so far from home and amongst strangers. When he is with you, we think you will take good care of him. He thinks of taking a school for one quarter if he concludes not to stay there, and will be home in the spring.

If he thinks of making his home there, we may as well give up ever seeing him any more, but I cannot think of that.

The other Wellington was on the Missouri River, actually only about thirty miles northeast of Independence. During the past four months Niles had been exploring the region. He opened a part-time law office in Harrisonville, thirty miles to the south of Independence. While business wasn't particularly brisk, he had been encouraged to believe that if he stayed, his chances of being sent to the Missouri Legislature were better than average.

The most discouraging feature of the Missouri frontier was the prevalence of sickness. Fever and ague sooner or later affected everyone who settled along the rivers and streams, and there was no other land suited to making a living.

Niles wrote to Cornelia on February 24, 1849, his first letter to her in four months:

If I mistake not, when I last addressed you, it was from Cincinnati and the boat was just ready to leave. I consigned the letter to a boy with directions to deposit it in the Office. Perhaps it reached you, and then again, perhaps it did not.

You know I have always contended that absence is all that is required to effectually sever the bonds of friendship and produce complete forgetfulness on the part of us poor human critters. Let my long *silence* be received as a practical demonstration of *my Theory*.

Perhaps you will now ask, "Why then do you write at all?" Wait a moment and I'll tell you.

In the first place, it rains so hard that I cannot stir out. In the second place, I am a complete cripple and could not walk if the weather was ever so fine. Yes, that same *Foot* which for years has been so ungovernable took a start last Friday to run away with me, and being unable to arrest its speed in any other way, I ran against a little stump, thereby not only stopping it, but spraining the ankle in a way that has kept it perfectly quiet ever since. Under all these circumstances, you will of course conclude that my only desire in writing is to pass away the tedious moments of an otherwise too long day.

I *have* (to use a Missouri expression) "seen a heap of the World" since I left RVille, and a "mighty site of people" too. Of the former, some has been so moulded over by the hands of man as to have but slight traces of its original features, but *more* has exhibited the grandeur and wild sublimity impressed thereon by the Creator's hand. Of the latter, some are equal in intelligence and in all that tends to elevate and charm to any with whom I ever met; while in others I have seen prominently displayed those characteristics spoken of by the fair authoress of "Prairie Land" as displayed in her steamboat companions and sundry others by her described. . . .

I have been for a day or two thinking how things looked about RVille and expect that I have only to imagine everything just as when I left— five feet of snow, to get it exactly! O! poor deluded beings, why will ye stay cooped up between those frowning hills, to be buried alive seven months out of the twelve, when by coming to Missouri you might enjoy an Earthly paradise, with only just enough of "Chills & Fever" to remind you that you are still on Earth and in all probability destined soon to leave its dreary scenes. Tarry not, but come away to the West. The winter has been very severe, the most so of any ever known in the country, though it is now mild as a New York April and looks as though it might remain so. . . .

I have not yet fully decided whether or not to make this country my future home. I received a letter from Mr. Hartsen a few days since. He has returned home from a long tour through Ill., Ind., Ohio and Wisconsin, and now prefers to commence practice in N.Y. State, and as we partly agreed last summer to unite our fortunes, it is possible I may return. Otherwise, you will hear of me somewhere up in the vicinity of Nodaway, Oregon [Missouri], or some of those [other] places in the NW part of this state. *That is,* providing I do not go to *California.*

I shall expect to go home in the spring at all events. My Father wrote that they would like me to come in May, and stay home while he and Mother take a trip to Albany, which it appears they contemplate doing towards the last of May. Only for *that,* I should prefer waiting till July, so as to be away from here during the warmest part of the season.

I like Missouri well, even *better* than I expected, and though it is somewhat doubtful whether I remain *here,* yet I expect if I leave to be sorry very often. I shall never regret my trip or anything connected with it, even though I do not stay. I am already doing some business, more than sufficient to defray all expenses. And my business is not all in the *Legal line,* neither, for I have acted the part of the Physician in at least one instance.

Col. Lauderdale is something of a Dr., that is, he keeps some medicines for his own family, and understands bleeding pretty well. *Bleeds his own Niggers.* One of the neighbors, a widow woman, had a negro taken with a pain in the side and sent for the Col. to come and bleed him, but the Col. was sick, so he gave me directions and the lancet, and away I went, examined Darkie's tongue, pulse, &c, after which I bled him profusely—gave him the dose which the Col. had put up for me and returned home—called next morning—patient still very sick—growing worse—made inquiry with regard to his diet.

Philicy had two hours before given him two warm biscuit—went to his mistress, told her to either feed him a green gourd and kill him at once, or see that he was properly taken care of—she took the hint and *Cesar* is now a well nigger, and I doubt not, were he taken with the cholera, would prefer me to any Dr. in the country.

I can assure you there is nothing like being able, as the yankees say, to turn a hand to anything. But I have no idea of flourishing as a MD, for they are so plenty now in this country that two have to ride on one horse. Lawyers are not so plenty. I have also become somewhat distinguished as a *cook* since my arrival here.

MISSISSIPPI RIVERBOATS

CHAPTER 14

CALIFORNIA BOUND

February–April 1849

I

"GOING TO CALIFORNIA? You're not serious! Not you, Charley Mulford—of all people!" For days, every man, woman, or child who entered Mulford's Store on Main Street had much the same thing to say to Robert's younger brother. Mary and Cornelia, hearing the news, rushed down to confront the assistant postmaster.

"What's this nonsense about going to California?" demanded Mary. "Harriet says you've written to Niles—she says you want Niles to go to the gold fields with you!"

"What she says is absolutely true," replied Charley. "I'm leaving as soon as I put my affairs in order."

"That's dreadful!" exclaimed Cornelia. "I thought you were the one sensible, practical young man who would keep his head long after all the others—and now you're the first to lose it! How can you dream of leaving all your friends and family and probably never see them again?"

"Hold on there!" Charley was taken aback. Although he knew better than to expect the town to praise him, he was unprepared for such vehement disapproval, especially from his cousins. "Just wait a minute! I don't see where I'm proposing to do anything like what you're all making it out to be! Thousands of others are doing the same thing."

"Then they're just as crazy!" snapped Cornelia.

"Look, if you feel this strongly about it, I'm willing to discuss it with you. But it will have to be done calmly, peacefully, and at another time! I have lots of work to do—so, if you'd like to talk about it, I can come by your house tonight after supper. All right?"

"Good," replied Cornelia. "We'll expect you at half past seven."

"I'll be there," Charley promised.

The whole family was waiting, from the youngest to the oldest, when Charley arrived to explain his bizarre behavior. The Niles boys thought it was a great plan, but even they were puzzled by the fact that Rensselaerville's first deserter should have been quiet, businesslike Charles Mulford. His demeanor was so adult that most people forgot Niles Searls was the older of the pair by more than a year. Unlike Niles, Charley never clowned or played practical jokes, and for this reason, no one ever doubted what he said he would do—until now.

"This may be the only chance I'll ever have to travel clear across the continent," he explained to the gathering. "I'm not going to make my fortune—I don't care about gold. But I want to see the west. I'd like to look at the trees and plants and flowers—to see the animals and birds and insects. I want to see the Pacific Ocean and stand on top of the Rocky Mountains—to see Indians and Mexicans and Russians!" He paused for a breath, then said, "What I'm trying to say is that I want to see something of the rest of the world before I'm too old or feeble to make the attempt."

"That's all well and good," replied Judge Niles, "but you're still just a very young man—how old are you, twenty-two? You've got many, many good years ahead of you. What's the rush?"

"The gold rush, I suppose," said Charley with a wry smile. When the adults failed to laugh, his expression grew sheepish. "I didn't mean to sound fresh. I meant only to suggest that by traveling at a time when thousands of gold seekers will be crossing the plains, I'll expose myself to less risk than usual. Indians, for instance, are said to be more apt to attack small groups of emigrants. I can assure you, Uncle John and Aunt Polly, I've given the matter a lot of thought."

"But it's all going to be for naught—you'll see that all that talk about gold is greatly exaggerated," insisted his uncle.

"I know! That's why I say that I don't care about gold—it's only the means to my end, not the other way around. And Niles feels the same way, I'm sure."

"And what about Niles? Suppose you can't locate him—what then?"

"I don't expect to have much trouble. I wrote and said I'd meet him at Wellington and that's a very small settlement."

"But if you couldn't find him—would you go on alone?" asked Mary.

"I suppose I would, but I don't expect to have to."

"And if he decides not to go with you?"

Charley smiled. "He'll go. It was Niles who first got me to thinking about exploring the west. It's the most natural thing in the world that he'd want to go. You've said yourselves in recent weeks that you feared he'd already gone. That's one of the things which forced my decision—the thought that he might leave without me! I don't think I'd ever forgive myself if he went to California and I passed up the chance to go with him."

"Well, I think you're doing a very foolish thing, Charles," stated the Judge. "But if I can't change your mind, I can at least try to influence Niles. I'm going to write and tell him not to go and to try to bring you home as well!"

"I'm sorry you feel it's foolish, Uncle John, but I'm not sorry you're going to write Niles. I'd feel badly if I discovered later that your reasoning could make him change his mind, but that you hadn't offered it. I want Niles to feel it's the right thing to do."

Not only John Niles, but Mary and Cornelia also wrote to Niles and listed all the reasons why he should not go to California. And while they wrote, Charley packed. On March 5, 1849, he left Rensselaerville for New York City and Brooklyn, to say goodbye to relatives. Then he went back to Albany and caught the cars for Rochester, where he took the night packet to Buffalo on the Erie Canal, crossed the Wire Bridge over the Niagara River into Canada, and traveled by stage all the way to Detroit. He wrote to Cornelia from a stage stop at Niles, Michigan:

... a rich time we had, too—2 load[s], 18 in all, and among them 12 Chippewa Indians and Squaws with a conductor and interpreter—what would you think of seeing me with two pretty squaws facing me accompanied by their copper colored companions?—I acknowledge there was no danger of my being *smut*, as Deb says, but not exactly in the sense she would imply—the balance of our companions were good company, I can assure you—and I had rare sport observing the doings of our company.

We arrived in London, [Canada] Tuesday 12 P.M. and were delayed as we supposed until 10 A.M., but proved to be 12 o'clock before starting. "Our host" was well acquainted with the [William Henry] Niles family and offered to carry me there if I would stay the day—should have gone as it was, had I known how long the delay would be. . . . after many delays, we arrive[d] in Detroit on Friday Evening, being 4½ days from Buffalo—left Detroit this morning 9 A.M.—arrived here 7 P.M., were to have started hence this evening enroute for Chicago, but will remain until morning on account of bad roads. . . .

By the way, I suppose you have one of the miniatures I had taken in New York; if not, Lucia will give you a choice in them, if there is one— they were taken while it rained "pitch forks" and having no time to spare, did not examine them much. . . . Who do you think showed signs of being most affected at my departure? It was one I should have thought the last—Robert Murphy—when shaking hands with me in Albany on the departure of the cars, he could but just speak and hardly that—no doubt some of my friends felt as much or more regret on parting with me, but none I saw showed it so much—perhaps, like me, they managed to conceal a feeling which, being shown, could do them no kind of good.

It is a most beautiful country in the vicinity of Niles—and a fine day we shall have tomorrow, as we have had today. . . . I shall be two days in going to Chicago, and two more thence to Rockford, Ill., where I shall tarry a day or two, and thence one day to Janesville [Wisconsin].

II

WHEN NILES RECEIVED the letters from Rensselaerville late in March, he did not know that Charley was in Janesville already. In his packet of mail were two letters from Charley, one from Mary, and another from Cornelia. Four days later he received a message from John Niles. All his plans were thrown into disarray by the several hundred words carefully chosen to influence him.

On March 30 he wrote his reply to Cornelia—at the top of his sheet he penned the words, "Wellington MO (not California)"—and went on to say:

It is now just 5 oclock PM. of as fine a day as you usually see in NYork any time during the pleasant month of May. At peace with myself and the world, I proceed to answer your *too kind* letter of Feb. 23, which was received last Sabbath morning. The same mail brought one from Mary, two from Charlie and one from Carman.

The effects of Charlie's letters were to throw me into a severe fit of the "fever," from which I have now only so far recovered as to be just able to write, and I doubt not that, only for the counter influence of yours and Mary's, I should have taken a *"Stampede"* at once and made off for the *diggings*. Thanks to you for my preservation from so horrible a fate.

After reading Charlie's letters I was forced to get up and walk two or three times across the floor before I could persuade myself that it was not a *dream.* Words will fail to convey any idea of the astonishment with which I pored over the pages of those letters.

Had it been Rufus, Filkins, Cope, or anyone else but Charley, I should have been less surprised, but I suppose I am bound to believe the story, though I cannot understand the process by which Charley was brought to embrace the project of going to California.

So you thought I had gone to Santa Fe or St. Francisco last fall, did you? and perhaps got my *wool* pulled by the Indians? Really, you do not pay me any great compliment if you did but know it. For, to suppose that I had started at *that* time of the *year,* over *that route,* would be just about the equivalent to thinking "Niles Searls is a *nice young* man with just enough of *common sense* to be led away by *silly schemes of silly fools.*"

In some things that may prove true, but then you must remember that we of the *legal profession* are governed pretty much by precedents, and the only adjudged case to which I could refer for light was *that* of the Mormons who were caught in the mountains a few winters since and had to subsist upon the dead bodies of their famished companions.

I have only to say that if the above *interpretation* of your opposition reveals the true opinion held of me by those who know me *best,* the *quicker* I *evaporate* and go to California or some other unknown land, the *better.* What I may have said upon the subject in my letters to you, I do not now recollect, but I can assure you of one thing, nothing was farther from my intention than to convey to you an idea that I was going.

Now I know you would like to have me come right out and say whether I am going or not. That will be committing myself upon a question which I have not decided myself yet—though for once I will answer frankly and say I want on many accounts to go, especially as Charlie's going—but do not much expect to do so. There, ain't that *definite?*

I can see more reason for my going and less objections than in Charlie's case—I am out of business and it will take me no longer to get into business on my return than at present—but I will not discuss the reasons for or against my going, but merely say I had expected to start for home (Canada) about the 15th of April, and then decide whether to return to Missouri, go to work in NYork State, or what next, but I am not now certain of doing even this.

From a merchant who returned from St. Louis the other day I learn that the cholera is making havoc in that place and on the river. One boat from New Orleans lost 20 of her passengers while coming up to that place and landed 16 more under its influence. The boat upon which my informant came up left two on the way who were reported sick with the same disease. This may be an exaggerated report—and perhaps I ought not to circulate it, as it may cause some fears about Charlie—I hope it *may be* false, but fear not.

If it *does* prevail on the river, I shall just stay where I am and not venture one step toward home, much as I want to go. They tell me the cholera did not rage on the plains or in *Santa Fe* when it was here before, from which some are in hopes it may not affect the emigrants on their way out to California, though I am not so certain of *that*, even. You can't frighten me by talking about the hardships of the trip to *Eldorado*, for I just believe I can stand them all—but just talk *cholera* and I quail.

When I wrote to Addison, which was several weeks since, I thought of going to Independence to stop in the course of a few weeks—but from the crowd that has congregated there since then, I desire to keep clear—and still they come, by the hundred. I shall look for Charles about the 5th of April, from that to the 10th, and most happy shall I be to see him. I must confess that I shall be sorely tempted to go with Charley, for better company could not be found anywhere. He is always the same, not today friendly and tomorrow filled with enmity, and then I think he will enjoy the trip even better than I should, though for reasons somewhat different.

But I have said enough concerning this affair—much more than I should, but for the feeling which you have *all* manifested upon the subject. I appreciate the motive, which induces you to dissuade me from this enterprise, and rest assured, *dear Cornelia*, that *neglectful* as I have been, I would not barter that affection which leads you to feel thus interested in *my welfare* for all the gold which I expect to get *if* I cast aside your admonitions and go with Charles. I received a letter from your Pa yesterday, which I think I must answer before long . . .

I go to HarrisonVille next Monday or Tuesday, and from there to Independence. . . . Only for the fear of missing Charles, I should go on next week to Atchison Co. (the NW County of the state), as I have some thought of making that or the adjoining counties my future *home*. . . .

Eight oclock PM. . . . From my window I can see the *Prairies* on fire in *several directions*. There is scarcely a night that the horizon is not lit up with long streaks of light from the burning prairies. It may be seen to a distance of fifty or sixty miles, and presents a most magnificent view. Sometimes damage to a considerable amount is caused by these fires, yet nothing in comparison with what I had hitherto supposed.

I wish you could be here this evening to enjoy a right sociable time with me—then I would tell more long yarns in a minute than I can write in an hour. Perhaps, though, you have become so *dignified* since you took charge of the *Academy* that you would hardly be willing to play the agreeable with your humble cousin, especially since he has abjured civilization and gone to live among the outer barbarians of Missouri. . . . Remember me kindly to *Uncle* and *Aunt* and tell *Addison* that in all probability I shall wait for him to get ready before I go to the modern *"Ophir."*

A postscript had been appended to the letter which read:

PS Since writing the above, John Lauderdale has come in from Wellington and brings word that there are two cases of *cholera* there—both negroes who were landed from a steamboat last evening. One of them was reported dying when John left. They are in the same building with the Post Office, so that I don't know as I shall venture there to put your letter in—Don't tell of this, as it will make *Charlie's* friends feel *bad,* and can do no good. You need not be uneasy about me. If this is mailed anywhere except at Wellington, you may read the last of it and *guess* the *reasons.*

The letter was postmarked at Lexington, Missouri. A few days later, Mary received a letter from Niles which spoke more about the cholera:

[I] should not perhaps have written just yet, were it not that I spoke something about the cholera, and am fearful that you might again deem me dead or absent if I neglect longer to write.

I must confess that I feel rather ashamed that I did not write for so long a time after my arrival, but see no way to get out of it but to laugh at you for thinking anything was to say more than common. I can only say that I had not the remotest idea of your being at all uneasy about me.

The recent outbreak on the Mississippi was the first appearance of the dreaded disease in ten years. Cholera first reached the shores of North America with the Irish emigrants of 1832. It traveled down the St. Lawrence River to the Great Lakes. It infected the troops at Rock Island and went down the Mississippi to Jefferson Barracks, at St. Louis.

In 1833 it killed at least sixty of St. Louis' leading citizens. Cholera was re-introduced from Canada and Europe in 1834 and from Cuba in 1835. But this newest outbreak in 1849 showed early signs of being the worst. Scarcely a boat came up the Missouri River without its share of victims.

Less than two weeks passed before Mary received a new letter from Charley, who was now moving up the Missouri on the steamboat *Bay State.* Charley said:

Here we are, slowly on our way to the place of outfit—the far famed Independence—with a load consisting of about 225 passengers and a large amount of freight—a very large load for these western boats.

NILES SEARLS

I arrived in St. Louis Friday morning and found a letter from Niles awaiting me, the contents of which you have heard, perhaps, through his own letters to R Ville. He says he had considered to go before the receipt of my letter, although he, like myself, made little noise about it, and would be pleased to accompany me.

You perhaps have heard of the failure of my plans in regard to the Iowa City company, in so much as Abraham Palmer had concluded to remain until fall or spring, and did not receive my letter until he had made business arrangements which made it impossible to leave at present. There would have been no difficulty in my obtaining passage with a company starting from Iowa, but did not desire to—as Palmer was not going with them—until I heard from Niles.

My route since writing to "Nella" has been from Niles [Michigan] around Lake Michigan to Chicago, thence via Elgin to Rockford—staid two days. Thence via Beloit to Janesville—found friends well—remained six days, waiting for letters from Searls, Iowa City, and home, but receiving none, returned to Rockford, and thence via Dixon to Rock Island, [Burlington] and Iowa City—remained over Sunday—returned to [Burlington]—and per steamer *Auburn* left for St. Louis—and arrived *after many* days.

I had the [bad] luck to get aboard a boat which had no freight, and at every little landing she stopped to take in "the plunder"—we were two and a half days going down, but ought to have been but 1½ days.

The Mississippi hardly came up to the idea I had previously had of the "father of rivers"—it is true, it was seen somewhat disadvantageously (what a long word!), as the water was said to be higher than it had been since 1844. Its banks appear to be low and mainly covered with a dense growth of heavy timber, with much sameness to them, but occasionally a bold shore or high bluff projecting into the river enlivened the prospect in a measure. Its innumerable islands, covered with cottonwood, were also somewhat pleasing.

The scenery of the Missouri is, I think, far more pleasant—one side is a bold and bluffy shore, covered with a beautiful growth of timber and flowers, with here and there a neat cabin in some romantic spot, with an abundance of peach and cherry trees surrounding them. It puts me in mind of the scenery of the Hudson most of anything I have seen.

The Red Bud, or Judas Tree, in particular is most beautiful at this season—it grows from the size of a peach tree to that of a medium size apple tree, and is covered from the ground to its smallest limbs with small, locust shaped flowers, and in the distance looks like the flowering almond. . . .

I just told a room mate of mine, a fine young fellow, that I was writing to a young lady, and wishing to improve the opportunity, he sends all the love he has to you, saying he does not expect to see any ladies from this time until he returns, and wishes to leave his love where it will be prized. Nine-tenths of our passengers in the cabin are [would-be] Californians and are a very respectable appearing body, so far as I am able to judge. Many have their outfits complete—with mules and waggons on board, but from the reports now current, those that outfit at Independence will be the best off.

Independence has been for years the outfitting place, and nearly everyone, expecting it would be the same this year, have shipped their goods for St. Josephs above, thinking thereby to avoid the crowd, but it has proved the contrary, as report says there is now at St. Josephs ten when there is one at Independence.

Independence has calculated upon the trade and, expecting mules, oxen &c would be high, have gathered them from all directions, but not meeting with a ready sale, for a want of customers, many are obliged to sell very low . . .

I shall stop now at Wellington and consult with Niles as to our mode of starting—we shall either go with pack mules or mule waggons, and not with oxen, I think. Niles wrote me there were plenty of chances to join companies there. The whole western country is moving—every boat is crowded. St. Louis is so busy it is almost impossible to pass along the levee, it is so crowded.

The trees and flowers are very forward there. Lilacs, daffodils and tulips are in bloom, and everything indicates the approach of spring. You, I suppose, are now making garden and arranging all things as nice as you please—if you *will,* plant a *forget-me-not* for me, and take *good care* of my corner *by the fireplace.* . . .

Your cousin
Chas W. Mulford

P.S.   Our boat strikes a sand bar occasionally and causes pretty rough times, so when you come to a *rough place* in my writing, please consider it was penned while crossing a bar and oblige   Chas.

CHAPTER 15

INDEPENDENCE, MISSOURI

May 1849

E ARRIVED HERE yesterday evening [May 2, 1849], having sent our baggage per steamboat from Wellington, and coming on ourselves on horses purchased for the trip we are now about commencing," wrote Charley when he and Niles got to Independence.

Charley's horse, "Major," was already a veteran of life on the plains. According to Niles, Major "knows more about camp life than Charlie and I both put together." Jo was the name of the Indian pony which Niles rode—"next to Charlie, the best of anything that has life in these diggins."

The two young men had decided not to buy a mule team and wagons after observing the hazards and problems involved. One day they watched as some wild mules were broken to harness. First the animals were lassoed, thrown, harnessed and dragged into place. Then a driver mounted the wheel mule (the tamest that could be found) and ropes with choking nooses were placed around the necks of the other mules.

Each rope was held by a man who had to walk, run, jump, fall, or be dragged, as occasion demanded, so long as the procession continued to move. When progress ceased, the men untangled themselves from mules and rope ends, repaired the damage, and prepared to give it another go.

Because the mules were wild and stubborn, it took a good deal of trial and error to discover which pairs would work best together. Then, when two had been matched, the next task was to find four mules who would pull in unison—usually the forward pair preferred to kick those in back. When, at last, the mules were broken sufficiently so they would pull the wagons, they were sold for sixty dollars apiece.

Two men from St. Louis, Turner and Allen, offered an easier alternative. They announced plans to transport 120 gold-seekers and their belongings in small spring wagons, six men to the carriage. The fare to California was $200, meals included. The "Pioneer Line," as it was called, would provide enough heavy freight wagons to carry baggage, equipment and provisions for the whole company, which also included wagonmasters, teamsters, hunters, and commissaries.

Turner and Allen were to furnish tents, cooking gear, and rations. The passengers were expected only to take turns driving their carriages and cooking their meals. Teamsters would be responsible for the animals and would harness and unharness the mules for the passengers. The Pioneer Line had contracted to carry government mail through to Sutter's Fort in sixty days, thus delivering the passengers as well by the fourth of July. If they made it by that date, it would be record time for crossing the plains.

Niles and Charley quickly arranged for passage and were told by Captain John Turner that there had been a slight delay. The train would not be leaving until May 9, thanks to some unforeseen problems. They arranged to board with a local farmer, Mr. Caldwell, who lived one and a half miles outside of town. Charley began a long letter to Cornelia, to be posted before they left Independence:

You have already learned through Niles of our intended departure by the Pioneer Line, so there is no need for me to describe the peculiar advantages gained by joining the company. The last part of the train will perhaps leave on Monday next, but in the meantime, wagons are constantly leaving as fast as loaded, and join the camp, some nine miles on the Santa Fe road. We are patiently awaiting the arrival of our trunks from the river, some three miles from town, and shall send them on immediately, while we take up our abode with a farmer's family, one and a half miles from town, thereby enabling us to visit *folks* a little more easily than in camp. . . .

The mails are very irregular in this region, and it is difficult to get a letter after it arrives. The Post Office is in a very small building—large enough for the ordinary business of the place, but under present circumstances is very much crowded. So, to avoid trouble to the clerks of the office, a list of the letters arriving by each mail is made out before any are delivered and pasted upon a board hung outside the door.

If any person finds his name there, by cutting it out and handing it through a broken window, it is delivered to him after waiting a half hour for the P.M. to find it—but woe be to him that finds nothing like his name registered there—as none of the clerks will look until the written name is handed them. . . .

I again resume the pen after a night's rest upon the floor, rolled up in our Indian blankets. This is the first step towards camp life. We have gained admission into the family of an old planter who already has more boarders than beds to accommodate them with, but finding a good table, we are well contented to put up with some inconveniences. You perhaps have ere this wondered at the oddity of my sheet, but when you learn that all Californians are furnished with nothing but *foolscap*—as the name is best suited to their proposed journey—you will not be much surprised. . . .

I think no one can start in better spirits than Niles and myself. The dangers of the journey are greatly magnified in the eyes of the eastern people, and western men laugh when we Yankees talk of Indians.

Niles was writing his own thoughts for the people at home:

I have been watching the falling rain all the morning and thinking what good times a fellow will have in such weather on the plains. Several came in here this morning for breakfast, being unable to strike fire in camp to cook with. . . .

You would hardly know Charlie and myself, were you to see us now. Charlie's face has been burned so that it has peeled five or six times, and now it looks about the color of a piece of sole leather, while I am turning Indian as fast as possible. Could you see us travelling about with our display of revolvers, rifles, bowie knives, all in our belts and about us, I am sure you would pronounce us as two very savage looking young men.

Charlie's whiskers begin to start right finely, and I think, with a little nursing, will soon cut a figure. We talked some of having our miniatures taken, dressed in full costume, but shall defer it until our return.

We took our first lesson at sleeping in our blankets last night instead of in bed. We both affirmed that we slept first rate, yet I doubt it a little. We shall commence our journals in a few days, and shall be able, I think,

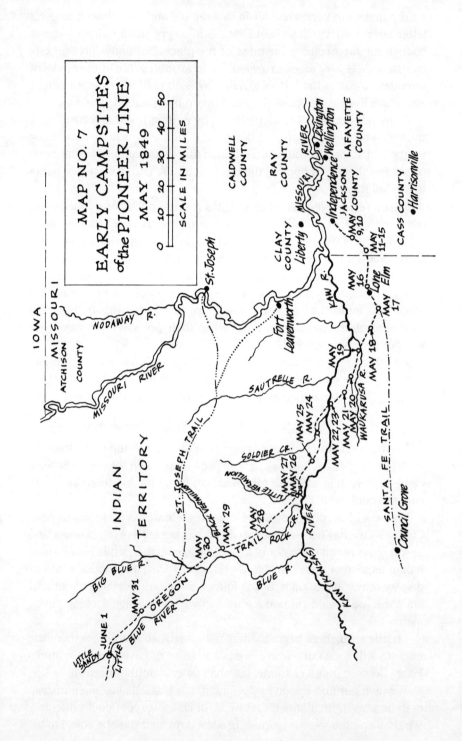

MAP NO. 7
EARLY CAMPSITES of the PIONEER LINE
MAY 1849

SCALE IN MILES
0 10 20 30 40 50

to keep a pretty full account of our travels.

I have already seen enough to convince me that it will take Charlie two years to cross the plains. Not a flower does he see but I must hold his horse while he gets down and plucks it. I think I will study botany a little while on the plains, just enough to prevent my appearing a perfect ignoramus on the subject, if nothing more.

Then he changed the subject to talk of things at home—home was a favorite topic of conversation around Independence, taking a backseat only to gold and Indians. He offered advice to Cornelia, now teaching at the Rensselaerville Academy:

How long are you going to act in the capacity of teacher? Perhaps you recollect that I used to advise you to teach, and now let me advise you not to teach too long. Remember, also, that teaching, if followed as a profession, invariably spoils the temper and most commonly renders the subject the most despicable of all human species.

Take my advice, therefore, dear Cornelia, and quit teaching before long. Don't for anything become a peevish old maid of a school teacher. . . . If I remember right, it was one year ago tonight that I took such a glorious ride down the Champlain canal and railroad after being admitted [to the bar]. A year is gone. How quickly has it flown and what changes has it brought, and who can anticipate what will occur during the next!

On May 9, a Wednesday, Niles and Charley left the Caldwell farm and rode out to the Pioneer Camp. The company was not ready to start, so they spent most of the day watching the preparations. Charley described the scene to Mary:

Oh, if our eastern friends could but see our camp ground, they would no longer wonder at our anxiety to journey across the plains. On a high roll of the prairies, with the Santa Fe road on the left and boundless green at the right, our white tents array themselves, scattered here and there as the taste of the occupants may have directed them.

Near us a crystal spring pours its limpid waters forth, and with a warm sun, I can assure you it is a great luxury. The prairie is dotted with flowers, and most all the pink verbena, the same we cultivate at home. Wild peas of different colors, star grass, and a great many new subjects to operate on when the time comes.

It was raining outside the tent and Charley was seated on a trunk, using a saddle for a writing desk. Nearby, Niles was standing beside a stack of trunks, using the topmost for his desk, and others were similarly engaged. Said Niles, "I write a sentence, then stop to keep up my end in joking." He pictured camp life somewhat differently for Cornelia's eyes:

The day has been spent in breaking in upwards of 100 mules . . . every animal was caught by the lasso and choked down, then harnessed and placed before the wagons, there to perform more antics than all the dancing ponys in the world combined. The whole day has been thus consumed, and now the baggage train is moving off, sometimes *rocket like,* and sometimes *snail like* across the broad, undulating prairie, while *we,* the *passengers,* the *gentlemen,* the *gold diggers,* the *sportsmen,* are crouched together beneath a small tent ⅛ full of baggage, where we are endeavoring to cheer up the disconsolate by telling them of the hardships to come. . . .

The novelty of our situation tickles some of us *almost* to death and frightens others as bad. Of course, I am among the frightened—yet for the life of me I can't help but laugh . . . all is glorious confusion.

Three men from Ann Arbor, Michigan, joined Niles and Charley to form the nucleus of Mess 17. Two were in their early twenties, both named Charles, to add further confusion. Charles C. Cranson was the son of a retired farmer and Charles M. Sinclair had been helping his older brother operate a dry goods store. The third Ann Arbor recruit was fifty years old—David T. McCollum was a bookkeeper and "conveyancer," had served two terms as county register of deeds, and was a merchant.

McCollum was an abolitionist and a member of the Sons of Temperance. Once he had signed an agreement with a business partner in which he promised not to speak evil of the Congregational Church if the other man would refrain from denouncing Methodists. Soon after arriving at Independence, McCollum came down with "bilious fever" and still was weak from the effects of it. His younger companions wondered how such an old and infirm man would make it across the plains.

One "old" man didn't even start the trip, and his loss came to be sorely felt by all the others, even though few had met or even heard of him. His name was Moses "Black" Harris and he was supposed to have guided the Pioneer Line over the trail to California. Twenty-three years earlier, Harris and a fellow Kentuckian, Bill Sublette, came out of the Rocky Mountains on snowshoes to guide General William H. Ashley to the 1826 rendezvous of hunters and trappers at Bear River.

Harris had once offered to lead a filibustering expedition north to the Columbia River hunting grounds to wipe out the Hudson's Bay Company, and on another occasion he was with the Bible-toting Jedediah Smith and had to climb a high peak in order to ascertain their location. It was a rough climb to the top and a bitter wind was blowing. When Harris crawled back down, cold, hungry, and exhausted, Smith demanded only to know what he'd seen.

"Damn your hide!" he swore at the pious Smith. "I seen the city of St. Louis—and a feller takin' a drink!"

Never again would Black Harris take a drink, at least not with living mortals. In 1849 cholera accomplished in Independence what years of dangerous escapades elsewhere had failed to do. The Pioneer Line had to rely on less talented guides to bring them safely across the plains and mountains.

Niles began making notes in his journal:

After sundry mishaps such as breaking wagon tongues, harnesses, &c, we at length got under way and proceeded two miles, where we again encamped for the night. Our first business, after picketing our horses for the night and pitching our tent, was to seek for wherewithal to satisfy the cravings of appetite.

After an hour's delay, we succeeded to the number of four in procuring some coffee, bacon, pilot bread and sugar. One of our number soon levied upon a fence rail with which a fire was kindled, and culinary operations were for the first time commenced. Another hour and we were seated in a circle around our humble supper, eating by moonlight *this,* the first fruits of our own cooking.

No useless table was spread. The Earth is to be our future bed, seat and table, and we reclined upon her bosom. We partook of our creature comforts with a relish that in our former plentiful hours was wholly unknown.

May 10th—Rose this morning from our bed upon the ground with sensations similar to those I imagine must pervade the frame of the inebriate after a week's spree.

We have succeeded in forming a mess today and in procuring our carriage and camp equipage and are beginning to feel quite at home in our new situation. . . . Our mess is made up, with a single exception, of young men . . . all intelligent, moral men, and, with perhaps one exception, are all enterprising industrious persons . . .

The last-mentioned exception was the sixth member of Mess 17, John J. Eastman, who came from a place near Concord, New Hampshire. Already "Yankee," as they called him, was showing signs of extreme laziness. "Work and he must have had a falling out when young, for he is so plaguey lazy he can hardly eat," said Charley. No further progress was made that day.

May 11th—Rose this morning under the influence of a severe cold contracted from exposure in camp and in sleeping on the ground. The most deleterious consequence which I apprehend is the effect which it appears to be having upon my eyes. They are now very weak and today scarcely permit my reading or going about.

His old nemesis had returned, after a long reprieve. On the next day Niles found his cold no better and his eyes much worse, "so bad as to be unable to leave my tent without suffering considerable pain." Nevertheless, he believed the general health of the company was as good "as under all the circumstances could be expected. Some few are complaining, but judging from the number of Doctors in the train, if any suffer from sickness, it will not be for the want of medical advisers." No fewer than ten passengers made use of the title "Doctor," but it was an open question as to how many were merited.

Moses Harris was not the only Pioneer Line fatality at Independence. Reverend Davis Goheen, a prospective passenger, also died of cholera. Others were ill, but it was uncertain if their ailments were cholera or some other disease. The passengers were eager to get moving, not only to reach their destination sooner, but to escape the spread of cholera which was closing in from behind.

Niles described the antic parade of wagons in his journal:

At nine oclock A.M. word came to "hitch up," when we again had a repetition of the sport of catching wild mules. When duly prepared, which was not till late this evening, the baggage train filed off in advance, the passenger carriages bringing up the rear in ludicrous style.

At one moment we might all be seen rolling on at a slow pace with all the solemnity of a funeral procession, while in the next, some refractory team, enraged at their recent captivity, would plunge from the procession and, after a few gyrations by way of ascertaining if their locomotives were in moving order, dart off across the broad Prairie at the top of their speed, and in utter defiance of all restraint.

Ever and anon, some startled passenger, aroused by the speed from his golden dreams, would throw himself from the carriage at the risk of life and limb.

Our team consisted of two mules, one a venerable, sedate looking chap, whose experience, if told, would fill a volume. To him a wagon was no novelty, and the duties now devolving upon him were but a repetition of what he had performed for the last twenty years.

Not so with his youthful companion, who, for the first time a captive, wore his bonds with but a bad grace. Sometimes he would dart ahead, as if running against time, then pause and plunge for a few moments, vainly trying to extricate himself from his fancy covering of harness. Sometimes on all fours, and sometimes biped-like, he continued pushing along, for be it said to his credit, there was no refusing to go, till, at length, finding that resistance was useless, he calmly yielded to his fate and, with an occasional exception, walked on sullenly, champing his bit.

Charley described his domestic duties in his serial letter to Mary:

We now begin to be fairly initiated in camp life and will be ready soon to cook with the best of you. Today I made bread, the first we have made in our mess, and if you think you can beat me, you are welcome to your opinion—that is all. I have my opinion about it. We all called it first rate for the first time trying. In making coffee I own no superior, and if we are not yet perfect in other things, we are *a'most,* as Missourians say.

The first duty of the day is for one of the mess to gather wood while another brings water. A third, with a spade, cuts a hole in the sod about three feet long by one wide for a fireplace and makes a fire. A fourth mixes bread and puts the water to boil in the camp kettle. A fifth cuts the ham and attends to it and makes coffee, and number six washes the dishes after the meal. So between us it is light work and soon done.

We have ample provisions and almost as much variety as at home, with the exception of milk and eggs and fresh meat. All things go on finely, much better than I had anticipated. I always thought you cooks had hard work, but now find it is nothing but play. . . .

The supper is over—dishes washed and wood gathered for Sunday, and now I'll finish if possible. Making biscuit, or bread, as western people call it, was again my portion, with previous good luck.

A beautiful day we have—such as you eastern people seldom see, that is, with the scenery to accompany it, which makes it so charming. The grass is just high enough to give the prairies a light green appearance, and flowers begin to peer up . . .

On the Sabbath, a day of rest, Niles visited a neighboring farmhouse and brought brought back a pail of milk and two pounds of honey so Charley could prepare a special dinner: fried ham, boiled rice, soda biscuits, pilot bread, hoe cake, honey, and milk. "This morning I made a *Hoe cake* (or corn bread, as western people call it) from *Penola* (parched corn meal and sugar), and succeeded very well," wrote Charley to Cornelia.

The previous day had provided an opportunity to explore the country and do some fishing. "I went fishing yesterday in a stream called the Big Blue, 1½ miles distant, but did not get even *'one glorious nibble,'*" he told her, adding that "some staid longer and had better luck—one caught a Mud Turtle, another two small fish, while I came back with 3 fresh water clams—and from them made an *oyster supper*." Life was very easy and romantic at the moment. He described their tent, which was shared by the men of two messes:

If you have ever seen a tent pitched small enough for 12 persons to occupy, it will not be very difficult for you to imagine you see me seated on the ground, leaning against the tent pole, with a carpet bag supported by a pair of boots for a writing desk, actively engaged in striving to sift from the dross some few items of camp life of interest to you in your eastern home.

Niles is stretched at full length on my left hand, enjoying the luxury of a good snooze after the labor of the morning's meal, while others are in the same condition around, only they have no Rubber Bed to lay on, as we have—We find camp life much more pleasant than I had anticipated. ... The tent we occupy in company with another mess is very comfortable, and, by tying a candle to the pole in the center, is well lighted and very pleasant. We have music and singing every night and draw a crowd from tents around to hear *us*. We have a violin, flute well played, two good singers, and others from camp come in and help ...

We take turns cooking—2 of us this week—2 next and so on around. Niles has his turn next—then I guess we shall live well, as I believe he knows how and will do it first rate.

Give my very best respects to Deb and Maria—and all other inquiring friends—do not fail to write me at San Francisco.

PIONEER LINE
SPRING WAGONS

CHAPTER 16

FORT KEARNY

May–June 1849

ONTRARY TO EXPECTATIONS, the Pioneer Line did not cross the Big Blue on Monday. A cold wind out of the northeast blew throughout the day and showers pelted the tents. The storm's intensity increased during the night. A downpour at two in the morning soaked the tents and everything in them. Lightning crackled and thunder shook the plains; sleep was impossible.

Winds of gale force pushed and pulled at the tents until it seemed they would fly away at any minute, yet somehow the stakes held. When morning came at last, the wet, tired, and bedraggled company crawled out from under soggy canvas hoping they had seen the worst of it. "Some of our boys concluded . . . that if they had not seen the elephant, they had at least had a peep at his proboscis," wrote Niles in his journal.

And cholera overtook the Pioneer Line. Robert "California Bob" Beadell, a teamster, was stricken during the storm and had to be left behind when the wagons moved out at three in the afternoon. Some friends stayed behind to keep him company until the end.

Niles and Charley rode on ahead to the Big Blue and were amazed to see how high the waters had risen since the storm. When the train caught up, it was hard to persuade the mules to enter the flooded stream, and harder yet to keep the spring wagons from being swept downstream in the current. In time each wagon made it across and was then hauled up the steep, muddy bank by ropes and teams placed at the top of the bluff.

The carriages then were driven another mile or two, to a high, open bit of the prairie where the next camp was set up. Meanwhile, at the Blue, the job of hauling the heavy freight wagons across the river and up the bank proved more difficult than what had gone before. By now the men and animals were tired and the slippery banks had been eroded by the carriages and mules in the first contingent.

Not till midnight did most of the baggage wagons reach the camp, and only then could the wet and shivering passengers collect their tents and blankets and make ready for bed. Some wagons still remained behind, stuck in the mud. California Bob Beadell had died during the night and was buried beside the trail by his friends.

During the day the train moved only ten miles, starting at eleven and stopping at four in the afternoon. The road was in terrible condition, both because of the storm and because of the hundreds of wagons just ahead. Niles rode off to find firewood, after discovering that his mess had neglected to bring any from the last encampment.

The rains encouraged wildflowers, which began coming out in great profusion. Charley spent hours each day introducing Niles to the many species, and instructed him in basic techniques of botanical identification. The weather improved somewhat and the sun shone from time to time.

On Thursday two passengers from the eleventh and twelfth messes, O. Trowbridge and William Millen, came down with cholera and were left behind with some friends to look after them. Shortly after noon, the Pioneer Line passed the junction of the Santa Fe and Oregon trails and took the right-hand fork which led to the Wakarusa River.

In his journal Niles wrote:

Owing to the damp state of the atmosphere, our blankets are saturated with moisture and, notwithstanding our efforts at keeping them properly aired, are in a bad condition for forming our bed. We are again encamped far away from any wood and are entirely out of wood. A wagon was sent off and obtained a meagre supply, of which we obtained a single stick four feet in length as our share, with which and a quantity of rosin weed we were to do our cooking for the night.

Charlie undertook the preparation of some bread or cakes and having seen the cooks at home warm their water before commencing, he did not hesitate to pour in a quantity of boiling water which converted his flour into a most beautiful paste. After sundry efforts at making it into bread, without success, the paste was condemned as being nothing better than a foul imitation of gutta-percha, and thrown aside. Our supper was therefore composed of a few crumbs shaken from the bread bag,

and some cold boiled ham. Not content to yield the point without another trial, Charlie, a second time, commenced preparing bread and succeeded finely, as usual.

In the morning, as they were preparing to leave camp, Charley's horse
escaped. The horses had been saddled and left to graze for a few minutes
when Major suddenly took a mind to sprint in the direction of an Indian
dwelling which the company had passed on the previous day. Niles
climbed into Jo's saddle and hurried off in pursuit. After two or three
miles Jo fell while running, but recovered without dislodging Niles from
his seat. He continued the chase and eventually caught up with the errant
steed.

". . . for the future think we shall be more careful, as it is nothing
uncommon for a horse on finding himself thus at liberty and pursued to
escape and run for a whole day without the possibility of being overtaken," he wrote in his journal that evening after supper.

An opportunity to send mail back to the states arose when a young
woman came along on her way home. Her husband had died along the
trail and the young man who was driving her wagon offered to carry
letters for a fee. Niles and Charley gave him the messages they had been
writing since leaving Independence. On the outside of his letter to Cornelia, Charley scribbled one final note:

Niles is writing away as fast as possible and is laughing to himself at a
great rate—if he tells any whoppers about me, take it was some few
grains of allowance, for he is in fine spirits and seems determined to
have a spree of some sort. I hope Nella will excuse us for not paying the
postage on this, as we cannot do it and send it by a teamster. Yours as
ever, Cousin Charlie.

When Sunday came again, Captain Turner ordered the train to move
out at 8:30 A.M. Never before had the Pioneer Line got underway so
early. Because of chronic late starts the company had fallen far behind its
schedule, one reason why Turner ignored the Sabbath curfew on this
occasion.

Even those passengers who knew nothing of overland travel had noticed that most other emigrant parties rose earlier, moved out sooner, and
traveled farther each day than did the Pioneer Line. More companies
passed around them with each new day. Concern grew among the passengers that they would not reach California until too late in the season
to take part in the mining. Those who recalled the Donner Party's travail
worried about snow in the mountains.

Fortunately for their peace of mind, none considered the most serious threat of all: the possibility that they would run out of food as well as time. Only the teamsters and wagonmasters worried, but no one listened to their complaints.

A new storm dropped torrents of rain on Sunday afternoon and evening, making it impossible to build campfires, so the unhappy travelers went to bed after a cold supper and rolled up in damp blankets. In the morning the storm quieted, but a new concern filled the minds of those who shared quarters with Mess Seventeen. Niles noted in his journal:

(Monday) May 21st—The rain of last night has abated, the wind still remaining S. W. and blowing very briskly. With a few hickory barks which lay in the bottom of our carriage, I managed to kindle sufficient fire to boil our coffee and with the assistance of some pilot bread which we obtained late last night from the Commissary, we made a breakfast, all taking hold with a hearty good will except Sinclair (from Michigan) who has been slightly unwell for several days and this morning is severely, if not dangerously, sick.

His symptoms are similar to those of cholera patients which we have had among us almost continually since we left Independence.

The whiffletree to our carriage has given out and we were assisting to repair the injury when the storm, accompanied by a gale of wind, overtook us. The violence of the wind was such as to render it almost impossible for a man to retain his equilibrium. The united efforts of those in the carriage were hardly sufficient to keep it from oversetting. Hailstones the size of the end of a man's thumb, driven by the blast, pelted us with unprecedented fury.

Our horses and mules, rendered frantic with fear and pain, were with difficulty prevented from making their escape together. The storm having abated, we rigged our gearing and resumed the journey, dripping with wet, and at 4 o'clock encamped on the eastern bank of a small creek four miles from the Kansas.

Sinclair has been growing worse during the day, having had several spells of vomiting. A physician was called this evening who has administered some medicine and pronounces his case to be cholera, but thinks him in a fair way to recover.

On the following day they crossed the Kansas River by means of a ferry operated by Indians and half-breeds. The river was between 150 and 200 yards wide. The loaded wagons were lifted by as many men as could gather round and were pushed aboard two boats, working in tandem. The loaded boats then were propelled across the stream with long poles handled by the Indians.

Collected around the bank were quite a number of Indians of the Pottawatomie tribe, dressed in their usual grotesque costume, and painted or daubed with vermillion. Our camp today has been the resort of a large number of Indians with whom many of our company have been trafficking. They are all of the Pottawatomie tribe. This tribe was originally from Wisconsin, and some of our passengers were acquainted with many of them in that place.

Charles Sinclair was not improving, but neither was he getting worse. It was hoped he might recover.

On May 24 the trail became so bad that a detour was made over an old road which Moses "Black" Harris had laid out years before. While waiting for a new approach to be built down the steep banks of Soldier Creek, Niles and Charley discovered an apparently abandoned Indian village. As they were inspecting the Pottawatomie dwellings, a heavy rainshower began to fall. Quickly they took shelter inside one of the huts.

The structures were of varying sizes, from twenty to thirty or more feet in length and about fifteen wide. Rows of hickory saplings had been driven into the ground to form walls and the tops of the saplings had been bent over to meet those of the opposing wall and then tied together in the middle to form an arched roof. Over this frame were placed long strips of peeled bark, each about one foot in width and five feet long. To hold this covering of bark in place, a second, outer scaffolding of saplings was erected all around the building and these were tied together with flexible willow withes to hold the whole thing tightly bound.

Each cabin had a single low entrance, and inside, around the walls, were placed bunks made of woven reeds tied to a pole framework. Niles and Charley laid down upon these pallets, pronounced them comfortable, and promptly fell asleep.

When they awoke, the rain had stopped. Returning to camp, refreshed and dry, they encountered their messmate, Charles Cranson, who had come from Ann Arbor with Charles Sinclair, the sick member of their group. Cranson had just bought a horse from an Indian for forty dollars and was anxious to hear their opinions about the animal.

"That's a nice looking horse, Charley," Niles declared. "How does he ride?"

"I don't know yet—I've got to find a saddle for him, but I think I know where I can get one tomorrow."

"How's Sinclair?" asked Mulford.

"Not very well. I'm really worried, because he doesn't seem to be improving at all. He's suffering terribly, I think, but he never says a thing."

"Why don't you let me watch him tonight?" asked Niles. "I've been napping all afternoon in a Pottawatomie wigwam and I probably won't sleep at all tonight anyway. Get yourself some sleep."

"Thanks, Niles, I think I'll take you up on your offer. I can hardly hold my eyes open after the last two nights. But be sure to call me if there's any change, or if—if anything happens."

"Sure, Charley. I'll let you know. Is he still in the wagon?"

"Yes. It's better for everyone that way, I think. He doesn't disturb the others so much and they don't disturb him."

In the morning Niles wrote in his journal:

(Friday) May 25th—Last night I watched with Sinclair. It rained nearly the whole night and to me it was the most dreary night that I have passed since we left the States. The rain, in spite of all our efforts to the contrary, beat into the wagon upon the head of our poor sufferer. To keep a fire was out of the question, and all that could be done to relieve his wants was to administer medicines and use encouraging words. Those who passed the night in the tents were completely soaked with water.

When this series of rains and storms will end I know not. It appears as if everything, even the very elements, warred against us.

They crossed Soldier Creek and traveled nine miles. Sinclair was watched by Charley that night. They went another nine miles, crossed another stream, went four more miles and reached the banks of the Little Vermillion, filled with seven feet of rushing water. The wagons were emptied and tents pitched to protect the contents against showers. The bodies of two wagons were waterproofed with tar along the joints and detached from their undercarriages to serve as boats.

They began the job of ferrying the equipment across on Saturday night. Niles wrote in his journal:

The baggage and provisions are across and they are now taking the wagons over. Much difficulty has been experienced. One wagon has been carried away by the current and has been drawn under some drift where, it is feared, it cannot be recovered.

There are several companies encamped in our vicinity awaiting the fall of the stream. One company from Mo. has lost its captain by cholera, and several others are at the point of death. They entertain some thoughts of disbanding and returning home.

Near us are several comfortable log houses erected by Uncle Sam for the Pottawatomies, and from which they have been driven by the Pawnees. We shall enter the territories of the latter tribe in a day or two, and some fears are entertained of trouble with them.

The next day was Sunday and Niles wrote that Sinclair had become weaker. "His attack of cholera appears to have subsided, but a frail constitution seems hardly capable of enduring what he is passing through." The business of ferrying continued and by the time it was completed it was four in the afternoon, too late for travel. The patient had taken a turn for the worse during the day. Said Niles in his journal:

Poor fellow! Who that possesses a soul can look unmoved upon him amid his sufferings. Far from home and the friends he loves, with few of those kind offices which take from pain its severest pang, his case seems truly distressing. Charlie has been all attention to him since his first attack and, alike regardless of comfort or exposure, has done everything in his power to smooth our new companion's pathway to the grave. I shall take his place tonight in watching over his, apparently, dying pillow.

To everyone's surprise, Sinclair continued to hang on, yet it was apparent to all that he could not long survive. "He seems conscious of his situation and manifests no fear at the near approach of death. The extremities are becoming cold and the foe is slowly but surely creeping on to the vitals." The Pioneer Line traveled eighteen miles and then another twenty, and yet the patient continued to live.

If alive, we shall remain with him here tomorrow in our camp, ½ mile west of the Vermillion . . .

(Wednesday) May 30th—Our company left camp this morning at an early hour, but in accordance wth our preconceived intention, our mess, together with No. 11, remained upon the camp ground with our esteemed and dying messmate.

Calm and collected, he spoke of his approaching end without fear or trepidation. His mental faculties were unimpaired up to the latest moment of his life, and when no longer able to use his voice he showed conclusively by signs and gestures that he fully comprehended the remarks addressed to him.

Gradually yielding to the embrace of the monster, death, he quietly breathed his last at four o'clock P.M., May 30th, aged 23 years. One-half mile west of the ford of the Vermillion and about one hundred yards to the left of the road in a beautiful elevation of the prairie his grave was prepared, near that of another which, from the defaced inscription upon the wooden cross at the head, we learned was that of "St. Louis," who died June 9th, 1844. Unable to procure other conveniences, we wrapped him in his blankets and with sorrowful hearts consigned him to the "cold earth," there to remain till the last trumpet shall call him forth to meet the reward of his many virtues. . . . the words of one of my dearest friends were brought most vividly to mind, who in dissuading *me* from going to the shores of the Pacific, remarked that "California Gold would cause more bereaved friends and relatives than the late Mexican War."

The burial completed, we hitched up and rolled till 11 o'clock at night, when we camped for a few hours, Distance eight miles.

(Thursday) May 31st—Started out at an early hour and by 7 o'clock A.M. reached the bank of the "Big Blue." Near the river, shaded by an old oak, we saw the grave of Mrs. Sarah Keyes.

The ten men who stood solemnly beside the grave were the remnants of two messes which had left the states no more than three weeks previously; already two of their companions were dead. Sarah Keyes was the seventy-year-old mother of Margaret Reed. Both had been members of the ill-fated Donner-Reed party and the older woman had been on her way to meet her son at Fort Hall. Thinking of what had happened to Margaret Reed caused each to wonder what further horrors lay in store for them on the trail ahead. Without a word, the ten men hurried to catch up with the main body of the train.

Sixteen-year-old C. B. Dodson of Chicago came down with cholera on May 30, two more were stricken on June 1, and on the following day Reuben Cincannon, a teamster, died and was buried. By that evening several more persons were sick with the disease. On June 3 Richard Smith of Kentucky, a member of Mess 5 was sick and not expected to recover.

It was precisely at this time that Mr. Allen, coproprietor of the Pioneer Line, decided to take several of the baggage wagons and most of the sixty or so replacement mules and head back to Independence, where he said that he was going to put together a second Pioneer Line. Some suspected that Allen had had his fill of the adventure and was simply trying to minimize his losses. In any event, Captain Turner was forced to discard about a ton of cured meats at the June 2 campground.

Most passengers were unaware of what had occurred, because the delay was explained as being the result of an accident which damaged one of the baggage wagons. The loss of these extra mules and wagons was soon felt by those who stayed with the train. It was only the first in a long series of miscalculations which began to plague the Pioneer Line.

A French employee of the American Fur Company met them on June

3. He was returning to St. Louis with two wagonloads of buffalo skins from that company's fort at Laramie. He told them the Platte River was too high to cross and might be for several weeks. Three or four thousand wagons were ahead of them and had cut up the road so that it was barely passable. Grass had virtually disappeared at all the best camping grounds.

Meanwhile, behind the Pioneer Line were thousands more, still coming, pushing at their very heels. However, the weather was improving and they traveled twenty-five miles one day, their best distance yet.

A new hazard presented itself: "We have been last night and this morning tormented by clouds of beetles. They were so numerous as to almost overpower us. Not a dish could be cooked in which they did not protrude, and during a portion of the night might continually be heard the thumping noise occasioned by hundreds of them flying against the tents."

In the morning it was Niles's turn to prepare breakfast. When he went to the back of the wagon to grind coffee beans in the mill at the rear of the carriage, he found it full of beetles. Cleaning the mill as best he could, he then began to grind the morning beverage. Upon withdrawing the wooden drawer at the base of the mill, he realized that pulverized amid the coffee were the remains of more than one beetle which he had failed to remove from the apparatus. With a shrug of his shoulders, he decided not to waste the mix, but to let his unsuspecting messmates make the final decision.

"What did you do to the coffee, Niles?" asked Charley.

Here it comes, thought Niles. "Why, what makes you ask?"

"Well, it just tastes better than usual. In fact, it almost tastes good!"

"It's just an old Canadian recipe, Charley. I'm glad you like it."

"A Canadian recipe? You'll have to teach me how to do it."

"A few Indian herbs make all the difference," explained Niles. "I'd like to give you the recipe, but it's an old family secret that I swore I'd never reveal, under penalty of death."

Charley eyed him suspiciously. "I don't believe a word you say, Niles, but from now on, you can make the coffee. Whatever you did, it's an improvement."

"I'll be glad to oblige, at least as long as my supply of herbs lasts. After that I guess we'll have to go back to the old way."

Later in the day, when Mess 17 had its big adventure, Niles was not around to participate, but for once he was not sorry. In his journal he described the events of the day:

Charley took possession of both horses this morning, while I took a seat in the carriage. After proceeding about two miles, feeling chilly, I got out to walk and was soon in advance of the train; feeling somewhat exhausted after my night's watch [on Indian patrol] I lay down to await the coming of our carriage and was soon in a sound sleep.

When I awoke I found two hours had elapsed and our company had passed me long since without being conscious of my whereabouts. Knowing that I must be several miles in the rear, I struck out on foot, following through the bottom and over the bluffy points bordering on the creek.

After having travelled till the perspiration stood in big drops on my brow, and almost despairing of reaching the company, mounting a small eminence from which was an almost impossible descent into a deep, sandy ravine, I looked forward and to my utter astonishment saw our team and mess in the bottom of the valley—but in such a plight that I recognized them with the greatest difficulty.

In descending the steep declivity, the pole strap had given way, letting the carriage forward upon the mules. Springing forward, they rolled—mules, carriage, and passengers—to the bottom of the hill. Fortunately, none of our companions were severely injured, though the whole top and body of the carriage were literally crushed to atoms.

A more chaotic profusion of provisions, cooking utensils, remnants of wagon seats, covers and curtains you never witnessed. I could not but laugh at the ridiculous figure cut by my comrades. Yankee [Eastman] sat on the ground, looking for all the world as though he would shed tears, while the squire [McCollum] was stamping around among the stove baggage like a wild man.

Half an hour sufficed to store our traps and the wreck of our wagon top into the body of the wagon. After which, all mounting, we rode on and overtook the train, cutting very much the figure of a Yankee peddler's cart or an Albany beer wagon.

Jacob Keller, a teamster from Bluffton, Indiana, came down with cholera during the day and was dead by nightfall. Richard Smith was still alive, but not improving.

June 5th—Mounted our little wagon this morning, the box of which is completely filled with baggage, over which we threw the remains of the seat cover, forming a kind of deck over the whole. Stretched out on this, we all lay in the boiling sun, knowing it to be of little use to mourn over our situation.

We made all the fun possible, and ridiculed those who were so foolish as to be confined like wild beasts in cages, when at one dash they could secure their freedom and enjoy the pure air of the plains. We have a promise of repairs when we stop for noon, but do not think we can receive any till we reach the Platte, from want of timber.

The Pioneer Line arrived at the Platte River one day later. Heavy rains had increased its width so that it now covered the entire valley, from bank to bank, a distance of three miles. Its depth, however, did not exceed three feet. The train was halted for two days to rest the animals, air the baggage and provisions, and give the passengers a chance to bathe and wash their clothes. Richard Smith was buried here.

On the way to Fort Kearny on June 8, a storm once more struck with devastating force. Two carriages were overturned by the wind and one was crushed. Mules and loose stock stampeded and ran for hours, and Captain Turner was struck on the finger by a hailstone which dislocated the joint. Three inches of rain and hail came down in ten minutes. Wrote Niles:

Our only course was to turn our teams to the leeward and, in the language of the seaman, "scud before the gale." At the close of the storm we again got underway and reached the fort, glad to behold once more the residence of civilized men.

The fort was not much to look at. Formerly known as Fort Childs, established in the summer of 1847, it consisted of a few sod buildings and some tents. The original plan called for a picket wall around a long adobe building, enclosing about four acres of land. Blockhouses were to be built at two opposite corners. Mounted Missourians known as the "Oregon Battalion" camped on the site in 1847 and erected the walls for the adobe building, covering it with a brush roof. They also put up turf walls for several other buildings before returning to Missouri in the fall.

Since then the place had been occupied by two companies of mounted riflemen who had done no further building of walls or blockhouses. The sod buildings had so badly deteriorated as to afford little protection in wet weather, and the only building under construction was the hospital. No timber was available along the Platte, so progress was slow. For the present, a tent sheltered the hospital.

On May 23 and 28, two companies of the First Regiment of Dragoons arrived at the fort, now called Kearny to honor the general who had marched to California during the Mexican War. On May 29 the new commanding officer, Lieutenant Colonel B. L. E. Bonneville, arrived with Company D, Sixth Infantry. When the Pioneer Line reached Fort Kearny on June 8, Bonneville's three companies were just getting settled in their primitive quarters.

The only civilians living at the fort were a family of Mormons whose livestock had disappeared while they crossed the plains to Salt Lake in 1848. To recoup, the family opened a boarding house for emigrants. Many took advantage of this last opportunity to enjoy home-cooked food in a civilized atmosphere. Niles and Charley savored every crumb of a supper which included fresh-baked bread, butter, milk, gingerbread, doughnuts, liver, ham, and pickles.

A correspondent for the St. Louis *Republican* was keeping track of the wagons as they passed the fort. He spent a good deal of time interviewing passengers of the Pioneer Line before writing this report:

FORT KEARNY, Indian Territory, June 10. Dear Sirs: The cry is still they come—5,095 wagons at sun down last night had moved past this place toward the golden regions of California, and about 1000 more I think are still behind. . . . The Pioneer line of *fast* coaches reached here on the 8th, advertised to go through in 70 or 100 days, I forgot which—the end of one month finds them but 300 miles on the road. The passengers were loud in denouncing all fast lines and the Pioneer Line in particular. A strong feeling of discontent prevails throughout the entire company, owing entirely to the want of sufficient transportation, and the chances are thoroughly in favor of a general explosion.

The devil himself would find it difficult to give satisfaction to an incongruous crowd of 120 persons, drawn from all parts of the world and thrown together for the first time, as is the case in the Pioneer Line.

There are to be found lawyers, doctors, divines, gentlemen of leisure, clerks, speculators, &c. &c. tumbled in together and obliged to stand guard, cook victuals, bring wood and water, wash dishes, and haul wagons out of mud holes.

BUFFALO HUNT

CHAPTER 17

ROCKY MOUNTAINS
June–July 1849

*A*FTER PARTAKING OF a hearty breakfast at the Mormon house, we again took leave of civilized society," wrote Niles. "It really seemed odd to eat from a table and to hear a lady ask, 'Do you take sugar and cream in your tea?'"

The day was Saturday and the road was dry. The weather continued good on Sunday and the traveling went well. Only Charles Cranson complained of not feeling well. When on Monday it was discovered that a calculation error had left the company short of flour, a wagon was sent back to Fort Kearny to remedy the problem. Meanwhile, Cranson's complaint was diagnosed as "bilious fever," the common name for typhoid fever.

On Wednesday, June 13th, Niles noted in his journal:

A considerable uneasiness and discontent has prevailed among our passengers for several days, owing in a great measure to our slow progress. All sorts of abuse has been awarded to Captain Turner, some blaming him for not going faster, others for traveling at all during the continuance of the present bad state of the roads.

Our baggage train has been heavily laden and the unprecedented rainy weather has rendered our progress slow and toilsome. Captain Turner resolved to lighten up by destroying everything not essential to our comfort. Liquors to a large amount were turned out, and extra articles of various kind broken up, after which a meeting was called in the corral at which Captain Turner explained his views and intentions, at the same time requesting each mess to carry their bedding in their carriage till our arrival at Fort Laramie, from which point it is probable we may pack through, leaving the baggage to come on at leisure.

Niles explained the decision in a letter to Cornelia and Mary:

It was resolved that the baggage should be relieved as much as possible by the destruction of several things not necessary to our welfare—tobacco, whisky, raisins, vinegar, &c., was destroyed to a large amount, and all the little extras such as molasses, dried peaches, &c. were issued to the passengers in just such quantities as they chose to take—the consequence was we were relieved of one and a half ton of freight and have ever since lived like *nabobs*.

The mistaken notion that raisins, dried peaches and vinegar were "not necessary to our welfare" was to have tragic consequences, but not one of the ten doctors traveling with the company seemed to realize how these foods might have protected the company from scurvy. "Captain Turner's request was cheerfully acceded to," wrote Niles.

Not everyone was pleased, however. Two of the teamsters, realizing that Turner's inexperience on the trail was likely to get them into deeper trouble, walked away from the train one night and never returned. "The rats are already leaving the sinking ship," said one dissatisfied passenger.

On Friday the train halted just beyond the forks of the Platte to wait for the wagon which had been sent back for provisions. Niles and Charley decided to explore the bluffs above the valley of the South Platte. Said Niles afterward in his letter to Cornelia and Mary:

The scenery along the bluffs of the Platte are beautiful beyond description. The bottom along the river over which the road passes is usually about three or four miles in width, perfectly level, without a solitary tree except along the river. The bluff is a succession of high peaks divided by innumerable ravines, altogether forming the most romantic scenery I ever beheld.

Charley and I ascended one of these points this morning and after admiring the beautiful expanse around us for some time, engraved upon the hard surface of the chalky earth not only our own names, but also those of Cornelia D. Niles, Mary Niles, Deb Wickes, Lucia Mulford, Harriet Mulford, Polly Cook, Maria Jarvis, Harriet Rider &c. So you will perceive your name will for some time at least stand recorded on the Everlasting Hills of the Platte.

Later in the day, things went less well. Niles told most of the story to his cousins, but left out the most telling detail:

We have met with a serious loss since we encamped here. A number of us went into the bluffs to hunt buffalo and, seeing a large wolf, dismounted to load our guns, when by the accidental discharge of a rifle in the hands of a passenger, Jo (our Indian horse) was shot in the hip, and though not killed outright will, I think, either die or have to be shot, to prevent his destruction by the wolves, as it is not probable he can travel if he lives. I would almost as soon lose a friend.

To add to our mortification, just after the accident, a herd of buffalo was discovered at a short distance from us and after a short chase three of them shot. Charley and I had enough to do beside hunting and lost all the sport.

What Niles neglected to mention, both in the letter and in his journal, was the fact that the passenger who had fired the rifle was none other than his closest friend, Charley Mulford. Distraught, Charley swore that Niles should have the full use of Major from then on, but Niles refused, saying they should share the horse in the event of Jo's death.

To his cousins, Niles explained his eagerness to get a message back to the States by referring to a report which had gone out to Independence that nearly half the passengers on the Pioneer Line had died of cholera. "The fact is," he wrote, "we have lost seven men since starting"—which was literally true, although two others had died before they could start. He did not say that one of the dead men had been sharing his food and quarters until he died. "We have now reached the dry country—have no dews or rain for several days and no more cholera or sickness in camp of any kind, except one case of bilious fever—again, no mention of the fact that the single case of illness was also in his own mess.

The horse appeared much better in the morning and traveled twenty-three miles with the train. On Sunday, Niles resumed writing his letter:

It is with the utmost difficulty that we remember the recurrence of the Sabbath. Every day is pretty much the same, we travel just as much on that day as any other. Instead of the sound of the church-going bell, we are saluted with the crack of the driver's whip and the horrid oaths which are showered in volleys at the poor mules.

Our course is still up the south fork and we shall travel some thirty miles above the crossing at which [Edwin] Bryant forded in '46 before we pass over. [This year] Bryant started ten days in advance of us, at the

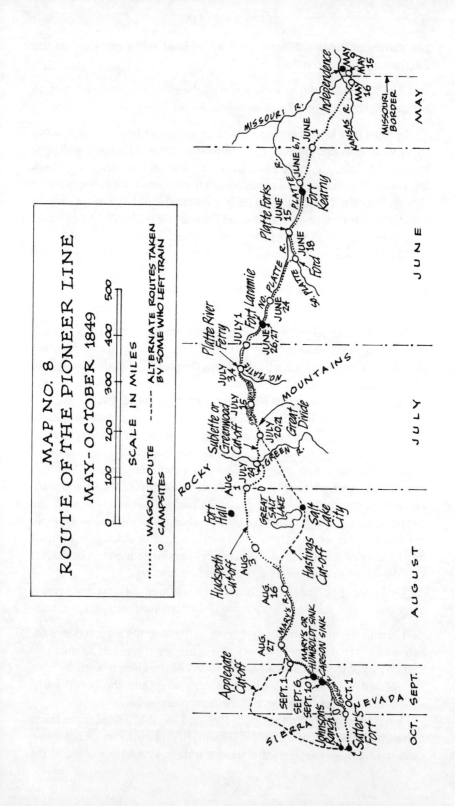

MAP NO. 8
ROUTE OF THE PIONEER LINE
MAY–OCTOBER 1849

SCALE IN MILES
0   100   200   300   400   500

—— WAGON ROUTE
○ CAMPSITES
······ ALTERNATE ROUTES TAKEN
BY SOME WHO LEFT TRAIN

MISSOURI BORDER

MISSOURI R.

Independence
MAY 9
MAY 15
MAY 16

KANSAS R.

PLATTE R.
JUNE 1
JUNE 6,7

Fort Kearny

Platte Forks
JUNE 15

Fort Laramie
JUNE 24
June 18
So. Platte Ford

No. Platte R.
JUNE 26,27
JULY 1

Platte River Ferry
JULY 3,4

NO. PLATTE

SWEETWATER
JULY 15

ROCKY
JULY 20,2

Great Divide
MOUNTAINS

Sublette or
(Greenwood)
Cut-off JULY

GREEN R.
JULY 24

Fort Hall
Aug. 1

Hudspeth Cut-off

GREAT SALT LAKE

Salt Lake City

Hastings Cut-off

AUG. 3

AUG. 16

MARY'S R.
AUG. 27

Applegate Cut-off

MARY'S OR
HUMBOLDT SINK

SEPT. 1
SEPT. 6
SEPT. 10

CARSON SINK

CARSON
OCT. 1

Johnson's Ranch

Sutter's Fort

SIERRA NEVADA

MAY   JUNE   JULY   AUGUST   SEPT.   OCT.

head of a Kentucky company with pack mules, and is now but fifty miles in advance of us, with animals nearly ruined and company on the point of mutiny—at least, such is the report brought to us by a trader. . . .

I had an exciting chase after a herd of buffalo yesterday and succeeded in wounding one, but afterwards he made good his escape. I chased them for several miles, and in the melee lost a borrowed rifle—*just like my luck!*

Niles, like many other emigrants, carried a copy of Bryant's book, *What I Saw in California,* a detailed account of his trip across the plains in 1846. That night, in his own journal, Niles wrote:

We saw four buffalo crossing the bottom towards the hills about noon, and, in company with Dr. Spears, I immediately commenced a pursuit and were soon alongside of our game. After discharging the contents of my rifle into the body of one of them without bringing him down, I dropped the gun and advanced on him again with a large rifle pistol.

Owing to the largeness of the percussion cap, it slipped from the tube and my pistol missed fire. Both of the Doctor's holsters also missed, and, after running for some distance, we finally gave up the chase. Returning to near the spot where I supposed I had left the gun, I searched in vain for it and was at length compelled to return to camp, minus buffalo and minus gun.

Upon reaching the upper ford on Monday, the company found the South Platte only about half a mile wide at this point, as compared to a mile or more at the lower crossings. The water was only about two or three feet deep and the company had little trouble in crossing, unlike the difficulties encountered by hundreds of wagons downstream.

Cranson's condition worsened at the ford. On Sunday he had begun to experience severe pains in his limbs, resembling, Niles said, a paralytic stroke. On Tuesday, his fever disappeared but the paralysis continued. Now he was delirious most of the time. Soon after thay had crossed the river and started north to meet the north fork, Cranson died.

Jo managed to keep up with the train for 107 miles, but at last, in the valley of the North Platte, he could go no farther and was left beside the river to fend for himself.

"To thus abandon an animal that had faithfully served us to the best of his powers seemed really cruel," wrote Niles, "but it was the best we could do."

"On our second day's march after striking the North Branch, we came in sight of Chimney Rock some forty miles distant," wrote Charley to

Cornelia. "Saturday evening we camped about ten o'clock within two and a half miles of it, so rising early and doing our duty in the mess, Niles and myself started to visit this curious specimen of Nature's work." Charley went on to tell of their excursion:

[Chimney Rock] is composed of a species of soft sandstone and was formerly one of the bluffs of the valley of the Platte, but the action of wind and water has separated it from the hills around. After a long and tedious ascent, we reached the chimney, or the perpendicular rock around which is a platform of rock, making a good resting place.

The whole rock is said to be three hundred feet high, the perpendicular part, or chimney, is about one hundred feet high. The chimney is covered, as high as can be reached, with the names of those passing this season. That you might say your name has visited the western wilds, I engraved the names of C. D. Niles, M. C. Niles, Maria and Deb, together with many other acquaintances, Niles and myself being engraved near them, of course. . . .

It being Sunday, we, with the assistance of a Bible and Prayer book, celebrated the day in a manner that perhaps has never been witnessed on that lone spot.

On the day before they arrived at Fort Laramie, the last storm of the year showered the company. No more rain would fall during the remainder of the trip. Fort Laramie, according to Niles, was in a "a barren, desolate region. I see nothing that looks like living except the vast amount of provisions which are thrown away by the emigrants."

Charley described the fort for Cornelia:

It is a large, square block of buildings, made of adobe, or sun dried bricks. There are four entrances, from the north, east, south and west. These open into the square. The stores and dwellings are entered from the inside of the square. The fort has been owned for a long time by the American Fur Company, but on Tuesday was bought by Uncle Sam for the round sum of four thousand dollars.

About three miles back, we witnessed for the first time the process of "lightening up," as it is termed. A large number of wagons had been burned and destroyed in various ways, and much of the contents lay around partially destroyed. It was probably the remains of goods left by companies concluding to pack through, and as nothing can be sold at the fort to advantage, was left and destroyed.

Large numbers of emigrants have provided themselves with two year's provisions and have overloaded their teams so much they are obliged to throw away or sell a large portion of their loads. Flour has been bought in large quantities at the fort at $1 per hundred lbs. Bacon, coffee, soap, from one to one and a half cents per lb. Many have thrown away large quantities of breadstuffs, guns, clothing, &c., &c.

Our train is now busily engaged in exchanging their heavy wagons for lighter ones, and disposing of all extra baggage. It is the intention of the train now to reach the diggins in sixty days, without fail. . . .

I have passed a great variety of flowers on our route, although we are too early to see the greatest display, as it has been spring, as it were, ever since I started. We have traveled and ascended just fast enough to present the same stage of vegetation nearly all the way. It has been a source of much regret that I have not been enabled to examine but few of them and to preserve none, as the duties of the mess, together with writing, employs all the time we have while in camp. I have seen some twelve or fourteen varieties of wild peas, some of them very pretty—a good many varieties of Phlox and many other flowers well known at the East. All of them are bright colored and pretty.

There was plenty of news from California, all contradictory. "One day we meet some returning emigrant who informs us to a certainty that there is no feed for our stock ahead, that there is no gold in California, that cholera is destroying the whole population, &c." Niles reported. "The next, we meet another who informs us the roads are good, good feed, good health, plenty of gold, &c., &c."

"Were gold my only object," he declared, "I think I would return even now, for I can't conceive it possible that all will obtain it in any great quantities."

No one envied David McCollum the task of writing home to Ann Arbor to reveal the tragic fate of his two younger companions, Sinclair and Cranson. To his former business partner, Jonathan H. Lund, McCollum wrote:

We started the 13th of May from 10 miles west of Independence, and arrived here this day. I have been sick two weeks with the bilious fever at Col. Grant's 10 miles west of Independence, and was well taken care of—paid $5 doctor bill and $2 per week for board and trouble, cheap enough—and my health at present is very good.

Now the news will be melancholy. C. M. Sinclair's health was good till after starting from our encampment on the 13th ult. Then he was taken sick with a liver complaint and was well taken care of for a number of days, and finally died on the 30th of May and was buried on the west bank of Vermillion River. C. C. Cranson was well and hearty until the 10th instant. He then was taken sick of bilious fever and died on the 19th instant, and was buried about four miles east of Ash Hollow and about

530 miles west of Independence. I am alone in the journey except strangers. . . .

Dr. Ormsby is encamped but a short distance from us. He has sold his wagon and intends to pack his mules for the balance of the journey. They are all well. . . . Our train will continue to proceed with wagons clear through, if possible. I ride about two-thirds of the time and walk the balance. We go from 10 to 28 miles per day and make the best of it. The journey is long and fatiguing and the Lord only knows when we shall get through, should we live and have our health. . . .

The property of Sinclair and Cranson must be sold, and will bring but a trifle. I have all they left in my possession and shall do the best I can with it and pay over to their friends if I live to return. I have not heard anything from home later than the time Dr. Ormsby left. As for gold, I cannot tell whether I shall get any or not. I have endured hunger and thirst—heat and cold, wet and dry, and look more like an Indian than a white man. My hands are the color of brown mud and rougher than a hemlock board.

I have written to Wm. M. Sinclair and E. Cranson, and shall put them in the fort, and the Capt. says they will start for Independence by the 4th of next month.

Caleb Ormsby, a pioneer Michigan physician who began his practice in 1824, had come from Ann Arbor a week or two after McCollum, Sinclair and Cranson. He had lived in that place since 1835, since which time, instead of practising medicine he had gone into business. An unsuccessful candidate for Congress under the banner of the Free Soil Party in 1848, he was on his way to California to recoup recent financial losses. He, like McCollum, was considerably older than most of the emigrants in 1849.

On June 30th, the day after the departure from Fort Laramie of the Pioneer Line, Caleb Ormsby wrote home to his wife:

We have here finally resolved to pack. Four of us have eight good animals. We shall ride four and pack four. The object is to reach California with the least possible delay. The change must necessarily lead to a great sacrifice, taking with us what is barely sufficient to get us through. The rest we sacrifice, or nearly so.

The wagon I sold for $35. This was considered a remarkable fortunate sale. I sold to the Pioneer train, and had I not of met with that opportunity, it is not likely that I could have got half that price for it. Many are sold at from $5 to $20 and many are left by the road side. . . .

I have just returned from the Fort (2 miles distant). I there visited Mr. Hodge, the sick man from Jackson. . . . Near him I saw a man stretched on a couch in another small tent. I enquired of a woman at the tent what the trouble was.

"Why, sir, a wagon ran over his head; we thought he was dead, but he seems to be some better."

He was her husband. . . .

Leaving them, I called on Capt. Perry, who said, "Within the last hour another emigrant has been brought into the hospital, shot to pieces—three emigrants now laying in the hospital from gun shot wounds." A few days since a woman had her head run over by the wheel of a wagon, but by some fortunate depression in the ground she escaped with life.

A man was killed by the accidental discharge of a gun in the hand of his friend—another shot intentionally by his mess mate. The murderer afterwards came into our company and wished to travel with it, doubtless thinking he had got ahead of the report, but I happened to have wind of it—suspected him—charged him with murder—he owned it, mounted his horse and put forward.

A man was killed by the fall of his horse in pursuit of a buffalo—and so on and so on, a constant scene of disaster. But all this is nothing compared to the havoc that has been made by cholera, a regular line of graves mark the course of the emigrants of 49. . . .

The Pioneer Line had not gone far past the fort when Niles heard someone call out his name. Turning, he recognized Clinton Bledsoe, a friend from Lafayette County, Missouri. He was heading back to Laramie with three badly injured men, all Missourians whom Niles had met. A pack horse whose load had slipped ran away from his owner and caused some oxen to stampede, and the men had been run over by the wagons. Two, Henry Bledsoe and James Walton, were so badly injured that it appeared impossible they could survive. The chances for Thomas Seawell were only slightly better. Clint was taking them to the fort hospital, after which he would hasten to rejoin his company, now far advanced along the trail.

That night, for the first time, the passengers slept under bright stars which illuminated the skies over the Black Hills. To save weight the company, counting on good weather for the remainder of the trip, had abandoned all its tents at Fort Laramie. The days were hot and dry now, but at night heavy dew formed on the men's blankets. Although Niles discovered that it felt pleasant and invigorating to sleep in the open, he worried that it might prove to be an unhealthy practice.

Grass was very scarce. What little there would have been in normal times had been taken by the faster-moving trains. After traveling out of sight of the Platte for a few days, they returned to its banks to cross, and found it to be ten to twelve feet deep. Ferrying was the only practical method of crossing; Niles described the technique:

Emigrants are crossing from a short distance below us to a point thirty miles above, at every place practicable. The usual method is to prepare some two or three "Dug Outs," pin them together by means of cross timbers, thus forming a kind of scow capable of carrying a wagon. The builders, after crossing, sell out to some other company who, in turn do the same to a succeeding one.

Our company has purchased two of these rude machines, one near us and one two miles below. The carriages will proceed to the lower ferry in the morning and cross, while the baggage train does the same here. By thus passing over at once, we hope to steal a march on a large portion of those waiting on the south bank, the number of which within thirty miles is estimated even as high as two thousand wagons. . . .

From the bank of [Deer] creek some of the messes procured a supply of coal, which when ignited seemed to burn freely. We shall ferry the river tomorrow, and also endeavor to exhibit our patriotism in some degree, sufficient at least to show we have not forgotten the "Glorious 4th."

On the same night, close by, John Evans Brown and his friends slept in the hills near their mules, to protect them from Indians. Brown noted "Six trains were in sight and all night our ears were deafened by reports of guns and pistols fired in celebration of the coming day." In the morning, Captain Turner graciously allowed Brown's smaller company to cross on his ferry. Niles Searls recorded the holiday in his journal:

July 4th—The day was ushered in by the discharge of fire arms in all directions. Everyone was astir betimes and for all I could see, the hurrahing was very much the same as in the States. After breakfast we hitched up and rolled down to the ferry, but had to wait till 1 o'clock P.M. before the boat was at liberty.

Charley improved the time by preparing a 4th of July dinner. Fresh fish, peach pies, &c, were among the constituents of the repast. At 1 o'clock the cloth was laid—Yes, *cloth,* for this time we spread a large piece of canvas upon the ground upon which we placed our dinner. If the viands were not equally rich with those enjoyed by our friends in the States, they were at least enjoyed with quite as much zest.

We have passed the day with reading, chatting, feasting and telling stories. The wagons were not all passed over till 11 o'clock at night, but was at last completed without any accident, though we were near being sunk by overloading the boat with passengers.

The celebration was continued by a few till near morning.

Five days later, on the evening of July 9, the company enjoyed an unusual treat: several ladies, members of a nearby train, entertained the men with a choral concert. The morning, however, brought sobering news: the wagonmasters threatened to leave the train unless immediate and radical changes were made. Some of the passengers were said to be ready to join them.

According to them, the mules still were overloaded. Because of the difficulty of finding grazing, it was doubtful how much longer the animals could hold out. For several days' march, dead oxen had strewn the road. In one place Niles saw eight in a single pile. "A blind man might find his way by the odor," said someone.

Upon reaching the Sweetwater Valley and a good supply of grass, the train halted and the company held a meeting. Colonel William H. Rumsey was elected to head a committee to consider alternatives and report back with recommendations before the day was out. Niles recorded the result:

After an absence of a couple of hours they returned, and the meeting being called to order and Col. Rumsey in the chair, resolutions to the following effect were offered:

(1) That the baggage of each passenger be reduced to seventy-five pounds, including arms, ammunition, bedding, &c.;

(2) That the number of passenger carriages be reduced to twelve;

(3) That a committee of five be appointed to associate with Captain Turner in taking supervision of the train and recommending such measures as they from time to time may think proper;

(4) That Mr. Campbell be allowed four mules of his present team and withdraw from the train.

The resolutions were accepted. On the next day the discarding of baggage began:

Trunks were opened, their contents scattered on the ground. The most choice articles packed in bags and the residue left in confusion upon the ground or carried off by immigrants encamped around us. Law and medical books, ammunition, merchandise, clothing—whatever exceeded the weight limit and was deemed not vital to survival was tossed to one side.

Our teamsters and Mexican herdsmen were soon arrayed in the cast off finery of their unfortunate fellow travelers. To look upon the profuse destruction of property was enough to cause a sigh.

They now were part of a larger mess with ten members. In addition to themselves and "Squire" McCollum of the old Mess 17, there was Fred Pearks, who had joined them at Fort Laramie after "Yankee" Eastman withdrew (to join another mess), Robert Brogdon, Doctor Hutton, Horace Gouth, William Ware, Mr. Bierce, and Mr. Royer.

Soon after the new mess was formed, McCollum began complaining of diarrhea, and he continued to be sick for several days. Finally he was found to have such a high fever on July 17 that Niles volunteered to ride back a few miles to get Dr. Spears, who was tending to a patient. After treatment, McCollum began to improve, although he was unable to sit up for a day or two.

When they crossed the summit, it was hard to believe that the smooth road over which they were passing was actually the "Great Divide" of the Rocky Mountains. But soon a decision would have to be made— should they follow the old route to Fort Hall or take Greenwood's cut-off over the desert and save sixty miles? After much angry debate, it was decided to take the shorter trail. Unfortunately, the leaders were reading Joseph Ware's newly published *Emigrants' Guide to California,* which called the cut-off "Sublette's" and estimated the width of the desert as thirty-five miles without wood or water. But Ware had never seen the desert, much less traveled it.

Had they consulted Bryant, they would have read that "from Big Sandy to Green river, a distance of forty-five or fifty miles, there is no water." Bryant was sure, for he had been there. But Niles's copy of Bryant had long since been discarded to make room for more important baggage. His journal tells the result:

July 23d—Were called at 1 Oclock A.M. to prepare for our march across the desert before us, and before daylight were on the march. The road was excellent, with a level country, and by 11 Oclock we encamped to rest our animals, having made 20 miles of the journey, and as we supposed, with only 15 before us to Green River.

After traveling some 12 miles, Charley discovered he had left his revolver and Bowie knife at the last camp, and returned with the horse to recover them. He will not overtake us before tomorrow.

As we proceeded onward, the plain became an entire mass of loose shifting sand. The wind commenced blowing a gale about noon, driving clouds of burning sand directly in our faces. The heat was intense. Sunburned as we are by exposure, I observed the faces of many of our passengers blistered by the heat.

Having been much on foot, we were all fatigued long before night. Our water was exhausted, but still we expected, on mounting every hill, to behold the river. Thus we toiled on till the golden sun sank behind the western horison. The mules began to exhibit signs of exhaustion, and some were taken from the harness, unable to go farther and haul their loads.

As if to render our progress more difficult, we now approached deep ravines into which the trail descended by precipitous roads, and again ascended by ways equally difficult and dangerous. In descending into one of these ravines, Reed, a driver, was thrown from his saddle mule, the wagon passing over him and injuring him severely.

[Reed being] unable to drive his team, I volunteered to take his place, and for the first time attempted to drive an eight mule team. At 10 PM we had come, according to our computation, upwards of 40 miles, yet no signs of any river were found. It was apparent that our guide books were erroneous in regard to the distance, and in consequence of their blunder, we were compelled to pass the night without food for man or beast, and undergo the parching thirst incurred during the march till our arrival at the point which we expected to reach this night.

The mules were no sooner liberated than their natural instinct became apparent by their making off in the direction of the river. They were with difficulty forced back and closely corraled till morning. For my part, tired and disappointed, I threw myself upon the ground and was soon dreaming of home and absent friends. Distance 45 miles.

July 24th—A more woebegone looking set of fellows than emerged from camp this morning could not easily be found. Some satisfied the cravings of appetite by eating raw bacon, thereby adding tenfold to their thirst, but the majority preferred waiting breakfast till we reached the river.

The wagons were let down several long hills by means of drag ropes, and, by the united assistance of men and mules, hauled to Green River, a distance of 7 miles, making in all, 52 miles from Big Sandy. Had the authors of our guide books been along during the last few miles, I fear they would have paid dearly for their ignorance.

The sight of the river, however, a fine swift stream descending from the snow covered mountains on our right, and a hearty draught at its brink soon soothed our perturbed feelings and revived our spirits. The channel contains from six to ten feet of water, and is crossed by a ferry established by some Mormons from Salt Lake.

The terms for ferrying are $2 per wagon, and from 60 to 75 are crossed per day. The stream is lined with wagons waiting to recruit their teams after the unexpected drive. Charley came in about noon, having rode nearly all night. We were all safely ferried over by sunset and shall remain a day or two. Distance 7 miles.

CALIFORNIA TRAIL

CHAPTER 18

GREAT DESERT
July–October 1849

*A*NYONE WITH THE ABILITY to solve simple arithmetical problems could have demonstrated how the Pioneer Line would fail. It was all there in the numbers: Since leaving Independence they had traveled for eleven weeks and gone half the distance to California. When they left Fort Laramie four weeks earlier, they carried provisions for eight and a half weeks. If they continued to travel at the same speed for the second half of the journey, it would take eleven more weeks. If they continued to eat at the same rate, they would exhaust the provisions in four and a half weeks. Theoretically, they could complete the trip if they increased their speed by 50 percent and cut their rations by an equal amount.

The trouble with the theory was soon apparent. The food hadn't been rationed soon enough. At Soda Springs (August 2) the last of the coffee and sugar was given to the passengers. Two weeks later, nothing remained for the men to eat but flour and rancid bacon. And no one had the slightest idea how much grass and water was available for the mules, which would have to work harder to move the train faster.

Of the original six-man mess to which Niles and Charley had belonged, only three men still lived. John "Yankee" Eastman died on the last day of July—of "consumption of the lungs." Niles found it too exhausting to write in his journal every night, so he made notes once a week. The Pioneer Line covered 146 miles during the week ending August 5. The following week netted another 110. Niles described a typical day:

Left camp on Reeds Creek early Monday morning, pursuing a south-westerly direction over the broken range of mountains bordering on the northern rim of the Great Basin. Under the scorching influence of a torrid sun we threaded our way, vainly seeking for vegetation and water by which to rest at noonday.

On, on, we journeyed, hoping as we toiled up each steep ascent to find the cherished object of our desires in the next valley. The orb of light reached his meridian and sank low in the western heaven without respite from travel. Already had we reached the point at which report said was a limpid stream. In the place of cooling waters we found the parched bed of a mountain torrent, without a particle of aught beside.

Around were the jaded teams of numberless emigrants who, like ourselves, had hoped to find repose from travel. Women bewailing their hard fate and helpless children crying for water form no pleasant theme for my notes, therefore I dwell not upon this subject.

I determined to walk forward till we reached water. Darkness brought no hope of rest, and till 11 o'clock PM we continued our journey, over a region devoid of all interest. Straying a short distance from the road, I threw myself upon the ground, determined to indulge the forgetfulness of repose. On rousing from slumber, I pursued my way with no companion but my revolver, and no certainty when I should rejoin the company.

At 3 AM I found them encamped by a beautiful spring of pure water. The journey of a day illustrates that of a week. We have traversed Goose Creek Valley and are now encamped in the valley of a nameless stream which sinks in the sands of the desert.

Artist James Wilkins, traveling slightly behind them, heard on August 8 that the Pioneers were just ahead, with animals in "poor condition." But not only the animals suffered. Wrote Niles:

Our men are becoming emaciated and querulous. Luxuries in the way of foods are among the things to memory dear. Rancid bacon with the grease fried out by the hot sun, musty flour, a little pinoles and some sacks of pilot bread, broken and crushed to dust and well coated with alkali, a little coffee without sugar—now constitutes our diet.

The men need more and must have it or perish. Yet at our present rate of progress, even these supplies must fail long before we can reach

California. . . . The men know we must all inevitably starve unless relieved, and yet feel like cutting the throat of him who would remind them of it. The thought is not invigorating, 'tis true; yet with health we can and will reach the goal of our desires, the Mecca of our hopes! Upon a hundred and fifty skeletons of mules, we can subsist long enough to scale the great barrier in our way . . .

But what of the sick? How are they to be cared for when the emergency arrives and, disorganized as we must inevitably become, each seeks his own safety? God only knows what fate awaits them. . . . We have discussed the question of dividing the train and pushing ahead with the sick and such others as choose to walk, leaving the heavy wagons and remainder of the men to come on at a slower pace, but as usual cannot agree upon any course of action, hence I conclude we shall go on as before.

Teamster W. Maxwell of the Pioneers, who had contracted and recovered from cholera on the Platte, now came down with scurvy and died on August 24. The rest of the company made it to Lassen's Meadow, where the main trail headed south and a side trail, known as the Applegate or Lassen Trail, took off to the west. The latter was said to be a shorter route, but no one knew for sure. But, as Niles said, "it at least affords a change and inspires hope." A guide was sent ahead to examine the route.

Charley is down with fever and needs unremitting care or I should now leave the train in company with a number who, on foot, turn to the west by what is termed a cut-off. . . . Fred Pearks and Bob Brogdon of our mess are preparing their packs to try it. It seems like leaving the ship and taking to the boats, but were Charley able to go, I should chance it. It seems hard to part with the old friends with whom we have toiled for so many weary miles . . .

Meanwhile, the company busied itself cutting grass and making hay for the animals. More and more of the wagons from other companies were turning on to the Applegate cut-off. Niles and Charley decided to send a message to their friends, choosing Addison for their correspondent and selecting their words with care:

Mary's [Humboldt] River August 31st 49

Cousin Addison

The far famed Pioneer Line "through in sixty days" arrived at this point (80 miles above the sink) last night after a rough passage of 110 days. We are about to leave the river and turn to the right across a barren desert of from 60 to 70 miles in extent and are laying up to cut grass for the subsistence of our stock across.

By taking this route we shorten the distance very materially, being enabled to strike the head of the Sacramento in 200 miles. Three members of our mess will leave this morning on foot and expect to reach the settlements some ten days before us. As we have already been out much longer than we expected, I avail myself of this opportunity of sending a line to allay any anxiety that may be felt on our account.

In the few moments allowed me for writing, I can say but little except that Charley and I are O.K. and have enjoyed the trip admirably. We left Fort Laramie June 28th and were till the last of July in reaching the pass. This slow progress was occasioned principally by the want of grass for the animals. We were compelled to throw away about half our baggage in order to save the rest and prevent being left on foot. Since leaving the "pass" we have made rather better time and though often nearly out of provision, we have always succeeded in getting supplies from emigrants who had plenty.

We know exactly what it is to live on half rations and to endure all the privations and fatigues incidental to the plains. We have had no rain, not even a decent shower since leaving Laramie. The whole country traversed has been a barren, trackless waste, with the exception of the river valleys, along which there is usually a little grass.

Dust, dust, dust, has been the order of the day, and unless that article can be turned to account, I would not give 25 cents for all the country passed over.

We have had but very little sickness in camp for the last ten hundred miles. I have taken no medicine and have not been sick a day since leaving the States. We are all anxious to terminate the journey as soon as possible. . . . As it will be some time before I get where I can write home, I wish it would not be asking too much that you would drop a line to my father informing them where I am, that I am well, &c. Charley spoke of writing before the boys started, but I do not think he will have time.

I think we shall be about from fifteen to twenty days in getting through. Our mules are pretty nearly used up and our progress over the Sierra Nevadas will be slow. You need not be uneasy if you do not hear from us again in a month, as we may stop in the diggins awhile before going farther. We hear from California every few days by emigrants returning to the states. Of course, you know more of the news from that region than we, so I will say nothing of the various reports that meet us.

The accumulated love of nearly four months to Cornelia and Mary and all sorts of fine things to all the friends

Yours in haste

Niles Searls

He had offered the excuse about Charley in case he were too ill to write, but Mulford summoned up enough energy to pen a single page:

80 miles from the Sink of Mary's River
California August 31 1849

Cousin Add,

Niles has been writing for a few minutes past and I too had intended to give my friends a short epistle, but as matters have turned it must now be very short, for want of time.

Niles has of course told you all about our doings and travels since we last wrote—if not, we will do so soon on our arrival in the "land of promise"—You will please tell Nella and Molly it will not be long before they will hear from me—I had also intended to have given Robert a line or two, but time prevents—

We have enjoyed excellent health during our journey, and aside from being much longer on the road than we have expected, it has proved a very pleasant trip—we are now 180 miles from the headwaters of the Sacramento and shall probably reach Sutters Fort in about 20 days—remember me to all friends, not forgetting to reserve to yourself a share of the kind regards of your cousin

Chas. W. Mulford

After the men set off on foot, their guide returned with an unfavorable account of the cut-off. Because of the company's rapidly deteriorating condition, it was decided to continue south to the sink of Mary's River. At the sink the thermometer registered 140 degrees. "I never felt the heat till now," despaired Niles. "The whole atmosphere glows like an oven. The water is bitter and nauseous. Off to the southwest, as far as the eye can extend, nothing appears but a level desert. This we must cross!"

They traveled only at night now. On the following day while resting in the desert, Niles began to run a fever and the day took on a dreamlike character. At sunset they moved out again, but at 3 A.M. they were mired in deep sand.

It soon became apparent that they were going no farther. The animals fell to the ground, exhausted and unable to free the wagons. Some would never rise again—others were released from harness and allowed to head for the Carson River, some ten or more miles distant. The sick men remained in the wagons, tended by friends, while those who could walk followed the mules to the river.

Now it was Charley, recovered from his own illness, who took care of Niles. He and many others had come down with scurvy. James Wilkins caught up with their wagons about dusk on September 10:

... we came up with the Pioneer wagons left on the road, their mules being unable to drag them further. They had taken [the mules] out, and drove them on to the river to recruit. The passengers, those that were able, walked on, but there were a great many sick, and unable to walk. These had to stay with nothing but salt water to drink; amongst them a Mr. James was expected to die with the scurvy. They, like us, had nothing left but bread and bacon, and for these they were indebted to the ox teams on the road. Three dollars a pint was offered for vinegar.

A soft, heavy, deep sand commenced here, and continued to the river (about 10 miles), thro which our horses laboured severely. We sighed for our cattle, and judging from the smell which saluted our nostrils every few minutes, for it was dark, they must have lain pretty thick on the ground.

Here we met Turner going back with a few mules to fetch one of his wagons containing those most severely sick. About 10 O'clock we arrived at the river and found the Pioneer passengers asleep around an immense log fire, for here are actually some large cottonwood trees, the first we had seen since leaving the settlements. We toasted a slice of bacon and eat a cracker that we had brought with us, and lay down beside the fire to sleep. I did not rest much, it being too cold, but got up and sat by the fire till morning.

Meanwhile, Royer had brought several canteens full of water back to the sick passengers and their companions. When Captain Turner arrived with eight of his best mules, they were harnessed to a single wagon containing all of the invalids. Slowly, the last contingent of the Pioneer Line made its way over the desert to the sink of the Carson. Here they camped for almost two weeks, endeavoring to prepare themselves and their mules for the assault on the Sierra Nevada, last obstacle between them and California.

On the 15th of September Mr. James died of scurvy. Captain Turner offered $500 to anyone who would fetch in his three provision wagons. They were in sand up to their axles, sixteen miles out on the desert. No emigrant train could or would try. Either they lacked the teams, or were unwilling to risk losing those they had.

Turner and Allen had planned the California expedition based upon their experience in the Mexican War. They had been attached to the army on its second expedition to Chihuahua, in charge of a large number of wagons. Wilkins commented that it was being remarked among the emigrants "that a man may have traveled to Santa Fe and Chiwawa, and yet derive no information necessary for a trip to California."

Ironically Allen, who had taken the extra mules and wagons back to

Independence to outfit a second train, now was only a short distance behind Turner's group. Augustus Garrett, a passenger with the first train, told Wilkins that Turner was offering $3000 to anyone who would take his receipts and pay his expenses for the trip. Turner claimed he had done all a reasonable man could to provide for the comfort of his passengers, and had purchased additional provisions from emigrants "at enormous prices."

William Ware and Horace Gouth left the train, as did many others. So many of the able-bodied passengers were taking off on foot or horseback that Wilkins remarked, "[Turner's] loads will be light from this onward and I think he will get through." Only five men were left in the mess to which Charley and Niles now belonged. Only Charley was not disabled. Hutton, McCollum, and Niles were down with scurvy, and Mr. Royer was sickening with what shortly proved to be the same thing.

But Turner could not afford to wait any longer. On September 24 the pathetic caravan began to wend its way through the Carson River canyon. Six days later the tired survivors rested near a snow bank high in the Sierra Nevada. Niles wrote:

September 30th—I breathe more freely. We have traversed the Carson River to the mouth of the worst canyon opening into the valley, and that, of course, we turned into to find our way to the summit. For eight miles we literally climbed and hauled the wagons by ropes and mules over the jagged rocks, which in places were higher than the wagons. . . . At the west of the canyon, we emerged into Hope Valley—rested a day, and then spent another in getting to the first summit and were caught in a storm of sleet by which forty mules were frozen to death. . . .

I am deathly sick, and must get better soon or play Moses by looking at the Promised Land and never entering therein. Hutton is dying. Royer is down with scurvy, and a score of others are showing the effects of starvation or, what answers the same purpose, the effects of spoiled provisions that do not nourish.

Judging from the effect of scurvy on others, I am good for about three weeks—and then—and then—Well, at the end of a week if no better progress is made, I will, if able, confiscate a mule and ride for life.

October 1st—The summit is crossed! We are in California!

Colonel Rumsey came alongside Niles and pointed to the hazy out-lines of the Sacramento Valley in the far distance.

"Niles," he said quietly. "There is the goal of our ambition, the end of our enterprise. Somewhere out there lie all our hopes."

"The only hope I have is that I shall stay alive long enough to get to

Sutter's Fort," replied Niles, smiling wanly at the older man. Colonel William Rumsey, six feet tall and ruggedly built, had taken a fatherly interest in Niles early in the trip. He often invited Niles and Charley to ride and hunt beside him, which pleased the younger men, for Rumsey was respected and admired by everyone in the company.

"Where's Charley?" asked the Kentucky veteran.

"Up here, Colonel!" called Mulford. "I'm engraving a few names on this rock — the members of the Rensselaerville Young Ladies' Reading Society!"

"Well, come on down. We've got to get moving—the others have almost left us behind."

In the two weeks it took to reach Sutter's Fort, Doctor Hutton and three others died. A fourth man died at the fort, and Royer died soon after. The rest survived.

They were amazed when they saw the incredible tent city which had grown up along the river, two miles from Sutter's Fort. Charley, Niles, and David McCollum set up their tent among the others at Sacramento City. On October 20, 1849, a few days after their arrival, McCollum wrote to his old partner in Ann Arbor:

Nearly half the passengers in the Pioneer Line, by which I came, have had the scurvy, and four have died with it, and many on arriving here cannot walk or stand, and but few of us are really healthy or able to work at present . . .

Upwards of one-sixth of our number, who left Independence in good health, have died on the road. But the mess to which I belonged suffered the worst . . .

The land for thirty miles to this place is of the choicest quality, but poorly timbered and watered and rain does not touch it frequently for six months. The river is full of vessels of all kinds within forty rods of where I now sit writing this letter on my knees under a large oak. This place contains say 5000 persons, and the houses are mostly little light frames or posts set in the ground and covered with cloth. All kinds of provisions are very high. . . .

But you may ask, how I live? I will tell you: there are three of us who have a tent made out of 2 old wagon covers, and we purchase provisions and board ourselves, cook, wash and bake at a cost of about 8s each per day. We are all some unwell, and are trying to recruit our strength, and then do something, or try and get home again: which may God grant as a great favor!

The Gold Diggings are from 30 to 100 miles in all directions. Some are making money digging and some are losing. The truth is, it takes a hardy man to dig and get an ounce a day, and on an average they do not get that. Although now and then a man makes his *jack* in a month or two, but such instances are rare. I advise all men to stay at home and not come here. . . .

Wages are high here for mechanics and hard laboring men. Chopping wood $6 per cord, but out of the tops of great oaks with long heavy crooked limbs, and many cannot chop over one or one and a half cords per day. Mowing and curing hay and putting it in cock $16 per ton. Carpenters from $10 to $14 per day. Labor of all kinds when wanted 8s per hour; but a person wants steady employment. Clerks in stores, more applicants than any other kind, and but few wanted, every man doing his own business.

Doctors plenty, say every tenth man a doctor. Lawyers enough. But above all trades here give me the bakers'—they coin money. A pie they sell for 75 cents, a loaf of bread 50, and one small card of ginger-bread for 75 cents. Liquors high, and much drank at 2s a drink. Gambling of all kinds—high and low. But I have not heard of a theft yet in this place. Should a man be caught stealing he surely would be hanged, and all know it. Property is more exposed about their canvass houses and tents and lying in the streets day and night, than ever I saw it in any other place, and still nothing taken.

Niles wrote to Cornelia a week after McCollum penned those words. His letter was eight pages long and told in detail the story of the trek from Lassen's Meadow to Sacramento City, including his bout with scurvy. Said Niles:

. . . the scurvy had taken advantage of my defenceless state to pounce upon me. I looked upon it as a *scurvy trick,* but submitted with the best grace possible. I was able to hop about and drive the carriage till we reached the first ridge of the Sierra Nevadas, in ascending which I worked too hard and used myself up completely.

A precious road we had over the mountains, I can assure you. Driving a wagon from G. Conkling's woolen factory to the top of the "Falls" over the bed of the stream would be easy compared with the road by which we ascended the mountains.

When within about thirty or forty miles of the settlements two of our party came forward and brought back a few onions, two of which I succeeded in purchasing at the rate of one dollar each. On our arrival here we found that vegetable food in any quantities could not be had at Hotels and boarding houses, even at the most exorbitant rates, so we pitched a tent in the shade of some wide spreading Oaks, retained our mess utensils and went to living on our own hook.

Beside Charles and I, we have Mr. McCollum of Mich., a middle aged man who has messed with us from the beginning of our travels . . . I hope soon to be in condition to undertake business of some kind. . . . Charles has just engaged for a month as bookkeeper for a firm in town. Salary of 150 and boarded. . . .

I attended religious service this morning for the first time since leaving the states. No churches are completed as yet in Sacramento, but the extended grove offers room enough for religious exercise. . . . Charley has just put away the dinner dishes and laid down in the tent to rest a short time before going to Church. Mack is reading the new constitution of the "State of California" aloud. . . .

Around us are tents scattered through the grove in which the city is built, and canvas houses of all sorts and sizes. The whole town has sprung up within a few months and though containing several thousand inhabitants and doing an incredible amount of business, is yet in its infancy and presents a ragged, hurly-burly appearance.

It is two weeks ago today since we entered town and I need not add that after a journey of upwards of five months, we were glad to reach our point of destination. Had the trip been prolonged for a few weeks longer, a large number, and I among them would have found our graves in the mountains. When we arrived here, I was unable to walk without assistance, and though I have improved rapidly ever since, still I can't walk without limping slightly in one trotter. . . .

Charley met with a Dr. Baldwin who formerly studied with Dr. Lay in Rensselaerville it seems. He has been to the mines, but found it too hard work and has now gone to San Francisco. Robinson, formerly of R Ville, we hear has arrived, but we have not seen him. Of Wm. Williams we have heard nothing.

CHAPTER 19

NEW CAREERS

June 1848–October 1849

I

*T*ALLMAN ROLFE left San Francisco with Ed Kemble and John Yates on June 14, 1848. The trio disembarked from the old whaleboat a week later at Sutter's embarcadero on the Sacramento River. At the fort, they went first to Sam Brannan's store to tell him what they had done. Kemble was somewhat apprehensive, but Sam wasn't surprised to hear they had stopped publishing the *Star* to go to the mines.

"But I'll tell you one thing, boys," he said. "Don't waste your time on the American River."

They all stared at him in amazement.

"But Sam," said Tallman. "Isn't that where all the gold mines are?"

"The early ones, yes—but it's so overcrowded along the river that there's not nearly enough room for everyone who's come. There are too many miners and not enough space!"

"Where would you suggest we go?"

"North. North to the Yuba and Feather rivers. I hear there's just as much gold up there as on the American, and a lot fewer miners. But it won't last, so get there right early. By the time the others arrive, you'll have made your pile."

The three quickly conceded the wisdom of Brannan's counsel, and with his help began to pick out the supplies they would need.

II

JONAS SPECT, formerly of Pennsylvania, Ohio, Missouri and Oregon, was sailing down the coast from Astoria when Marshall discovered gold particles in the sawmill's tailrace near Coloma. Spect hadn't heard much about it until he was about to return to the States by the overland trail. He and a friend who was going with him decided to take a quick side trip to Sutter's Mill to see what was going on.

They arrived in time to see the sawmill begin cutting logs, and they watched some of the miners working in the river and along its banks. Because Sutter and Marshall claimed ownership of all the land near the mill, they charged rent for each mining claim. This rent, set against only fair to mediocre mining luck, was resulting in net gains that did not much impress Spect and his friend. It seemed to them that most men were averaging no better than $2.50 per day.

The two men said goodbye to Marshall and continued to Johnson's Ranch, the agreed-upon meeting place for the company which was to cross the plains together. At Johnson's they waited for two weeks and only one more person arrived. Everyone came to the same conclusion: the trip was off, the participants having been lured away by promises of gold. Spect's friend headed for the American River to try his luck, but Jonas stayed at the ranch and persuaded Bill Johnson to go with him on a prospecting tour of the Bear River.

They passed the area where Doctor Gildea and young Ben Bonney had spent the day collecting flakes to fill a bottle. They stood in the place where Gutiérrez showed samples to Bidwell. For three days Spect and Johnson splashed around in the stream, but in the end, both came back to the ranch with empty pockets.

Spect thought their failure had something to do with the size of the stream—it was smaller than the American. In fact, it was so much smaller that most folks called it "Bear Creek." Spect argued that the Yuba would be more likely to produce comparable results, but because Johnson's wife, the former Mary Murphy, had left him to obtain a divorce, he was unwilling to go off and leave everything in the hands of his Indians. As an alternative, he offered to outfit Spect and furnish an Indian to do the labor, if they could mine on shares. Jonas agreed.

He and the *nisenan* servant arrived on the Yuba on the first of June. They worked for several hours before anything promising turned up. The next day was the same, a few flakes here and a few more there, but never enough to satisfy hope; certainly not enough to pay for provisions. Then, late in the day, Spect found three small nuggets. It wasn't much, but it was enough to raise his spirits.

Having discovered that certain supplies had been overlooked, he sent the Indian back to the ranch to fetch them and set up his camp for a more extended visit. In the morning, while searching for additional evidence of a "strike," Jonas encountered two local ranchers who were prospecting along a nearby creek. One was Michael Nye, the other William Foster.

They exchanged greetings and soon were exchanging information, for all had lived in Missouri before coming to California. Nye had come with John Bidwell in 1841. Six years later he bought some land from Sutter near the joining of the Yuba and Feather rivers and was raising cattle for a living. He and Foster had come to the river to see if any of the gold might be close enough at hand for them to profit by it.

Foster, whose ranch adjoined Nye's, came to California in 1846 and was trapped in the mountains with the Reed-Donner party. With him were the three Murphy sisters, Harriet, Sarah, and Mary. Foster had killed and eaten two Indians sent by Sutter to aid them. Sarah was Foster's wife, Harriet had married Nye, and now Mary was the estranged child-bride of Jonas Spect's partner, Bill Johnson.

Other ex-Missourians arrived on the Yuba a few days later. A party from Benicia included the Long brothers, Willis and Doctor John, and the well-known rancher, John Marsh. Back in Independence, Marsh had run a general store in the 1830s, and his customers included Michael Nye, Lillburn Boggs, and Johann Sutter. Marsh had left Missouri and come to California three years before Sutter, telling the Mexican authorities he was a physician. When Nye and Bidwell came to California in 1841, they traveled first to Marsh's ranch at the foot of Mount Diablo. Although well known, Marsh was not well liked, at least by some, Bidwell among them. The feeling, one gathered, was mutual. Fortunately, Bidwell was mining on the Feather, not the Yuba River, and so things ran smoothly.

By mid-June the temperature was rising day by day and soon the sand and rocks were so hot that John Long's dog refused to walk across them to the river. He waited till the sun went down before venturing to the water's edge to drink. More and more miners began coming to the Yuba. Now the area near the tent of John and Willis Long was being referred to as "Long's Bar"—later it would be called simply "Long" Bar, and people would come to think it named for its size. During the summer of 1848 everyone called the adjacent camp "Marsh's diggings," but that name didn't stick.

When Tallman Rolfe, Edward Kemble, and John Yates arrived, they were disappointed to find the river canyon swarming with activity. Again they took counsel.

"What do you think?" asked Kemble. "Shall we stop here, or keep going north?"

"I favor going north, if you mean by that the Feather River," said Tallman. "I'd like to see what Bidwell is doing up there."

"Why don't we stop here first, at least for a day or two, and see what we can learn about mining?" suggested Yates. "I don't know about the two of you, but I'm very ignorant about the entire process!" His companions approved his idea.

They soon observed that everyone used the same tools: pick, shovel, and gold pan. It was obvious what the pick and shovel were for. Less obvious was the use of the pan, which was shallow, flat-bottomed, and slope-sided. Watching, they saw a miner fill his pan with sand and gravel dug from beside the river. He walked into the stream, squatted in the shallow water at the outer edges, submerged the pan beneath the surface and began to rotate the pan until the dirt was saturated with river water.

Then he raised the pan above the stream, continuing to rotate or swirl the pan all the while. As the lighter grains of sand floated to the top, he washed them over the edge and out of the pan. The process was repeated over and over: dipping, lifting, swirling, dipping, swirling, lifting, until at last only the heaviest pieces of black sand and the gold (if gold there was) remained in the flat bottom. The gold was put aside in a tiny sack or jar or box.

The pan was refilled with sand and gravel and the washing began all over, the process being repeated hour after hour and day after day. Meanwhile, the miner's back and legs ached and screamed, as muscles pulled and strained to maintain the unnatural and ridiculous posture of stooping or squatting all day long. Feet, hands and wrists were constantly washed by the icy waters of the Yuba, while back and arms baked in the glaring rays of the summer sun. It would be hard to invent a more fiendish torture to which a man would willingly submit.

But, having learned that much, there was little more that the three young men could discover at the Yuba, for when it came to giving out information, the working miners were both deaf and silent. The friendliest treatment came from those who simply ignored their questions, while others offered to chase them off the bar. At last, the three would-be miners took their leave. Tallman was not sorry to go, for he still could not be fully at ease in the presence of Missourians—just to hear them talk grated on his nerves. He felt better when the Yuba dropped from sight and they began hiking over the ridges which overlooked the twisting route of the Feather River.

A gradual and subtle change was taking place in the relationships among the three young men. In the city, where Kemble was at home and held authority, at least in their place of employment, the youthful editor was accustomed to instruct his older companions. When they left San Francisco, he acted as the leader of the party by unspoken agreement.

As they sailed up the Sacramento River, Yates began to assert himself. His military training overcame his self-consciousness, for in this enterprise he was Kemble's equal. Tallman continued to defer to Kemble, willing to accept a lesser role in the adventure.

But as Yates and Kemble traveled farther away from familiar scenes and activities they became ill at ease. With the exception of Ed Kemble's brief excursion to Sutter's Mill, neither one had spent time outside urban or suburban communities. They had traveled to San Francisco by ship, thus losing the opportunity to spend time in the wilderness among strange animals, peoples, and sights. This trip for gold was their first opportunity to explore the rugged and unsettled regions of California. The new experience did not frighten them, but they were unsure of themselves.

At the same time, Tallman was renewing familiar and pleasant contacts. He felt at home in the wilderness, where he had spent several years and been happy. With the advantage of experience, Tallman quietly assumed leadership among the three. Kemble, who never before had thought much about the fact that Tallman was older and more experienced, even as a printer, now was aware that his survival depended to a certain extent upon the older man's skill and maturity. Yates also deferred to Tallman whenever a situation arose for which he was unprepared—he had learned how to accept orders in Stevenson's Regiment.

For the first time Tallman understood what it was to have other people look to him for advice. He had been taught to listen to the words of his elders—now he was being treated as an elder. It was an interesting experience, although he wasn't sure how long he wanted it to continue.

III

MINING WAS NOT his cup of tea, Ed Kemble decided. After a few weeks of working wth his friends at Bidwell's Bar, he told Tallman and John Yates that it was all well and good if they wished to stay in the shadowy canyons of the Feather River, but as for him, he was returning to a more sensible way of life.

They said goodbye and wished him well and that was the end of the matter, for they expected to see one another again when winter arrived. Kemble hurried back to Sutter's Fort in the company of some people who were going for supplies. When he got there, Sam Brannan put him to work waiting on the customers who by now numbered in the hundreds weekly. He also brought Brannan's books up to date after weeks of neglect.

Kemble didn't mind the work—it was a great improvement over mining—but he itched to smell printer's ink again. One day he said to Sam:

"If we don't publish the paper again, someone else is bound to fill the void. I hear the *Californian* is going to appear again soon."

"Let 'em," replied Sam. "I thought you told me there wasn't anyone left in the city to buy or advertise—at least that's the excuse you gave in June for shutting the paper down."

"I know, I know—but things have changed. People are moving back and wages have increased. By the time winter comes, everyone will be out of the mines and back in the city."

"Don't be too sure. We're going to build a new city right here."

"Do you mean here at the fort, or are you talking about Sutterville?"

"Neither one. Sutterville is a joke. That's no place to build a city and I told Sutter so."

"Why not?"

"It's too far from deep water. Ships can't get in there unless Sutter is willing to dig a canal half a mile long. You can get small boats and barges in, but we're going to be seeing bigger and bigger vessels on the river. The only place for them is along the embarcadero."

"But the land is so low up there. Sutter says it floods every winter."

"Sutter talks too much. He won't listen to reason, but his son will. Besides, Sutter is exaggerating—it doesn't flood every winter—just in the bad years, maybe once in every twenty or so."

"How do you know? You haven't been here twenty years!"

"Well, neither has Sutter! But if we have to, we can build up the banks, create a levee. The important thing is to realize that there's nowhere else to build the kind of city that's needed."

"What about the paper?"

"Are you back to that again? I don't care if it never appears again, I'm tired of the newspaper business. I've found a way to get really rich."

"Would you be willing to sell the *Star?*"

"To you? Of course! If you want it, I'll sell it to you. You can have the press, the type, everything."

"How much would you want?"

"I don't know—I'll have to think about it. Let me think about it tonight and I'll give you an answer in the morning."

"Fine. Just don't set the price too high—I'm not sure how much I can scrape together."

Kemble bought the *Star* for $800. He resumed publishing in September 1848. Two months later he bought out the *Californian,* called his new paper the *Star and Californian,* and brought in Edward Gilbert as co-editor. Gilbert had been associate editor of the Albany, New York, *Argus* in 1846, when he resigned to join Stevenson's Regiment. He had persuaded John B. Frisbie, an Albany lawyer and captain in the New York State Militia, to accept volunteers in his company so they could go to California with Colonel Stevenson. Gilbert was elected first lieutenant of the reorganized company.

While waiting for their ship to leave New York, Gilbert sent a dispatch to the *Argus* which was printed on August 19, 1846. It read, in part:

Every man of this expedition feels that he is engaged in an enterprise than which none greater will be found recorded on the historical pages of the nineteenth century. He knows that his country looks upon him as the pioneer in an undertaking which is to make his beloved republic the greatest nation on earth—which is to shower into her lap the profits of half the commerce of the world; and which is to extend the benefits and blessings of education and republicanism over three-fourths of the continent of North America.

It was Gilbert who had talked John Yates into joining the company, and who had made it possible for him to go off to the mines while technically still on duty with Company H.

With the advent of 1849, the firm acquired a new press, a new name, and new management: operating the *Alta California* would be Edward Kemble (former New York printer), Edward Gilbert (former New York printer and editor), and George C. Hubbard (former New York printer and ex-lieutenant in Company K of Stevenson's Regiment). All three were in their twenties.

IV

TALLMAN ROLFE, former Missouri, Oregon, and California printer, did not go back to San Francisco, but instead spent the winter working for Sam Brannan. Not until April 1849 did he see Ed Kemble again, and it was at Sutter's Fort that they met. Kemble appeared with the announcement that he was going to start the first newspaper on the Sacramento. He also brought along the old wooden Ramage press on which the *Californian* had been printed before he bought it out.

The first issue of the *Placer Times* appeared on April 28, at a time when the combined population of Sutter's Fort, Sutterville, and Sacramento City was approximately 150 persons. However, this was a misleading statistic, for hundreds more were passing through the city on the way to and from the mining districts. Sacramento merchants were doing a lively business.

On February 28, the first steamship to round the Horn, the *California*, came into San Francisco Bay with about 350 passengers from the States. Her sister ship, the *Oregon,* followed a month later with four or five hundred (no one could get an accurate head count, the ship was so overloaded), gold hunters and politicians. Down at Panama thousands more waited impatiently for transportation to California.

The *Placer Times* got off to a fast start, but Kemble found he was as ill-suited to the valley as to the mountains. He became sick almost at once and never quite regained his health while he remained in Sacramento. He sold the paper and equipment in June to another former officer of Stevenson's Regiment, lawyer Theron R. Per Lee of New York.

Back again at the *Alta California,* Kemble and Gilbert calculated that during the first six months of 1849 approximately 9,500 persons came to California by sea. Another 5,500 came by land, but none of these overlanders could have come from the eastern states, because it was too early in the season. Most of these early emigrants by land were from Mexico and Oregon. Two-thirds of the newcomers by land and sea were thought to be foreigners, mostly from Mexico and Chile.

Ships continued to arrive throughout the summer, and in August the first of the overlanders swarmed over the Sierra Nevada; they did not stop coming until November. Tent cities popped up in all the mining districts—"mushroom" cities they were called. Paper cities also appeared, less visible but more profitable for the men who invented them. The *Alta California* listed a few such towns early in the summer: "Fremont, Vernon, Boston, Sutter City, Webster, Suisin, Tuolumne City, New York of the Pacific, Benecia, Martinez, Napa, Sonoma, St. Louis, San Rafael, and Saucelito."

Sacramento City, with fewer than 150 in April, was now said to have 2000 residents. Sam Brannan had a new store on the corner of Front and J Streets. He got into the city building business with some friends, Jacob Snyder, Henry Chever, and Sam Hensley. They bought some land from Sutter on the west bank of the Feather River, opposite the mouth of the Yuba. Snyder, a thirty-four-year-old surveyor from Pennsylvania went upriver with Tallman Rolfe and George Pierson to survey the new town of Yuba City.

On August 25, 1849, Tallman Rolfe and David A. Chever placed an advertisement in the *Placer Times:*

Notice to Miners.

ROLFE & CHEVER, having established a store at Yuba City, will keep constantly on hand a large and general assortment of Dry Goods, Groceries, Provisions, &c. which will be sold low for cash or Gold Dust.
Yuba City, Aug. 20, 1849

ROLFE & CHEVER,

Wholesale and Retail Dealers,

Yuba City, corner of Water and B sts.

In September David's brother, Edward E. Chever, rode to Yuba City on his mule to visit the store. He reported that the walls of the place were palisades of rough split posts set upright in a trench, with the soil tamped firmly back around the base. A ridge pole extended from one end to the other, and from it cotton cloth had been stretched to make a roof. The store was located quite near the Feather River, close to an Indian village.

Elections were held August 1 to select local judges and *alcaldes,* as well as official delegates to the constitutional convention to be held at Monterey in September. There were thirteen polling places in the Sacramento District, which included all the mining camps east and north of Sutter's Fort. Two of these precincts were on the Yuba River, one at Doctor Atkinson's trading post and the other at Foster's and Nye's trading post.

Eight delegates were selected to represent these thirteen precincts: four lawyers, two farmers (Sutter was one), one merchant, and one surveyor (Jacob Snyder). Four had been in California three or more years: Sutter, Lansford W. Hastings (whose route cut-off had such dire consequences for the Reed-Donner party), Snyder, and William E. Shannon, formerly with Stevenson's Regiment (another New York lawyer).

Those who had come with the gold rush were M. M. McCarver (farmer from Oregon and Kentucky), Elisha O. Crosby (lawyer, New York), John McDougal (Indiana, Ohio; fought in Black Hawk War at fourteen years of age, was superintendent of Indiana State Prison at twenty-three), and Winfield S. Sherwood (lawyer, New York).

One of the San Francisco delegates was Edward Gilbert, who editorialized in the *Alta California:*

Every person appears to be convinced that the slavery question, under the complexion that it now wears in the Atlantic States, defeated the numerous attempts made in the last Congress to give to California a territorial organization, and all men ought to be as firmly assured that, unless the citizens of California settle that question for themselves, and do so at once, it will prevent, defeat, or at least protract for years to come, the establishment of any government in the country.

Independent of the moral considerations which weigh so heavily in the balance against slavery, and which we have neither time nor room to repeat, as a matter of expediency—as a means of giving to this country a government—it is necessary that the people should insert in their constitution a clause forbidding the introduction of negro or other slavery.

Among the emigrants who came to California in the summer of 1849 were some who came by way of the new Mormon city at Salt Lake. With the help of one such company a letter came to Tallman Rolfe full of news about his family, now safely established in Utah. Gilbert and Benjamin were busily occupied constructing houses for the new arrivals. No lime was available, so they plastered walls and ceilings with clay and sand mortar. Gilbert's wife had produced a daughter in 1848, which made a total of three nieces and nephews for Tallman in that family. Benjamin had decided to join the church and soon would be marrying a young woman from Vermont.

Horace and Sam were being taught by their father to be carpenters, and Ianthus was expected to arrive in Utah from Massachusetts at any moment. Sadder was the news about the youngest members: David, whom Tallman had never seen, had not survived the march to Zion. Mary Ann, born in Nauvoo, also had died. When, his family asked, could they expect to see Tallman? He was sorely missed and it was time for him to come home.

Tallman recalled the words of Sam Brannan and those of recent arrivals about the Salt Lake community. Life in California, however rough it might be in the midst of the gold rush, seemed a far better choice to him. Although anxious to see his family once more, he had no desire to step back into their chosen way of life. He wondered how it would seem to his younger brother after four years spent in New England among the gentiles. Perhaps he could persuade Ianthus to come to California.

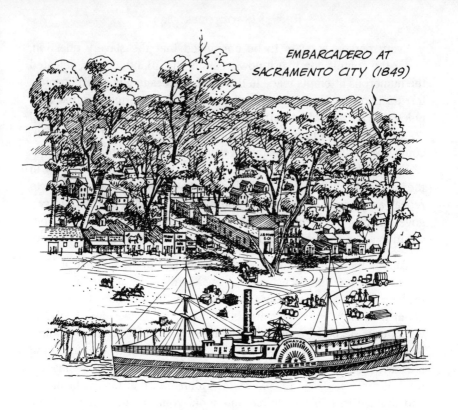

EMBARCADERO AT
SACRAMENTO CITY (1849)

CHAPTER 20

CONSTITUTIONAL
QUESTIONS

October–December 1849

I

*I*T'S A DEAD-RINGER for the New York Constitution! Or nearly
so, at any rate."

"How can you tell, Niles? I've never read the constitution of my own
state, and I don't know anyone who has," said "Mac" McCollum.

"You probably didn't have to, but I did. I studied it at law school. I
don't say I know it line for line, but it's pretty much the same as this, I
know."

"Do you think that's good or bad?"

"That it resembles the New York version? Good, I'd say. And the

234

differences all appear to be improvements, in the California model."

"Because it prohibits slavery?"

"That's one. Another is that it gives women property rights that don't exist in other states. That's a carry-over from Mexican law—in fact, so is the anti-slavery plank. Apparently the Californians at the convention insisted on both points."

"I never thought of Mexican women having more rights than Americans," said Charley.

"Well, it's a fact, though if this constitution is approved it won't be entirely true. All a woman has to do to improve her lot is come to California!"

"How many would believe you if you told them?" laughed Mac.

"Not many, I suppose."

"What are some of the other differences? Or is that all?"

"Well, there's the clause which prevents the chartering of banks and the printing of paper money. I'm not so sure that's all to the good, but I guess some would call it an improvement."

"Count me among them!" exclaimed McCollum. "Bankers are swindlers and that's all."

"I don't know that it's fair to call every one of them by that name, but there's no denying we've seen more than enough of that stripe. Every failed bank ruins thousands of innocent people—mostly those who can least afford it, too," said Niles.

"That's the Lord's own truth," agreed the older man. "Read me what it says—I want to write and tell my partner. He'll be tickled to hear about it!"

Niles flipped through the pages of his copy of the proposed constitution on which Californians would be voting in November. One thousand copies had been printed, bound, and distributed by the *Alta California* job printing plant within a week after the convention closed. Another 250 copies in the Spanish language had been prepared for the *Californios* to study.

"Here it is," Niles said:

The legislature shall have no power to pass any act granting any charter for banking purposes; but associations may be formed under general laws, for the deposit of gold and silver; but no such associations shall make, issue, or put in circulation, any bill, check, ticket, certificate, promissory note, or other paper, or the paper of any bank, to circulate as money.

"I guess that says it," said Mac with satisfaction. "But what about those other fellows, the politicians? If this is approved and we elect some of those politicians who are out making stump speeches all over the place, what kind of money will they be getting? It must be a confounded lot, to judge by the amount they're willing to spend on drinks for the voters!"

"The governor gets ten thousand dollars a year."

"That's a lot of money in Michigan, but it won't last more than a few months in California," said Mac.

"It certainly won't," agreed Charley, who worked part-time for a Sacramento City merchant, keeping his books. "The prices being charged are almost unbelievable!"

"The lieutenant governor receives twice what the legislators are paid, which is sixteen dollars a day while they're in session. They also get sixteen dollars for every twenty miles they have to travel to and from their homes."

"At thirty-two dollars a day, the lieutenant governor could receive as much as the governor, but only if the legislature met every day but Sunday throughout the year," computed Charley. "That's not likely, I suppose, but it's better than what the senators and assemblymen will get."

"Teamsters and carpenters are paid just as much."

"I don't suppose they'll get rich on those salaries."

"All the more reason why you'll have to watch 'em!" snorted McCollum. "They'll get theirs some way or another. They're just the same as bankers—steal you blind, if you're not watching every minute!"

"Politicians and bankers are like everyone else," replied Niles. "There's good ones and there's bad ones. Our job is to encourage the good ones and throw the others out."

"How do you spot the difference?" asked Mac. "That's what I'd like to know."

That the California Constitution bore striking similarities to the New York document was not a matter of coincidence, for much had been copied from the older version. The *New York Herald* proudly told its readers that New Yorkers were playing a prominent role in setting up the new state. Most of its information was passed along by its San Francisco correspondent, E. Gould Buffum, City Editor of the *Alta California* and veteran of Stevenson's New York Regiment. Before coming to California, Buffum had worked for the *Herald* as a printer and reporter.

On December 9, 1849, the *Herald* said:

The influence of the New Yorkers in California is stamped upon the document of the convention, which is evidently framed upon our State constitution, in its general features. The officers and soldiers—regulars and volunteers—from New York, bore a highly distinguished part in the Mexican war, and they were conspicuous in the conquest and military government of California.

We now find the New York politicians giving shape and character to the organic law of the new commonwealth, according to the latest New York fashions—not even excepting the occasional doctrines of socialism which are infused into our political charter. Free soil, free religion, free speech, and a free press, are secured, and a free access to the gold mines is also to be undisturbed, as far as the State has any power over Uncle Sam's property.

No duelling, no imprisonment for debt, no turning a man out of his house for debt, no squandering away of the wife's property, are tolerated. No banks, except *faro* and *monte* banks, sand banks, snow banks, and gold banks, are allowed. Shinplasters are tabooed, and specie and gold dust are not to be displaced by the spurious issues of swindling promises to pay.

II

TWICE DURING OCTOBER it rained, but the first really big storm didn't arrive until November 3. Then it rained without stopping for five days, bringing mining operations to a complete halt. It was nearly impossible to negotiate the muddy mountain trails after two or three days, and candidates for office under the new constitution cursed the weather as they tried to visit all the camps before election day.

Not only was travel difficult, but the rain made it necessary to address the voters indoors, usually in saloons. Few stump-speakers disapproved of demon rum, but buying endless rounds of drinks for thirsty miners was expensive.

On the Thursday preceding election day, skies cleared and soggy miners came out to bask in the sun. Office-seekers took prompt advantage of this opportunity to present their credentials to all and sundry, for every male was eligible to vote. By Sunday, miners began to show some interest in Tuesday's plebiscite. At Sacramento City, Niles was chatting with his neighbors when David McCollum approached and asked:

"Would you mind coming over here and explaining something about the constitution? These fellows don't have the least notion of what it's all about. I told them you knew it backwards and forwards!"

Niles laughed. "Where are they?"

"On K street, by the corral. I tried to tell them what I could remember, but they asked so many questions I got confused. It's better you told them so they get it straight."

"There seems to be some kind of a crowd by the corral. Maybe we should go somewhere else to talk."

"That's the bunch that wants to ask you questions."

"That crowd? I didn't know this was to be a stump speech!"

"It's not a speech they want, Niles, just the simple facts. Just tell them what you told Charley and me the other day. They've had all the speeches they want to hear for a month of Sundays!"

Mac asked the men to let the two of them through the crowd. Niles looked around for something on which to stand and saw some ox yokes lying near the fence. He climbed gingerly onto the pile and looked around at the upturned faces.

"Mac says you have some questions about the constitution. What in particular did you want to know?"

"We want to know what it's all about!"

"Only don't give us no lawyer's talk—your friend says you can explain it in everyday American!"

"All right. I'll give you a brief outline of what it contains." Niles proceeded to enumerate the main features, referring from time to time to the bound document he'd brought along. As he spoke, others came to hear what he was saying. Passing miners listened for a minute, became interested and signalled to their friends to come and hear.

He answered questions as long as his listeners required, but when someone asked what candidates he would recommend, he told them he had no advice to offer, having been there too short a time to know the men involved. Satisfied, the crowd began to break up. Niles climbed down from the pile of yokes and was about to leave when a large self-assured man in his forties clapped a hand on his shoulder.

"Well done, young fellow," he said. "You know your subject and you have a nice way with a crowd. I gather you've had some training in the law."

Niles thought he recognized the speaker as one of the Assembly candidates to whom he had listened earlier in the week. "I'm a member of the New York State Bar," he replied. "My name is Niles Searls and unless I'm mistaken, you're Mr. Bigler!"

The older man laughed. "Right you are. Here, have one of my cards."

Niles read the message on the proffered pasteboard: "John Bigler, Candidate for the First California Assembly, Sacramento District. Vote Tuesday, November 13, 1849."

"I'm a lawyer, too," continued Bigler. "I was admitted to the bar nine years ago after spending a few years as a printer and editor. I came overland this year with my wife and daughter, certain that in California there would be a great demand for someone of my varied talents." Bigler laughed again. "Can you guess what I've been doing since I arrived?"

Niles shook his head.

"For two months I've supported my family by cutting firewood, sewing calico bed comforters, carrying mail, assisting an auctioneer, and by loading and unloading boats! But I'm not discouraged yet, and next week you'll see why."

"Then you think you'll be elected?"

"Think? Young man, I know I will!"

III

ON ELECTION DAY, November 13, 1849, the rain came down in torrents. Two-thirds of the voters stayed in their tents and boarding houses and never ventured forth, according to an estimate the *Placer Times* issued relating to the Sacramento area. Not many felt like braving the storm merely to select from a list of strangers those who would run a state which might never exist.

Those who did go out to cast a damp ballot overwhelmingly endorsed the constitution. Forty-seven percent selected Peter Burnett to be the first California governor. Burnett, a former Missouri acquaintance of Michael Nye and the Long brothers, had mined with them for a short time after coming down from Oregon. In 1844 he had helped organize Oregon's early provisional government and had served on its first supreme court. Soon after reaching California in 1848 he was informed that President Polk had named him Justice of the Supreme Court of the newly created territory of Oregon. Burnett refused the post, saying his family couldn't live on what it paid.

He went to Sutter's Fort in the winter of 1848–49. Sutter's son, also newly arrived, retained Burnett as his legal advisor and real estate agent for the brand new city of Sacramento. He was to receive one fourth of all money paid for building lots. When General Riley, California's military governor, named him one of four judges on the Superior Tribunal in the summer of 1849, Burnett sold his half interest in certain Sacramento City lots for $50,000, held onto some others, and moved to Monterey.

Having little to occupy his time in his new position, he spent much of his time observing the deliberations of the convention, also meeting at Monterey. As soon as its work was completed, Peter Burnett announced he was running for governor. He toured the cities, towns, and mining camps, where his carefully cultivated backwoods style sat well with ordinary miners. He poked fun at fancy manners, though in the city he could be as elegant and graceful as occasion demanded. Rival candidates who spoke with eastern accents were at a disadvantage. The only other westerner in the contest, Johann Sutter, did not campaign at all.

One of the losing candidates for the office of lieutenant governor was Colonel Albert M. Winn, president of the Sacramento City Council. Unfortunately for his ambitions, Colonel Winn alienated the sporting vote by pressing for a city charter which taxed gamblers. There had been two elections on the subject, and the first had failed. In October a second try had succeeded. At the polls, Eli B. "Jim" Lundy, a well-known gambler and bully, had insulted Winn and issued a challenge.

A duel was prevented when friends intervened. Each combatant had a reputation as a skilled marksman and each had killed at least one opponent in the past. Winn, born in Virginia, came to California from Vicksburg, and was said to have an impressive military background. He was forty-nine years old, elderly by gold rush calculations.

Jim Lundy hailed from Canada, where his family owned a farm near Niagara Falls. The road leading to the family estate was known as Lundy's Lane, and in the late summer of 1814 a bitter fight took place in which both the Americans and British suffered heavy casualties. The Americans finally retreated and the day was recorded in the history books as the Battle of Lundy's Lane.

Lundy and his friends worked hard to defeat Winn, throwing their support to John McDougal, who had fought in the Black Hawk War at the age of fourteen. John was well liked around Sacramento, nearly as well as his brother George, who ran a store at Sutterville, and before that operated a ferry across the Sacramento River. George had come to California with Bill Swasey in 1845 and fought alongside Frémont in the Mexican War—alongside, but not under, for unlike John, who fought in two armies in two wars, George was a free spirit who refused to submit to any man.

Two men were elected to serve in the United States Congress whenever California should be admitted as a state. One was George Wright and the other was Edward Gilbert, co-editor and co-publisher of the *Alta California*.

John Bigler, who had been so confident, finished tenth in the race for nine Assembly seats in the Sacramento District. He was challenging the result, but Niles Searls wondered if the middle-aged lawyer had once more encountered one of life's defeats. Too bad, he thought. He had begun to develop a fondness for the old gentleman.

The storm continued for a full week, but Niles was impatient to find work, so he went out anyway. Because of something John Bigler had said, he headed for the embarcadero, where new steamers landed several times a month. Smallest was the *Mint*, which had been going up and down the river since October. The propeller-driven *McKim* went into service in the same month, and it boasted sixty berths.

Newest of all was the handsome paddle-wheeler, *Senator,* which could reach San Francisco in a single day, leaving at eight in the morning and arriving between five and six in the evening. The upstream trip was slower and required an overnight passage, but one could leave San Francisco in the morning and have breakfast next day in Sacramento. Cabin fare was thirty dollars each way, deck fare was twenty, and berths on the upward journey cost five dollars extra.

Niles was not interested in traveling, but hoped to find work as a longshoreman. He was lucky—a man had been injured and a replacement was needed. In good weather there would have been plenty of idle men hanging around the docks, but in this downpour, only Niles was available.

"I'll pay you a dollar an hour," said the dock boss. "Now hop to it. The boat has to be loaded as fast as possible—we're behind schedule already."

Niles was glad of the chance to work again, and he put every ounce of energy into the task. But before long he was breathing hard and trying desperately to keep up with the other members of the work gang. Near the end of the first hour, the boss called him aside.

"Here," he said, handing him a dollar. "Take this. You're in no shape to work here. You been sick?"

"I had scurvy for a while, but I'm better now."

"Not near enough for this kind of work. Better find some other line of work."

Niles accepted the money and advice. Removing his hat, he wiped his sweating brow and neck. He looked up and down Front Street. On one of the small frame buildings he saw a hastily scrawled notice that read: "Cook wanted." Above the doorway, painted directly on the rough-sawn boards was the legend: "Restaurant."

The room inside was steamy and crowded. The mingled aromas of salt pork, coffee, tobacco and sweat filled the spaces between bodies and walls. Niles threaded his way carefully past the patrons till he found the owner in the kitchen at the rear.

"I came to see about the cook's job," he said.

"Good. Take off your coat and go to work."

"Do you want me to take the job notice down?"

"No. Leave it up till we see if you really can cook."

Given the limited assortment of foodstuffs in the larder, it wasn't hard to satisfy the patrons or the owner. At the end of the day, Niles was told he could take down the sign. After a few days he found the task was not greatly different from feeding his messmates on the plains. He especially enjoyed the opportunity to eavesdrop on table conversations and learn what was happening around the city.

"There was quite a fight at the Round Tent the other night," he told Charley. "Two gamblers shot it out. The reports I heard said no bystanders were hit, but it doesn't seem possible, does it?"

"Not with the crowds they usually have. Those gambling saloons are good places to stay clear of," said Charley.

"I hear they've put up an enclosed walk between the Round Tent and the Eagle Theater so the theater goers can buy drinks between acts."

"Doesn't surprise me. I'd like to visit the theater some time, but I think I'll wait till I've saved some more money. I don't want to be without money in California."

"You've hit it on the head, Charley," Niles agreed. "Without money or friends, you're in terrible trouble."

The Round Tent was on J, between Front and Second streets. Large enough to accommodate as many as 100 persons, it contained eight tables which were leased out to dealers for eight dollars per day each. A bar at one side of the tent was a major source of revenue, and musicians played lively tunes throughout the day and night.

Paintings of plump, pale, and bare-skinned ladies lined the tent walls, but the effect of erotic and lush decorations was dimmed by the leaking roof and walls. The gummy floor of the tent was churned and kneaded by the muddy boots of miners, from whose hats and coats water constantly dripped.

In a few days Charley handed Niles a copy of the *Placer Times* which described the shooting:

A quarrel took place the other evening between two men named Cheeks and Lundy, in consequence of some misunderstanding in regard to a fiscal operation performed on a monte table. During the first part of the recontre Lundy fired two shots at Cheeks, one taking effect in the hand and the other in the foot.

Although there were 30 or 40 persons in the room, no one else was injured by the shots discharged. Notwithstanding the wounds he had received, Cheeks challenged Lundy to fight him on the spot, when a ring was made, and the two gentlemen "went in" on scientific principles.

We understand that Lundy was severely punished, so much so that he has not been able to get about much since.

"It seems Lundy is a strong, heavy man who likes to pick fights. The other fellow, whose name is Weakly Cheek, is tall, but fairly slim."

"Weakly Cheek? You're joking! What kind of a name is that for a gambler?" Niles laughed.

"That's his real name! But he's far from weak—he gave Lundy such a beating that he's likely to lose an eye."

"I guess we can be thankful the blackguards are content to attack one another. I suppose the marshal will ignore the whole affair."

"That reminds me—before the fight, Lundy had Cheek arrested for taking four hundred dollars from him and Cheek is out on bail. But after the fight, Lundy's lawyer went to the clerk and withdrew the charges, and Cheek and two others have filed a complaint against Lundy! He's charged with assault and battery with intent to kill."

"Well, I hope they convict him—he's a hard case. He's the same fellow who threatened Colonel Winn in October, I've found out. I can't say I'd like to make his acquaintance."

IV

"IF I HAD A LAWYER worth a damn, I could win that suit!" declared a customer at the restaurant where Niles worked. "That's what makes me so angry!"

The man to whom he spoke nodded his head and went on eating. During the meal they discussed the legal dispute which had caused the outburst and Niles tried to listen whenever he was within earshot. As they were paying their bill and about to leave, Niles said, "Excuse me. I couldn't help overhearing what you said about needing a lawyer. I happen to be one myself and I'd like to try that case for you on a contingency basis."

"If you lose I don't have to pay you?" asked the stranger.

"That's right. All you'd have to pay is court costs."

"Why don't you meet me tonight at the City Hotel—about nine o'clock?"

"Better make it ten—I'll still be cleaning up here at nine."

"All right, ten it is. Here's my card."

Niles went to the City Hotel that night and was offered the case. A week later he came triumphantly home to his tent and told Charley:

"I did it! We won the case and I've earned a three hundred dollar fee!"

"Congratulations! The beginning of a great California law practice! When is your next case?"

"My next case is to mine some gold on the American River. With this money and what I've saved at the restaurant, I'm ready to outfit myself. How about you—are you ready to head for the mines?"

"You're joking! Why, it's snowing in the mountains! I just hope Mac is O.K. He left for the mines three weeks ago and we haven't heard a word from him."

"Don't worry about old Mac, Charley. Remember how we all thought he'd never make it to California because he was so old and feeble? Well, he made it and three of the youngest men died—you and I and old Mac are all who survived of the lively bunch that called itself Mess 17."

"I know. I think about it often. Why do you suppose we didn't fall by the wayside, too?"

"'Cause we're too mean to die, Charley!" said Niles lightly. "I don't know. I guess it wasn't time for us to go, that's all. But Mac's not in the mountains, he's in the foothills, and it's not snowing there, it's raining. I met a fellow yesterday that I knew in Missouri. He's here to buy provisions for himself and some other Missouri men I know. They're mining up at Mormon Island and he wants us to go back with him. How about it—aren't you more than fed up with bookkeeping?"

"I guess I am, but I don't itch to wade around in rivers at this season of the year. I was thinking of going to San Francisco. I'd like to take a look at the Pacific Ocean. Why don't we go there instead? We might find interesting work for the winter."

"We can always go to San Francisco. Who knows how long the gold will be around? And it's a good chance to work with some fellows who have found a fairly good claim."

"If you really want to, why don't you go with them? I'd rather head for the bay. When you're ready you can join me there and I'll pick up our mail when it arrives later in the month."

"Then you can't be persuaded?"

"I'm afraid not. I'll wait for summer."

On December 6, 1849, Niles left Sacramento and followed the American River to Mormon Island. Charley boarded a San Francisco-bound steamer on December 13. While they were gone, two storms buffeted Sacramento City. The second, which was stronger than the first, swept across the valley with the force of a hurricane. Buildings were blown apart, tents and shanties overturned and scattered. The Eagle Theater, built two months earlier at a cost of $75,000, was damaged so badly it had to be closed for repairs.

Johann Sutter shook his head sadly from side to side. No one paid the slightest attention when he warned that Sacramento City was in danger.

SACRAMENTO CITY
UNDERWATER

CHAPTER 21

SACRAMENTO FLOOD

December 1849–March 1850

I

*A*T SAN FRANCISCO it also stormed, but less severely, so it didn't interfere with Charley's exploration of the city and surrounding country. On December 23 he wrote to Cornelia:

You will perhaps remember to having heard me say before leaving R Ville that in years previous I had determined, if life spared me long enough, to make an overland trip to the shores of the Pacific—this journey I have this day completed.

Having ascended one of the neighboring hills, I could just discover the gleaming of that broad expanse of waters and a vessel under full sail, striving to enter this far famed haven, towards which so many wandering spirits are wending their way.

There is a satisfaction in thus safely accomplishing my trip which words can hardly express. An All Seeing Eye has guided my path through dangers, trials and scenes which required to be witnessed to be fully realized. . . .

I arrived here from Sacramento City some ten days since, and have been very busily engaged playing "the gentleman," seeking some employment in preference to working in the mines during the rainy season. Niles started for the Mormon Island diggings about a week before I left—since which time I have heard nothing of his doings. He is now, as well as myself, enjoying good health, and I presume is, ere this, counting up the ounces and half ounces—the results of his daily toil. He was intending to join a party of acquaintances from Missouri.

It is almost an impossibility to obtain situations in mercantile employ at present, as a very large number of persons have come down from the "diggins" to spend the rainy season and are seeking employment—while at the same time, business is less brisk than before the rains set in.

The city of San Francisco is situated at the base of a range of hills which surround the bay and harbor and extend to the water's edge—as the city increases (as it does very rapidly), it extends up the hill sides and in time will present quite an imposing appearance, as viewed from vessels in the harbor.

The clayey nature of soil renders the streets almost impassable from the continuous rain—mud—mud—mud is the order of the day—rendering it very unpleasant—nor do the continuous rains render it more agreeable. For the last week it has rained six days, almost all the time—I would much prefer one of our old fashioned snow storms, such as you are enjoying in abundance about these days, I presume.

The city authorities are busily engaged filling up and grading the streets, and buildings spring up like mushrooms—one week the foundation is laid, the next it is finished and occupied. Carpenters and most mechanics find steady employ at prices varying from $10 to $16 p. day.

The markets are well supplied with Beef, Mutton, Pork, Venison and Wild fowls and game of all kinds. Among the things I noticed in market the other day: a fine fat Grizzly Bear; sweet and Irish Potatoes, Cabbages, Squash and Onions comprise the list of vegetables, all of them quite high.

The Sandwich Islands furnish what few fruits we have, consisting of Oranges, Limes, Bananas and Cocoa Nuts—pretty sparingly at that. I saw today, for the first, about a dozen Pine Apples, probably from the same quarter. There is a great deal of traffic between this port and the Islands, principally in the articles of Sugar and Potatoes. A great many persons have gone there to benefit their health and avoid the rainy season—the passage to and from occupies from 2 to 4 weeks, usually about 20 days. It is a very fine trip, I think, and have thought strongly of trying it myself, but have not yet determined.

There is here the greatest mixture of foreign residents I ever saw. All parts of Europe are represented, I think. South America has sent large delegations from Peru, Chile, and other States; the Chinese number from 300 to 500, which together with the Sandwich Islanders, New Zealanders, Malayas and some from Australia make up a well mixed population. The Chinese are a very industrious class and are mostly employed in eating houses. They have some 6 or 7 large eating houses with tables and fixtures in Yankee style, set well filled tables, give better fare for the same price and are better patronized than any houses of the kind in town. There are large quantities of Chinese goods in the market, being direct importations from China—some of them in Chinese vessels.

The hills around town present a somewhat barren appearance and are covered with a thick growth of low bushes bearing very pretty clusters of red berries, much like the mountain ash. Fire wood is enormously high, varying from $40 to $60 per cord—there is no timber in this vicinity, and it is principally brought from the Sacramento and San Joaquin rivers. The Spanish and Native Californians carry their wood and water upon the backs of donkeys and mules. It is somewhat astonishing to see the little donkeys toiling up the steep ascents with a load almost equal to themselves in size.

The water from the old Spanish wells and springs is very fine. It is said the lands near the mission, some three miles distant, are very fertile and productive. I intend to visit them as soon as convenient. I learn they are making large preparations in that section for supplying this market with vegetables the coming season.

I received your note of June 22d shortly before leaving Sacramento City—which is the last—but I presume I shall receive another soon, as Niles gave my name with his own for an express man to get letters for us, and I passed him coming down the river. So, when the mail arrives from Sacramento, I shall expect a line from you and Niles too. . . .

We are expecting another steamer about the 22d inst. The process of obtaining letters from the Post Office would be somewhat amusing to you, could you once witness it. There are two places of delivery, each from windows fronting on a piazza—the one for letters from A to K inclusive, the other from K to Z—the order of delivery is first come, first served, so as the applicants arrive, they fall into line, single file, each before his respective window. The office is constantly thronged, the number varying from 30 to 200. You are obliged to wait from one to six hours before your turn comes, so I can assure you, we do not get letters without toiling for them, but when obtained, the labor is well repaid, and I can assure I would willingly stand at my post tomorrow from Sun to Sun to hear from home, dear home.

Early on the following morning, the day before Christmas, Charles and the rest of the townspeople awoke to find the central part of the city ablaze. After watching the first great fire in San Francisco's history, he sat down to describe it to Mary:

This morning, at 5 o'clock, we were awakened by the cry of "fire!" and in a few minutes the flames made the spot apparent from all parts of the town. It originated in a gambling and eating house fronting on the public square, and almost instantly communicated to the adjoining buildings and spread with frightful rapidity, destroying a large number of the most valuable buildings in town. Its progress was finally checked, after consuming nearly all the square of buildings, and with a loss of several lives and a number wounded.

The entire loss cannot be ascertained, but is computed at $2,000,000. The Parker House alone cost $300,000 a few months since, and together with several others of nearly the same value, were filled with valuable furniture and goods. Gambling is carried on here to a very great extent, and as nearly half the tables in town were in this block and were destroyed, we have concluded after all "there is no great loss without some small gain."

Today has been very warm and pleasant, and "a few more such" would cause the mud to disappear very rapidly. How different with you—methinks I hear the sleigh bells sounding "as in days of yore," while the merry laugh rings loud in Our Reading Circle—the turkeys and chickens are ready for the morrow, and mince and pumpkin pies abound. If business was not so urgent, I should be happy to give you a call about dinner time, but really, it don't look well to beg an invitation, so I say no more this time.

How does our circle of young folks number now? Has cupid or absence thinned its ranks still farther? I hope not—if Deb has changed her address, give her my best respects, wishing her good luck—if not, add a few words of kind advice, telling her to "wait a little longer," and not to give up to Maria her right and title in my miniature.

With the winter evenings, I presume you have resumed your reading society, or some thing of like nature—at least I hope so, for the remembrance of those evenings is sweet. . . . And how many sleigh rides have you had—the Cairo folks, have they visited you, and does May King sing "Lay down the shovel and the hoe" as of old—Caroline and Rose—what has become of them—have they tried teaching again? . . . Do give me full particulars.

. . . A Merry Christmas and New Year to all, and to all, Good Night.

Before adding his letters to the outgoing mail, Charles wrote a short postscript:

Monday, Dec. 31. The mail steamer arrived yesterday morning and return mail closes in a few minutes. I have no line from home as yet, but got a line from Wisconsin. I hear Niles has returned to Sacramento City and obtained employ in a Hotel, but have received no line from him.

II

UNKNOWN TO CHARLEY, Niles was delirious with fever in the Odd Fellows Hospital at Sutter's Fort. The rains had forced him and his companions away from the diggings and sent them back to Sacramento. For a short time he worked at a hotel before falling so ill that his employer had him taken to the fort.

The hospital had been started by Doctor J. S. Martin and Reverend William Grove Deal, the latter also a physician. Colonel Albert Winn persuaded the Odd Fellows, whose local chapter he had organized, to underwrite the operation and for awhile the members each contributed five dollars a week to sustain the hospital.

In November the Odd Fellows voted to buy the hospital, subscribing one thousand dollars for the purpose. The Masons decided to join the endeavor and a board of directors was chosen from representatives of both organizations. Doctor Deal then stepped out of the administration so that he might devote more time to his religious and political activities. Doctor Benjamin R. Carman took his place.

Those patients who could afford to were asked to contribute to the cost of care, but payment was not a condition of admission. At Sacramento Hospital it was a different story. This private institution was owned and operated by Charles Abbott and Doctors Robert M. Stansbury and J. W. H. Stettinius. Patients at this hospital, located outside the fort, were required to furnish full security for payment before being admitted.

Charges at Sacramento Hospital ranged from ten dollars (for wards) to sixteen dollars (single rooms) per day, and this covered board, lodging, medicines, medical and "other necessary attendance," and the washing of bed linen and towels. No victims of "mania" were accepted, and surgical operations were extra.

At Third and K streets, Doctors James Stillman and John F. Morse opened a hospital two days before Christmas. Their building had cost the owner $15,000 and the doctors were renting this "finest building in Sacramento" for $1500 a month. Built of Oregon pine, it was thirty-five feet wide by fifty-five feet long, one and a half stories high, the half story consisting of an attic dormitory which ran the whole length of the building.

Doctor Stillman, until recently himself a victim of diarrhea, chills and fever, believed malaria, or "bad air," was the principal cause of illness among the miners. Wrote the doctor:

The people at home can have no conception of the amount of suffering in the vicinity of this city. Hundreds are encamped in tents, through the rains and storms, scantily supplied with food and covering. Men are driven from the mines for want of food, and are begging for employment, asking only subsistence.

Yesterday there were twenty-five deaths. The sickness does not arise from the severity of the climate, but largely from overwork, scanty and bad food, disappointment and homesickness. It is a great satisfaction to us to give them shelter and other things, for the want of which they are dying. If we are bankrupted, it will be in a good cause.

When the *Oregon* steamed out of San Francisco Bay with Charley's letters for Rensselaerville, Niles lay perilously close to death on a cot in a crude adobe room at Sutter's Fort. A raging fever had kept him bed-ridden for a week. When his doctor remarked that it was New Year's Eve, Niles hazily recalled the last moments of 1847, when he and his cousins vowed to remember the event on each succeeding anniversary. It seemed unlikely he would see them again—he did not expect to see even Charley before he died.

Once more he lost consciousness; outside it began to rain, the first rain of the new year. It rained again the next day and the next. For several days the storm continued, with a few brief moments when the low winter sun hurled long shafts of brilliant light through holes in the clouds, but the openings closed as quickly as they appeared.

According to the *Placer Times*, the rainy season was about over—this they had been told by the "oldest inhabitant," who had resided there for eighteen years. Since not even Sutter had been around that long, it was not clear who had made the optimistic forecast. Its accuracy was at once thrown in doubt.

As the waters rose higher, some half-hearted efforts were made to construct dams and levees around the sloughs, but with each lull in the storm all work stopped. The tents had almost dried again when a new storm rushed in from the south, bringing warmer air and plenty of moisture. It brought rain even to the higher elevations of the Sierra Nevada, causing snows to melt and add to the torrent from the skies. Soon every gully, ravine, creek, stream, and river was running full.

When saturated soil could absorb no more, water ran across the contours of the land to the lowest elevations. From north, east, and west it came tumbling off the mountains toward the one long narrow exit to the sea. At last the accumulated waters of all the great rivers of the Sacramento system breached their banks, and spilled out in waves across the wide, fertile valley, making one great sea which stretched from one mountain range to the other, leaving exposed only the tops of hills and trees. By these signs alone could anyone have guessed where to find the river's natural bed.

Sacramento City was under water.

III

Luzena Stanley Wilson, her husband and two sons fled to the safety of the Trumbow House, a hotel on K Street near Sixth. Until very recently, she and Mason Wilson had owned an interest in the Trumbow House, purchased for $600 dollars. The bottom story contained two rooms, and the upper half-story was a long, single dormitory with a window at each end.

Downstairs, the main room was long and dimly lit by tallow candles stuck in the necks of whisky bottles. The room was dark because from floor to ceiling the walls were completely covered with tiers of bunks. In a corner of the room a bartender dispensed liquor from a narrow bar, and in another corner a card game usually was in progress. The second ground floor room was Luzena's, for this was the kitchen, and her job had been to feed the boarders.

The Wilsons had sold their interest in Trumbow House for $1000 in December so that Mason could invest the whole amount in barley at fifteen cents a pound. Her husband had expected to make a fortune speculating in grain. They moved out of Trumbow House and into a small canvas dwelling a few doors down the street. Mason piled sacks of barley against the windward side of the tent to insulate it against the winter gales. When it rained, they slept beneath a cotton umbrella to keep the water off their heads.

Luzena was from North Carolina and Mason was from Kentucky, but they had been living in a cabin in Missouri when the gold rush began. He was thirty-nine and she was almost twenty-nine, and their boys were aged four and one when Luzena announced that Mason wasn't going anywhere without her and the children. They came across the plains and sold their cattle for enough to buy into the Trumbow House when they got to Sacramento City.

Now the city was under water and the Wilsons were sharing the dormitory of the hotel with forty other persons. After a few days the waters receded enough for them to take a look at what remained of their household. Some of the canvas still flapped from the pole frame and they managed to repair the walls and roof. Between the supports they found great piles of driftwood and the bodies of several drowned animals. In one corner sat the stove, rusty and covered with slime and sediment. Sheets of mold hung from underneath the beds. The barley was a total loss.

Mason cleared the room and built a free-floating platform which rose and fell with the tide. For six weeks they continued to live in the swamp-lands of Sacramento. Because the bed was not on the platform, at night Luzena would wake and feel along the bedpost till her hand touched the water. If it reached a certain notch on the post, she woke the others and they got up and packed their belongings, just in case. Always a boat was tied at the door, ready for their escape at any time of the day or night. The barley sacks began to burst—the grain was sprouting. They were penniless for the first time in their lives, Luzena realized.

"I want us to leave this place," she told Mason one day. "I want to go to the Deer Creek diggins."

"How can we? We haven't any money," he replied sadly.

"Find out how much would it cost," she said.

Seven hundred dollars was the price to move four persons, one stove, a few articles of bedding and clothing, and two sacks of flour. That was the end of that. "We can't raise that kind of money," said Mason.

"Let me talk to the man," she said. "Where is he?"

The teamster told her he'd take them if Luzena would "go security for the money."

"So help me, I'll pay you if I live and we can earn the money," said Luzena. She returned to their dilapidated shelter and began to pack what was left.

IV

"DON'T ANYONE MOVE or I'll shoot to kill!"

Judge Wilson froze. Several armed men suddenly had burst through the doors and windows of his temporary courtroom at Marysville. As they aimed their weapons in his direction, Wilson recognized their one-eyed leader as Jim Lundy. Too late, the judge regretted his earlier decision to grant bail to the notorious gambler, who was awaiting trial for murderous assault.

Lundy motioned to George Armstrong, on trial for theft with two confederates, calling out, "C'mon, George, get moving! We're taking you away from here!"

Armstrong left the prisoner's dock and ran towards Lundy. As the pair backed toward the open door, Judge Wilson shouted:

"Stop! By God, stop! I order you to stop and surrender your weapons!"

"Shut your mouth, judge, and sit down, or I'll make you sit down for good! You move one more time and you're dead!"

Lundy reached the doorway and stood there with his gun aimed in the judge's direction, Armstrong at his side, grinning nervously.

"Drop your gun, Lundy," said a quiet voice behind him, and the gambler felt a sudden, firm pressure against his back.

"Damn you!" cried Lundy, slowly letting go of his Colt's revolver. The sheriff reached forward and caught it. Seeing no one but Sheriff Robert B. Buchanan with a gun, and he being occupied with Lundy and Armstrong for the moment, Lundy's partners seized the opportunity to disappear out the other courtroom door. The sheriff watched them go. He couldn't stop them now, but he took a good look at their faces. He'd get them next time if they were foolish enough to appear again in Marysville.

"Bring those men to the bench, sheriff!" thundered the judge.

The sheriff complied and Judge Wilson waved his gavel in Lundy's face.

"I hereby revoke your bail and order you to pay a fine of four hundred dollars!" he stormed angrily. "Plus, you are to receive fifteen lashes on your bare back—and unless your fine is paid by sundown, today, I order that you shall receive twenty-five more!"

The clerk, Stephen J. Field, raised his eyebrows as he wrote out the sentence just delivered. Only eleven days had elapsed since his arrival at Nye's Landing, and the scene he had witnessed was just one more in a long series of barely credible events. Until 1848 he had been his brother's partner in the New York law firm of David Dudley Field and Stephen J. Field. During 1848 he traveled to Europe for the second time in his life, and in the fall of 1849 he came back to America and headed for California.

His very first act was to look up Colonel Jonathan Stevenson, former commander of the New York Volunteers, to collect a $440 dollar debt owing to his brother. After ten days in San Francisco he saw that the city's normal business had been totally disrupted by the arrival of flood victims from Sacramento City, so he decided to visit the valley.

At a time when everyone else was coming down the river, Field boarded a steamer bound for Sacramento City. He had heard of a new town called Vernon which sounded promising to his green ears, and at Sacramento he transferred to another steamer which he was told would take him to that place. However, when the boat reached the site, close to the juncture of the Sacramento and Feather rivers, Vernon was underwater. Field had no choice but to stay with the steamer until it reached its destination on the Feather River.

On January 15, 1850, Stephen Field disembarked at Michael Nye's landing. Among the first persons he met were Charles Covillaud, Theodore Sicard, John Sampson and a Señor Ramirez, who at that moment were looking for a lawyer to draw up a legal title to land they had bought from Johann Sutter. Field happily joined the venture upon learning they planned to establish a new town beside the Feather and Yuba rivers, opposite Yuba City.

It was decided to call the new city Marysville in honor of Covillaud's new bride, the former Mary Murphy Johnson, sister-in-law of Michael Nye and William M. Foster. Field had been elected *alcalde* and instructed to go to Sacramento City where District Judge R. A. Wilson would swear him in officially. He located the judge, no easy task in the flooded city, and when the judge heard that the new city of Marysville was high and dry, he decided to take the District Court business up-river until his own courtroom could be cleaned and renovated. Wilson and Field traveled together and the judge appointed his companion clerk of the court. On his return to Marysville, Alcalde Field appointed Robert Bloomer Buchanan sheriff of the new city.

The first case in Judge Wilson's court was a charge of stealing cattle lodged against Samuel Hicks, Nelson Gill, James Nicholson, and Michael Watson. The owners, Covillaud and Foster, could not prove ownership because the cattle were unbranded. Before dismissing the case for lack of evidence, Wilson instructed Field to give notice in the *Placer Times* that in the future all persons convicted of stealing cattle, unbranded or not, would be sentenced to two years on a chain gang.

Two days later, Michael Watson was back in court with Ariel Nelson and George Armstrong, all having been caught with a quarter of beef bearing Covillaud's brand. It was during this trial that Jim Lundy tried to free Armstrong and was thwarted by Sheriff Buchanan. Stephen Field contemplated his new venture in wonder. Marysville was a fast town—at least in its first couple of weeks.

V

A PAIR OF MINERS passed through the new city on their way to the Deer Creek diggings, but so far as they knew it was Nye's Landing still. The younger of the two was Benjamin Parke Avery, twenty-one years old and a native of New York City. The other, Evariste Franchére, was a Frenchman whom Avery had met at Mormon Island.

Avery's father ran a New York hotel until his death in the 1832 cholera epidemic, when Ben was four. At twelve he began serving an apprenticeship to a banknote engraver. In the summer of 1849 he came to California and mined at Mormon Island until October, when he took off for Reading's diggings near Mount Shasta. Along the way he met up with a party of miners who told him about the rich diggings at Deer Creek and Gold Run. Intrigued by their tales of "pound diggings," which paid twelve ounces of gold per man per day, Ben Avery promptly changed direction.

Shortly after he crossed the Bear River at Johnson's Ranch, he overtook a pack train heading for Deer Creek. Among the party of Missourians was a man named Caldwell—"Doctor" Caldwell was what the others called him, though Avery never knew him to minister to any patients, except to those miners in need of medicine for snake bites. For Caldwell, he discovered, operated a trading post on the creek about seven miles below Gold Run. He was coming back from Sacramento City with a load of provisions—whisky, flour, bacon, salt pork, biscuits, gingerbread, sugar, salt, coffee—everything that miners would need to survive the long winter.

When the party reached Deer Creek, Avery saw that the store was nothing more than a square canvas shanty where whisky could be obtained for four bits a drink. Moldy biscuits went for a dollar a pound. It was the only trading post on Deer Creek, so Doc Caldwell was free to charge what the market would bear.

For awhile Ben tried prospecting on a claim said to have been abandoned by old Caleb Greenwood. To his surprise he found gold, but not "pound diggings." He kept moving upstream in the direction of fabled Gold Run, stopping as he traveled to sample dirt from the side ravines. Although he seldom probed deeper than a few inches below the surface, he usually found a little color in his pan. Because he was on the north bank and Gold Run is on the south side of Deer Creek, he never reached his destination, but he found a ravine with such good prospects that he went back to Mormon Island to fetch his partners.

He got there in November, by which time the rains had begun and only Franchére was interested in his proposition. They went to Sacramento City to buy provisions, but then the rivers were so high that they hesitated, for Avery could not swim and was afraid of the crossings. They waited, and while they waited it stormed until finally Sacramento flooded and Avery and Franchére took refuge on the bark *Orb,* at a cost of seventy-two dollars for a nine-day stay.

After further delays, they made their way through the snow to the Deer Creek diggings and Avery's prospect, arriving in late January or early February. Ben's first sight of the changed scene filled him with disbelief.

"Will you look at that!" he cried. "The whole ravine is full of miners!"

"I think we better look for another place," said the Frenchman.

"That won't be easy," grumbled Ben. "From the looks of things, every kill, crick, and ravine is crawling with miners. While we've been holed up in the valley, these fellows have been making their piles!"

A tent city now spread over the slopes and in the hollow at the foot of American Hill. Giant evergreens towered above the cabins and tents. In the middle of a small flat area was Dyer's cabin, where whisky and brandy sold for six and eight dollars a bottle, and across the ravine was Doc Caldwell's newest store. The "upper store," it was called, to distinguish it from his earlier establishment seven miles lower on the creek.

Although a few log buildings had been erected, most shelters were made of brush or canvas. The snow appeared not to impede the miners, who went on with their activities in all but the very worst weather. Sometimes it was necessary to knock snow from the tents to keep the roofs from falling in, but after working all day in the cold water, men warmed and fed themselves at giant campfires built against the trunks of trees and laughed and sang and played fiddles and flutes as if enjoying a summer's outing in the woods.

Not long after the arrival of Avery and Franchére, who now were mining at a new claim, an election was held to choose an alcalde and a sheriff for the camp. C. F. Stamps, a native of Tennessee, was chosen alcalde. Now forty years old, he had come to California with his wife. She ran a boarding house and he had a trading post and they had spent the winter at Deer Creek.

After the votes were counted, some of the townspeople crowded into the cloth building known as Miner's Hotel to celebrate with some champagne from San Francisco. Peyton G. Womack and A. B. Kenzie owned the Miner's Hotel and Martha Womack did the work. As they celebrated the occasion, someone brought up the matter of a name for the camp— something with more elegance than Deer Creek diggings or Caldwell's upper store. O. P. Blackman's suggestion of "Nevada," meaning snowy or snow-covered in Spanish, was applauded as an ideal appellation, for it was as appropriate as it was poetic.

Luzena and Mason Wilson arrived at Nevada after twelve miserable days traveling over sixty miles of muddy roads and swollen fords. The sun finally shone forth on the March day on which they slowly descended the slippery path into the fledgling city. It brought pleasurable warmth to the shoulders of the hundreds of miners standing knee-deep in the icy waters of Deer Creek. Shouts rang out above the roar of the stream and Luzena wished there was some way she could sneak her family past this scene of frenzied activity without being noticed. She was ashamed of their appearance, for all were covered with red mud from head to toe. But she soon realized that everyone was too busy to glance in her direction—under the mud she looked like just another traveler.

The teamster who had brought them to Nevada on credit took time to help them unload before heading for Dyer's saloon to satisfy his thirst. Luzena and Mason quickly set to work building a rough shelter out of brush and pine boughs. Then he, too, disappeared, going off into the woods with his axe to cut shakes. All but Luzena's cookstove was inside the brush house. The stove sat underneath a huge pine.

It was mid-afternoon. Luzena decided to get acquainted with her new neighborhood and see about earning the money which she owed the teamster. With her boys, she began to stroll down the camp's main street, pausing for a few minutes in front of the Miner's Hotel. A cloth sign announced, "Meals $1." She bent over and picked up little Jay before addressing her older son:

"C'mon, Tommie. Let's go see the man build a house."

"Where, Ma?"

"Just come along and you'll see. Now, watch your step and don't step in the dung."

"I didn't. Where's the man building a house?"

"Hold your britches on, Tommie, you'll see in a minute. See? There he is. Here, take my hand and step carefully around this hole."

Hearing the unfamiliar voice of a woman, the carpenter stopped his work and turned around. Staring at her in open-mouthed surprise, he removed his hat and wiped his perspiring brow with a dirty rag.

"How d'you do, ma'am! You must be new in town!" He grinned with pleasure.

"I'm just fine, thank you, and I've just arrived. I'd like to know where I could get a couple of boards like—well, just like those boards," and she pointed to a stack of freshly sawn sugar pine planks, each one-inch board measuring eighteen inches wide by sixteen feet long.

He frowned. "I really don't know. I had a hard time getting these and they cost me a pretty penny. About how soon would you need 'em?"

"By sundown, anyway."

"That soon?" He looked her carefully up and down. "How many did you say?"

"Two. I only need two. I'll be happy to pay you for them," she said forcefully, blushing crimson at his bold stare. "I don't have a lot of money at the moment, but I can pay you in a day or two."

He looked at the child in her arms and then at the four-year-old tugging at her hand, itching to explore the building site. He swallowed hard and said:

"I guess I could let you have two of them boards. D'you s'pose you could pay maybe a dollar apiece for 'em?"

"Why, yes, I could. That seems very reasonable. I don't imagine you'd want to sell very many at that price, would you?"

"No ma'am, I certainly would not!"

"I thought not. I want you to know how very grateful I am to you—now I can go ahead with my plan!"

"It's none of my business, but do you mind tellin' me what you're going to do with them boards, ma'am?"

"Oh, I don't mind at all—in fact, I'd be pleased if you'd tell everyone you know! I'm going to make a table for my hotel."

"Your hotel? Which one is that?"

"Do you see that cookstove setting out under the tree where I'm pointing? That's my hotel! By the way—would you mind awfully to carry the boards up the street for me?"

The carpenter hadn't minded. And the storekeeper had been happy to deliver the provisions she purchased on credit. Some miners passing by were astonished to see her chop several stakes with her own hands and drive them into the ground. When Luzena saw them watching she asked them to come over and lift the boards (which the friendly carpenter had tied together with several cleats) from the ground and onto the stakes. After it was adjusted to her satisfaction, she thanked the men and invited them to have supper at her table that evening for a dollar each.

When Mason returned with a load of shakes, he was amazed to see twenty men eating supper at the door of his brush house. It was dark outside, but the table was brightly illuminated by several blazing pine torches.

"What's going on?" he asked his tired but happy spouse.

"This is the beginning of the El Dorado Hotel," she answered with a grin. She wiped her face and hands on a clean corner of her apron, kissed her husband and said, "If you mind your manners, I might consider goin' partners with you."

"LONG TOM" MINING

CHAPTER 22

RENSSELAERVILLE ROVERS

February–May 1850

I

WHAT HUMBUG IS THIS? I was told you were deathly ill, but you look better than I do!"

"Sorry, Charley. I don't know where you get your information. I've been taking life easy for a change. I must say that I've missed your bright and shining face, however!" said Niles with a wan smile.

"How are you feeling? Can you leave this hospital before long?"

"I hope so. It's been a few days since I did much shaking."

"Good. I need you for a business venture that's almost ready to put in operation. You won't have to do much and it won't tax your strength either."

"I'm ready to do something useful for a change—what have you got in mind?"

"Well, I've located a farmer who'll supply us with potatoes and onions. His place is south of San Francisco, out by the Mission Dolores."

"Fine—buy us a bushel! But what's the plan?"

"We're going to buy more than a bushel—we're going into the vegetable business, Niles! I'll buy them and ship them to Sacramento. You'll set up a stand on Front Street and sell them on the levee!"

"You mean I'm to become a vegetable peddler after spending all that time to become a lawyer? What will my family think? It's bad enough that I should have run away to California—but a vegetable peddler—how will I ever explain?" Niles chuckled. "You're a marvel, Charley! You've figured out exactly how to make the best use of my talents!"

"Of course! All you have to do is sit outside in the sun, get well, and make a fortune while you're doing it! Come on, let's ask the doctor when you get to begin!"

Within a week, Niles was trading onions for gold. Whatever Charley could find to buy at a reasonable price (and some things which weren't so reasonable) he sent up-river on the steamer. His experience in the mercantile business while working at Toledo, Ohio, and at Rensselaerville now stood him in good stead. He knew what to buy and told Niles what to charge and how to sell. They intended to close the business when the rivers dropped, at which time they would try their luck at mining. Sometime in March, Niles wrote Charley to say that business was falling off. The miners were leaving Sacramento and so should they.

Charley wrote Mary Niles on March 25, 1850, from San Francisco:

I acknowledge with much pleasure the receipt of your letter of Jany 5th addressed to Niles and myself, and improve the earliest opportunity to answer it, but own that I am unprovided with materials with which to make it as interesting to you as yours was to us.

Niles is at Sacramento City and, I presume, is engaged about these days fulfilling like duties, and I think, between us both, you will be well advised of our doings.

I have already written five letters for the next steamer, and after this is finished I think friends at home will have no reason to complain of a lack of correspondence on my part.

Last Monday I took a walk down the bay to the mouth of the harbor, and as the waves washed the sands at my feet, accomplished my task of journeying from the Atlantic to the Pacific. During my walk I found a large variety of beautiful wild flowers, many of them entirely new to me, but among them recognized three old faces—viz Honesty or Satin Flower, House Leek, and a plant we used to call Crane's-Bill Cactus. The banks are covered with strawberry and other flowers down to the beach and in some places almost to the water's edge.

If the sands of the shore do not prove treacherous to their memory, future generations can there behold that eastern friends are *not always* forgotten on the shores of the Pacific, for as the waters washed my feet, I buried a bouquet, and with my finger engraved in bold characters upon the beach the names of friends most dear; and may the flowers long continue fresh to their memory, is my humble wish.

I can assure you, the names of the members of "Our Reading Circle" were not forgotten, and as their names are now engraved upon the shores of Long Island on the Atlantic—on the hills of the Platte river— the summit of the Sierra Nevada Mountains and the shores of the Pacific, their fame has spread far and near, even from the shores of the Atlantic to the Pacific, and future generations may talk of the fame which "our little circle" has already gained.

I am much flattered to hear of the pleasure with which my letters were received when read before "Our Circle," but had I known they were destined to be *honored so highly,* it would have been well to have prepared them with a little more care—but I trust they, as well as yourself, will forgive and *forget* the many little errors in my correspondence. Ere this reaches you, your evening meetings will be discontinued, I suppose, else I would pen a few lines addressed to that august body, but will now defer doing so until *the long evenings* commence again— and remember, if you form any new society in place of the old one, I shall consider myself a member, and as soon as informed of your doings will give you a few slices of "life in California."

He went on to allay concern Mary had expressed about Niles's welfare and his own:

In speaking of Niles you thank me for my care of him, and inquire if he was not able to take care of me in our journey across the plains. He did, indeed, take a brother's care of me, and it was needed, too, for I was at one time quite sick. It would certainly be very ungrateful in me not to give him due praise, and I was exceedingly thankful to have recovered sufficiently to be able to walk and care for him during his illness, and I do not think my care was worthy of praise, as it was merely returning kindness for kindness.

I perceive you are still filled with care and anxiety for our welfare, and, like all good friends, are determined to believe we are still unwell and perhaps suffering; but I can assure you never two mortals enjoyed better health than Niles and I do at present. Tell Nella I weigh above *her old* standard 140 pounds and can beat her five pounds, which is 17 pounds heavier than I ever was at home—and Niles is, I believe, in pretty much "like condition."

As to the scraps from our journals which you desire, I must beg to be excused, as the few papers I have are at Sacramento City, and therefore beg you to await the time when distance will be no impediment to verbal intercourse. As to when that time will arrive, the *bright future* will determine.

I am now anxiously awaiting the Panama steamer, and immediately after its arrival shall leave for Sacramento City and thence to the mines, accompanied by Niles—we shall start thence as soon as possible. Your letters you will please direct hereafter to Sacramento City, as I can get them more easily thence—and do not be disappointed if you do not hear from us as regularly hereafter, as our communication from the mines may be somewhat difficult.

But I beg of you all, do not fail to write often to us, as we trust each steamer will bring from each of you packages more precious than Gold dust. Give my *best* respects to *Rose, Deb* and *Maria and "all the rest," in particular*—likewise to all friends in general. Remember me to your parents and Addison, and forget not to reserve for yourself and Nella a large share of the love of

Your cousin, Chas. W. Mulford

When the steamer arrived with a letter for Niles from Rensselaerville, Charley brought it with him on his last trip up the river. It was from Cornelia and she had begun writing it on January 19:

As it is to be my privilege to have a letter ready for you by the next steamer, and my time is not always at my disposal, I thought tonight I would commence a letter, and then fill it out at any leisure moment, and then the time for its departure would not find me unprepared.

As we have no particular news to write since the date of the last letters, this may be a kind of journal, or scraps of the everyday life of friends at home. By the last mail we received your letters to Mary and I, dated Oct. 31st and Nov. 25th—and I can assure you, our anxiety to receive your letters can be little less than yours to receive news from the States. We *devour* every word you write and every line prompts a dozen questions concerning you, which are left for our imaginations and *dreams* to answer, until the arrival of another steamer sets us to "looking" again for letters.

And you have a way of telling things so clearly, and telling such news as we want to hear, that your letters are valued more than we can tell. The portion of your letters the oftenest perused is that in which you speak of *yourself.* Tell us how you look, how you feel, what you eat, and wear, when you laugh or *cry,* &c &c, and we will value it more than the most extravagant story of the gold speculation. Oh, for one good, long peek at your journal.

Tonight Robert received a letter from Charles, sent by a passenger to

New Orleans. He says you had, to date, received but one package of letters, and that one of June, the first we wrote. We wrote again in October, and then by the last steamer. Robert always directed to the care of Sibley; all of ours have been directed to San Francisco. We hope by this time you have received all that have been sent, if they will be any pleasure to you in your absence from home and friends.

You said "you were prepared for unlooked for changes" among friends at home, but time has dealt well with all thus far, and were you now among us again I do not think you would detect any great changes among us in R.Ville. . . . Each week finds us fulfilling the same round of duties, and each Saturday Eve finds us as we are now, with the cares of the week cast aside and seated around the table in the dining room, each spending the time as they fancy best.

I am sitting (for shame, to commence with No. 1) by the south end of the table next to the dining room door with my paper before me. Hamy is on the corner reading the last Godey's Lady's Book. Next comes Mary, with her head leaning on her hand (we have no girl, and it has been her turn to do the week's housework, and she is tired, because she *would* clean the floor, "as she was as strong as Cornelia" if not so *fat*). She is reading "Life of Johnson" and looks just as when you saw her last (only she has on a new green calico dress). Ma has just donned her spectacles and commenced the "Observer" and at the other end of the table sits Addison reading aloud the Congressional news to Pa, who lies on the sofa with his eyes bound up, they being quite sore.

Now and then Pa speaks of a letter from Oswego, received tonight, relating to some property he has been thinking of purchasing there, but it is all talk. I have no fear of his moving there, for if Addison concludes to go on with his studies and get a profession, we shall remain here; if not, Pa will go into business somewhere and Addison with him. And I think Addison will choose to study.

You never said a better thing than that you were going to return ere long and go on with your profession. Take good care of yourself, and when you have seen enough of California, don't wait to gain a *fortune,* but come back to our home in R.Ville, or if that then is changed to Oswego or some other spot, remember it is your own home still, and its inmates are ever ready to welcome you. . . . If we go, we shall go the 1st of May, but will know ere we write you again—shall probably not go to Oswego.

Lewis Tompkins has returned from Canada and says your friends are all well and had received a letter from you dated Sacramento. Alice was married, but I don't know to whom. Last Saturday Pa and I went down to Coeyman's Landing and returned Tuesday (in an awful storm of *snow and wind*)—Went to Uncle Nath. and found all well. They are about building a plank road from Coeymans L. to the Widow Andrews, 7½ miles. One is much talked of here, also, from Albany, but it is yet uncertain. I wish it were not so very far to California . . .

If I had time, I would write to Charley too, and tell him of a fine donation party we had a while ago at Mr. Washbon's. I have not as much time to write in these days as usual, as we have no girl and Mary is not at home and I chief cook and bottle washer . . . Mary, you must know, has this week taken upon herself the dignities of school mistress. You know this school in the session house is the first step in the ladder to fame to the girls here, and each must try her skill in it. It was offered Mary this week, and just *for fun* she took it for one term. . . .

First Niles, then Cornelia and Addison, and now Mary—each had been challenged to try his or her skill. Niles hoped Cornelia would pass along his earlier advice "not to teach too long . . . teaching, if followed as a profession invariably spoils the temper."

II

IMMEDIATELY AFTER CASTING their votes in the first county elections in California, Niles and Charley boarded the steamer *Sacramento,* bound for Marysville and the northern mines. The current was strong; night fell soon after they passed from the Sacramento into the mouth of the Feather River. The steamer was tied up for the night and passengers and crew were serenaded by swarms of mosquitoes and a background accompaniment of crickets and frogs along the river's bank.

The steamer reached Marysville on the following day and the pair made their way on foot to Bidwell's Bar, thirty-five miles to the north. To their dismay, they found the water at the camp was too high to work. Those few who were trying to mine were earning no more than six or eight dollars a day. After prospecting about for a week, Niles and Charley took off across the mountains to Foster's Bar, only to find that the water on the Yuba was equally high. On May 5, 1850, Charley wrote to Cornelia from Long's Bar, not far from Marysville:

It had been our intention to prospect higher up the river, but learning from those just returned that the snow was still four feet deep about twenty miles above, and of course the miners were unable to work, concluded to come down, and accordingly arrived here in one day's journey—distance 35 miles.

Next morning, in prospecting around, we found the claims on this bar were all taken up, so if we wished to work were obliged to buy. This is in

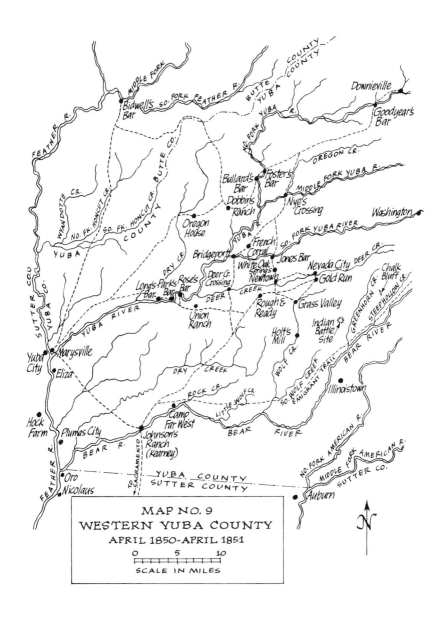

Middle Fork
So. Fork Feather R.
Feather R.
Bidwell's Bar
Butte County
Yuba County
Downieville
Goodyear's Bar
Wyandotte Cr.
No. Fork Yuba R.
No. Fk. Honcut Cr.
So. Fk. Honcut Cr.
Oregon Cr.
Butte Co.
County
Bullard's Bar
Foster's Bar
Dobbin's Ranch
Middle Fork Yuba R.
Nye's Crossing
Washington
Yuba
Oregon House
Yuba
So. Fork Yuba River
French Corral
Bridgeport
White Oak Springs
Jones Bar
Nevada City
Deer Cr.
Chalk Bluff Cr.
Dry Cr.
Deer Cr. Crossing
Newtown
Gold Run
Long's Park's Bar
Rose's Bar
Deer
Creek
Nevada City
Greenhorn Cr.
Steep Hollow Cr.
Sutter County
Yuba Co.
Yuba River
Union Ranch
Rough & Ready
Grass Valley
Bear River
Yuba City
Marysville
Holt's Mill
Indian Battle Site
Eliza
Dry
Creek
Wolf Cr.
Hock Farm
Plumas City
Rock Cr.
So. Wolf Creek
Emigrant Trail
Illinoistown
Little Wolf Cr.
Camp Far West
Bear
River
Johnson's Ranch (Kearney)
To Sacramento
No. Fork American R.
Middle Fork American R.
Feather R.
Bear R.
Oro
Nicolaus
Yuba County
Sutter County
Auburn
Sutter Co.

MAP NO. 9
WESTERN YUBA COUNTY
APRIL 1850-APRIL 1851

0   5   10
SCALE IN MILES

N

accordance with *the law* amongst men: whoever stakes out a claim consisting of 30 feet in width across the bar is entitled to it so long as he works on it as often as every tenth day. We accordingly bought a claim and at noon commenced work—and here we are, hard at it every day but Sunday, and this is here emphatically a day of rest, for all, whether from religious feelings or not, are willing to quit their work one day in seven.

The claim had been purchased for $150 from four men who were on their way to the Feather River. Along with the claim Niles and Charles had also acquired a rocker and some tools. At noon on Friday, April 19th, they had commenced mining, and by Sunday morning they had taken out enough gold to pay for the claim.

During the first week after arriving here, we stopped at a boarding house and meantime made a tent so we could retreat from the heat of the day—but a week last Friday commenced living by ourselves. Now, I suppose you would like to know how we look in and about our little ranch.

Just imagine a neat little tent, nine feet square by six feet high, made of bleached muslin—as white as the fuller's art can make it—and you will see our home. This you must *believe,* from what you know of its occupants, must make quite a respectable appearance, but if you will just take a peep with me into its interior:

As you enter, you will be so kind as to incline your head a little, lest the ridge pole of our tent should strike you into a conviction of its beauties. As its size would indicate, the most permanent thing to meet the eye at first is our cord couch, on which we nightly seek the land of visions, or as we commonly call it, our bed, consisting of blankets spread upon Mother Earth as soft as ordinary sized rocks can make it. This is the spot from whence we nightly wander to the home of our childhood. In that little bag at your right hand is the wardrobe of two miners, as well as various little nick nacks, amongst which you may safely conclude will be found certain miniatures which miners are known to possess.

Don't you think that half gallon coffee can makes quite a show? By the way, it is quite an important personage here, for although it looks so black and smutty outside, I believe it is pretty near right within, at least judging from fruits—for it makes good coffee, first rate tea, and then it boils our beef very tender, makes good soup, and various other things too numerous to mention—besides it would boil first rate dishwater, only we don't need any, as all our dishes consist of two or three tin plates, one cup, one knife, two forks and an iron spoon. They get along very well without washing, for Niles scrapes his plate with a chip and I eat mine clean.

I fancy I hear you ask if that thing by the coffee pot is not a shovel—why, I should think you would know better. You see, that is our frying pan. To be sure, it was a round pointed shovel once, but while digging the other day the handle broke and it has been a frying pan ever since, as you ought to know from the looks of it. To be sure, when we fry very fat pork, the gravy runs off some, but you know there is always enough left for *sop*.

Come now, don't you call that lard in that wooden bowl, for it is butter and was "mighty yeller" when we got it. They say tea leaks its strength by being left open, but the butter *hasn't*. When we first got it, it was mighty strong, and as we thought strong enough to take care of its self, left it alone in the tent. After a day or two the sun looked at it so strong through the white cloth it began to look streaked and finally turned pale. Looks sick, but it *isn't*, for it is so strong, when we use it on bread we have to take two swallows of coffee to get it down and one more to get the taste out of our mouths.

That is pretty fair looking pork at your left hand, is it not? The fresh beef we must boil tonight to have it cold at breakfast. That vinegar goes good with cold meat and greens, and by the way, we must gather some more of those Primroses just for greens. We have these loaves of baker's bread, just like those, every day. Don't you think we eat a few—but you have not seen our fireplace yet. Just step out with me and I will show you.

You see that pile of stones there, do you? There is where our kitchen is. And this is our table; to be sure, there is not much grass on it, for the soil is poor, but it answers very well, though—then we are not troubled with brushing off the crumbs when we get through, for they mix with the sand and we can't see them. Niles lays down there, and I sit on that stone when we eat. For a continuation of your letter, see the enclosed one to Mary.

One week later, on May 12, Charles resumed his description, addressed this time to Mary:

I suppose as a matter of course you have had foresight enough to have read Nella's letter before commencing yours, and therefore I can without difficulty to yourself or me, suppose you have been out walking with Niles while I have been showing Nella the internal beauties and arrangements of our little ranch, and while I resign Nella to Niles, if you will step with me, I will harp on the extensive grounds we have here, devoted to flowers, as I presume Niles has devoted but little of his time to floral themes.

Now—this way, if you please, here is the path. We'll go round this rock, and now your hand—we jump over this and bear to the right a little to avoid those Redbud bushes. Once we are here, to be sure, the grounds are not laid out with much regularity, but I believe Dame Nature had the whole say about its being. But she had some taste, though—just see those Lupens, white, purple, and blue, and the Larkspurs, too—what a variety of colors. Those white flowers are pretty, they are a kind of syringa, and the satin flowers are larger and the peas and clover different from any we have at home. That vine must be a kind of Passion Flower, and this is the Fringe tree—but is not that orange Spiderwort a rich flower?

This is a Marigold, this a Candytuft, and that Coryopsis. Then there are a hundred other kinds, here all very bright colors, but I'll not detain you, I see you are tired, so we will go home by way of the claim.

This is our claim and we wheel our dirt over there at the slough—and it is as much as one can do to work while the others pick and wheel dirt to him. We wheel the dirt just about as far as from your father's house to the street, and now I see Niles has supper ready. Let us try it.

Here is a plate for you and that for Nella, but you must both drink tea out of that cup—that's the way Niles and I do. But as to bread and milk, we must manage Dutch fashion and all eat out of the same pan. This, by the way, is our regular Sunday supper: bread and a quart of milk, but tonight we have rice, too. Come, sit down—you sit on that stone (my regular seat) and I'll bring one for Nella, then I'll follow Niles and lay down. It is quite a knack to learn to eat laying on your side, but experience has made us quite adept in it. No cake tonight—all our cakes are slapjacks, and they are mighty scarce.

But must you leave so soon? Very well. I see Niles will go home with you, so good night. I will have a look at the miniatures, if I can see the originals no longer, but remember me to Deb, Maria, and other friends, not forgetting to reserve for yourselves a lion's share of the best respects of your cousin,

Charlie

Dear Cornelia and Mary,

I perceive that Charley has been illuminating you very extensively with regard to the arrangements in and around our domicile. Truly, he is obliging. After describing everything in detail, even going into the *modus operandi* of cooking and eating, he leaves me, as he says, to finish the story and how am I to finish it? Not by describing the process of washing the dishes, surely, for he has already informed you that no such labor is ever performed.

I see nothing left for me to do except make my bow and retire. Before doing this though, I'll just say a few words and kindly permit me to acknowledge the receipt of Cornelia's kind letter of Feb. 6th. It spied us out in our fine home just as we had consumated one of our hardest day's work. Never was friendly missive more welcome—it brought glad tidings to two "strangers in a strange land." . . . Surrounded as we are by a busy multitude, we yet live a very retired life, scarcely recognizing those about us. We pass our time, when not engaged in labor, at home and alone.

It is impossible to say how long we will remain here, or what we will do next. Most likely, though, we will stop about two weeks, then go up this Yuba River. When I say mining is the hardest work in the world, I but speak the truth. "Paddy on the Canal" leads a life of ease in comparison. . . . The weather is extremely hot, about equal to July at home. Cornelia asks how we look, what we wear, what we say? I reckon we look natural as life, and as for me, I wear the same clothes that I *always* did, except the coat. I have a new sailor jacket, a kind of knit stuff, just the fit for anybody from Col. Jarvis to James Lack. I presume I shall appear in other habiliments soon, for I begin to comprehend the force of an expression in common use here, *viz* that "rents are enormous."

To make washing easy, we wear the real striped shirts. The natural inference is that the pan in which we pound our coffee is also *striped.* The sun is nearly set. I must conclude. I hope Cornelia will not take it for granted that I wish this to be considered a full answer to her letter, and as for Mary, I will not and cannot till I get it, which I hope may be soon, as I sent by an Expressman this morning for them. Remember me kindly to Uncle, Aunt, and all the friends generally. I remain

Yours and ever N. Searls

III

COMMUNICATION TO THE EAST remained sporadic, notwithstanding efforts of the two adventurers to maintain contact with their families. On April 5, 1850, Niles Searls's parents wrote from Wellington, Canada, to their Rensselaerville relatives in considerable distress:

Dear friends

I take this opportunity of writing a few lines by way of enquiry of you to ascertain any knowledge that you might have received of Niles and

Charles by Letter or other wise since your last letter to us, we have not received any from him   we have been waiting a long time with great anxiety of mind for a letter from Niles and almost despair of ever hearing from him again, if you have received any letter from them since your last to us, please write to us and let us know all about it.

No doubt you would like to know something about our family and Relatives here   our family are all in good health at presant   we have all of us had a turn of influenza colds but are now in good health

Joanna has poor health and is at presant about the same as when you saw her last summer   Alice has left us   she was married last Oct to William Babbit a Tailor by trade and has gone to Bellville to live. the children that are at home with us are all attending school.

Stephen Niles and family are all in as good health as usual   Arnold Dorland has had a severe attack of inflamation on the lungs a short time since but is recovering at presant   his older son Philip is still in a poor state of health

the winter here has been quite mild and a prospect of an early spring the ground is pretty well settled. and the roads good. pleas excuse this imperfect scrawl as I am not in the habit of writing and a trembling hand these combined make a bad piece of work

write as soon as you get this and oblige yours

Abram Searls
Lydia Searls

to John Niles
and family

Nearly two months had elapsed since Charles Mulford and Niles Searls had left Sacramento City "like true Yankees, with cakes of ginger-bread under each arm," as Charles put it. When Mulford returned to the city late in May to mail their letters and pick up any correspondence addressed to themselves, he stopped in to see William Williams, another Rensselaerville youth who had made his way to California. From him he learned that Sacramento had acquired a second newspaper, the *Sacramento Transcript,* and had experienced its first fire. Only days after they had left the city, eight commercial buildings had burned to the ground on Front Street between J and K streets.

The election which had taken place on the day of their departure had produced many new county officers. Charles was interested to see that the district attorney for Yuba County, in which they were now mining, was a man named Samuel B. Mulford. He decided to call on the attorney next time he passed through Marysville—perhaps they had relatives in common.

The outgoing alcalde of Marysville, Stephen Field, had created a stir by his dispensation of justice in the case of a soldier from the army camp at Johnson's Ranch. The ranch had been sold the year before and a pair of speculators, Henry Robinson and Eugene Gillespie were selling lots in the subdivision known as Kearney. Not far from the new town, the United States Army had established a military post which it called Camp Far West, occupied by a detachment of the Second Infantry, commanded by Captain Hannibal S. Day.

Discipline at the fort was a constant problem, so when a soldier was accused of robbing a civilian early in the year, Captain Day gladly gave permission to the Marysville authorities to try him. Private John Barrett had been convicted of stealing $1200 in gold dust, but when he refused to divulge its whereabouts, Judge Field handed down a harsh sentence. In two previous cases Field had called for the thieves to receive one hundred lashes on their bare backs. In Barrett's sentence Field ordered that the defendant be transported to Camp Far West and whipped fifty times. If he failed to reveal the hiding place of the booty within twenty-four hours after being flogged, he was to be given an additional fifty, followed by fifty more each day until a total of two hundred and fifty lashes, "well laid on," had been given the prisoner. The last four punishments could be remitted, but only if he talked.

At the conclusion of twenty strokes, Private Barrett broke down and confessed. The gold was found and restored to its owner, but because no provision had been made for remitting any of the first fifty lashes, he was taken out and flogged thirty more times. Field justified the extreme measure by saying it was better than hanging, which he supposed would have been the man's fate at the hands of miners. Captain Day requested permission to discharge Barrett dishonorably, "branded as he is with infamy and disgrace by the lashes, so deservedly inflicted." When permission was received, Barrett was branded once more, this time with the letter "R" for "rogue," and drummed from the service. Ex-Private John Barrett headed for the mines and two years of obscurity.

Before mailing his letter to Mary and Cornelia, Charley Mulford added a final note:

Sacramento City May 27

I have barely room and time to say I have just got a letter from the office for Niles postmarked R'Ville April 5th. I presume it is from some of the cousins. I long to know its contents, but must wait three days before my mule will carry me to Niles. He is still on Long Bar, and on joining him we shall pack to the headwaters of the Yuba.

NISENAN WARRIORS

CHAPTER 23

TWO PEOPLES

Summer 1848–May 1850

I

I T WILL GO BADLY if the *wolesem* choose to stay. The wolesem are not friends to the *nisenan*." So Wema had spoken many moons ago, and now it had come to pass. The white people had come again, this time to stay, or so it seemed.

Two summers earlier they began to arrive from the great valley in the west. In time Wema had learned that they were searching for small pieces of a yellow material which often was found in the bottoms of streams or along the banks of rivers. The nisenan had never bothered to give the substance a name, for it did not seem to them to be a useful material. The wolesem called it by such names as *odo* or *kol-deh*, and their passion for the flakes never ceased to astonish Wema.

At first he wondered if his people had not overlooked in this substance some important or valuable quality which the wolesem had discovered.

272

But close observation disclosed nothing more than the fact that it had some symbolic or superstitious significance for them. It was obvious that it was not good medicine, for the nisenan had witnessed much violent behavior which seemed to be connected with its possession. When they learned that the whites used it as a medium of exchange, the nisenan began to offer it in trade for tobacco, cloth, coffee, or whisky. The nisenan people did not wish to keep it long in their own possession, however, preferring not to become victims of its bad medicine.

At the end of the first summer the white intruders had gone away and some thought they would not return. Wema, however, was not surprised when even greater numbers began to arrive in the following summer. This year they did not stop only on the main river, but many continued moving eastward, exploring the narrow canyons of the smaller stream which flowed past Wema's villages. They intruded farther into nisenan territory than before, and this time there were many more persons searching for the yellow substance.

When the processions of foreigners began to arrive from the eastern mountains, as they had been doing for six summers, it was not like the other years. Instead of going to Johnson's Ranch as in the past, many stopped beside the Bear River, far up in Wema's territory. As more of them came down off the mountain, some traveled north from the Bear River, walking and riding right through the middle of nisenan villages. When they reached the camps of whites who had come up the stream from the west, they set up their shelters beside the ancient sites of Wema's summer villages, forcing the nisenan people to move to less desirable locations.

Even when summer was giving way to winter, the invasion had continued, and so indifferent to the manner of their trespass were the wolesem that the insult was like a knife to the heart. It was clear that they did not expect to be opposed in whatever they chose to do, and because the assumption had proved correct, it was resented all the more by Wema's people.

It was true that the invaders showed little desire for the theft of such valuable foods as seeds, acorns, nuts, and berries, but they were interfering with the hunting of game and the catching of fish. What they didn't poach, they frightened away. Not only was it nearly impossible to approach many of the best fishing spots because of their presence, but the streams had become so disturbed and muddied that the fish could not remain in their homes to feed the nisenan.

Hunters sometimes were warned by the whites to stay off the ancient trails, just because they had camps nearby. Wema had advised his people to avoid contact with the interlopers except when trading *odo*. However, as time passed and the number of wolesem grew, it was becoming harder to avoid encounters with evil or drunken ones, and Wema heard more and more complaints about threats or obscene proposals being made to his people. Most nisenan women took pains to stay out of sight when the whites were around, but some of the younger women were overcome by curiosity. Occasionally they could be coaxed into wolesem camps. Much of the time nothing unpleasant happened, but now and then the *odo* hunters took gross liberties. When the frightened women tried to escape they were sometimes laughed at and permitted to leave only after a great deal of fondling of their breasts and bodies. In a few instances, women had been raped and injured.

Wema worried as winter approached, and he saw that only a part of the wolesem were leaving. Some were building log shelters, and it looked as if many were preparing to remain throughout the winter. As Wema's people packed their belongings and began to move to the winter villages below the snowline, many wondered if the white people knew how cold their camps could be. If snow forced them to move later in the winter, would they not then invade the winter quarters of Wema's people? Much as the nisenan wished to leave the summer camps, they did so with heavy hearts and forebodings for the future.

II

THE HEADLINE IN the *Alta California* called it "Another Outrage upon the Indians":

Complaints have reached Sacramento city, of a disturbance having occurred in the vicinity of Deer Creek between the white men and the Indians, attended with quite a severe loss of life.

The difficulty originated, it is presumed, from a theft of animals, committed by some vagrant Indians, whereat several infuriated whites charged a party of peaceable Indians in the neighborhood and commenced indiscriminate slaughter.

The Sacramento *Transcript* contains the following particulars:

"We have been informed by a gentleman from Deer Creek that, one day last week, some twelve men, who had been soldiers in the Mexican war, attacked a party of Indians whom they accused of stealing animals, and killed four or five men and one squaw.

"The Indians, after running some time before their pursuers, turned round, seeing so few in chase, and the pursuers became the pursued, until they gained a stronghold on a rocky part of the mountain, where the Indians attacked them furiously, wounding, it is believed fatally, two of the whites, one in the shoulder and the other in the arm.

"The seige lasted two days, during which the Indians lost seventeen men and one squaw, besides those before mentioned. A man called Bill Ebben is the leader of the assailants. A party of two hundred was organized at Deer Creek, and were expected to start in pursuit last Thursday morning."

Two weeks later, the Sacramento *Placer Times* reported that "At Deer Creek . . . Indians stealing everything and getting two or three of their rancherias burnt down in consequence, whereupon in revenge they murdered one of the boys and then war commenced. Seven whites and seventy or eighty red skins are supposed to have passed out."

III

GEORGE HOLT had barely enough strength to drag himself through the heavy brush to the neighboring sawmill of James Walsh and Zenas Wheeler. His body hurt terribly and his clothes were drenched in blood. Whenever bushes or brambles caught at the broken arrow shafts still hanging from his body, he cried out in pain. When he thought he could go no farther, and just as he began to lose consciousness, he saw the mill.

Fortunately, Jim Walsh chanced to be looking in his direction when Holt pitched forward. As he ran to the wounded man, Walsh called out to his partner:

"Zenas, quick! Bring the whiskey and a bucket full of water!"

"What's happened?"

"It's George Holt—looks like he's been shot up by Injuns. C'mon, Zenas, get a move on, before the man dies!"

Jim Walsh tried to ease George's body into a position which brought less pressure on the arrows. Some of the shafts had broken off, but others were still intact. It would take a doctor or a surgeon skilled in the art of removing arrows to get them out, for the points were barbed and could not be retrieved like those used to hunt game. Removing them was as painful or more so than being hit in the first place, and even after they were gone there was still the danger of infection by erysipelas.

Zenas Wheeler rode his mule four miles north to Grass Valley, where he hoped to find someone to take care of Holt and where he also hoped to raise a posse to go after the Indians. But neither at Grass Valley nor at the Rough and Ready camp could he find a doctor willing to remove the arrows.

"Why don't you get the army surgeon from Far West?" he was asked. "He's the one to do a job like that."

"In fact," said another, "you should get the soldiers to come up here and teach them redskins a lesson. That's what they're here for, but you never see hide nor hair of them when there's trouble. Go down to Camp Far West and make the Army stop all this killing!"

Eventually he had convinced John Day, a former officer in the Mexican War, and some of Day's friends to return with him to the sawmill. Day had offered to carry a message to the army post from Walsh and Wheeler.

"You lead the way, Wheeler, and we'll follow," said the ex-captain, "but keep an eagle eye out for Indians. We don't want to step into another ambush."

IV

THROUGHOUT THE WINTER the *wolesem* had been hard at work erecting two strange buildings beside the creek. One was downstream from the other, and each was attached to a thing which rotated. It was as if one had put many feathers, not just three, on the end of an arrow, then turned the shaft round and round.

However, instead of feathers, the fins on these giant shafts were made of wood and were partly submerged. When water in the stream pressed against them they moved away from it—or tried to, because in time each fin or blade again was forced back into the stream, which once more pushed it away. Wema's people, to whom this was a curious sight, came often to watch the revolving things and wonder what they meant to the wolesem.

One day they brought a nisenan from the south to view the mysterious shapes, which also resembled the wheels on wagons. This visitor, who was related by marriage to Wema's people, was not astonished by what he saw, thus disappointing his hosts. He smiled and said:

"Ahhh! You, too, have a Sutel Mill."

It was their turn to be astonished. "What is that?" they asked.

"Kapitan Sutel has built one just like that near the village of Kuloma. It is a place for sawing trees into thin pieces. A tree can be cut into smaller slabs without using an axe."

"And they do this inside a building? That seems very awkward. I would rather work outside, where there is more room," said a northerner, bemused.

"That is the magical thing about a Sutel Mill—one does not have to work, because the thing inside will cut the tree."

"The 'thing' inside?" The southern man's relatives looked at him in wonder. "Is it a cage for a wild creature which can tear trees apart?"

They began to suspect that a madman had married into their clan.

"It is not like any living creature I have ever seen or heard about, but it can move about and cut wood that the wolesem feed it!"

"Who would believe such colossal lies?" cried an outraged cousin. "Next you will tell us that it must drink water from the stream!"

"You are right—that is the reason for the turning wheel. The cutting thing cannot saw trees unless it drinks water. If the wheel does not turn, the cutting stops."

"Go back to your own people—apparently they are gullible enough to believe such nonsense!"

The man from the south laughed. "You northerners are very ignorant about the wolesem, I see. But one day you'll see that I speak the truth."

After the Kuloma man had gone home, Wema's people discovered that it was indeed true. When the white men began to feed trees into the Sutel Mill, the tribesmen watched by the hour as the magic saw sliced through the logs. The sawdust piles grew at an alarming rate. The peculiar wheel slapped round and round, dipping into the cool water of Wolf Creek and stroking the stream in rhythm with the saw's movement.

The mill operators were friendly and invited their audience to come closer. By signs the men explained how the force of the water turned the wheel's blades, which then caused the long metal saw blade to move up and down. Wema and Walupa visited the mills one day late in April, and were concerned by what they saw.

Like others of his tribe, Wema realized that if the Sutel Mill continued to slice trees, the nisenan forest would soon disappear. No one had asked permission to cut the trees or to build the mill. Although the foreigners who operated the mill were not harming his people directly, the result of their activities would affect future generations. Recently the white people had killed many of the tribesmen because it was said they had taken animals and supplies without permission. Now the wolesem were taking trees from the nisenan in the same way. According to the white system of justice, Wema's people had the right to take the lives of the log-thieves.

On May 6, 1850, ten miners from Deer Creek attacked a native village because it was said that its inhabitants had stolen some cattle. Most of the villagers escaped, but two were killed. On the following day, warriors attacked Samuel and George Holt at their sawmill. When the rain of arrows caught them, George had seen his brother collapse even as he felt his own body absorb the blows of many feathered shafts.

Despite his injuries and the fact that his only weapon was a small pocket knife, George Holt had jumped from the building and fled to the woods. The warriors fired several more arrows in his direction, but now that he presented a moving target obscured by brush, they could not get clear shots and so abandoned pursuit. As Holt pushed his way painfully through the underbrush along the stream banks, he wondered if his brother had been able to escape. In the confusion he had not known whether Sam had fallen deliberately or had been dropped by arrows.

V

"A REDSKIN'S COMING OUT OF THE WOODS!"

John Day had been telling Jim Walsh about his planned trip to Camp Far West when the warning cry had sounded. He immediately took command: "Everybody take cover! Don't shoot unless I tell you to. Do you see any others, Bob?"

"Not so far—and he don't appear to be armed."

A solitary, naked figure was moving slowly in their direction. Halfway across the clearing, the stocky Indian halted and raised one arm. John Day stared in amazement.

"That's the chief—Wema's his name!" he said, taking a long hard look at the stationary figure. "What d'you suppose he wants?"

"That's him, all right," agreed Walsh. "He's got plenty of nerve coming here after what his bucks did this morning."

"I've a good mind to put a piece of lead between his eyes," said Wheeler, raising his rifle.

"Don't!" ordered Day harshly, putting his hand on the rifle's barrel and holding it down. "Look over there among the trees—the woods are plumb full of Indians. You pull the trigger and we're all dead!"

The others looked and saw that he was right. "What shall we do?" one of them asked Day.

"My guess is he wants to talk. I'll go out to meet him while the rest of you keep your guns ready to plug that damned chief if anything goes wrong. But, for God's sake, don't shoot unless I say the word."

"S'pose they let loose their arrows at you?"

"Then shoot him quick—but I doubt you'll have to. If they meant to kill us they wouldn't have given warning."

"Guess you're right, Captain. But how are you going to talk to him? You can't talk Injun, can you?"

"I can't speak digger language, but I know a little Spanish from the war. Most diggers know a little Spanish themselves." John Day walked away from the others.

He took his time moving across the clearing, not wanting to do the wrong thing. He hoped that he had guessed right about the chief's intentions. At last, three paces in front of Wema, he halted and said in Spanish:

"¿Qué quiere? ¿Qué hace?"

The chief answered in the nisenan tongue: "Wole wono."

"Did you say 'wolawono'?"

"Wole wono, han. Sí," replied Wema.

"No comprendo wolawono, chief. No comprendo. No sabe. How about it—¿Wema sabe español?" Day pointed to the chief.

"Sí, panjól." Wema pointed to Day, saying, "homble" as he did so.

"Hombre, right! Me hombre all right, and don't you forget it!"

Wema grinned. "Homble—wole,".he said, again indicating Day.

Day pointed to himself and repeated Wema's words: "Hombre—wole." Wema nodded agreement, but when Day repeated the words while pointing in the chief's direction, Wema shook his head and frowned.

"No," he answered. Touching his own body, Wema said "Homble—majdyk."

"Maiduk?"

"Majdyk—sí," said Wema.

"I get it. Me wole, you maiduk—is that it?"

Wema nodded and smiled. Then the smile went away as he pointed towards the woods and his tribesmen, saying, "Wole."

"Wole? Haven't you got that mixed up? Looks to me like maiduk in those woods. Maiduk?"

Wema nodded. "Majdyk wada. Wole wono."

"There you go with that 'wolawono' business again. What in hell is wono?"

Suddenly Wema clapped both hands to his chest, opened his mouth as if to cry out, and rolled his eyes skyward. Then, before Day knew what was happening, the chief closed his eyes and dropped his head so that his chin rested on his chest.

Day felt an icy chill race up and down his spine. Although there had been no sound of any kind, it looked for all the world as if Wema had been wounded fatally. As John Day steeled himself for the expected volley of arrows, Wema's head went up and his eyes flew open.

"Wono!" spoke the chief.

Day was dripping with sweat, his face white with shock. You miserable old savage! he thought. I figured you were dead, and me as well. *Dead!* Suddenly he realized that was what this naked chief was trying to tell him: wono meant dead. John Day, still shaking, gestured in the direction of the woods behind Wema.

"Hombre—wole—wono," he said, carefully.

Chief Wema nodded. Then he called out an order to his tribesmen, following which a young Indian stepped out into the clearing with the body of Samuel Holt slung over his shoulder. Hearing a noise from the direction of his white friends, John Day quickly told them not to move. "It's all right, boys—don't shoot. I think he's got Sam Holt, and it looks like he's dead."

Anger was slowly replacing Day's earlier fear. He had seen many corpses in Mexico, so the body did not shock him, and he did not grieve as a friend, for he had scarcely known the dead man. What gave rise to his outrage was his belief that a white American possessed of valuable skills had been wantonly murdered by worthless savages, the lowest of the race. Either through ignorance or meanness, he reasoned, these miserable creatures had destroyed a superior life.

He willingly would have attacked the chief with his bare hands, but he recognized how slim were his own chances of surviving. With immense effort he restrained his fury and tried to elicit more information from Wema. After much effort on both sides, Wema was able to make Day understand that Holt had died because the whites had killed Indians, but the ex-soldier either could not or would not understand that Holt had been executed for stealing from the Indians.

Eventually, Wema gave up trying. He turned his back to Day and walked into the woods, followed by the youth who had delivered Samuel Holt's body. John Day picked up the lifeless form and carried it to the mill.

VI

IT HAD BEEN TOO LATE to head for Camp Far West, so they had eaten supper in Walsh and Wheeler's cabin and were preparing to spend the night at the mill. Afterwards John Day and Zenas Wheeler had gone for a walk while Jim Walsh laboriously composed a letter to the military commander. The day had been warm, and now, in the cool of early evening, the men still could smell the sweet fragrance of wildflowers among the tall grass of the meadow.

"Look at that sunset, Wheeler. It's as bloody red as the day has been."

"Peculiar, isn't it? Don't usually get a sunset quite like that. Kind of like a sign, maybe."

"Maybe." Day looked at the sky for a long time. "Tell me, Wheeler, which way is north? I'm a little confused."

"Why, it's that way—you can line up with that big pine over there—see that real tall one, by itself?"

"That's what I guessed. So why is there a sunset to the southwest of here?"

"Oh, Lord! It must be a fire!"

"I think you're right. It looks to me as if someone's set fire to the Holt place."

"We'd better get down there and lend a hand!"

"Forget it, Zenas. There's nothing we can do. Do you want to chase around in the woods at night and have them Injuns lift your scalp?"

"I guess you're right, John. Damn, but it makes me mad, though! We never did any harm to those redskins and look at the thanks we get. We treated 'em decent, let 'em come down and watch us. I figured we were friends."

"It's no use trying to figure 'em, Zenas. Only thing to do is show 'em who's boss, and if they won't take orders, kill 'em or run 'em out. And that's what we're going to do!"

In the morning, John Day and a companion rode to Camp Far West, where they delivered Walsh's letter to Captain Hannibal S. Day. On the way they had stopped at the site of the Holt sawmill and found both it and the cabin burned to the ground. They transmitted this information along with the letter.

To their dismay, Captain Day replied that he could spare no more than eight men, including Doctor Murray, the camp physician. Only two companies of the Second United States Infantry were stationed there at the time, and Day actually tried to convince the men that the miners were better able to deal with the Indians than the military. The commandant also hinted that they might even have caused their own problems. The disgusted miners had no choice but to go back to Wolf Creek in the company of five privates, one corporal, a lieutenant and the camp doctor.

After George Holt's wounds had been treated and the arrows removed, he was taken to the store at Stocking's Flat. There were men nearby who called themselves physicians to look after him, now that the surgery was done. A hundred or so miners who had heard about the assault on Holt's Mill rode down from Deer Creek and joined the platoon from Camp Far West. For two days the combined posse combed the countryside, but the villages were deserted and only one Indian could be found.

On May 11 the soldiers went back to camp and Captain Day filed a report which pointed out that the death of Samuel Holt had been preceded by the killing of two Indians for the alleged theft of cattle. He noted that the cattle had later been found, unhurt, never having been stolen. It was Captain Day's opinion that the attack on the Holt brothers was "purely in consequence of a lawless aggression of white men in the first instance." He warned that, unless something were done quickly to change the situation, the Indians would seek revenge on any white man, guilty or not.

Unlike Captain Day, California Governor Peter H. Burnett was not immune to pressure from the miners. As rumors of Indian attacks and raids traveled like wildfire through the mining camps, sales of guns and pistols increased; demand drove the price of Colt's five-shot revolvers back up to seventy-five dollars after a decline in price during the winter. The miners demanded protection and the governor responded by telling State Senator Thomas Jefferson Green to organize two companies of volunteers to pursue the Indians and tame them.

Green, who had earlier been named a Major General in the as yet non-existent First Division of the California State Militia, accepted the assignment with pleasure. First he hurried over to the town of Nicolaus and persuaded its recent founder, Nicolaus Allgeier, to raise one of the companies. At Oro, just above Nicolaus on the Feather River, a second company was being formed by Charles H. Hoyt, cousin of Lieutenant William T. Sherman, and former owner of the land on which Camp Far West stood. The town of Oro had been founded by General Green himself, and was the new seat of Sutter County government thanks to Green's political connections, which were excellent.

The Sacramento *Placer Times* reported these moves with approval:

Brigadier General A. M. Winn has received a letter from Major General Thomas J. Green, First Division California Militia, forwarded by Brigadier General Eastland, and enclosing one to his Excellency, Peter H. Burnett, Governor of California.

We have been favored with the perusal of these letters. They are dated at Oro, the headquarters, at present, of General Green. Serious Indian troubles are announced on that frontier. A volunteer company, under command of Capt. Nicolaus Allgeier, had prepared to march against the savages, and other parties were being formed. The Indians are reported to number several hundred and to be headed by white men and some Chilians. An engagement is said to have taken place on Deer creek, a few days before, in which four whites and fifteen Indians were killed.

General Green has very wisely determined to take the field, both for the protection of the citizens and to protect excesses on their part.

On Friday, May 17, a report that 200 Indians had been seen in the vicinity of Camp Far West sent the volunteers out in hot pursuit. Four or five Indians were killed and six prisoners taken by a mounted posse led by Lieutenant James Bell of Captain Allgeier's company. On the same day, the body of Charles Mott, or Matty, a Nicolaus teamster, was found pierced by fourteen arrows. His wagon and merchandise had been burned and four pair of oxen killed.

During the next two days, Saturday and Sunday, Green's fifty mounted volunteers visited the empty villages in the vicinity of Deer and Wolf creeks. On Sunday evening, acting on a tip, the First Division made camp alongside the Bear River. In the morning, Green and his men left their horses in camp and crossed the river on foot. Their destination, a village just below the Illinoistown trading post, was found deserted. This was not too surprising, for Green was told that local traders had been battling the Indians throughout the winter. The white merchants had tried to force the nisenan tribes to stay on the north side of the Bear River, and the Illinoistown road was lined with Indian scalps prominently displayed on trees.

Although the village was empty, there were signs that a large group of Indians recently had headed north across the river, so the militia went back through its icy waters to camp. Here Green learned that his scouts had sighted several hundred Indians on top of a cone-shaped hill two or three miles north of the river. One Indian suspected of spying on the scouts had been shot and wounded, but had escaped.

VII

FROM THE HILL on which they waited and watched, the nisenan villagers could see far into the Sacramento Valley when they faced the west. In the opposite direction the snowcapped outline of the Sierra Nevada stretched for miles along the distant horizon; in the foreground, the gray and white cliffs of Chalk Bluff stood out against the dark green forest. The Deer Creek mining camps of the white people lay to the northwest, but they were hidden from view by the timbered ridges which paralleled the streams in that area. It was a scene not greatly different from that which their ancestors had viewed many centuries before.

Wema was not fooled by this illusion, nor were his people. Not only were there many camps on the other side of the ridge, filled with thousands of wolesem, but for two weeks the soldiers had been chasing the nisenan people from village to village until it now appeared they would soon be overtaken. Because the whites rode horses and the tribes walked (with the exception of the *jom*), it was inevitable that the day of confrontation should come. The men might have escaped by traveling swiftly and silently up the canyons and ravines until they lost their pursuers in the dense chaparral, but women, children, and old men were slower and could not keep up. If left behind, they would be killed or enslaved.

Wema, Bukla, Walupa, and Pulel had been discussing future strategy for days, knowing that the time of reckoning was approaching quickly. Although the nisenan warriors were brave and outnumbered those of the wolesem, all knew that the enemy force was superior, by reason of their greater mobility and better weapons. Although arrows were effective and lethal at close range, pistols and rifles were deadly at two or three times the distance. This meant that an archer must work within an extremely dangerous perimeter of fire in order to be effective.

Until the arrival of the white man, the limited range of the bow and arrow had not been important, for all California tribes on the western Sierra slope used the short bow. It was the logical choice in country where opportunities for long shots seldom occurred. Hunting was ordinarily done by archers who concealed themselves beside animal trails and waited for their targets to appear, usually no more than ten or twenty yards away and sometimes closer. Both the hunter's skill and his equipment were adapted to these special circumstances.

Even carrying a bow through heavily wooded or brushy terrain dictated the use of shorter weapons which would not tangle in the undergrowth. The length of a new bow was usually determined by holding the piece of yew or cedar from which it would be constructed in a diagonal position across the front of the user's body. The piece of wood was gripped in both hands, one placed beside the hip and the other outstretched in the opposite direction and lifted toward the sky at an angle midway between the horizon and directly overhead. The distance from one hand to the other was the proper length for a bow.

Although native yew was the favored wood for making bows, it was hard to find. Because it grew only in dark and moist canyons, and very slowly at that, few such trees ever reached maturity, and those few often were nearly inaccessible. Most bows were shaped from branches taken from the red incense cedar (called *man*). After being seasoned in a warm and sheltered place, the *man* wood was scraped with flint or obsidian until it assumed the desired shape.

So that it would not break when bent, the back of the bow had to be coated with deer sinew, soaked and chewed and then applied in strips over a thick layer of salmon glue which had been allowed to dry. Then, as the deer sinew itself began to dry and consequently bent the bow in the wrong direction, more of the glue made from boiling salmon skins was applied over the sinew strips. After several days the backing and glue were hard and dry and it was safe to begin limbering the weapon.

The arrows used were of many types. Some were designed for shooting birds, while others were for larger game, and most of these could be removed easily from the target and re-used many times. Those to be used against the wolesem were not of this type, however, but were barbed and then dipped in rattlesnake venom.

Jepe, who had been watching the soldiers for several days, arrived to tell Wema that the enemy was not so numerous as they had thought.

"There are no more than fifty-five *soltánu*," he said. (The first soldiers known to the nisenan had been Spanish *soldados*.) "They will be here soon."

"From which direction?"

"From the south."

"Fifty-five won't be enough to surround the hill," said Walupa.

"What are you thinking, Walupa?" asked Wema.

"They can't prevent some people from slipping through their lines. If we conceal the women and children in ravines part way down the hill, they can wait until the wolesem have gone by. While we keep the soltánu occupied on top, our families can slip away."

"I like that plan," nodded Wema. "The whites will be in such a hurry to close the circle higher on the hill that they will not pay close attention as they climb. They will avoid the ravines because of their horses, anyway."

"The women and children, and even some of the old men can find their way to the Chalk Bluff. They all know the way. But they must remain hidden and avoid the main trails."

"Good. But we cannot fight for long on the hill. We, too, will have to flee before the wolesem close the trap."

"Yes, we will have to come down from the hill ourselves, but we should not go in the same direction as the others, for fear of leading the soltánu to them. We shall have to be like the quail and its young."

"Then we shall travel west, where it is steep, rough country. The horses will have slow going."

"Excellent! We'll show our broken wings from time to time, but see to it that they see no more. In the meantime we must arrange the families into traveling groups and get them hidden. And Jepe, I want you and Bukla to locate several escape routes for us. The more choices, the better, because we don't know yet how they'll come at us."

VIII

To His Excellency, Peter H. Burnett, Governor and Commander-in-chief, California Militia, from Thomas J. Green, Major General, First Division:

. . . After examining their position, I ordered Captain Hoyt with twenty men to take station at the foot of the hill upon the left, and with Captain Allgeier, Lieutenant Bell and the balance of the men, in all thirty, I charged up the most accessible side of the hill upon the right, into the camp, and drove the Indians upon Captain Hoyt's position, where a smart skirmish ensued.

We pursued them for several miles in the hills and ravines, killing and wounding a number and took eight prisoners . . . We had none killed. Wounded: Captain Hoyt, Lieutenant Lewis and Mr. Russell. My Aid, Major Frederick Emory, was accidentally shot through the thigh by the discharge of a rifle. All doing well.

The day previous, in attempting to capture one of their spies, his determined resistance caused him to be shot, and in camp we found his remains upon a funeral pile nearly consumed. Here we found a large amount of supplies, consisting of beef, sugar, tea, and other articles robbed from the wagons, and the clothes of the murdered teamster, Matty.

On the afternoon of the same day I sent the following note, with a flag of truce, to the chiefs, by an old woman who had been taken prisoner:

Wolf Creek Camp, May 20, 1850

To the Indian Chiefs Weima, Buckler, Poollel,
    and others:

Your people have been murdering ours, robbing their wagons and burning their houses. We have made war upon you, killed your men and taken prisoners your women and children. We send you this plain talk by one of your grandmothers.

When you cease to rob and murder our people we will cease to make war upon you, and then you can come in and get your women and children, who will be taken care of in the meantime. If you wish peace, come down to Johnson's old ranch, on Bear river, and report yourselves to Captain Charles Hoyt, who will protect you until your Great Father shall speak.

Thos. J. Green,
Major General
First Division
California Militia.

NISENAN CREMATION

CHAPTER 24

FIRST TREATY

May 1850

I

*S*HE COULD HAVE BEEN SAFE by now, far from the dreaded *wole-sem*, had the widow and her family gone off with the other women. But that was impossible. Her dead husband, a *nisenan* scout, had painfully worked his way back to Wema's camp after receiving mortal wounds in a skirmish with the *soltánu*. Because of the expected attack, the usual cremation ceremonies had to be abbreviated—there was not enough time to follow tradition.

Properly, the cremation should have occurred on the following day. Instead, it began almost immediately. Family members were not permitted to take part in this first rite. Only after the remains were nearly consumed and the fire extinguished was the family invited to gather round the body. Then, as the fire was being rekindled for the final burning, Owl's cry warned that the attack was beginning, and soon all could hear the crashing of horses in the brush below.

Even if there had been time to escape, the widow would not have abandoned her spouse's remains, so she and her female relatives waited as the soltánu came charging up two sides of the hill. The unarmed women and children were seized by several white men, whose companions rode off in hot pursuit of the men. For some unaccountable reason the soldiers had poked about the fire, seemingly as distressed and angry with the grief-stricken widow as she was with them.

When the wolesem warriors came back from the chase emptyhanded, torn, and bloody, the widow was glad. Before she could think about her own fate much, she and the other women and young people were led downhill to the wolesem camp and she began to be afraid. The hungry eyes of the soltánu explored her body, lingering often upon her uncovered breasts. She thought that she would not like to be exposed to such searching examinations without the protection of her skirt. It did not disturb her if nisenan men occasionally observed her bathing naked at the river, but they did not look at her with such undisguised lust as these soldiers did. It was because they had no women of their own, she knew. She also knew that they did not treat nisenan women with respect.

She was taken to a cloth house and pushed inside. Here she found herself in the presence of three men, two of whom she guessed to be chiefs of the wolesem. The third one began to speak to her in a strange language, and it took awhile for her to realize that he was trying to speak her tongue. His pronunciation was outrageous and he was speaking in a dialect which she had only heard once or twice in her life. If she concentrated very hard, however, and he repeated the words often enough, she could make out the gist of what he had to say.

"Talk chief," said the interpreter. "You talk chief, O.K.? You talk chief, say stop! No kill Americans! American chief stop kill nisenan. Understand?"

She was puzzled. What did he mean? Yes, she understood his words, but his meaning was unclear. Obviously the fighting had stopped or else the soltánu would not be here in the camp. Was that what he meant? If so, he must think her stupid. She said nothing and waited to see if he would speak again.

"Understand: Chief Wema? You know Chief Wema?"

She nodded yes. Everybody knew Chief Wema.

"Know place Chief Wema live?"

She didn't know, not now. She shook her head.

"You find chief! Tell chief Americans want smoke pipe."

"The soltánu wish to smoke the pipe with our chief?" she asked.

"Yes! Good! Tell chief Americans not kill your people."

"What are you talking about? You have killed my husband! What stupid talk is this? What do you mean *Melikin* don't kill our people? They do it all the time!" she snapped angrily.

The interpreter could not follow her rapid speech and held up his hand in protest: "Stop! Talk more slow—no understand fast talk!"

Very slowly, she said, "Do you think I am crazy or stupid? Your people have killed my husband—for nothing!"

She waited while he translated her words into the wolesem language and listened as the chiefs chattered back and forth. Their pink faces changed to bright red. The interpreter turned to her again and said:

"American Chief say bad thing your husband die. American Chief say him sorry."

She did not reply, so the man went on:

"American Chief want stop war. American Chief go home now. Take nisenan women, children to Johnson's Ranch. You tell Chief Wema, come Johnson's Ranch, smoke pipe. Stop war. Then women, children go home. Understand?"

She nodded.

He pressed her for a reply: "What you say Chief Wema?"

"I'll tell Chief Wema the soltánu have taken my family prisoner and are taking them to Chansen Lanjo. I'll tell the chief you wish him to come to Chansen Lanjo and smoke the pipe with the wolesem chief. I'll tell him you will end the war and release the prisoners."

"Say again, more slow." He'd lost most of her words, she could tell. Scornfully, she imitated his broken speech, even corrupting her excellent diction in order to mimic his awkward pronunciation. When she had finished, the interpreter smiled with relief. Pleased with his success in making the woman understand, he turned proudly to his chiefs and spoke in their language. The chiefs talked to one another. Then one went away. When he returned, he carried something white and flat and thin which he handed to the other chief.

After examining it for several minutes, the second chief had folded it carefully until it became very small, small enough to fit in the palm of his hand. He gave it to the go-between, who handed it to her. "Give to Chief Wema," he said. "Good medicine. Save Chief from harm. Tell Chief carry *papel*. American see papel, no harm Chief Wema. Understand?"

She looked at the thing in her hand with great curiosity. So this was the substance called papel about which she had heard but never before seen. It was slightly stiff, like an animal skin before it had been softened, but so much thinner and more delicate. The man said it was good medicine, but how could one trust wolesem to speak the truth?

II

AFTER THE AMERICANS released her, the widow hurried back to the site of her husband's remains. Already the scavengers had been at work and they had disposed what the fire had not. At the top of the hill she dug two holes with a sharp manzanita branch. It took a long time to make both holes deep enough to satisfy her. At last she stopped digging and began to gather the bone fragments which had belonged to her man—the warm, strong and handsome person who had shared her house for twenty-four winters. She laid the bones in one of the holes and covered them with the ashes of her husband.

Under normal circumstances, she would not have done these tasks herself. Other women would have burned the body and buried the remains, but today they were far away and could not help the lonely widow.

Next she took a sharp-edged rock in one hand and a hard piece of oak in the other and began to cut her long black hair between the tool and the cutting board. She cut until her head was closely cropped all over and then carried the shorn tresses to the second hole and buried them. Had a fire been available she might have burned the hair, but she had no fire drill. She covered the bones, ashes, and hair, pressed the soil firmly with her feet, and laid pine needles, acorns, leaves and twigs across the surface so that no sign of her excavations remained. Finally, she carried a number of large rocks to the burial spot and piled them on it to discourage wild animals.

The widow walked about in the woods on top of the hill until she found a bleeding pine from which she could obtain pitch to apply to her scalp. When head and hair were thoroughly coated with the sticky substance, she came back to the former camp. Locating the firepit where the tribe's meals had been prepared, she rubbed handfuls of ashes into the pitch on her head.

With one tarry hand she drew a line across her cheek from the corner of her mouth to the bottom of her ear. Then, with the other hand she repeated the decoration on the opposite cheek, so that her face seemed to be bisected by a continuous line running from ear to ear and passing through her mouth. This done, she sat down once more and reached out her black and sticky hands to hold herself in a tight embrace.

For two or three minutes she seemed not to move or to make a sound. Then she bent slightly at the waist and began to rock slowly back and forth, moaning quietly as she did so. Soon she was moving more quickly and she had begun to weep. Forward and back, forward and back, she rocked, the rhythm of her cries matching the motion of her body. Before long her voice had become a rising and falling wail, full of grief and misery and longing.

Except for the low whisper of the wind, the forest had grown silent. The birds and animals on the hill stopped their talk and warnings as if listening gravely to the keening of the nisenan woman. As she sat and rocked and wept and wailed, the widow's tears etched a lacy pattern across the black and gray finger trails left by her hands as she clutched her chest and shoulders.

III

JEPE SAW THE WIDOW walk out of the soltánu camp. Because he wondered why she had been let go, he waited and watched the camp for a long time afterward, curious to see if the wolesem would follow. When instead they broke camp and moved in the opposite direction, going west, Jepe went to Wema and told him what he had observed. The chief at once ordered Jepe to overtake the woman and bring her back to his hiding place.

By the time Jepe caught up with the widow, she was preparing to leave the site of her husband's grave and join the other women and children at the Chalk Bluff summer village. Instead, she accompanied Jepe and told Chief Wema what the wolesem had said. Her words satisfied him that the soltánu had gone back to Johnson's Ranch, so he proposed that they all rejoin their families as soon as possible.

On the way to Chalk Bluff one of the men voiced the apprehension of all. "What if Chansen Lanjo is a trap? They may be using the hostages as bait."

"That's a chance I'll have to take," Wema replied. "We can't continue to run. They outnumber us. We have no choice."

"What do you hope to accomplish?" inquired Walupa.

"I don't know. If I explain how things are with us, I think the wolesem chief may realize it's not possible for his people and ours to live in the same country. If they were reasonably civilized, it would be one thing, but when they behave like barbarians, there is no way to avoid trouble. The sooner they leave, the better it will be for everyone."

"And if they decide to kill you?"

"You'll have to elect a new chief, I imagine," Wema dryly replied.

When Wema headed west a few days later, bound for Johnson's Ranch, he rode the shaman's horse, borrowed especially for the occasion. The animal was growing old, but its pace was fast enough to suit Wema, unused as he was to riding. Bukla and Pulel went along on foot to keep him company, and a dozen younger men acted as his armed guard.

General Green was not at Camp Far West when they arrived, on May

25, 1850, so they had to wait until he could be found and brought to the government camp. The nisenan delegation was very uneasy in the presence of armed soldiers and Wema was about to withdraw when General Green and his aides rode into the fort and gave the Indians a warm greeting.

He invited them to sit with him in the soltánu lodge, where he announced that he and the other white leaders wished to bring an end to the fighting forever. This was good news to Wema and he suggested that one practical method of accomplishing this result would be for the wolesem to withdraw from Wema's territory. Green was amused, which angered Wema, so the General quickly apologized, but added that such a solution was out of the question. The Americans were going to stay and Wema's people were simply being requested to make room for them. There was plenty of land for all, said Green, and the American chiefs would guarantee to protect the Indians from bad treatment at the hands of the whites if Wema would agree to two conditions. Through the interpreter, Green explained them:

First: If any nisenan tribe member should kill or steal from an American (or break any other American law), Chief Wema was to deliver the guilty party to the American chiefs for punishment.

Second: Wema's people were not to carry weapons in or near the white people's camps. This was to prevent misunderstandings.

In return, the Americans were prepared to promise four things to the Indians:

1. Any white who wronged a nisenan would be punished by the Americans.

2. The nisenan people would be allowed to work in the gold mines. American chiefs would settle any disputes which arose concerning contracts between them and the whites.

3. The women and children being held hostage would be released.

4. The Americans would pay Wema, Bukla, and Pulel one thousand dollars each, twice a year, for a total of ten summers and ten winters.

Wema, Bukla, and Pulel affixed their marks to the paper.

IV

"IT IS MY OPINION, as well as the opinion of others better acquainted with these Indians, that they will observe the treaty in good faith," wrote General Green in his covering letter to the governor. "It is to be hoped that no acts of aggression will be commenced upon them by the whites. These Indians can be made very useful to the miners if they have even a small portion of justice extended to them.

"Heretofore a few persons have monopolized much of their labor, by giving them a calico shirt per week and the most indifferent food. This is not only wrong, but highly disgraceful, when they would be content with the pay of one-fourth of the wages of the white men."

Green did not bother to call to Wema's attention a small escape clause which read: "The Government of the United States shall have six months from this date to confirm, amend, or annul the treaty." He saw no reason to suppose Congress would fail to ratify such a reasonable document.

The *Placer Times* applauded the agreement in an editorial on May 29, 1850:

This is a movement in the right direction. We hope indiscriminate outrage and revenge have had their day. Nothing has so disgraced the early history of our state as the atrocious and inhuman persecutions that have been inflicted upon these weak, ignorant and naturally inoffensive Indians.

That they have retaliated, as far as lay in their power, the barbarous assaults and promiscuous slaughter that have been visited upon them is their credit and not their crime. There is no difference in the enlightened opinion of all who are familiar with the subject.

We have seen but one expression, and that of unqualified denunciation upon those whose beastly passions have led them to commit the murderous deeds, a recital of which has often led us to suppress.

We believe that there are good men enough, now that the initiative has been taken, to carry out the example of conciliation which is here set forth, and we anticipate favorable results from its publication and general circulation in the different mining and Indian regions.

But unknown to Wema or his nisenan followers, the first California Legislature on April 22, 1850, had passed a set of laws regulating conduct of Indians and whites, without concurrence of any Indian tribes. Entitled "An Act for the Government and Protection of Indians," it sought to minimize conflict and provide a basis for law and order.

This Act provided that local justices of the peace were given jurisdiction over all complaints for, by, or against the Indians. Whites could not simply drive Indians off the land, but must apply to the local justice to have certain areas set off for the "necessary wants of such Indians, including the site of their village or residence, if they so prefer it."

The Indians could not be forced to abandon homes or villages where they had resided for a number of years, and either party feeling aggrieved could appeal to the county court.

Any person having or wishing to obtain a minor Indian for a servant could legalize the arrangement simply by going before a justice with the child's parents or friends and registering the child's sex and probable age. The judge would issue a certificate granting the white petitioner care, custody, control and earnings of the minor until the age of majority was reached. For females this was defined as fifteen years, for males it was eighteen.

Should the child be maltreated, the person into whose hands the Indian had been delivered was subject to a fine of not less than ten dollars and the justice had the discretion of placing the child in the care of some other person. If one wished to establish a binding work contract with an Indian, a justice would approve and file the written document in his office—no other contract would bind the Indian. Anyone who kidnapped or forced an Indian to work was subject to a fine of at least fifty dollars, if convicted.

Anyone who furnished intoxicating liquors to an Indian "except when administered in sickness" was subject to a fine of at least twenty dollars for each offense, or imprisonment for at least five days. An Indian convicted of stealing horses, mules, cattle, "or any valuable thing," could receive any number of lashes not exceeding twenty-five, or a fine not to exceed two hundred dollars. If he was to be whipped, the justice could appoint a white man or Indian, at his discretion, to execute the sentence in his presence and he was not to permit unnecessary cruelty in the execution of the sentence.

Any Indian who was able bodied and could support himself and who was found loitering and strolling about, or frequenting saloons, begging, or leading an immoral or "profligate course of life," could be arrested on the complaint of any resident and brought before any justice, mayor or recorder, and if it was determined by that official that the Indian was a vagrant, he could be hired out within twenty-four hours to the highest bidder for any term not exceeding four months. The money received for his hire, after deducting costs and necessary expense for clothing the Indian, would go to the Indian's family, if he had one. If he had no family, the money would be credited to the county Indian Fund. However, if the vagrant, when arrested and before judgement, could provide the official with a bond, and good security, that he would conduct himself properly for one year, he could be released.

All fines imposed on Indians and fees recovered were to be recorded and turned over to the County Treasurer so a statement could be kept under the heading of "Indian Fund." It was the duty of justices and other peace officers to instruct Indians about the laws which related to them, give them proper advice, and if any tribe or village refused or failed to obey the laws, the justice could punish the guilty chiefs or principal men by reprimand or fine, "or otherwise reasonably chastise them."

Justices could require the chiefs and influential men of any village to apprehend and bring before them or him any Indian charged or suspected of an offense. When an Indian was convicted of an offense punishable by fine, any white person might give bond for the Indian, conditioned upon the payment of fine and costs, and in such case the Indian would be compelled to work for the person who provided bail until the fine was cancelled. However, the bail bondsman had to treat the Indian "humanely, and clothe and feed him properly," and the allowance given for his labor was to be fixed by the court when the bond was taken. Complaints could be made by either whites or Indians, but no white man could be convicted of any offense solely upon the testimony of an Indian.

General Green waited until after Wema and his two companions had finished signing the treaty before explaining the already enacted new laws to them. He had not wanted to confuse the Indians with too much information at once. Now, however, it was his duty to inform them of their rights and obligations.

When he realized that conditions had already existed without his agreement or knowledge, Wema was incensed. When the whites tried to explain that, unlike treaties, legislated acts were not negotiable, Wema replied that even if this were so, information had been withheld from him during the negotiations. Had he known of the existence of such laws he might never have signed, he stated, thus confirming General Green's shrewd guess. Furious, Wema demanded that the jom's horse be brought to him.

As Wema and his companions headed glumly in the direction of the village at Chalk Bluff, General Green hurried home to the city of Oro. The first meeting of the Sutter County Court of Sessions was due to commence on June 10, but no buildings had been erected for the use of its judges. County Judge Gordon N. Mott and his two associate justices, P. W. Thomas and Tallman Rolfe, were threatening to hold court in the town of Nicolaus unless suitable quarters were provided soon at Oro.

Judge Rolfe, twenty-five years old, had been elected to the post of Justice of the Peace at Yuba City's spring election. Judge Mott, an Ohio veteran of the Mexican War, then appointed Rolfe to a seat on Sutter County's governing body. After a slow and shaky start, Yuba City at last was beginning to grow. Its population was nearing five hundred, half that of neighboring Marysville, and it boasted a hotel, called the "Western."

Tallman Rolfe was both surprised and amused to realize that his roommates both hailed from Missouri. He wondered wryly what his family would make of him sharing quarters with a couple of "pukes from puke county."

MINERS' BALL

CHAPTER 25

NEW PROSPECTS

June–July 1850

I

"SHHHH! DONT MAKE SO MUCH NOISE!"

"Can you see them?"

"Yes—they're just crossing that upper ridge. Look carefully—there! against the sky."

"Let's get moving. We don't want to lose them."

"Not much chance of that with all the noise they're making."

"Well, we don't want to take any chances."

The seven conspirators moved slowly through the wooded hills north of Nevada City. The sun was about to rise, the day was June 7, 1850, and ahead were several dozen men on mules, and twice as many heavily laden pack animals. The procession was led by Thomas R. Stoddard, who among other things claimed to be a former Philadelphia newspaper editor and veteran English sailor. He also claimed to know where gold was easy to find.

A few nights earlier, Luther Schaeffer had been joined by five young miners from Gold Run, who came by his camp to report strange happenings in their neighborhood.

"No one will talk to us about it," said one young man, "but it looks to us like a lot of men are about to leave for the mountains."

"That doesn't sound very mysterious," replied Luther. "That's just about the commonest thing I can imagine."

"That's so; but men who are working valuable claims seldom have time for prospecting."

"I guess you're right," acknowledged Schaeffer, "but are you sure they're prospecting? Perhaps they're just off for a day or two while the weather's nice."

"With mining tools and supplies enough to last two or three months? No, they're onto something or they wouldn't risk losing a sure thing."

"But if they've heard about some rich diggings, why hasn't the rest of the camp found out about it?"

"That's what puzzles us. News like that is hard to keep quiet."

"Pretty near impossible, I'd say. Have you tried asking around town? If they're outfitting and buying supplies, they must have let something slip. One or another of them is bound to have talked to a saloon keeper or gambler or someone."

"That's just what we thought. We came by to see if you and your friend want to help out. If any of us finds out something useful, we'll share the news. What do you say, is that fair?"

Luther looked at his tentmate, a young fellow from Providence, Rhode Island, who answered, "Why not?"

"All right," said Luther, "we'll help you. Any special place you'd like us to go? No sense everyone talking to the same people."

"Why don't you fellows visit the Main Street hotels while we stop at the saloons and stables and the Broad Street boarding houses. How's that?"

"Sounds good. We don't much care for the faster night life, anyway! Where should we meet afterward?"

"How about right here, tomorrow night, about the same time?"

Luther and his friend from Rhode Island went first to the Nevada Hotel to exchange gossip and small talk with Nick Turner and his wife Harriet, two of Nevada's earliest residents. Thirty years before in Tennessee, Nick had been christened Joshua Nicholas Turner—his Ohio-reared wife was five years younger. In the fall of 1849 she had set the "hearts of the sturdy miners to beat strong and fast," according to Joseph Morrison.

On the first of May they had opened Nevada's first frame-built hotel. Nick was eager to discuss the details of his building, which had been constructed entirely of lumber sawed from a single pine tree and was thirty-eight feet wide by forty-eight feet long, a story and a half tall. He was equally informative about business affairs (board and room was twenty-five dollars a week, all meals prepared by Harriet), but he had no explanation for the mysterious activities at Gold Run.

Saying goodnight to the Turners, the pair went on to the Miner's Hotel and conversed with Peyton and Martha Womack, owners in partnership with A. B. Kenzie, a twenty-two-year-old lad from Missouri. Theirs had been the first boarding house in town, with walls and roof of cotton cloth and meals a dollar apiece. The Womacks could shed no more light on the problem than the Turners, so the sleuths moved down the street to the El Dorado.

It was a high-sounding name for what was the least pretentious boarding house in town. In the two months or so since Luzena and Mason Wilson had been there, they had saved enough to pay off their $700 debt to the teamster. Now there was a solid roof over Luzena's open-air stove and the brush hut in which they lived—Mason planned to frame a building and enclose the walls before summer's end. In time, if the town continued to grow and business prospered, Luzena expected to add a room or two so she could provide beds as well as meals. She wanted to manage a first-class hotel.

In the meantime, she was preparing a hundred or more meals each day, at the same time endeavoring to keep a watchful eye on her two boys. She overheard a great deal in the course of serving her customers, but when asked if by chance she had heard of the business at Gold Run, she reminded the youths that it wouldn't be right for her to eavesdrop on the private conversations of her boarders. In a kindly way, and careful not to give offense, she explained that even if she should accidentally overhear a word or two, it was none of her business; her policy was to respect their right to privacy.

Luther agreed that this undoubtedly was a prudent course and wished Mrs. Wilson great success in her endeavor. Wiser, but no better informed than when they set out, the young men went home and retired. On the following evening they were relieved to hear that one of the Gold Run miners had discovered the secret.

"Out with it!" cried Luther. "Don't keep us guessing!"

"It seems there's a fellow who has showed around a lot of gold he claims to have found in a place he calls Gold Lake."

"Gold Lake!" laughed Luther. "Gold Lake! Marvelous!"

"Don't laugh—I'm telling you what he told them—the lake really is called Gold Lake!"

"Oh, I can just see it: a lake of molten gold, surrounded by golden sands and golden rocks! Is that the best he can do?"

"I admit it does sound ridiculous when you look at it like that, but it's not quite that bad. He says he called it Gold Lake because the diggings are so rich beside the water. And he certainly seems to have the evidence to back up his story. He's got gold—lots of it. Some pretty good-sized nuggets, I'm told."

"But if the place is that good, why is he running around telling everyone about his find? Why doesn't he keep his mouth shut like any sensible miner would?"

"Because he's afraid to go back alone. You see, he says the Indians attacked his party last fall and he had to run for his life. He's never seen the others since and supposes the Indians killed them."

"If that's the case, I can see why he might be cautious about returning. Did you find out how many are going?"

"They say he offered to take as many as fifty men if each promised to pay him a hundred dollars when they got there."

"What if it's all humbug?"

"He says then they can lynch him!"

"He's a bold one—either that or a complete lunatic!"

"The question is, do you fellows want to come along?"

"I didn't know we'd been invited."

"We haven't. That's the nice part. We don't have to pay the hundred dollars, either."

"I doubt they'll let us come unless we promise to pay," said Luther.

"I doubt we'll tell 'em we're coming!" said the messenger impatiently.

Comprehension dawned and Luther grinned. "Say when and where."

"That's more like it! Friday morning just before dawn, on top of Sugar Loaf."

On the first day out, the aspiring claim-jumpers traveled northeast to the camp of Washington on the South Yuba. The weather was hot. Already temperatures had reached the high nineties in mid-May, and one day it had been one hundred in the Deer Creek diggings. When the seven young men laid down at day's end, they ached and itched from head to toe; in order not to arouse suspicion they had elected to follow on foot. Now their adventure began to assume some negative aspects.

Sleeping on the hard ground did little to relieve their soreness or their doubts, and when they heaved their packs off the ground in the morning, the loads seemed to have grown heavier while they slept. This fault was remedied by abandoning all "excess" baggage, much to the surprised pleasure of the Washington residents who were quick to gather up the windfall. Then the gold hunters crossed the South Yuba precariously on a log which had been felled across its swift-flowing waters.

They made their way up the canyon of Poorman's Creek, pushing up the rough and brushy slopes while the hot sun beat down upon their heads and backs. Late in the afternoon they made their way in a ragged procession to the top of the ridge separating the Yuba's south and middle forks. At the summit they rested and looked down to the snakelike path of the river two thousand feet below. Night had fallen by the time the exhausted adventurers staggered to the bottom of the canyon and into the cooling waters of the middle Yuba.

The long trek was taking a bloody toll: clothes and bodies were torn and bruised from the thorny chaparral; mosquitoes had attacked in regimental numbers, raising itching welts on every inch of exposed flesh, much of which was burned to a brilliant hue of red by the summer sun. Despite these wounds, the camp slept soundly on the second night out.

The day following was much like the one before, but thirst became a major problem. For most of the trek they encountered no water, so it was with a great deal of pleasure that they found themselves at last on the banks of the North Yuba, beside the bustling camp of Downieville. For two dollars they sat down to a fine supper at the French Restaurant and washed away their thirst with great draughts of red wine.

In the morning they enjoyed an appetizing breakfast at the same establishment and parried questions put to them by a puzzled citizenry. But a few hours later, having reached much higher elevations, Schaeffer and his friends were asking one another some of the same questions: why were they marching about in the midst of snow, high in the Sierra Nevada?

The drifts grew deeper with each passing mile, and after two more days of cold, exhausting and aimless wandering, it had become evident to Stoddard's official and unofficial followers that their leader was lost, confused, or lying. A few of Stoddard's company were ready by now to take up his earlier offer and hang him to the nearest tree, but most were willing to grin and bear the knowledge that they had been taken in by a raving madman. Heading back to Downieville, they encountered late-comers on their way to "Gold Lake." Try as they would, the wiser heads could not dissuade the new arrivals from going on with the search.

When the gold hunters came back to Nevada and Gold Run and told of the hoax, the town was vastly amused. For weeks the story of Gold Lake was good for a hearty laugh at the expense of the sheepish victims, all of whom soon were doing much better at the old diggings along Deer Creek and Gold Run.

Although the gilded lake lost its sheen at Deer Creek and Downieville, at Marysville and Sacramento it continued to glitter alluringly. A full month after Stoddard's exposure in the mountains, the *Placer Times* was still reporting:

GREAT DISCOVERIES OF GOLD—GOLD LAKE. We were inclined to give only an average degree of credit to stories that have reached us during the past few days, of the unprecedented richness with this locality has developed. A few moments passed in Marysville on Saturday convinced us that there is much more show or reality in this last *eureka report* than usually attaches to the like.

In a year's experience of local excitements from the same cause, we have seen none equal to what now prevails in that town. It has visited all the inhabitants indiscriminately, lawyers, doctors and judges, traders, teamsters, mechanics and gamblers.

Our readers know we are the last to justify the circulation of unfounded or exaggerated reports, but we deem it right to conceal nothing of what may prove (for aught that we can see to the contrary) one of the most astounding discoveries in the modern history of diggings.

The specimens brought into Marysville are of a value from $1600 down. Ten ounces is reported as no unusual yield to a panfull, and the first party of sixty, which started out under the guidance of one who had returned successful, were assured that they would not get less than $500 each per day.

We were told that the previous morning two hundred had left the town with a full supply of provisions and four hundred mules. Those who could not go were hiring others in their stead. The length of the journey and the quantity of provisions required, there being no stores in the region, rendered an outfit rather expensive. Mules and horses had doubled in value, and $400 were considered no more than enough to furnish a proper start.

The distance to Gold Lake was first reported two hundred miles; the best informed, however, say that it is but little more than half of that. It lies at a very considerable elevation among the mountains that divide the waters of the South Fork of Feather from those of the north branch of the Yuba. The direction from Marysville is a little north of east.

The story has of course spread ere this far and wide among the miners high up on the Feather and Yuba, and the spot will be as crowded as all other good places are, ere the tardy adventurer from this region could reach it. The region of the Gold Lake wonders is a new one, however, and lies between what are established to be diggings of unsurpassed richness.

It is our belief that it is better for one who has got some initiation into the gold mysteries (if there be any), not to be content in old 'used up' localities, but to push along to the great field yet unexplored. . . .

II

THE CITIZENS OF NEVADA had more down-to-earth projects to occupy their attention. Former *alcalde* Stamps and Reverend Lamden managed to collect enough subscriptions to construct the town's first church house. Volunteer carpenters were nailing wide, hand-split shakes to a row of posts driven into the ground at two-foot intervals. The posts fenced in a rectangular space and acted as the walls for the building. Here and there some openings had been left for air, light and egress, but there was no way to close the windows and doors.

The church was on the upper slope of Main Street, and the dirt floor followed the hill's natural contours. It wasn't very handsome, resembling a barn more than a house of worship, but it was better than nothing.

Life seemed to have turned against Mr. Stamps in recent months. Soon after his election as alcalde the new California law called for a second election. This had resulted in Albion H. Olney being chosen to serve as Justice of the Peace, rendering the old Mexican office obsolete. Two months later, Mrs. Stamps died after a lengthy illness. Perhaps these events had contributed to Stamp's desire to provide Nevada with a church, a place for the renewing of spirit and faith.

Mr. Lamden, a minister back in the States, agreed to preach the first few services. During the summer he was joined by the Methodist preacher, C. A. Leaman, and Reverend R. R. Dunlap, a Southern Methodist from the Missouri Conference. The three took turns conducting Sabbath services; though the church was non-denominational, many took to calling it the "Methodist" church. Because Methodists had a reputation for arriving early in the frontier settlements, a few had spoken of it by this name even before Leaman and Dunlap came to Nevada, and one who made this error was the local correspondent for the Sacramento *Transcript*, who said of the booming village:

Nevada City, July 22d

MESSRS EDITORS—Perhaps some persons in your city would like to know where Nevada City may be found. If they will jump on to an ox team and undergo six days travel over what appears to have once been a part of the great "Pacific," thence trudge over some very long hills—wondering at the immense pines, some of which measure eight to ten feet through and thirty to forty feet to the first branches, and sufficient in number to supply all California with "clear stuff"—go on a little further and see the work of man in search of the precious article—the deep ditchings of Gold Run—a little farther, and we come suddenly to the brow of a hill—look across Deer Creek: you will see a city containing twenty-five or thirty stores, five or six commodious hotels in California style, a population of 1500 or 2000—this is Nevada City.

Gambling is carried on extensively in one of the establishments. A quarrel took place between a *monte* banker and a person betting. The issue was, the "gent" betting pulled out one of "Colt's best," and without shooting the right one, wounded three others; one in the back part of his head, another through the left breast, but the third one was so badly wounded it was thought it would cause his death, the ball passing through the fleshy part of his right breast and out near the shoulder.

But I am glad to write you, all are getting along very well. They were persons who were entirely uninterested; the one for whom the shot was intended escaped unhurt.

Health is generally good here, especially among those who wintered about Nevada. You can purchase here almost anything to be had in your city. Merchants are doing a fair business. Some miners are very lucky and strike rich leads; some dig six inches on the hill's surface, others go down to the rotten granite, ten to fifteen feet, then dig under the hill the same as if they were working out coal veins. The average is half an ounce to three pounds to a man; water getting very scarce.

The above diggings are called the Coyote diggins. An accident happened among the miners a few days since—the caving of a prospect covered the digger up to the chin. It looks very strange here to see several hundred persons gathered for sabbath services, and only one or two ladies in the congregation. The gold found about Nevada is fine and in small grains.

Punishment of criminals is very severe; Judge Lynch is well known; an instance will show what I say to be true. Lawyers stand but poor chance to do anything, they must dig or starve. An individual who had been mining took a notion to a good mule not belonging to him, but he did not travel far before he was overtaken and brought before a jury who were called to give their verdict in the case by the owner of said mule.

He was found guilty of theft, not only of the mule, but also the earnings of the young man who had placed confidence in him, gave him his bag of gold dust to take out $5, and he put the amount, eleven ounces, down in the chance of *monte* and lost the whole, but vamosed the ranch—stealing the mule to assist him in reaching your city.

The verdict of guilty was given by the jury and his punishment twenty-five lashes on his bare back, and compelled to work at $5 per day till the eleven ounces were returned. I have to write that one cut more was given for interest. So rogues must look out and know where Nevada City is situated.

Provisions are at fair prices: potatoes per lb 35¢; turnips, beets &c. 35¢ per lb.; flour retailing 25¢ per lb. The Yuba river falls but slowly, and the hopes of many are blighted almost entirely—not only the miners but the traders having depended on the claims being rich, but disappointment is their own.

There are fears of trouble about the tax on foreigners, notice being given to American citizens to "jump" their claims unless they pay their taxes. I fear to trouble you with items, not wishing to be in the way of some more interesting writer.

Yours respectfully, QUARTZ.

III

HAMLET DAVIS WAS erecting a two-story frame building for his new store at the corner of Broad and Pine. On the second floor he was going to have a reading room with a supply of newspapers from every major American city. Davis, Stamps, Olney, and Mason Wilson were the elder statesmen of the camp, each of them being forty years old; the average age of local miners was about twenty-six.

Davis, a bachelor, hailed from Kentucky, but had been a storekeeper and merchant in Illinois and New Orleans before coming to California in 1849. After mining for two months on the Yuba River, he opened a store in Sacramento City prior to the flood. In the spring, Ham Davis set out for "Caldwell's Upper Store" with a stock of dry goods, but when he arrived, "Caldwell's" had become Nevada.

He opened a store in a canvas tent until the frame building could be completed. Then he, George Washington Kidd, and Mr. Bedford laid out Broad Street and Pine Street and offered to give seventy- by ninety-foot building lots to anyone who would put them to immediate use.

Kidd, another Kentuckian, was thirty-three, and before coming to California had spent time as a cabin boy and steward on the Mississippi steamboats. Like Hamlet Davis, he had a store on Broad Street, but his secret ambition was to command his own boat on the Sacramento. Meanwhile, he traded goods and invested his money, while his wife

Phoebe Ann, twenty-three, managed the Missouri Boarding House with the aid of a seventeen-year-old Mexican lad.

Over at Grass Valley things were changing and expanding, too. James Walsh and Zenas Wheeler decided to abandon their original mill site near that of the ill-fated Holt brothers, and with a new partner, G. P. Clark, they put up a sawmill beside Wolf Creek between Grass Valley and Boston Ravine. Already the road to their place was known as Mill Street, and it joined Main Street alongside the Beatty House. One day Jim Walsh let John F. Morse see several specimens of gold quartz which had been uncovered in the course of building the mill. Walsh was trying to come up with a practical way of separating the gold from the rock.

A new family with several grown daughters came to Grass Valley and it wasn't long before all the young men for miles around were stopping by to talk about the weather. When it was time for Nevada City to hold its first fancy ball, two of the city's businessmen, Ed Truex and O. P. Blackman, called on the Grass Valley family.

Blackman was twenty-four and a native of Vermont, while Truex was from New York and twenty-five. Nevada's most eligible bachelors (for so they saw themselves) rented horses and showed off a little and arrangements were completed for two of the young ladies to attend the ball. When the big day arrived, Truex and Blackman put on their best blue wool shirts, tucked their wool trousers into new boots, borrowed a team and wagon and drove over to Grass Valley.

It was dark when they arrived, and as they were admitted into the log house, the young men sensed that something was wrong. For one thing, the parents were frowning and the young ladies were nowhere in sight.

"We've come to pick up the young ladies, ma'am," said Blackman, looking anxiously about the room, unable to imagine where they might be concealing themselves.

"Just where did you have a mind to take 'em this time of the night?" demanded the mother.

"Why, don't you remember? You said they might go with us to the ball at Nevada."

"Oh no, not much! They don't leave this house!"

"Wh-Why not?" stammered O. P. "I thought you said—"

"We s'posed your ball was in the daytime. If the gals'd be home before dark, we wouldn't have minded, but our gals don't go traipsing around at night with young fellers. Not a chance!"

All their arguments were unavailing, and at last the unhappy bachelors left the house. As they drove away, Blackman said to Truex, "Did you see what I saw?"

"D'you mean the two pair of feet sticking out from under the bed-covers in the corner?"

"That must have been our dancing partners. Do you suppose they always go to bed so early?"

Back at the ball, the imbalance in the sexes was compensated for by the willingness of some miners to tie handkerchiefs round their arms and temporarily assume the role of ladies. The event was the hit of the social season, and afterward Luzena Wilson told a friend, "I had men come forty miles over the mountains just to look at me—and I never was called a handsome woman in my best days, even by my most ardent admirers."

Impressed by the pace of life in the new mountain community, the Sacramento *Placer Times* told its readers:

NEVADA CITY—This must be a fast place. Mr. Davis, of the firm of Brown, Davis & Co., has been in town, making arrangements for the opening of a reading room over their store, where they intend to have the latest advices from all parts.

We find also numerous jobs from merchants in every line coming to our office: drug stores, hotels, livery stables and all the other con-comitant pursuits of a veritable city are represented upon "posters" of every size and style.

These are sure signs of business, and of the good sense of those who are engaged in its various branches. The population of Nevada City is estimated at about 2,000, but there are supposed to be four times that number within a circuit of four miles.

A tri-weekly line of stages runs from Nicolaus through in one day, a distance of 50 miles, connecting with the steamer *Dana.*

STEAMSHIP AT SAN FRANCISCO

CHAPTER 26
DOWNIEVILLE EXPRESS
June–September 1850

I

EARLY IN JUNE 1850, Niles Searls and Charley Mulford inspected Downieville, high in the Sierra Nevada. According to all accounts, miners were removing from one to two pounds of gold per day from the rich claims along the North Fork of the Yuba. Upon reaching the diggings they found that the stories for once were true, but every bit of ground had been claimed and occupied by the time Searls and Mulford got there.

The town of Downieville was named for Major William Downie, who had come to the forks of the Yuba in November of the preceding year. Downie and a few others stayed there throughout the winter, occasionally going down to Sacramento or Marysville to purchase provisions. From the handful of prospectors who were present to name the town in February, the place had grown to several thousand miners, fifteen hotels and gambling houses, four bakeries, four butcher shops, and hundreds of tents and cabins. Richard Galloway, the Justice of the Peace, dispensed justice while his spouse served meals in their log cabin restaurant.

The opportunities in mining seemed about closed, but there was a bright opening in the express business. Every mining camp needed one or more persons who would carry mail and packages to and from the post offices at San Francisco, Sacramento, and Marysville, and miners were willing to pay one or even two dollars per letter for the service. Niles and Charley purchased a pair of mules and began carrying express articles between Downieville and San Francisco, by way of Sacramento and Marysville.

Niles coaxed the two mules back and forth between Marysville and the mines, and Charley operated the business on the riverboats. They had other competitors, including Samuel W. Langton, but there was ample business for everyone that summer. On August 12, 1850, Niles was in Sacramento, having come down from Marysville while awaiting Charley's arrival from San Francisco. While there, he decided to write his cousin Cornelia:

I was very much disappointed this morning in not being able to leave town on my usual semi-monthly trip to the head waters of the Yuba River. . . . I came down here on Saturday. Met Charley at MarysVille on his way up the river. I think he will be down by tomorrow and will very likely write by the steamer of the 15th.

I expect Charley has written something already with regard to the business in which we are at present engaged (running an express) which will enable you to comprehend the reason of our journeying up and down the country. We go as far as MarysVille by public conveyance, then with mules the remainder of the way (eighty miles).

The last time up I met with Orsamus Sexton of Palmyra, N.Y. I was not aware of his being in this country till I saw his name on our Express List. He came out last year and appeared to be busily engaged mortising holes in the ground.

Chancellor Hartson, the young man who wrote a note to me at RVille, as stated by you in your last, arrived here overland, safe and sound, two weeks ago. We spent a few hours very pleasantly in discussing scenes at [Cherry] Valley—sights on the Plains &c. He has gone to the mines. The emigrants are pouring in by the thousands from the Plains, many of them in a suffering condition. Some, it is said, have actually starved to death already. Several relief parties have been sent out to meet them with provisions and animals.

The country is very healthy indeed at present, far more so than one could with reason suppose. My health, from the 1st of June up to two weeks ago, was not very good. I was able to be up and doing most of the time, it is true. I was more than half sick. I had almost concluded to start for home in the steamer of the 1st of the month, but got well and have given up all idea of leaving Cal. for the next seven years.

I say *got well,* so I *did,* all except the ague and fever, which I have had for a week in the *natural* way. I find it rather pleasant (the odd days, I mean, when I don't have it), so much of variety. First, cool as a cucumber, though the thermometer may stand at 112°—then *warm* enough to be comfortable in any latitude, however low.

Had I reason to believe myself the original inventor of "shakes," I should surely take out a patent for the discovery—as it is, the proficiency already made leaves some room to hope that I may *still* make some improvement on the old method that will entitle me to the favorable notice of a liberal public. When I *do,* I'll just happen through RVille and give instructions. Won't you and Mary get up an advertisement for me? Head it with "Shakes made Easy." This has been my day for an exhibition, but not getting sufficient encouragement, I took quinine this morning and postponed the *performance.*

Matters in Cal. jog along about after the old sort. New cities spring up daily, and old ones increase in magnitude marvelously. Some [miners] get rich and go home, and other get discouraged and do the same. All the luxuries of life are as plenty here as in the states, for anything I can see to the contrary. How different appears everything from what it did last Oct.! . . .

I have some long yarns to spin which I shall forget before my seven years are expired. Every trip up in the mountains is an adventure affording something new. Two weeks ago some Indians attempted to come an "Anti-Rent game" over me by stopping me in an out of the way place, to relieve me of my personal effects. Fortunately for me, they were armed only with knives, and the appearance of my six barrelled persuader convinced them their only safety lay in flight.

They evidently supposed me to be unarmed. Several persons have been robbed by the rascals of late. They are great cowards and only dare to attack the defenceless. I don't think there is the least danger to be apprehended from them to one prepared for an emergency.

Charley is well as usual. Wm. D. Williams is still here. We all board at the same old place when in [Sacramento]. Mr. Rich, our landlord, is as fine a man as ever was, and Mrs. Rich can't be beat in all California. In a house with from 50 to 60 boarders, there is considerable advantage in being the oldest residents and having the privilege of ransacking the establishment at pleasure. In short, I feel just as much at home as I used to at Uncle Alex. Watson's.

I thought I would write another sheet and enclose to Mary, but I hear the bell of the steamer from San Francisco and must go to look after some packages and letters which I expect up, so goodbye

Niles Searls

Two days later, violence erupted in Sacramento City. In May, John T. Madden had been charged with unlawful occupation of a lot on the southeast corner of 2nd and N streets. The Recorder's Court ruled against Madden, who appealed the verdict. On August 8, 1850, County Judge Willis sustained the judgment. Immediately, other settlers who, like Madden, disputed the legitimacy of Sutter's land grants and were squatting on parcels they had not purchased, began circulating handbills which warned they would "fight with our lives" over the land.

Their leader was Dr. Charles Robinson, and on August 10 he called for armed resistance. Mayor Hardin Bigelow countered by announcing that no writs would be served for arrest, thus calming the crowd who came to hear Robinson speak. But on the next day warrants were issued for several men who had interfered with the sheriff when he tried to serve a writ on Madden. One of those who had opposed the sheriff was a former correspondent for the *New York Tribune,* a man named James McClatchy.

McClatchy and Richard Moran surrendered on August 13 and were jailed aboard the city's prison ship, the *La Grange.* Captain Maloney, a Mexican War veteran and commander of the settlers' militia, marched his company to the river on August 14. At first it was thought that they meant to attack the jail, but then the men turned away from the embarcadero and marched up J street. At the corner of 4th and J they were met by a party of armed citizens led by Mayor Bigelow.

Bigelow ordered the settlers to surrender their arms. A series of shots was heard, and leaders on both sides fell to the ground. Mayor Bigelow, shot from his horse, was wounded and the city assessor was killed. Three persons from the squatters' company were hit, two of them fatally. Captain Maloney was dead and Dr. Robinson wounded.

One day later, on August 15, Sheriff McKinney and a posse of twenty men attacked the settlers' camp near Brighton. Three squatters and McKinney were killed in the ensuing battle. McClatchy and Moran were released from the brig, but Robinson was charged with murder.

Meanwhile, Niles left for Downieville and Charley returned to San Francisco to await the arrival of the end-of-the-month steamer. When it came, the news it carried shocked all of California: President Zachary "Rough and Ready" Taylor was dead. In reaction to this news and to the information that statehood for California was still in doubt, a public meeting was held at the Western Hotel in Yuba City on August 29 to respond to these matters and to select a candidate to represent Sutter County in the California Assembly.

Chosen to present the adopted resolutions was Justice of the Peace Tallman H. Rolfe. Among the resolutions he read were the following:

1st, That we regard the unnecessary delay of the admission of California, as a State, into the Union, as at once prejudicial to the interests of the people of this country, and as tending to lessen and weaken the bonds which bind us to the glorious Union of the States.

2d, That the only question at issue as to the admission of California, is as to the Republicanism of the Constitution, and that we condemn, in the most unqualified terms, the connection of this question with others, at once foreign and prejudicial.

3d, That the people of California, having adopted a Constitution radically Republican in all its parts, that we demand a speedy and unqualified admission, or immediate rejection, on this the only question involved.

4th, That we are unwilling, as fondly as we are attached to the Government and institutions of the United States, to be *"taxed without representation,"* and that, in the event of the refusal of the Congress of the United States, to admit California as a state into the Union, we will deny the constitutional power of the United States to levy and collect taxes from us, and will not quietly submit to its exercise.

5th, That while we deplore the sectional divisions which distract the Congress of the United States, and delay all actions for the good of the people of the territories, we appreciate the unavoidable necessity which has forced our fellow citizens of New Mexico to form a Constitution and apply for admission as a State into the Union, and that we deeply sympathise with them, and wish them success and prosperity.

6th, That in common with our fellow citizens of the Union, we deeply lament and deplore the death of our late Chief Magistrate, Gen. Zachary Taylor—distinguished alike as the hero, battling for the honor of his country on the plains of Mexico, and as the representative of the sovereignty of the people of the great republic of the United States.

II

CHARLEY MULFORD had expected to trade runs with Niles on his return from San Francisco, but he complained of not feeling well when the two met in Sacramento. Niles persuaded his partner to stay there and recuperate, saying he would take the mules to Downieville as usual.

Charley wrote cousin Cornelia on September 11 from Sacramento City, describing his illness:

My Dear Coz Nella,

Your favor of July 9th arrived in due season about two weeks since, and most joyfully was it received, perhaps none the less so from the fact I was at the time confined to my bed with a severe fever and was but just able to peruse the contents of my letters and that was all—but I had plenty of time to think over the news they contained.

My fever was intermittent and came so near being congestive the doctor cupped me, and by the aid of powerful medicines, *and plenty of them,* succeeded in breaking the fever within a week—but it left me very weak. I have now almost recovered my strength and am nearly recovered from one of those detestable calomel sore mouths, *the pleasures of which* I presume you can fully appreciate.

I was very fortunate in being taken sick here, rather than elsewhere, as Mrs. Rich, with whom we always board while in town, takes a mother's care of Niles and I, and I received every care I could ask for.

Niles is now on a trip up the river on business connected with our Express, of which I believe I have previously written you—we are now about closing up our business on the Yuba, but perhaps may continue it in some other direction. Niles now enjoys excellent health, and is as rough, rugged, and saucy as I have usually been, until my present sickness.

As to news—aside from the little I have already related concerning ourselves—I believe there is none of interest to you. Of Gold, gold stories, and miners, I suppose you have already heard to your heart's content, and therefore it will be but little news to tell you that miners as a body have done very poorly indeed this season—nearly all the large damming companies on the river (when they expected such large returns as the water fell) have proved entire failures—thereby ruining thousands who have expended their season's labor and all their previous earnings in living meantime and awaiting the fall of the water.

To be sure, there are some few instances where large fortunes are suddenly realized in the river diggins, but they are far too seldom to affect the mass of miners. It has heretofore been supposed that the summer months were the mining season proper—but I have come to the conclusion that miners did much better during the winter months of last year, and will [do so in] the coming winters, so as the rains begin to fall—succeed much better in the dry diggins than they have in the river beds this summer.

The air now feels like autumn and a cloudy sky puts us in a mind of the approaching rainy season—we had a few drops yesterday, not enough to lay the dust, but enough to say rain, and that is all. In about six weeks we shall begin to expect showers in earnest, but not before that time—this is a delightful country in one respect during summer, for travel where you will—in any direction—there are no umbrellas and overcoats to carry—no fear of getting caught in the rain, nor of overtaking any of the thousand and one showers we are constantly having at home—to be sure, the roads are somewhat dusty—but then there is plenty of room, and an independent codger like myself can travel to suit himself, and if the road don't suit me, just turn my mule one side and make a trail of my own.

You speak of the joys and pleasures of the 4th of July in such glowing terms you almost make me wish I was there with you, but then it is well I was not there to mar your enjoyment with my long face, for if you will believe it, I have now been absent so long from such life-giving scenes my face has become as long as a string and as narrow as a piece of chalk—whether or no it will ever come in shape again on my return among you, I cannot tell.

I think, however, there is but little hope for me, for I presume you will all be married off and scattered to the four winds before I shall reach the home of my childhood, and there will not be even one old maid left for me to tire with accounts of the pleasures, trials and hardships of my travels—if there is one of my old circle left on returning, she has a serious task before her to listen to all my treasured yarns, and she may as well be prepared to be questioned a few also. . . .

With regard to that bushel of love Deb sent Niles and I to be divided between us, we have had considerable trouble in the division—to start with, they have no measures in this country—everything goes by the pound, so of course we could not divide by measure. Then again, notwithstanding my endless enquiries as the weight of a given quantity of love, I can learn nothing satisfactory. Some think it a solid, ponderous substance, while others say it is flashy and light, a mere nothing in weight—fluid and all. Finding it impossible to divide by weight, we are at a stand still—it still remains an undivided treasure. . . .

You speak of my roses being in full bloom, but say nothing of the gardens, neither your own or Lucia's—I have been quite anxious to hear from them, but Lucia and Harriet [Mulford] are not very good correspondents and do not keep me very well advised of their doings—I wish you would touch them up a little for me. . . .

Saturday, Sept. 14th. Niles returned yesterday and went to San Francisco yesterday—he will probably write you hence. He was well—I have now almost fully recovered. Niles will return here in about 8 days—C. W. M.

Niles did indeed write. On the same day that he reached the bay city, September 14, he wrote to Mary:

I arrived here this morning from Sac City, and having completed the business of the day and taken an evening's stroll about town, I sit down to prepare a few lines for the Tennessee, which sails tomorrow.

I am surrounded by a crowd of *men—strangers*—beings between whom and myself there exists no sympathy. *How* consoling the reflection, that, tho' no link of friendship binds me to the itinerant throng on every side, there are those in the world who feel an interest in my welfare, can rejoice with me in prosperity and sympathise in adversity.

But how far am I separated from those loved ones. Why thus separated? Why do I wander from all I most prise on earth. Is it for gold? Or is it that my attachment for kind friends is weaker than that of others?

I answer as I have often done before, the love of *gold* never brought me to Cal, will never retain me here, and he who questions my *attachments* offers an insult not readily forgiven. I think my disposition must be more restless than that of most people. I never wish that I had stayed at home—but often *do* wish that I could have been contented to do so.

Did I believe in *Destiny*, I should believe myself *marked* for a cosmopolite, but as it is, I think I am possessed of a disposition too much inclined to wandering. I try to flatter myself that reason will eventually balance the romances of youth and make me what I sincerely want to become, a stable citizen—a useful member of society.

In a mood he rarely confided in letters, Niles went on to allude to matters closer to the bone:

A few days more and two years will have elapsed since we parted. Little did I think, Mary, when we separated on that morning, so long a period would ensue before we met again. Changed in many respects we doubtedly both have and will. One thing, however, affords me unlimited joy—it *is* that, however altered we may be in other respects, I flatter myself we will remain the same as regards our attachments for each other.

When substantial reasons are offered for the cessation of that attachment, *then* will I endeavor to conquer my feelings; till then, dear Mary, allow me the exquisite pleasure of loving and believing myself esteemed in return. What would I not give for an interview with you this evening. It seems as though it would more than compensate for all I have passed through since our separation.

I think I have felt a stronger desire to leave Cal today than at any former period. In front of the town are three steamers ready to take their departure for Panama tomorrow. Many of these with whom I am acquainted are to take passage, and I long to go, too—but I am not ready, cannot go. Our Express business requires my presence on the Yuba River again.

I left Charley at Sac City, who has written to Cornelia and will doubtless give you the particulars of his recent illness. He left here about three weeks since and met me at Sac, intending to go to the Yuba while I came here. He complained a little on his arrival and I persuaded him to let me go back in his place. He stayed, and in two days was dangerously ill with fever. My first intimation of his being sick was on my return to Marysville, where I heard that he was in a situation almost precluding any chance of recovery.

I came down and stayed with him until he began to get considerable better (a Yankee phrase). Since then he has improved rapidly and is now about well. He will not continue in the Express business any longer, but talks of going to Nevada City or in that region to stop for the winter. I shall finish our business when the next time I go up, and had about concluded to Vamose for home, but Charley and Billy both laugh and tell me I am joking when I talk of it, and I yesterday met with C. Hartson, who has pretty much persuaded me to go with him to Nevada [City] and practice Law.

He represents the chances of being most promising, and I have promised to go there on my return from above and see him. I shall procure the requisite books before leaving town, for *him* and for myself, if I conclude to go there. If I *do* stay in Cal this winter, I prefer that business to any other. I had intended to reach home by the last of Dec. and may do so still, but think my return before spring somewhat problematical. Charley is bound to stay at all events, and I don't much like to come without him.

I received your 10th July about two weeks ago. Your description of the hurricane amazed me very much. So Mr. Wood gave up coming here, did he? It's just as well, for a band of more disconsolate, disappointed beings such as the newly arrived emigrants, it would be difficult to find. Dr. Baldwin, formerly of RVille, sits opposite me at the table. He is practicing medicine—doing first rate; pretty good sort of fellow.

Ask Cornelia if she remembers going down the [Hudson] River on the Steamer Confidence when she was accompanying me. Well, that same little steamer is now on its way round the cape, and it seems to me just as if the sight of her will do me some good—it would at least if I could only find Nelly on board still. . . . Remember me kindly to all the friends, and do not expect me till I come, which will probably not be until spring.

While Niles waited for the arrival of the *Panama*, San Francisco burned for the fourth time on September 17, 1850. Four squares were destroyed, and the loss was estimated at from $250,000 to $500,000. The bay city still did not have an operating fire department, although the city council had passed an ordinance for the creation of one in mid-summer.

CHAPTER 27

TOWN LIFE

September–November 1850

I

*Y*OU WON'T COLLECT fifty votes around here, Field. You might as well head on back to Marysville."

The speaker, John Anderson, a prominent Whig lawyer, was addressing Stephen J. Field, candidate for the California State Assembly.

"Why do you say that, John? I've heard there are quite a lot of smart fellows around Nevada," replied Field.

"Because McCarty's got all the votes sewed up. The word's out that you're an abolitionist, like your brother."

"You know as well as I that I'm no abolitionist. Don't you read the papers up here?" Field was referring to editorial remarks in the Marysville *Herald* a week earlier. The *Herald*, which supported his candidacy, had said:

We presume the report arose from the fact of Judge Field being a northern man; strong ground, truly, for such a supposition. We happen to know Judge Field's opinions upon this question. Briefly, he believes that every State has the right to regulate the institution of slavery, or to say whether it shall or shall not exist in its own borders; and he has often expressed to us the opinion that the abolition agitation can do no good, and the General Government have no more right to meddle with slavery in the different States, than they have with slavery in Turkey.

"Men up here are too busy to read the papers—not like down there in Marysville where you fellows have nothing better to do than sit around drinking mint juleps and sherry cobblers!"

"You think that's what I do? That McCarty's spreading some mighty tall stories about me, it appears! Well, I'll straighten him out tomorrow."

"Why, what's happening tomorrow?"

"It's Sunday and everyone will be in town. I'll make a speech and show the people what kind of man I am—and what kind of a liar John T. McCarty is!"

"Well, don't say I didn't warn you."

"I'll thank you not to warn anyone else about my views until you hear me out!" replied the candidate.

Next day, Field climbed onto the platform on Main Street and began speaking. At first, only a few miners stopped to listen, but as the thirty-three-year-old ex-judge continued to talk, others gathered around.

"We need to give more jurisdiction to local justices of the peace," declared Field. "Having just come over that poor excuse for a road which leads from here to the county seat at Marysville, I know just how inconvenient it is to go all that distance to attend court sessions."

"That's the truth!" shouted one of his listeners.

"There's no reason why all contests over mining claims shouldn't be settled right here in Nevada!"

"Hear, hear!"

"What're you going to do about changing the county seat?" asked a miner. "It shouldn't be down in the valley—it ought to be right here."

"If I'm elected—excuse me, *when* I'm elected!—the first thing I'll do is write a new law to create the county of Nevada! Then you can put your county seat wherever you like."

"That's O.K.," replied one of the crowd, "but I've been hearing stories that you favor the abolition of slavery. Is that a fact?"

"It's nothing but a base calumny, a pack of lies, if you please, being spread by a boy who knows his only chance to win is to discredit me."

"What about your brother?"

"What about my brother? I have several."

"You know who I mean—your abolitionist brother!"

"Ah, my New York brother, David, who is a freesoiler. He is a noble fellow and may God bless him, wherever he may be, but I also have another brother who is a slaveholder in Tennessee—if I am to be declared an abolitionist because of my kinship to the one, logic says I must also favor slavery because of the other, so which shall it be?"

"Will you denounce your New York brother?"

"Of course not—any more than I would denounce some other relative—a woman, perhaps—because she might believe in things unearthly and spiritual. Instead, I shall tell you what *I* believe, and then you can make up your minds whether you wish to cast your vote for an honest servant or a lying scoundrel!"

"Which are you?"

"Listen to me and you'll find out!"

Field then outlined the theory of States Rights and stated his opinion that slavery was a domestic institution which each state must regulate for itself, without question or interference from the others. The audience, made up in large numbers of miners from the south and the west, cheered his remarks at every step of the way, and when he closed with a description of the future glories of California, as he envisioned them, shouts and applause told him he had gained back whatever votes brother David might have cost him.

John McCarty followed him to the platform, but Field effectively diminished his audience by offering to buy drinks for the crowd. It was a hot day, and most of the miners had heard all the speeches they cared to in one afternoon. Buying drinks for the electorate was an effective and approved method for keeping voters from paying too much attention to rival candidates.

Eight days remained before election day, October 7, and there were other offices to fill beside that of assemblyman. Among these were the superintendent of public instruction and a new attorney general for the state, a district attorney for the eighth judicial district, composed of Yolo, Sutter, and Yuba counties, a choice of where to locate the state capital, and a justice of the peace for Nevada township. John Edwards was a candidate for the latter position, but some of the younger men were not satisfied with this conservative older man.

"Don't you fellows know anyone we could run?" asked Charles Marsh, a young civil engineer from Wisconsin.

"I know someone who'd be great, but I don't know if he'll get here in time—he's in Downieville, but he's supposed to be here any day now," said Billy Williams.

"Are you talking about Niles?" asked Charley Mulford. "I doubt he'd do it."

"Why not?" replied Chancellor Hartson. "He'd be great at it! Billy's right."

"But Niles may not get here in time. What about you, Hartson? You're a lawyer—you went to Cherry Valley law school with Niles."

"I think Niles would be better. Let's wait and see. If he doesn't get here in a few days, then I'll reconsider."

"Good," said Marsh. "Now, tell me something about this Niles—what's his whole name?"

"Searls is his family name. Niles Searls," replied Charley.

"He's a first class speaker and everybody likes him," added Billy.

"The trouble is, everybody in Nevada doesn't know him. We'll have to start doing some campaigning right now."

"Before he arrives?"

"Why not? We'll tell everyone he's going to give a speech next Sunday here in town."

"And if he's not here by Sunday?"

"Then Hartson will give a speech!"

"How's your ditch coming, Marsh?"

"Pretty good. We figure it'll take us until November to complete. It's nine miles long, and a lot of rock has to be moved—we can't go just where we'd like to go, because it has to slope continually downhill, but not too much."

"What ditch is this?" asked Mulford.

"Bill Crawford, the Dunn brothers, a fellow named Carrol, and myself are having a water ditch built from Rock Creek to Coyote Hill so we can sell water to the miners. That way they can work their claims without having to haul dirt all the way to the streams."

"That's a big project—it must be costing a fortune."

"It is—close to ten thousand dollars, we figure. But it'll be worth it. We count on recovering our money in six weeks."

"Really? That sounds like a better business proposition than gold mining!"

"Of course! Almost anything is! But furnishing water for the mines is the best way of all to get rich, I'm convinced of that."

"Did you have to have it surveyed in order to get the proper pitch?" asked Mulford.

"Marsh does all that himself," replied Hartson. "He's a civil engineer—studied it in school."

"It's the only way I could have done it," explained Marsh. "The others all had money to invest, but I offered to trade my services for a share in the enterprise. When we're through, I'll have some money of my own, but I think I'll continue to invest my services as long as my partners will let me."

On October 2 Niles arrived, but for several days refused to take his friends seriously when they urged his candidacy. Finally, on the Saturday before the election, he gave in and began to participate in campaigning, more as a lark than out of any conviction that he might be elected.

Election day was warm and fair and there were no obstacles in the way of those who wished to vote—none except a great apathy among the electorate. When night fell, slightly more than 4000 votes had been cast in all of Yuba County, from Marysville to Downieville. It was later estimated that not more than 20 per cent of the eligible voters participated. Stephen Field beat his opponent by 300 votes. James McDougall was elected to the office of attorney general. McDougall's former Chicago law partner, Lorenzo Sawyer, was now a resident of Nevada City, where he opened a law office in competition with Niles Searls, whom the voters rejected for justice of the peace by a margin of ten votes.

II

WELL, HERE WE ARE in all our glory. Charley keeping a book store, and I procuring justice for my 'much injured clients.' What shall I write, Nella? Shall I describe Nevada, with its teeming population of seven thousand, and an additional ten thousand within a few miles around—or shall I tell you what a comfortable little ranch we have, all lined with cloth of snowy hue, with dining room in the rear . . . or shall I tell you that Charley's health is good and that mine was never better—excepting always that I have the chills and fever three days in the week and that as this was my day of performance, it has left me so nervous as to be scarcely able to write intelligibly?

Niles and Charley had joined Ed Truex and O. P. Blackman (Nevada City's "most eligible bachelors") in their Main Street store. Charley had a corner where he dispensed everything which went under the heading of "Books and Stationery." This included such items as blank books, pass books, memorandums, drawing paper, pencils, letter paper, note paper, and foolscap, envelopes, pens (quill, steel, and gold), inks (red, black and indelible), sealing wax and wafers, slates, playing cards, monte cards, maps, illustrated letter paper, periodicals, magazines, and newspapers. Also books of fiction, nonfiction, poetry, and religion.

Niles had obtained some law books and set up his office in another corner of the store, using a pork barrel for a desk and a nail keg for a seat (the latter furniture courtesy of Truex and Blackman, general merchandise). The "much injured clients" mentioned in his letter to Cornelia included six Frenchmen, J. Figuière, I. Isoard, Pierre Dreydemie, Joseph Durand, R. Mathieu, and Monsieur Mayet.

These miners had located a very rich claim on Buckeye Hill, known far and wide as the "French" claims. So rich was it that several Americans decided to take it over. As a pretext for jumping the claim, they cited the fact that the Frenchmen had failed to renew the licenses required at that time for all mining carried out by foreigners in California. When the Americans demanded proof that the Frenchmen had paid the twenty dollar fees for the month of September, the most recent receipt produced was for the month of July.

Only Figuière spoke English, and he explained that it was not their fault that the tax collector had not come around. He assured them the tax would be paid whenever an authorized collector arrived in the diggings. The Americans were unimpressed. The four of them, T. W. Colburn, his brother Charles, T. Robson, and Thomas Barton, hired a pair of Nevada lawyers, Hiram C. Hodge and T. G. Williams, who told the Frenchmen to stop work and leave the claim immediately.

The Frenchmen quickly hired Edward F. W. Ellis and Niles Searls to bring suit against the Americans before the newly-elected Justice, John Edwards. Ellis was thirty-one, came from Illinois, and was an active Mason, which may have been why he was chosen by the French miners. He was seven years older than Niles. When the case came to trial, Nick Turner, popular proprietor of the Nevada Hotel, was chosen foreman of the jury of six.

On the stand, Tom Barton swore that he and his comrades had stood by and watched the Frenchmen take out gold by the "bucketful." Finally, it got to be more than they could stand. The foreigners had taken enough of the American gold, they thought, and now it was time for American citizens to have a chance. After both sides presented their arguments, the case went to the jury, who found for the Frenchmen.

Now that the trial was over, the community was calm. News of the admission of California into the Union arrived late in October and created a brief flurry of excitement. Down at Rough and Ready, where between four and five thousand miners were said to be living, Rev. James G. T. Dunleavy opened the county's first ten-pin bowling alley. It was 90 feet long and the Methodist minister and his wife operated it in conjunction with a saloon they had been running since the first of the year. Dunleavy had embarked on a new course after the discovery of gold, one more profitable than his evangelistic endeavors of the past.

Judge Stamps, whose wife had died in the spring, had remarried, this time to Miss Chord on September 26. They were chivareed by bell gongs, and a large crowd ran up a bar bill of more than $200 at Nevada City. More specimens of gold quartz were being turned up at Grass Valley, and Doctor Wittenbach was experimenting with a device which he hoped would crush the quartz and separate gold from the rock. Wages dropped from sixteen dollars a day to nine as the summer season came to a close.

On November 12, 1850, Niles brought Cornelia up to date in the first letter he had written her since coming to Nevada:

We have now been in Cal over one year—have experienced all the vicissitudes of a life in the far famed country. I have been sick about one half the time since my arrival. Still, I cannot make up my mind to condemn the country in "toto" . . . The peculiar kind of life we lead here has enough of adventure connected with it to become exciting, and in some instances highly interesting.

With our blankets and the Texas code of practice (i.e. a revolver), we consider ourselves both safe and at home in all places. Often have I rode till it became too dark to follow the trail, then turned my mule loose or made him fast to a tree and slept as comfortable as possible amid the serenade of wolves.

We had an election of Justice of the Peace here not long since, at which election one Niles Searls was a candidate, and would doubtly have been elected had he got the most votes, but happening to be in the minority, he was defeated. I attribute it all to my first name being Niles, as I have observed said name to be very unlucky in elections.

We have had no letters from any of you for about three months, except one which Charley had from Robt [Mulford] about six weeks since. The Tennessee arrived four days since, and as Charley goes to San Francisco tomorrow, we shall, I trust, hear from you. I believe Charley will be vexed enough to upset the stove in the event of getting no letter, and I am bound to give your miniatures a good scolding.

I think the general health of the people is as good as usual, with the exception that the cholera has been prevailing in Sac City and San Francisco—It is abating at present. My old friend Hartson of Cherry Valley memory, who came across the plains this season, starts for home in from one to two weeks. His health has been poor since his arrival. . . .

Where is Addison? Tell him to write me, let him be where he will. I suppose, were I to see him now, I should scarcely recognise in him the heedless youth of two years earlier date. Two years! It scarcely seems possible . . .

Ten days later, in Sacramento City, Charley wrote to Mary:

My Cousin Molly,

Has I presume, wondered at my silence for the few last mails . . . I left Niles at Nevada City eight days since, intending at that time to reach San Francisco in time to write by the steamer which left Monday the 18th inst., but failed in so doing, and therefore our friends at home were again disappointed.

For 8 or 10 weeks past I have been moving to and fro so much it has been almost impossible to write, but now being located for a time at Nevada, I hope we can both write with more regularity. I perceive Niles has written Nella four full pages, and therefore has told of our doings and location, with the little news of our home in the mountains, and for me to tell of our city which has risen in the woods before the woodman had time to clear a spot for its site would be but a repetition to you. . . .

I have now completely recovered my health and strength and enjoy myself highly when at home in our little ranch at Nevada—it now seems quite like home, and being at all times ready to receive friends, if you are disposed to give us a call, we have one spare box, affording a substantial seat which is at all times at your service.

If inconvenient to give us a call do not fail to supply us with news of home or friends, and we will do likewise . . . with the exception of the previous letters from Robt we have not heard from RVille in a long time.

III

FOR SEVERAL WEEKS in September and October, Mary Niles and her parents had been away from Rensselaerville, visiting relatives. Addison also was gone, having been accepted for the fall term at Williams College in Massachusetts. Cornelia was caring for the younger children with the aid of Julia Hauh, the seventeen-year-old housemaid, and Deborah Wickes, who had moved into the Niles house to keep Cornelia company.

Deborah was teaching her own school and Cornelia was in charge of Mary's school in her sister's absence. Deb's sister Delight was assisting the new principal at the Rensselaerville Academy. Mr. Gallup was gone and had been replaced, first by George Cornell and then by Julius Pomeroy, before Will Allen graduated from Williams College and took over as principal in 1850.

On September 22 Cornelia and Deborah spent the afternoon writing letters; Deb to her beau Lloyd, and Cornelia to brother Addison. Said Cornelia:

School was pretty tiresome the first day, but I had made up my mind to take it easy, and it makes it seem more pleasant to meet Deborah every noon and night when I come home, and we are then both fresh and ready for any amusement. Julia gets us first rate meals (half our *happiness,* you know, depends on that).

The children are remarkably quiet and good, particularly Emma, and we have plenty of books to read, study, and I have converted Ma's bedroom into a little cozy parlor where we can enjoy the fire on the hearth evenings. We have received our company there thus far, and they have all pronounced us two very pleasantly situated old maids—we have not been alone one evening. . . .

Wednesday Eve Mr. Allen dropped in, and spent the whole evening, and I can assure we had a nice time. He makes capital fires, and shows off well in a rocking chair in the chimney corner, with the poker to amuse himself with. He brought me Harper's Magazine for July to read. . . . Deb says Mr. Allen is 21; did you guess him so young? . . .

Day before yesterday they commenced working at the plank road a little. Mr. Carpenter has come with tools, and they are pulling a few stone in the "spring lot" as Charlie calls it. One would think it was something very remarkable, from the number of people who are passing constantly to see the commencement of the work.

What a beautiful week our folks have had to visit in! But what an empty house this is. Your room is so desolate, and still I keep the door shut that I may not see in. I do not believe I could endure three weeks entirely alone—I should have the blues as I never did before, but Deborah is just the free and easy one to make such quiet seem pleasant. She seems to enjoy it as well as I.

We had lots of sport the other day, with an agent for some reading books. He spent most of the morning at Deb's school, trying to induce her to introduce his books, and she sent him to me. He met me as I was going home and said his health was very poor, and he would, if I pleased, just step in and fix himself a little toast, as he was a Grahamite and carried his own provision &c &c.—And perhaps there was a little grass about for his horse, or some oats in the barn maybe, and so in five minutes after he had introduced himself, his horse was in the barn and himself in the kitchen, hauling from his bag his loaf of bread and making himself quite at home.

Deb came home, all in a hurry to tell me about him, and laughed in his face as she ran into the kitchen and found him there. Julia and I were a little offended at his making himself so free, though I saw at once that he was a "character," and we were pretty *cool.*

He ate his dinner with us, and we thought it quite an adventure for three lone girls thus suddenly to move an addition to their circle of a fine looking, well dressed young gentleman. When we left for school, we left him packing his bag of bread and Julia looking a thundercloud, for fear he would not go away, but he soon took his leave.

The book salesman was an adherent of Sylvester Graham, a self-appointed expert on diet and health foods. Originally a Presbyterian minister, he became a temperance lecturer before "discovering" that the craving for drink was probably the result of poor eating habits. His vegetarian diet was based on unbolted wheat flour. Bread and crackers made from this flour was eaten only after it was slightly stale, and thorough chewing was required to achieve maximum benefit, according to Graham.

The new plank road, which was to pass in front of the Niles residence, was part of the improved highway to Albany. In wet weather it would be a distinct improvement over the muddy road which it replaced. However, traffic would be increased greatly on the quiet street which heretofore had gone only as far as the spring on the hill.

A few days later Cornelia wrote Mary that she had heard from Niles, "which letter I enclose, though I think it not as good as usual, and perhaps you had not better make it very public. No letters from Charles." On October 2 she wrote again to Addison and told him of the letter from Niles, saying it was short and that his health had not been good for some time until of late, but "*now* he had the fever and ague the 'natural way.' Thought of taking out a patent for 'shakes made easy.' Was with Charles still in the express business." She told Addison she thought it not at all impossible that he may come home yet this fall. "He had seen Orsamus, and Hartzen arrived in good health a fortnight before, across the plains. His letter was dated the day before the riot at Sac. City—13th."

Her October 2 letter continued:

We have not yet become accustomed to your absence . . . I do not miss Mary half so much as I do you. I shall have to hunt up some other nice little boy to look after, trouble myself about &c &c, to supply the "goneness." . . .

Mr. Allen seemed much engaged the other night about a Lyceum for the winter. Think they will be able to form one. Perhaps we shall start a paper for our Reading Circle. Mr. Allen spoke in favor of it, and says he wishes to attend the meetings and take a part.

By the way, have you any opportunity of learning anything about books suitable to be read at our meetings. Look about you and recommend something to us. We do not commence for some weeks, and do not talk much of them yet, but wish to be in readiness. . . .

Now, as for Mr. Allen's school, I can tell you quite encouraging news. He has now 32 scholars, and 9 of them girls and a prospect for more. I think people are much better pleased with him than before, and more than that, that he has improved himself.

Delight likes him well, but says his greatest fault is want of system and an inclination to be *too* obliging to the scholars to make all things move regularly on. He does not say "You must" but "Will you." Mr. Pierce has bought Dr. Aley's grey colt and Mr. Allen rides it quite often. Have not seen Pierce ride yet.

Mr. Allen enquired of you Monday, and said he thought he should have a letter before this from you. Won't you have more leisure when you get settled nicely? I want one of these days a letter describing your room furniture &c so that I can imagine all about you. Something about the people you find at your boarding place—what church you shall fix upon to attend regularly—how your wardrobe and fixins suit, &c, if you are well supplied. . . .

(Thursday Morning.)—Delight has been out, and returned with the news of a tragic occurrence which took place yesterday at Reedville, or near there. Two orphan children, nephew and niece of Dunbar's step father, went out nutting and had been lost two days, when, after much search they were found in a cornfield and pond, murdered brutally, and so strong suspicion was fixed upon Reuben Dunbar (who lived with the Dr. last winter) that he was arrested, and all our lawyers have gone down to get the case.

Fri. Mor.—Dunbar is committed. Pierce is lawyer for the people and [Chittenden] for Dunbar.

Addison capitulated to Cornelia's demands and provided her with a detailed list of his room furniture:

I am seated by my desk, not in the little, contracted room where I wrote to you before, but in a much more comfortable one on the main street, into which I moved last week. This is the same room [William] Allen occupied through his whole course and is about 13 ft. square, with 3 windows and one of the pleasantest rooms in W^{ms} town.

It is the upper room of a Dr^s office and the Dr. (Dr. Duncan) who rooms below, is one of the finest men in the world, and more than all, a member of the "Zeta Psi Fraternity" of which I am now a brother. Besides being more convenient, this room comes $4½ cheaper than the other.

You wished to know all about my room, furniture &c. Well, there is a carpet on my floor, which answers my purpose very well, though, as there are 2 kinds, it somewhat resembles Joseph's coat of many colors. I am writing on a neat red table, on which stands a book case with drawers and pigeon holes, and the shelves laden with lore.

In the other corner is a lounge, which I cushioned and covered myself, which fills the offices of bed and sofa, not the softest kind of bed, it's true, but still it affords me one long nap from the time I lay down till that dolorous Chapel bell rings us up to prayers and recitation. 2 chairs, a washstand and lookingglass complete the furniture of my room at present, but I think I shall have to get me a small side table and solar lamp sometime, as they are considered indispensible, and I can get them cheap and sell them afterwards for nearly the same I give for them. With these and paper curtains for my windows, I shall be completely fitted out.

Now, as for college life, I like it first rate. I have 3 recitations a day, which requires considerable study, it is true, but I have nothing else on my mind and nothing else to do (except the expense of things here, that worries me some).

I am acquainted with all my class and like most of them. I am not at all troubled about my standing in the class, and by taking things as they come and making the best of them, I think I shall pass 2 yrs. here *very* pleasantly.

I board now at a club in the next house and have very good board at probably about 1.50 to 1.75 $ pr. week. Mrs Chapman, where I boarded first, raised her price from $2 to 2.25 and the boarders all went to the Union house but me. I have joined the Philtechman Lit. Soc. and also the $Z\Psi$ fraternity. This last is a secret Soc. in name, but the exercises are literary and its principles the very best.

The members are all studious and moral, and it takes the highest stand of any Sec. Soc. in College. Allen was one of the founders of the W^{ms} Chapter. You can ask him about it. By joining, I have secured firm friends and *good* ones, good society, and many other advantages which you will have to come to college to understand. The expense is something ($8.00 badge and all), but I think the advantages, both during college life and afterwards, are worth 5 times that.

I must go and get ready for Church. I will finish afterward.

Sunday Evening.—I have been to Church all day and heard Dr. Peters. He is a most uninteresting preacher, but the sermons are middling good. You ask where I attend Church regularly. At the Presbyterian, of course, as there is no other, except a little Meth. Church where there is service occasionally, I believe. . . . All the students attend the Pres. and have seats set off to them in the gallery. By the way, I have donned the hat, in order to support the dignity of a [Junior] more properly. I wish you could see me once walk to Chapel. You'd think I was prex [Mark] Hopkins at least. . . .

My clothes and all are just about right, except my vest is giving out.

I'm afraid I shall have to get a new one before I come home. That will be only 9 weeks from next Tuesday. . . .

I have not had much opportunity yet to see or read much, though I shall soon. I have read some of Emerson's Essays and think the style beautiful, original and generally true, but I don't know as it would do for you.

When Mary and her parents returned to Rensselaerville, she resumed teaching her school and Cornelia began to catch up with her sewing. Mr. William Allen was becoming a prominent fixture in the village and in the Niles household. Wrote Mary to Addison:

We are getting to think very much of Mr. Allen. He seems to have cast aside that suspicious reserve that he had at first, and is very lively and agreeable. On Monday of this week, Mr. Allen and Delight, Lucina and Hopkins, Augustus and myself had a fine ride on horseback, and among other fetes, we rode home 6 abreast, cantered through the street in that way, and then filed off and went up the plank road as far as it is planked.

It was evening, but moonlight, and delightful. They all came to our house afterward and finished the evening in fine glee. Allen had his handkerchief stolen and instituted a suit against some of the company. The suit is still pending.

Last evening, the Calhoun girls, Tompkins's, Wickes's, Niles's, Allen, Pierce, More, Hopkins's, Cliff got together, went to the Academy, played fox and geese on the green. Pupils hopped on the piazza, chased each other around the house, sung &c, then came down and went up the plank road, stopped and sung and made speeches &c until 8 o'clock, then returned to their respective homes. What think you of dignity in R Ville? That it is getting scarce?

Perhaps your newly acquired dignity as Junior will be greatly shocked at the recital of such conduct among those with whom you so lately associated, but you must recollect that one of the principal actors in the scene was once himself a "grave senior," and is now a graduate of that college which you now claim as Alma Mater. . . .

We hope to hear from the boys again soon. I should not be at all surprised to see Niles at any time. I think he will come this fall, from what he said in his last.

In November, Cornelia described to Addison the interesting books she had read in the past several weeks, thanks to the equally interesting Mr. Allen:

"Picciola" is so interesting that I find it no task to get a short lesson in it every day when it is possible, and I can employ every other leisure moment, when I have not company or am not visiting myself, in reading Harper's Magazine, Female Poets of America, Judah's Lion by Charlotte Elizabeth, and more particularly just now, Emerson's Representative Men. This I have through the kindness of Mr. Allen, who, finding I liked Carlyle, asked me to read this.

Now you know I am not very wise, and cannot comprehend the deepest things "there be," so at first I read and reread to no profit—it was all jargon; but I tried again, and little by little, order came out of chaos, and beautiful truths and broad ideas became clear and comprehensible in some measure, and I do not tire of reading it, though I am not bound to believe all he says.

Have you been reading it? You spoke of it for the "circle," but I fear it would not suit all. We intend to commence our Reading Circle next week. . . . A Bible Class was commenced last week, which promises to be very interesting. Mr. Allen is the leading spirit of that, as he is fast growing to be of everything else. . . . Singing school is being talked of, and several other things, as Lyceums.

An "indignation meeting" was held last week upon the great fugitive Slave Bill, and they grew hot about it, I believe, particularly George Durant, [George] Cornell, Mr. Ransom &c. Another is to be held tomorrow, which we shall all attend.

Friday I went to the Academy and was extremely glad to see quite a number of spectators, knowing how cheering it would be to Mr. Allen, who has been so much neglected in that respect. His school appeared remarkably well. Had some capital speaking, particularly from Davis, who really did grandly.

Delight has now 14 girls, and I think the school slowly increases. As for Mr. Allen, I believe he is gaining esteem and respect day by day, and if he can only make it profitable for him to stay, the day will come when, even in Mr. Pomeroy's presence, he will not be cast in the shade in the eyes of the people of R.Ville. He never has deserved to be, but does not pass for all he is worth at first.

He has a very clear head, good taste, is perfectly upright, and has as kind a heart as ever beat. . . . He is taking lessons in drawing from Amelia twice a week, and she French lessons of him. . . .

We are now looking for letters from Niles to tell us whether he will return this fall or not—but I have faint hopes of his coming, because Charlie will not, and Hartzen wants him to go to Nevada and practise law with him. I believe Niles chooses to come home. Charles has been very sick indeed, but has nearly recovered.

COYOTE MINING

CHAPTER 28

COYOTE DIGGINS

November 1850–January 1851

I

"Would you like to visit our mine, Monsieur Searls? It would give much pleasure to me and my friends."

"Why, surely, Monsieur Figuière. I'd like very much to see your famous hole in the ground."

"Marvelous! Can you come with me now?"

"Nothing would suit me better. How about you, Charley? Want to visit the coyote diggins?"

"I guess so. Business has been slow all week, so I don't suppose it will change much before Sunday."

"I'll keep an eye on things," offered Ed Truex, who shared the premises. "I've been up on the hill a hundred times before. Besides, I'm expecting a shipment sometime today."

"Thanks, Ed. As soon as I locate my hat we can be on our way."

The three young men, two American and one French, climbed the pockmarked slopes of Buckeye Hill, dodging miners and mine shafts as they went. The hill, named for a dozen miners from Ohio, swarmed with activity, for the miners were trying to accomplish as much as possible before the winter storms began in earnest. It had rained on the last two days of November and snowed a little on the first couple of days of December, but now the skies were cloudless. It wouldn't last for long, they knew.

The coyote mines, so-called because from a distance they resembled the burrows of wild animals, were dug straight down to the bedrock. Some were only ten feet deep; others were as much as a hundred feet. Each shaft was like a well, even to the windlass above for winding the rope up and down, bringing bucketfuls of pay dirt to the surface.

Of course, not all the dirt and gravel brought to the top contained gold, but enough did to keep the men working harder than most had done in years. The buckets were emptied beside the mines until great mounds of earth were piled high on all sides, waiting to be washed when the winter rains filled ravines and gullies on the slopes of the hill. If the rains failed to come, the dirt would have to be hauled to Deer Creek to be washed.

Once the ditch was finished from Rock Creek, Charles Marsh and his partners would be selling water to the miners wherever they wanted it, but the cost was sixteen dollars a day, an ounce of dust, and not many claims could support such costs. On the other hand, a number of claims had produced as much as ten thousand dollars already and a few were said to have paid one hundred thousand, although it was impossible to verify such figures.

One thing was certain: it was backbreaking, dangerous work, especially for novices. For this reason, many of the better mines were those worked by experienced lead miners from Illinois and Wisconsin. Such miners never had trouble being hired, and inexperienced workers sometimes pretended to come from that region in order to gain employment. They had to learn quickly, however, to hold onto their jobs and avoid injury.

Niles had learned already, while prosecuting his first legal case in Nevada, that a coyote claim, by mutual agreement among miners, was thirty feet long by thirty feet wide and extended straight down to bedrock. After sinking the main shaft, the miners tunneled about in all directions until they broke through into their neighbor's drifts. While discussing the subject with fellow attorney Lorenzo Sawyer, Niles had been told that the hill was so undermined it was possible to go down one shaft and come up any other.

Remembering this, Niles walked uneasily over the undisturbed ground which lay between the shafts, wondering what force it would take to cause the entire hillside to collapse.

"Here we are," announced Figuière, with a flourish of his hands. His partners grinned and stopped their activities. "Monsieur Searls!" they shouted, rushing to embrace the man who had helped preserve their claim. Niles introduced them to Charley, who was then received with equal enthusiasm.

"Are you ready?" asked Figuière, addressing Niles.

Niles looked surprised. "Ready? For what?"

"To go down, of course! Just step into the bucket!"

Niles peered cautiously over the edge of the hole. "How far down does it go?"

Figuière shrugged. "Not so far. Perhaps eighty or ninety feet. What does it matter? You are going, are you not?"

"What does it matter? It matters a great deal—I'd like to go down and come back again all in one piece!"

"Never fear, Monsieur Searls—would we let something bad happen to you? Never! Get in!"

It was Niles's turn to shrug his shoulders. The bucket was actually a wooden box about two feet square and two feet deep. While the Frenchmen held the handle to prevent the windlass from turning, Niles climbed awkwardly into the bucket, gripped the stout rope firmly with one hand and bravely waved his hat with the other.

"Lower away!" he called out gamely.

"Not so fast," replied Figuière. "It's dark down there. Put your hat on your head and take this candle." While he talked, the Frenchman lit the candle at a nearby fire and brought it to Niles. "Don't let it blow out, or you won't see a thing!"

The windlass creaked, the rope began to unwind, and the bucket slowly dropped into a shaft that was four or five feet in diameter. By the flickering light of his candle, Niles saw that the walls of the shaft were lined with a loose mixture of loam, sand, and gravel, with a few cobblestones here and there. He reached out to touch the wall, and when his fingers contacted its surface, bits of dirt and pebbles crumbled away and fell in a shower to the bottom of the hole, echoing noisily all the way. He quickly withdrew his hand, noticing at the same time that the appearance of the wall was undergoing a change.

Instead of the typically red soil of the mountains, he saw that the wall now looked grey, even blue. He guessed it was some kind of clay. The walls seemed to be closing in around him; the small opening of light at the top now seemed very far away.

As the bucket neared the bottom, Niles could see gravel in the walls once more, but it resembled concrete, unlike the surface material. It was the first time he had seen what miners called cemented gravel.

Just then the bucket bumped to a sudden stop and the rope went limp in Niles's hand. He stepped out and onto the floor of the shaft. "O.K.!" he shouted. "Take it away!"

Niles looked about him. There was very little room. A heavy wooden framework had been erected around him and it was like standing within a cage which had spaces between the bars wide enough to permit a man to crawl through. He did exactly that, thinking it would be well to get out of the shaft before the bucket came back down with Charley aboard.

In a few minutes, his friend arrived, the bucket was sent up again, and returned with Figuière, who then explained the workings. It was crowded and uncomfortable in the tunnels, for they were not more than five feet high. Niles and Charley wondered how anyone could work under such conditions. Their candles cast ghostly shadows on the walls and ceiling.

Figuière explained the timbering, saying that the cagelike portion at the bottom of the shaft was described by miners as "squaring the circle." The hole was round, but the timbering square. All of the supports, whether posts or beams, were identical, being a foot square and four feet long. Two posts would be erected vertically on the bedrock, about two and a half feet apart. A third member would be laid horizontally across the posts, and all three were recessed into the wall of the shaft. Another such arrangement was repeated on the opposite side of the shaft, and then two more combinations of posts and beams completed the square.

Once this work had been performed properly, excavation could begin between the posts, and the cross beams would support the cemented gravel above them. As the tunnels were extended into the sidewalls, additional timbering kept the ceiling from collapsing.

"I'm surprised there's so much fresh air down here," Charley commented.

"An absolute necessity—the first miners found that out the hard way," replied Figuière. "But now we know how to have as much good air as we need."

"Do you have a pump?" asked Charley.

"A sort of a pump, yes, but it is amazingly simple. Do you see this hose which comes down the shaft and rests near the floor of the mine? Put your hand near the end of it, but take care not to block the opening completely."

They did as instructed and felt air being pulled into the hose. "The hose is exhausting air from the bottom of the mine," said the Frenchman.

"Where does it go?" asked Niles.

"Out the chimney."

"Chimney?"

"You will see when we get to the top once more. As you go up, watch the hose. You will see it suddenly vanish into the side of the shaft, just before you reach the surface. Now, let's go up."

When all three were again on the ground, Figuière took them to the small fire pit which had been dug at a short distance from the mine. A fire was burning in the pit, and the French miner explained that a small tunnel connected the bottom of the pit with the side of the shaft, and it was into this tunnel that the hose led. The draft of the burning fire drew air from the mine shaft through the hose whose lower end lay at the shaft's bottom. The resulting vacuum caused fresh air to enter the shaft from above, thus replenishing the stale air below. The fire had to burn constantly.

"Very ingenious," said Charley. "Did you think of it yourselves?"

"Oh, no. We merely copied what others had learned to do. It is the only way!"

"By the way," said Niles. "Have you had any more trouble with claim jumpers?"

"No. And we are all paid up. We are lawful once more!"

"I'm glad to hear it. Then someone finally came around to collect the foreign miner tax?"

"No. I went to Marysville and paid the County Clerk in his office. We're taking no more chances!"

"That's probably a very good idea. I see that Pierre has opened a restaurant on Broad Street."

"Yes, he and Charles are partners now. You must eat there if you haven't already. It's the only civilized food in Nevada! There you can eat and not be poisoned. Only the French know how to prepare food. It is a fact!"

On the way back to Main Street, Charley described his latest scheme: "I'm going to have lettersheets printed with a picture of Nevada. Someone is always coming in and asking why I don't have them. I've got San Francisco, Sacramento City, Marysville, everything but Nevada. They all want to show the people back home what this place looks like."

"Sounds like a great idea, but how will you go about it? I don't suppose such a picture exists, does it?"

"Not yet. I've found that I can have the sheets printed in San Francisco if I can furnish them with some kind of a sketch. I can't do it, but I'm going to talk to that sign painter, Withington, and see if he'll make me a drawing."

"Does he do that sort of thing? I thought he could only paint signs."

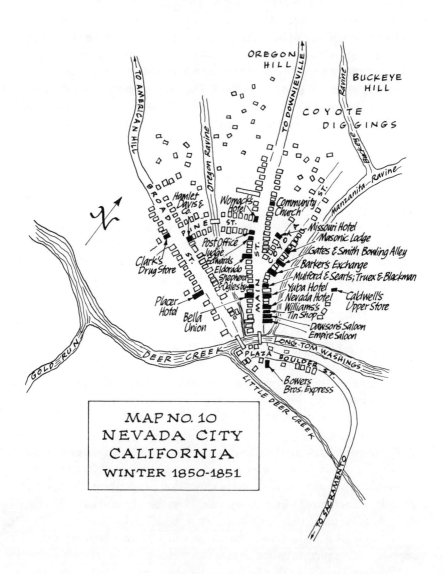

MAP NO. 10
NEVADA CITY
CALIFORNIA
WINTER 1850-1851

"He's pretty clever with his decorations, so I imagine he can do something at least well enough for an artist down in the city to improve on. By the way, did you know that he was trained as a carriage painter? He knows how to do all that fancy work like you've seen on those Albany and New York City rigs."

"Is that a fact? Not much call for that in California, I'd guess—not for awhile, anyway! Well, it sounds like a first rate plan. I know I'd like to have a few of those lettersheets myself. But how's he going to show the whole town with all these trees in the way? When you climb Prospect Hill you can only see a few of the buildings."

"I don't know just how he'll manage it, but I'll leave that to him. Artistic license ought to come up with some kind of solution."

"You know, I was just thinking that now there's a post office here in town, you'll probably have a lot more business. Not having to pay express fees down to the city will make it a lot cheaper to correspond."

"I'm banking on that—and aren't you glad we got out of the express business when we did?"

"I admit that sitting beside a warm stove on these cold mornings has distinct advantages over coaxing a balky mule through snowdrifts and icy streams. But my own business isn't doing too well at the moment. This town has entirely too many lawyers and not nearly enough trials!"

"How many lawyers do you suppose there are?" asked Charley. The young man began to name off Nevada City attorneys: "Ellis, Hodge, Williams, Sawyer, McConnell, Anderson, Barbour, Buckner, Caswell, Hubbard, Freeman, Townsend . . . and Bill Lyons."

"Don't forget Bowers," said Niles.

"Of Bowers Brothers Express?"

"No. Tom Bowers. And Dick Oglesby."

"Dick Oglesby? I thought he was just a storekeeper. Do you mean Oglesby of Oglesby and Shepherd, right across from Turner's hotel?"

"That's the one. He's a pretty interesting fellow, when you get to know him. He was only nineteen when he was admitted to the bar in Illinois. During the Mexican War he was an officer."

"He doesn't appear that old."

"He's not. He's twenty-four, same as me."

"I'll be twenty-four myself in February. He's been a busy fellow, I'd say."

"He's been pretty active in Whig politics back in Illinois. He says he's going back, soon as he can save some money. He and Ellis knew each other back there. They both say it's a lively place. They claim Illinois is going to have the power one of these days soon; say they're going to take it away from the Atlantic states."

"I doubt that! It's pretty nice country, in parts, but awfully backward. Mostly just frontier settlements. Not much in the way of schools. They're dreaming."

"I think you're probably right, but you kind of wonder after talking to those fellows—and Lorenzo Sawyer, too. You know, he was practicing law in Chicago with McDougall, the new Attorney General we elected in October. Sawyer thinks we should keep an eye on Illinois. Especially Douglas and Lincoln."

"Aren't they in Congress?"

"Lincoln was and Douglas still is. If you remember, Lincoln was one of those Whigs that opposed the war. Kept accusing Polk of starting the war illegally."

"Do you think it's true?"

"That he started the war illegally? I don't think there's any doubt of it! The southerners were looking for someplace to put new slaves."

"Don't let our neighbors hear you talk like that!"

"Think I'm crazy? Don't answer that."

II

"The mystery of the missing tax collector appears to be solved," announced Niles, putting down the latest issue of the Marysville *Herald.* "He's skipped the country, vamosed!"

"Doesn't surprise me," said O. P. Blackman, busy weighing potatoes in the back of the store. "What burns me is he probably took some of my gold with him."

"No doubt about that," answered Niles. "He had close to three thousand dollars of Nevada City money when he skipped. We can just be glad he decided to drop out of the Assembly contest. Can you imagine what he might have done then?"

"He wouldn't have been any worse than the rest of those politicians. They're all crooked as the Yuba River."

"They're pretty slick, I'll admit," said his partner, Ed Truex, carefully sweeping the floor and then scooping the dirt neatly into a gold pan in order to wash it later. "But they're not the only ones we've got to watch out for these days. The country's filling up with convicts from Sydney. They're coming into the state by the hundreds. I don't know why the authorities let 'em in."

"Like I said, the politicians are just as bad. Why should they object? They're probably working together, if you ask me."

"Well, Thomas Wilson certainly found his peculiar way to make a pile and go home," commented Charley. "I hope he loses it in a monte game!"

On November 29 the *Herald* had printed a query as to the whereabouts of the former deputy tax collector. It read:

> Thomas Ware Wilson—where is he? Great anxiety is manifested by the friends of Mr. Wilson to ascertain his *"whereabouts."* A few weeks since he was appointed by our worthy County Treasurer, Deputy Tax Collector for Yuba County. It is reported that heavy collections were made by the Deputy at Nevada City and neighborhood, viz, to the amount of $2000 or $3000, and that the Deputy has *"vamosed"* with the funds. His particular friends in these "diggins," and especially his sureties are particularly anxious to find out his location. Can anyone tell *whar* he is? *Il est sortie.*

The *Herald* received two responses, both appearing in the issue of December 3. One was extracted from a letter to a Marysville man from a San Francisco resident:

> I saw our friend, T. Ware Wilson, yesterday, in this city. He was on his way to Cincinnati. I presume he has left in the brig Gen. Worth for Panama. She was to leave yesterday. He bade me to give you his respects."

The second, from an anonymous subscriber, was addressed to Col. Robert H. Taylor, editor of the *Herald:*

> In the Herald of the 29th Nov., I was somewhat surprised to find an article inquiring the "whereabouts" of my old and valued friend, Thomas Ware Wilson. As persons in your "diggings, and especially his sureties, are particularly anxious to find out his location," I may, possibly, be able to enlighten them.
>
> Mr. Wilson has *vamosed* the State of California and is probably at this moment luxuriating at Panama with his ill gotten gains. He passed through this city in great haste about the middle of November, and, as I am credibly informed, took passage at San Francisco on the brig Gen. Worth, bound for Panama or Realejo.
>
> Mr. Wilson left in hot haste I assure you. The causes that impelled his locomotive speed were a mystery to me, until I saw the article in your paper inquiring his whereabouts. Can it be possible that Thomas Ware Wilson has been guilty of the act more than hinted at in your paper? I hope not.
>
> I am well aware that Mr. Wilson has been exceedingly unfortunate in his mining operations during the past year, and I am also aware of the

fact that he was involved in heavy debts, to the amount of several thousand dollars, all of which are unpaid; but I never dreamed that he was a dishonest man until I learned of his conduct in your county.

Mr. Wilson is a citizen of Hamilton County, Ohio, and where known, was much respected. He has a respectable family, who will feel this dereliction of husband and father, severely. He is a member of that respectable order named Odd Fellows, and has held many important stations in the order, requiring skill and ability. He was, I believe, twice elected to the office of Sheriff in Morgan County, Ohio, and never, until now, was he suspected of a mean action.

Trusting that this information will give relief to his friends, and particularly his sureties, I subscribe myself a

CINCINNATI BUCKEYE.

Sacramento City, Dec. 2d, 1850.

Two weeks later, copies of the *Herald* for December 13 and 17 arrived at Mulford's bookstore. They told of a murder which had been committed with interesting ties to Thomas Wilson and Foster's Bar, where Wilson's debts had been incurred. The first story on the murder reported:

Last Saturday [December 7], Mr. Charles Moore and his two partners left their camp, to come down to Dobbines Ranche, on the Yuba River. When about four miles from their destination, they separated; Mr. Moore came one road and his partners another; he had $2300, belonging to himself and partners.

His partners arrived at Dobbins Ranche, and waited there for him. After a short time, a Spaniard came to the Ranche, and said there was a man who had been shot, lying dead above. Mr. Moore's partners immediately went in the direction indicated by the Spaniard, supposing that Mr. M. was the murdered man. They did not succeed, however, in finding him that day.

The next day, Sunday, they took the Spaniard with them, and found Mr. Moore lying in a small ravine, dead, with three slug wounds upon him, one of which had penetrated his spine, and another had entered under the shoulder and pierced the left lung. The murderers had rifled the body of the money.

Suspicion attaches to three individuals, who are on the way below, to take passage for the Atlantic States. We understand that a party has left in pursuit of them.

Four days later, the *Herald* announced:

. . . Since then, an arrest has been made in Sacramento City, of the person supposed to be the murderer. He is an Englishman, from Sydney, by the name of James Stuart. When caught in Sacramento City, he was in the act of committing a burglary!

James Stuart's first conviction had occurred in England in 1836, at the age of sixteen. His crime was forgery and for it he was banished to New South Wales for life. Friends secured his release after he got there and he managed to work his way first to South Australia, then to Panama, and finally to California. In the summer of 1850 he was mining on Foster's Bar, fifty miles from Marysville, on the Yuba River.

He became part owner of a lifeboat used to ferry passengers across the river. From this and mining he earned enough to build a house and open a store at Foster's Bar. At the same camp was Thomas Ware Wilson, coproprietor with Edwin Burr (or Edward Barr) of the Great American Hotel, described in July by themselves as "new and magnificent."

Another store was operated by Oliver P. Stidger, newly elected justice of the peace and an associate justice on the Yuba County Court of Sessions. Burr (or Barr) doubled as the constable, or sheriff, of Foster's Bar. One day James Stuart, by his own admission, got bored with life on the bar, stole a chest containing $4300 in gold and silver, and buried it in his truck garden—all, that is, but $150 of it.

Stuart was accused, arrested and brought before Judge Stidger, who ordered Burr to take him to the county jail at Marysville, the only place where he could be confined until his trial. At Marysville, a crowd soon gathered at the jail and announced its intention of hanging Stuart. A special guard of sixty men was deputized to protect the jail, and in the morning his accuser offered to drop the charges if Stuart would reveal the hiding place of the chest.

Even in the face of the angry mob, Stuart was reluctant to part with the booty, but finally agreed to return all but $150, which he claimed was lost. While the others went to find the chest, Stuart bribed Burr with the gold he'd withheld and escaped to Sacramento. There he joined a gang of horse and mule thieves and acted as their fence, being unknown as yet to the Sacramento authorities.

Stuart took part in several armed robberies and burglaries in addition to operating as a go-between on sales of stolen items. Eventually he was caught breaking into a house. He heard about a young lawyer who was beginning to practice law in Sacramento and was in need of clients. For fifty dollars, Frank M. Pixley offered to defend him, although Stuart admitted his guilt. For twenty dollars more, a friend and accomplice of Stuart gave perjured testimony, setting him free.

A week or two later, when Stuart was caught in the act of burglarizing a lumberyard, Pixley came to his aid again. His fee was fifty dollars once more, but the picture changed before his client could be released from the Sacramento City prison brig. First, an Auburn constable identified him as the killer of the Auburn sheriff, also named Moore. Several hours later, Thomas Broadwater, partner of Charles Moore, came in and identified Stuart as the man who had murdered his friend.

Stuart was taken from the prison to appear before a Sacramento judge, but Pixley refused to allow his client to be examined. Stuart was returned to jail and in the morning a sheriff from Yuba County arrived with a warrant for his arrest. Pixley informed him that the warrant was invalid, having been incorrectly prepared, and the sheriff went back to Marysville to obtain a proper one.

While he was gone, Stuart turned over $600 in gold dust to Pixley. That same night, he escaped from the prison ship and vanished. He would not be seen again for many months.

III

CHRISTMAS DAY 1850 in Nevada City was beautiful and clear. Business was brisk, and several auctions were going in different parts of the town. The streets were crowded, and many more miners were drunk than was usual. In the evening, two balls were open to the public at ten dollars per ticket, one at Turner's hotel.

The weather continued fair right up to New Year's Eve. At ten o'clock in the evening, with Charley already asleep under the store counter, Niles sat down to write a letter to his cousins. His mood was nostalgic and sentimental:

Dear Cornelia & Mary,

Three years ago this night, we watched the departure of the old *year* and hailed the coming of the *new*. How vividly are the impressions of that night impinged on memory's tablet. The sentiments there imparted are as fresh as though communicated but yesterday.

Seated upon the *sofa* in front of the parlor stove, we talked of the past, the present, and the future—wondered if ever again we would be permitted to meet on a New Year's Eve and vowed in the warmth of youthful friendship that were'ere the coming year should find us, we would devote its last fleeting hours in commemoration of *that* occasion.

How little did we know what awaited us in the coming three years. How little did I *then* think that when I reverted to the engagement with a view to its fulfillment, it would be in the *far off* state of Missouri—*there* was I found, and *there* was the vow religiously kept.

Another twelve months passed away. In the Hospital, confined to my bed by a raging fever, which for a week had rendered me delirious, I heeded not the lapse of time, but when the Physician at my bedside mentioned that it was the eve of the coming year, the words roused me to consciousness. I cannot describe to you the sad, the bitter reflections of that night, standing as I *then* thought upon the threshhold of Eternity. I never expected to see you again.

With none but strangers to witness my exit from earth, I fervently wished that death had claimed me ere I left the home of my youth. Freely would I have hastened existence, could I first have seen my mother and sister, or heard one loving word from the lips of Cornelia or Mary.

Enough of this—the sands of a third year are nearly gone—in health and with the comforts of life around me, I am noting its departure and wondering if *either* or *both* of you think of me tonight. Tho' separated by America's vast continent, still methinks we may meet in spirit and converse in imagination at least.

I do hope that you may concoct a good long letter for me tonight—not one word have I had from either of you since the middle of the summer. Whether I shall ever get another letter from Rens Ville, begins to be a matter of speculation. Month after month have we looked in *vain* for some missive from your hands, till now we sit down by the stove after closing doors for the night and offer to *bet* that we will get no letter for the next three months.

Charley is quietly slumbering beneath the counter, all unconscious of the world around. He goes to San Francisco in the morning and said he would write you while there. We spent the early part of the evening with Wm. D. Williams, who, when I informed him I was going to write, requested to be remembered to you. He says he expects to be home the next New Years Eve. Charley too. I shall not stay in Cal, if *living,* another year. The climate has never agreed with me and probably never will. Either I go to *Oregon,* or come home in the course of the next season. Most likely the latter. . . .

The music in the various gaming houses has ceased—the din of voices in the street is fast being hushed—silence *profound* begins to reign over Nevada. The year, in a few minutes, will expire, and with it I shall close for the night. When I do so, it is with the fervent hope that during the flight of the *next* we may meet again, to renew the joy of other days. May this find you both as well and happy as I can wish, and believe me, to embody all of good that desire can contain in a single sentence, when I wish you a *happy, thrice happy New Year.*

IV

EARLIER IN THE EVENING, Niles, Charley, and Billy Williams had witnessed an elaborate practical joke staged at Dawson's saloon, just a few doors away. They and many others had been invited to a mock wedding, with everyone but the "groom" being privy to the joke. The part of the minister was played by gambler Jack White, and Tom Marsh, proprietor of Dawson's, was posing as the County Clerk.

The victim, a rancher from down near Bear River, had fallen head over heels in love with a pretty young prostitute from Galena, Illinois. Some said her name was Mary Mahaffey and others said it was "Maraha," but it may have been neither. All that anyone knew was that she was going along with the fun and had received $300 from the groom to purchase wedding finery.

Fifty dollars had gone to the "minister," an ounce to the "clerk," and several hundred went to buy dinner and drinks for the guests. Everyone, including the groom, had a marvelous time until he got ready to take his bride back to the ranch. Peter Decker, who was present, told his diary next day:

After the sucker was thus fleeced, his Deary told him he was a fool, swore he should leave the house or she would shoot him with a pistol she flourished. And not until then the truth flashing on the astonished victim's dull apprehension, after paying about a thousand dollars.

Six days later Niles wrote about the affair, adding some postscripts to the matter:

Good evening Girls. Pretty severe rain we have tonight. Did you say it snowed with you? Well, it's all the same—what else can you expect in your sun forsaken clime.

By the way, have you heard the news—that wedding is coming off over again in a few nights down at Dawson's Hotel. Did I not tell you about it before? O, beg pardon. You see, Miss or Mrs Maraha, who has one or two husbands already, persuaded a fellow with more money than Brains that she was dreadfully in *love* with him. So they were to be married and we were invited to the wedding—everybody knowing that it was a sham except the smitten swain.

With a gambler to officiate as Priest, everything went off in *ludicrous* style. The joke discovered, the unlucky *hombre* has wept ever since, and now they are going to try it over again—guess I shan't attend next time—it's carrying the hoax too far.

Then there was the party at Turners on Christmas Eve that I have said nothing about, either. How it was the best got up of anything of the kind in this region—how I picked out a *dreadful* pretty girl and got an introduction—how she told me she never danced a *lick* in her life—how she liked me a *heap* better than anybody else there—how I *vamosed* on hearing the news. Cal against the world for fun and adventure.

Charley is at San Francisco and I am alone and busily engaged in selling Books or Legal advice, just as the wants of community require. Charley said he should have his letters directed here for the future. Should you take it in your head to write to me for the future (a thing apparently improbable), continue to direct to Sac City, as I may not stay here more than two or three months longer.

I went out prospecting the other day, blistered my hands, spoiled a pair of new boots and dug two dollars, concluded I was not in luck and gave it up.

I have been reperusing Cooper's "Spy" of late. Mary, you read it once—do you recollect the famous surgeon, Archibald Fitzgreaves, whose only prayer was that Lawton and his comrades might cut *scientifically,* and leave something for his skill, instead of demolishing the enemy with the broadsword, as they were wont to do? Of all Cooper's works, his "Spy" has my preference. Though perhaps not as well written as some of the rest, it breathes a spirit of Patriotism throughout that ought to interest every American. . . .

We have a fine band of Lawyers in town, say upwards of twenty. Many of them are the finest kind of fellows—others again are just as mean as *Kayotes.* Our society, who can describe it. Composed of every grade of men from every land is as heterogeneous as you can imagine it. The restraints of *society* are thrown off, and every man exhibits himself in his true colors. Many who at home were considered models of virtue are here the most consumate scoundrels we have.

Conspicuous among the foreigners are the Chinese—industrious and quiet, they attend no ones business except their own. I never saw one intoxicated, or apparently *angry.* I dined at a Chinese Hotel the last time I was in Sac City and took things a la China, excepting the pies made of *"bow wow."*

I heard the report of a pistol a short time ago and have since learned that one Darkie shot another a few [doors] above here. Were such an occurrence to take place in Rens Ville it would create an excitement, but here it is too common to elicit much notice.

"Vile wretches," I think I hear you say. "How lost to every sense of justice and humanity are you become, when to look upon scenes of bloodshed and murder excites no indignation." Yes, yes, and won't we kick up a *dust* among the quiet, order loving citizens when we get home again. I pity the people if this band of *outlaws* ever return. No Sabbath— no temperance societies—no nothing that is at all civilized. I have concluded to open a monte bank in R Ville, and Charley will doubtless go into something equally meritorious.

My old friend Hartson has gone home, but expects to return in the spring with a Law library for himself and me, too, if I want it. Give my best love to all the girls with whom I am in any manner acquainted, I mean those who are unmarried. Tell them if they will wait till I go to Oregon, the Sandwich Islands, China, Van Diemans Land and sundry other places, I will come home and offer myself as a candidate for their favors . . . I think I will adjourn and take a look at the miniatures.

NEVADA CITY'S FIRST FIRE (1851)

CHAPTER 29
READINGS SPRINGS
January–April 1851

I

"DID YOU HEAR about the New Years Ball at Grass Valley?" asked Charley, when he returned from San Francisco in mid-January.

"I heard they were planning one. How did it come off?" asked Niles.

"Not so happily. One of the guests was killed when he stepped out of line."

"That's a sorry way to end the old year—or start the new. But I'm not surprised. When everyone is armed and drinking, shooting comes too easy. Who was killed?"

"I don't remember his name, but they say he was an ex-Mormon. He'd been drummed out of the Mormon Battalion and kicked out of the church."

"The one who's been causing trouble in the camps south of here? Allen, I think his name was."

"Allen! That's the one—Jack Allen. Well, he won't be causing trouble any more."

"We had a little excitement here in Nevada while you were gone," said Niles. "Doctor Knox's house caught on fire a few days back."

"I see the town is still here, so they must have put it out before it spread."

"They did. Or rather, we did. Everyone pitched in and we stopped it before it caused much damage. But it gave us all a pretty smart scare."

"I'd guess so. I worry a lot about fire in these cloth and shingle camps. I especially worry now that we've got our own building and our investment has grown. With so many stores and saloons on all sides, if one goes, it's pretty sure we'll all go."

"The buildings ought to be brick or stone, not wood."

"I agree, and just as soon as I can set aside enough gold dust, I intend to replace this shack with a substantial building."

"Do you think it's worth doing, when we're not likely to be in California for much longer?"

"I look at it as insurance—do you realize how much we stand to lose if the bookstore burns tonight? A lot of what I've saved is tied up here. In fact, Hamlet Davis and I are going to talk to a fellow who's interested in opening a brickyard. Davis means to put up a brick building."

"At this rate, we'll give Sacramento City a run for its money," laughed Niles. "That reminds me; not only do we have a Masonic Lodge and a hall, but I attended the first two meetings of the Odd Fellows in Nevada City while you were gone. On the seventh, I think it was, we set up a committee to draft a constitution and bylaws, and last Saturday we met and adopted the lot. So now we have a church and two lodges in addition to our gambling hells."

"All we need is a Temperance Society to balance things off."

"It may take a while longer to accomplish that!"

"Well, it's sure a relief to be back in the mountains and away from the things that are happening around Sacramento City and San Francisco— even Stockton and Marysville are getting bad."

"Anything new, or just the same old problems?"

"Everywhere you turn robberies and assaults and murders are being committed. Seems like the convicts from Sydney and Botany Bay are coming to California—they've heard we're easy pickings. I guess the word went out that we had lots of gold and didn't watch over it too closely."

"I wondered how long it would last. It always astonished me the way miners left gold dust sitting around in their tents or in their rooms and no one would take it—it seemed like everyone was suddenly overcome with brotherly love. Well, I don't suppose it will be long before they find out about us up here in the mountains."

On January 14, Nancy White, whose teamster husband was down in Marysville, woke up to find an intruder in her bedroom. Her female companion also was aroused and both were frightened and astonished when the robber made no effort to leave. Only when a man in the next room overheard their protests and raised an alarm did the man go away.

Five nights later, Doctor Lennox, formerly of Missouri, was killed by a shot fired through his window. Two men, Best and Fitzpatrick, were arrested and charged with murder. The trial began on the following day in the barroom of the Placer Hotel on lower Broad Street. Louis Best, also from Missouri, had come across the plains with the murdered man and it was said that the two had been quarreling ever since.

Best was not a man with whom most persons would choose to pick a fight. A hard-looking, tough-acting individual who ran a boarding house on Main Street, Best showed up in Justice John Edwards' court with a Colt's revolver and a Bowie knife tucked into the waistband of his trousers. Peter Decker commented that Best looked the part of a desperado.

The trial was expected to last for several days, but before a verdict could be rendered, Fitzpatrick took leg bail, which was interpreted as an admission of guilt, and Best was released to go back to the business of running his hotel. Not everyone thought he was entirely innocent of the charges, but all agreed he was cool under pressure.

Ten days later, a pair of English convicts settled a dispute with knives; one man was killed and the other arrested. Five people died of unspecified diseases during the next couple of days. It occurred to Niles that travel might suit his health better than sitting around this quiet mountain village.

Great gold strikes were occurring in the north part of the state, or so said the men who outfitted and supplied the miners who were heading north in ever-growing numbers. Pack trains were being dispatched from the coast at Trinidad Bay and from the valley at Marysville and Reading's Springs, near Pierson B. Reading's ranch. Gold was said to be turning up all along the Trinity and Scott rivers. Some sources claimed these were the richest and largest diggings ever found.

A Marysville correspondent for the *Alta California* reported that "provisions and mining implements are scarce and high; for instance, crowbars one hundred dollars each, tobacco, seven to eight dollars per pound, and other things in like proportion." The Sacramento *Transcript* said: "Packers are starting out for Redding's and returning from Scott's River daily. Mules are quite plenty, as well as provisions at Redding's Springs, but they command a good price."

The editor of the Portland *Oregonian* swore he had handled specimens from Scott's Bar and was told that some lumps were worth two hundred and even five hundred dollars apiece. Miners were flocking to the region, prospecting the Klamath and Umpqua rivers in addition to the Trinity and Scott.

Niles and Billy Williams decided to accompany some other young men from Nevada City, all of whom were interested more in business prospects near the new mines than in hunting gold themselves. Most had given up the hard work of mining the summer before. Billy got a friend to look after his tin shop while he was gone. Although not a tinsmith himself, the friend could sell the readymade items in the store and take orders for Williams to fill on his return. Inasmuch as Niles had been doing little more than to help Charley mind the bookstore, it was even less trouble for him to take a holiday. They left for Marysville and Reading's Springs in the first week of February. Charley broke the news to Mary on February 18, 1851:

Cornelia's letter of Nov. 18 enclosing one for Niles came duly to hand about 4 weeks since. . . . With us Spring has already commenced. Some two weeks since, I noticed the alder trees in bloom and the grass is now bright and green in wet places near the streams, but this is all—the hills and mountains are desert bare of verdure and herbage, and nothing but the giant pines are to be seen around us.

Niles and Williams, together with a party of acquaintances, started nearly two weeks since for Reddings Springs on the Upper Sacramento river and will be gone some three or four weeks. So I am now entirely alone—not one old friend to counsel with and talk over old times—but this cannot prevent my thinking of home and friends occasionally, for I can assure you many a ten o'clock at night finds my feet on the stove thinking of friends and old times. . .

At present I have but little idea how soon I may return to see you all, for I have a good easy business, a little ranch of my own, and as many customers as I can reasonably ask for. Were it not for the ties which will ever bind me to my early and dearest friends . . . there are inducements which might perhaps detain me for a lengthy period. One discovery I have made since leaving home and it is: the society of friends has greater charms for me than Gold, and therefore, one year longer is the limit of my stay in this distant region.

Today for the first time during the last six weeks we have a rainy day and it now pours down most beautifully. The miners have been very disappointed this winter from the want of water in the dry diggins. Their main dependence now is on the ravine diggins and last fall large quantities of dirt was thrown up ready for the rainy season to wash it—in such diggins the gold is in the surface dirt which is thrown out and washed until the granite is reached, varying from one to ten feet in depth.

The summer mining is principally done in the cayota diggins; in this kind of mining they sink a shaft resembling a great well, with a windlass to draw up dirt. The shafts are from 20 to 90 feet in depth and are continued until the bed rock is reached. The gold is usually found near the rock . . . if after the rock is reached the claim does not pay from ten to thirty dollars per day to the man, it is considered as not worth working.

In this way, considerable tracts of land are undermined, making them a perfect honey comb beneath, and last fall as the rains commenced, several acres sank down, thus rendering it unsafe to work them during the wet season.

A certain Mr. McDonald has just arrived to see Niles, an old Canada acquaintance—he has walked from Greenwood Valley on the American River, a distance of some fifty or sixty miles, and is sadly disappointed in not finding him. And now, good bye for the night, for I must do the honors of the ranch in the way of getting supper for Niles' friend.

Wednesday Morning 19th inst

Williams returned this morning—and reports Niles as on his way from Reddings to Scotts River in Oregon—accompanied by his friends and a train of pack mules loaded with provisions . . . it is reported to be 200 miles from Reddings or 400 from Nevada . . . We shall hear from him in about two weeks, and if he does not return, I will keep you advised of his doings—meantime, you had best continue to address him at Sacramento as heretofore.

Accompanying this, as you perceive, I send a view of our little city which I have had drawn and engraved for sale. By it you will perceive our town is very irregularly laid out, and is situated in a valley or nest like among the hills. It was very difficult to take the sketch, on account of the trees obstructing the view—the plate does not represent the trees in town, so you must imagine them nearly as thick as shown in the outskirts, and also that there are several hundred cabins in and around town not seen at all in the view.

In addition to the printed numbers to refer to in writing about the view, I have added a few to show you of my whereabouts—Main Street is the business portion of town, and like Broadway in New York, is pretty generally crowded with people. My little ranch is situated at the junction of Cayota and Main Streets between No. 1 and No.11—it is not shown on account of [Williamson's] auction store projecting into the street. At No. 14, Pine Street branches off from Main St., and it is thickly built up with Jew clothing stores and meat markets—Cayota Street is also a crooked one and on it the balance of business is done, as Broad St. is principally occupied by miners.

Writing to Cornelia a few days later, Charley commented:

You seem to have had the impression that Niles and I would return home before the appointed two years had expired, but surely you could not have got that impression from anything in my letters, for if I remember right, I have always referred to it as a period [too] vague and distant to talk about—but now I have set my limit and compassed my stay to a period not exceeding a year from this time, and at that time you may rest assured that, health permitting, you will see me face to face . . .

You say you all remain unchanged at home—this will indeed be strange if you continue thus—three years absence and all still the same—it is almost impossible—not that I could wish it otherwise . . . So Deb has not yet taken the matrimonial yoke—I wonder if [she and Lloyd] have not thought of the old adage, "look twice before you leap," and concluded to postpone matters for an indefinite period—very proper, I think . . .

I am pleased to hear you have commenced practicing horseback riding . . . you speak of riding 6 or 8 miles and back as quite a feat—and it is, too, for it is practiced so little with you. But what would you think of riding 40 miles before breakfast, 80 miles before supper, and 110 miles without leaving the saddle only for your meals—this I have done since I have been here, and think but little of it, as long journeys on horseback are so common here. I look forward with much pleasure to the time of my return to accompany you in your excursion, if you do not previously obtain a protector with stronger *legal* claims than I can urge. . . .

Monday Evening Feb 25th

Another Sunday has passed by, but how differently you and I passed the day—here it is the greatest business day of the week, as well as a gala day to the mining community. Here are auctions of all sorts—horses, mules, oxen wagons, and provisions, put up to the highest bidder. The streets are crowded, the gambling houses well filled, and the day often winds up with a fight in which one or more of the parties are wounded. I am within four doors of Barker's Exchange, one of the largest gambling houses, and am sure to hear the fuss when anything happens there. As soon as pistols are presented, the crowd scatters quickly, running over each other in all directions, each trying to get out of range of the pistols.

Shots are often fired while the crowd are standing thickly around them, and I hardly can conceive that there should be so many shots fired

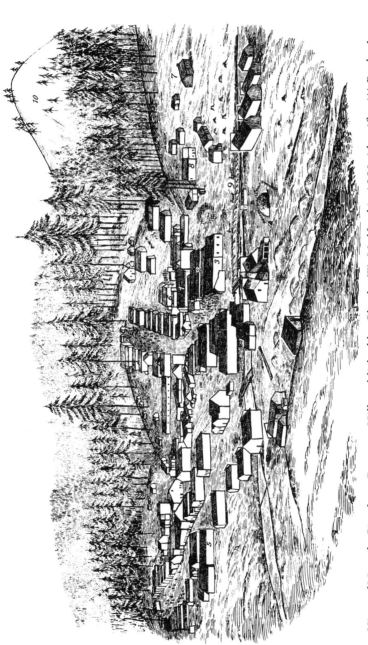

View of Nevada City from Prospect Hill, published by Charles W. Mulford in 1850, identifies (1) Barker's Exchange, (2) Nevada Hotel, (3) Empire Saloon, (4) Eldorado Boarding House, (5) Placer Hotel, (6) Missouri Hotel, (7) Dr. Caldwell's Upper Store ("first house in Nevada"), (8) The Cottage, (9) "Tom Washings," and (10) Sugar Loaf hill.

among them without more serious result. All a rowdy need do now is to run into the street and cry "don't shoot this way!"—the crowd comes around immediately and mount steps and woodpiles to see the "fun," as they call it, but soon leave again, disappointed.

Business has generally been very dull here, but now is beginning to brush up a little, as large numbers from the southern mines are passing by us now on their way to the Feather and Yuba Rivers. I am still engaged distributing "literature for the millions," and have been prospering reasonably well.

Billy Williams also began a letter to Cornelia on February 24, written, he said, at the request of Niles Searls. He told her that Niles had taken notes along the way to Reading's Springs, or Shasta City, as it now was called. These notes were intended to form the basis of a description of California which could be read to the Rensselaerville Young Ladies' Reading Circle. Williams explained how the plan had changed along with Niles's destination:

Some weeks since, Niles and myself were in San Francisco together; while there we heard that the Klamath River and its tributaries were very rich, indeed. We conversed with some men who had recently come from there and confirmed the report. We concluded when we got back to Nevada to take a trip up there, or at least go as far as Shasta City and see if that place did not present good business prospects.

In view of the excitement that already prevailed in this country in relation to the Klamath region, we thought perhaps Shasta City would be a good point to locate and do business, it being the nearest settled point to those mines. On arriving at Shasta we easily discovered that Shasta City was too remote from the Klamath region, and altogether "not what it was cracked up to be."

At length we arrived at Shasta City, after traveling some 6 days from Nevada. We stopped in Shasta 2 days and while there Niles concluded to go on into the mountains with some friends who accompanied us from Nevada City, . . . and learn for himself the truth or falsity of this new El Dorado. I, on the contrary, concluded to return to Nevada City, duly impressed with the belief that a "bird in the hand was worth two in the bush."

On parting with Niles, he requested your humble servant to write you what he had contemplated, viz, an article for the "Rensselaerville Reading party." For this purpose, he furnished me with a blank sheet with his signature. Of course, I cheerfully undertook the task. I did not at the time think of the difficulties of the undertaking—I was only anxious to gratify his slightest wish.

On my way down the valley, in thinking over the matter, it occurred to me that I had undertaken a really delicate job. It occurred to me that I had written many kinds of letters in my lifetime, letters, some of which tried very hard to be eloquent and sentimental, and others that might be considered by some as essentially dunning in their application.

In short, I have written all the way from a "billet doux" to a libelous paragraph in the "Microscope" and "Switch," but I never before wrote one like this. Imagine my situation, an old "bachelor," as Niles is pleased to term me, writing to an intelligent and pretty girl all about a dull, tame, but fatiguing journey up the Sacramento valley.

Had he requested me to write to you as to where he was going—his prospects &c, &c, I should have been satisfied, but no, the cunning rogue bade me do no such thing—he bound me up as a mere amanuensis. I am not to write one word but what tallies with *his views and feelings,* and of course I "obey his instructions."

Yet I enjoy a melancholy pleasure . . . for as I proceed, a thousand pleasing memories rush to mind. It seems but yesterday since I was in Rensselaerville in the midst of all that can contribute to human happiness . . . but it is years since time was when I could write to Rensselaerville to friends whom I highly esteemed in sincerity and boldness of heart, [and] time in its ceaseless flight has wrought great changes. Those friends have gone, some I know not whither. Others are slowly sinking into the grave, under the baleful influence of hopeless disease, and others have gone "to that home from whence no traveller returns," until at last I have no friends left in a village, my residence in which was the happiest period of my life.

At this moment memory grows oppressive and painful, and willingly would I blot it out were it in my power. . . . Here, for the first time, the thought occurs to me that I am writing to a comparative stranger—that I am trespassing on your patience and doing injustice to Niles. I set out to give a plain statement of facts, unvarnished by flights of fancy or relieved by allusions to the past, but before I was aware of it, memory seized the pen and fond recollection hurried it on. . . .

Now, one word as to the "sights" I am about to narrate. It purports to come from Niles. He, very regardless of his literary reputation, entrusted me to usher the little bantling into the world. . . . I confess I cannot conceal a smile when I think what a figure it will cut before the connoisseuries of your literary village—to think how bitterly they will chew the cud of disappointment when the precious morsel is unfolded to their longing gaze—how they will berate the tameness with which this subject is handled and pain over the literary imperfections of Niles; poor fellow, he is as unconscious of the literary outrage I am perpetrating in his name as I am incompetent to wield his pen . . .

On and on he wrote, chuckling to himself from time to time, thoroughly enjoying this opportunity to explore the world of flowery prose at Niles's expense. For several days, whenever he had a free moment, he added a few more paragraphs, but his literary masterpiece was destined to conclude with information that would shock author and reader alike.

II

THE EVENTS LEADING up to the disaster were complex and only in retrospect was it possible to see how inevitable it was that Nevada City should be victimized in such a fashion. In February the Sacramento *Times* printed a letter from the mining camp of Bridgeport on the South Yuba River. It told of the arrest and trial by miners' jury of an accused mule thief named Edward Stanton. After three hours, the dozen jurors ruled that he was guilty of stealing local mules and taking them to Sacramento for sale.

Stanton was sentenced to receive one hundred lashes on his bare back, and an accomplice was given eighteen. Said the *Alta California,* after reading the account in the *Times:* "The hundred was right. It was justice, and no lawyers to prevent it."

Two weeks later, the miners weren't so sure. Jack Knowlton was accused of committing the same type of crime, but in this instance the alleged thief was caught taking mules from the Bridgeport area to the mining camps high on the ridge between the south and middle forks of the Yuba. A posse overtook him and the animals in Grizzly Canyon and brought him back to be tried at Bridgeport.

After four days of deliberation, the miners' court called him guilty as charged and sentenced him to be hanged by the neck. The day of execution was set for four days after the trial. News of the hanging attracted thousands of miners to the scene, and the prisoner was placed under heavy guard to prevent the possibility of rescue.

Meanwhile, down in San Francisco, Charles Jansen was attacked by thieves in his store on February 19, the same day that Billy Williams came back to Nevada City without Niles Searls. After Jansen was knocked unconscious, the pair of robbers took nearly $1600 from his desk. Two men were picked up by police. One was William Windred and the other said his name was Thomas Burdue. Windred and Burdue were taken to Jansen's home, where he was recovering from the assault, and he tentatively identified them as his assailants.

On the way back to the city jail, an effort was made by a crowd of citizens to seize the prisoners. Shouts of "Hang 'em, lynch 'em!" were heard on all sides, but the lawmen got their prisoners safely across the plaza and locked them up. Later in the day the two men appeared before Justice of the Peace Shepherd to be examined. The courtroom was packed and the streets outside were thronged. After hearing some testimony, Shepherd announced that he was going to adjourn the proceedings until Monday, it already being late in the day on Saturday, which was also Washington's Birthday.

Immediately, a voice called out, "Now's the time—grab them!" Only the quick appearance of the Washington Guards with fixed bayonets prevented the mob from taking the prisoners. The crowd outside the city hall grew larger in the evening. Thousands stood in the streets and listened as the mayor and other civic leaders spoke to them, trying to cool the fever of the crowd.

At last, Sam Brannan came up with a proposal which was agreed to by all sides. He suggested the appointment of a committee of twelve to arrange for extra guards for the prisoners. Brannan was one of those selected to serve. The committee met at once. One member proposed that the people form its own jury to try the prisoners. Brannan went a step farther and announced to his fellow committee-members:

"I'm surprised to hear people talk about grand juries, or recorders, or mayors. I'm tired of such talk. These men are murderers as well as thieves. I know it and you know it." Sam looked at those around him, many of the richest and most respected members of the community. "*We* are the mayor and the recorder, the hangman and the laws. The law and the courts never yet hung a man in California, and every morning we read about new murders and robberies being committed. I want no technicalities to shield the guilty. I want to see them hung by the neck!"

The rest of the committee disagreed, but Brannan didn't give up. Even after they completed their business of selecting twenty persons to guard the prisoners, Brannan made a final attempt to get them to recommend that the accused men be hung at ten o'clock Monday morning. Four men voted for thus eliminating a trial. Eight others held firm.

The mobs were back on the streets on Sunday morning. Kemble and Gilbert in the *Alta California* cautioned that "Lynch law is a whirlwind which once let loose may sweep down all peaceable barriers before its angry blast." Sam Brannan snorted at the warning from his former protegé.

Again, speakers tried to soothe the crowd and quiet its dangerous mood. The mob listened but did not respond until William T. Coleman demanded that the prisoners be tried by a people's court on that very day. Lawyers would be permitted to participate, but the judge and jury would be picked by the crowd. The mob roared its approval. Justice Shepherd offered his formal protest, then stepped aside. Other officials protested also, but did nothing to interfere, except to refuse to surrender the prisoners, who were safely hidden in a secret location.

Judge and jury were selected. Suddenly, Coleman wanted to change his own rules and exclude lawyers. The issue was settled by the jurors themselves, who refused to participate unless the accused were allowed to have counsel. When the trial began, Burdue was identified by two prosecution witnesses as James Stuart, the accused slayer of both the Auburn sheriff and Charles Moore of Foster's Bar. Jansen's close friend and neighboring merchant, Theodore Payne, identified the two men as those who had struck and robbed the storekeeper, despite the fact that he had not been present at the robbery.

Other witnesses identified Burdue as Burdue and said he was innocent. Windred had persons who vouched for his whereabouts. All of this identification went on despite the absence from the courtroom of both the men being tried and of their accuser. When the jury retired to consider its verdict, another witness appeared who swore he was with Burdue during the hours of the robbery, but acting judge John F. Spence refused to recall the jury to hear the testimony.

The crowd grew restive as the hours went by. It was dark now and a hanging had been anticipated before the Sabbath came to an end. When the jury finally returned, the mob was stunned when its own hand-picked tribunal announced a split decision: three jurors refused to convict. Then the mob went wild. Windows were smashed, benches thrown, and a rush was made toward the jury, as if to assault them instead of the absent prisoners.

The jurors, each of whom was armed, drew their weapons and retreated to the jury room and shut the door. Finally, the authorities succeeded in clearing the courtroom and dispersing the angry crowd. The jurors left and the building was locked.

The hearing next day was in sharp contrast to the weekend's wild events. Justice Shepherd continued his interrupted session and ordered Burdue and Windred held over for trial, with bail for each set at ten thousand dollars. On March 5, 1851, the grand jury indicted the pair. Burdue's trial date was set for a week later, despite the sworn statement by Frank M. Pixley, James Stuart's attorney, that they had the wrong man.

In Yuba County, it came time to hang Jack Knowlton at Bridgeport. Thousands of miners watched as the victim was made to stand on a teamster's wagon, a rope wrapped round his neck, and tied off to the highest part of the bridge. The wagon drove off and Jack Knowlton was left to swing, a grim warning to other mule thieves.

Encouraged by these bold moves on the part of residents of San Francisco and Bridgeport, a number of the leading citizens of Nevada got together and decried the growing crime wave. They resolved to rid the neighborhood of wrongdoers, and certain suspected persons were warned to leave town at once or face the prospect of being lynched. The threatened persons complied, but not before making some threats of their own. They would return, they said, and when they did, the town would burn.

Within a day or two, a Nevada City man was accused of stealing a sack of flour. On the morning of March 11, he was given twelve lashes and told to leave town. In the evening, John Steele and some friends came down from Poorman's Creek, near Washington, and decided to camp on the ridge north of Nevada City, near Sugar Loaf Hill. About midnight, one of Steele's companions awoke and gave a shout:

"John! Wake up!"

"What's the matter?"

"The whole town's on fire! Look at that, will you?"

"Good lord—the place is a goner—they'll never be able to stop it!"

"The wind's coming from the east, down off the mountains. It'll spread the fire right across town. What do you think we ought to do?"

"Nothing much we can do. Nothing but watch the end of Nevada City."

III

IN PORTLAND, OREGON, Niles Searls read the latest copies of the California papers with dismay. In his absence, Nevada City had burned to the ground, taking with it Mulford's bookstore and his own law office. Billy Williams's Tin Shop lay in ruins. Everything they had was gone. He read the words over again:

AWFUL FIRE!!!

NEVADA CITY IN ASHES!

150 HOUSES DESTROYED!

Loss Estimated at $1,000,000!!!

One Man Missing

We have just learned the melancholy news that Nevada City lies in ruins. A fire broke out in that city on yesterday morning, at half past one o'clock, which has completely destroyed the principal business portion of the city, leaving only the houses scattered in the suburbs now standing!

We are indebted to Mr. John S. Lambert of Bowers' Express, who expressed the news through, leaving Nevada City at nine o'clock yesterday morning, and arriving here at 1 o'clock this morning.

The fire originated in the Bowling Alley of Mr. Gates, and was supposed to be the work of an incendiary. It appears that a difficulty originated between some Irishmen, one of whom threatened to fire the city, and strong suspicion is entertained against this person. Several persons were implicated in the affair, and the strongest vengeance is threatened against the incendiaries.

The whole city was in the very greatest state of excitement, and if the perpetrators are discovered they will be visited with dire vengeance for the wrongs they have done. We are indebted to H. C. Hodges, Esq., for the particulars of the awful catastrophe.

The bowling alley was of wood, as also the other buildings, and the fire spread with the greatest rapidity. The fire continued to rage from one o'clock until half past seven yesterday morning, when the fury of the flames was only stayed because they had no material to devour.

One man has been missed, and it is feared that he has fallen a victim to the flames—burnt in his own house. The following is the letter from Mr. Hodge:

NEVADA CITY,
March 12, 1851, 8 o'clock, A.M.

We have to record one of the most destructive fires that has yet been our lot to witness. About 12 o'clock last night the cry of fire was raised in our city. It commenced in or near Gates & Smith's Ball Alley, and is generally believed to be the work of an incendiary. It extended from Gates and Smith's on Coyota street, up said street on the east side, burning the store of Benson & Jeffries, Masonic Lodge house, Hammon's Hotel, blacksmith's shop, Ahart's Boarding house, Insurance Hospital, &c., and down the east side of said street to Main Street, then down Main Street to the bridge over Deer Creek, . . . all of Pine street, from the Post-office to the ravine near Brown & Davis, . . . thence from the Post-office and Justice Edwards' office, down Main street on the west side, . . .

The news story listed the property owners and their losses. Mulford's bookstore was shown at $4000. Williams's Tin Shop was $2000, as was the store of Truex and Blackman, where Searls and Mulford had shared quarters when they first reached Nevada City. Mr. and Mrs. Wilson's El Dorado boarding house was a $4000 loss, Turner's Nevada Hotel listed as $10,000. George Scott's Empire, the newest gambling house and saloon in town, open only three days before being consumed by fire, was said to have lost its owner $15,000.

Niles quickly arranged passage on the steamer *Sea Gull,* bound for San Francisco. It left Portland on Friday, March 28, and as the ship made its way carefully out through the mouth of the Columbia and into the Pacific Ocean, Niles began a letter to Mary:

When last I wrote you it was from Marysville Cal Feb 9th, in which I briefly stated that I was bound for the northern mines of Cal. Less than two months have elapsed, during which time I have traversed the wilds of northern Cal, penetrated through Oregon to the Columbia River and now find myself embarked for San Francisco.

My journey has been as those through a new country must ever be, one of hardships and privation.

We left Readings Springs—the last settlement on the Sac River, about the 12th of Feb. Our company consisted of eight men, two of them . . . the same with whom we came from Nevada.

We followed the Sac River through the mountains to its very source, sometimes toiling for hours and even days to reach the summit of the snow clad mountains, when after forcing our way for a short distance through heaps of driving snow, we would again descend down, down into some dark abyss, where the genial rays of the noonday sun never penetrate.

We were overtaken by a severe snowstorm, just as we reached the last summit of the mountains, but succeeded in pushing through it down the north side of the range till we reached "Chasta Valley" where, though safe from perishing, we were enveloped in snow for three days.

A short distance behind us was a large number of men and what became of them, God only knows. I have never seen them since, but by the Cal papers which I have seen since my arrival in the settlements of Oregon, I have learned that numerous of them perished. I left the settlements with a horse and a mule. The horse gave out and I was forced to leave him to die in the snows.

We reached the Klamath Diggins on the 23rd and found them a grand *Humbug.* Finding seven men ready to start for Oregon, and being half way already, I soon determined to gratify my desire to visit this region. We started again the last of Feb, and after swimming innumerable streams and having a few escapes from hostile Indians, at length reached the settlements in the head of the Williamette River on the 10th March.

I kept a journal of my travels, intending to send it to you, but either fortunately or unfortunately I lost it in swimming the Umpqua River—

therefore, I consider myself fully excused from the promise which I made before starting.

I have been luxuriating for a short time among the natives of Oregon, and now for the *first* time in my life am going to *Sea.*

When I began to write, we were laying to in front of Astoria, waiting for our "clearance" and a *"Pilot"* to take us over the Bar. Now we are under way, making directly for the long line of breakers which are rolling in sublime grandeur into the mouth of the river. How often in my school-boy days have I longed to see the Columbia River—now my desire is being gratified, and it affords me more pleasure than you can well imagine, but we are fast approaching the breakers. The ship rolls so that I can scarcely write. The doors and windows are being closed to keep out the spray. I must cease writing for the present and go on deck to see her breast the foam. When next I write, I may not feel quite so funny.

Good bye.

2 o'clock PM Saturday

For the first time since yesterday morning is the ship steady enough for me to attempt to write, and even now I am forced to hold the ink stand in one hand and wait for a calm moment to scratch a line.

The cabin looks like a well fought battle field. Men are scattered on every side, on the floor, in berths, and under the table, in all the agony of sea sickness. Contrary to my expectations, I have escaped and feel remarkably well. It has been very rough ever since we came out.

In crossing the bar, the waves made a clean sweep over the decks, producing no disaster, however, except the loss of a juvenile speciman of the genus *grunter,* which was washed from the forward deck and lost in the boundless deep. Poor fellow! What an agonizing squeal he sent forth as he was carried away to the leeward.

Our progress is but slow, owing to the wind's being directly ahead. We are running down the coast with all the headlands in plain view. If you would know how things appear around me, just take a seat in the dining room. Imagine all the chairs trying to jump over the table—the stove dancing an Irish Jig to the music of the dishes in the closet, with the shovel, tongs and a few sticks of stove wood all joining in the chorus. Then, if Addison is home, send him upstairs to sing out at the top of his voice, "Helm hard aport," "Bear a hand here my lads, down top gallants"—"brace the fore yard sharp up" "Ay, ay sir," these and a few like expressions will assist you greatly in your effort at comprehending the beauties and pleasures of a "Sea Voyage."

My page is out, my ink stand on its beam's end, so I will wait for a calm.

Humboldt Bay April 2nd

Arrived in this Bay yesterday morning, and shall leave in a couple of hours, having been detained by a gale of wind last night. When we left Oregon we expected to make San Francisco in from three to four days. The time is up and we are but half way. A strong wind from the southeast, accompanied by a heavy sea has prevailed nearly all the time. When off Cape Blanco it raged so that we could make no headway with steam and were forced to run off shore under canvas.

One of the seamen was washed overboard and lost. The storm has been very disastrous along the coast. We ran in to Trinidad Key night before last and found five vessels ashore at that point. On the beach at the mouth of this bay are four, all perfect wrecks. Many of the seamen were lost. [Captain Tichner] just came down and says we will be off in 20 minutes. More anon.

Friday Evening April 4th

At length, after over a week of buffeting against the wind, tide and current, our voyage is being brought to a close. We are now off the harbor of San Francisco, but shall have to wait till morning before we enter.

I left Charley in Nevada in good health and spirits, and in the everyday language of the world, "Doing Well." But what changes have been wrought. By a California paper which I saw in Portland, I have learned that Nevada has been consumed by fire and Charley is among the sufferers. Of course, he has given you more of the particulars than I can do with my limited stock of knowledge on the subject.

I need not say that I sympathize with him in his calamity. Really, it seems too bad. I suppose it's all for the *best.* No, I don't suppose any such thing, and were I in Charley's place I would give the man who set the fire his passport to a Better World in short metre.

San Francisco April 5th

I have just learned that Mulford left here on the 1st inst. in the *Columbia* for home. I go to Nevada this evening, where I shall learn the particulars. As the next mail for the States does not leave for ten days, I will keep this and add more at a future period.

San Francisco April 14th 11 P.M.

I just arrived here from Sac City per steamer *Confidence.* Before this reaches you, Charley will doubtless be home and can tell you more news in ten minutes than I can write in a week. I feel now as though my last friend had left me, and what is worse than it would otherwise have been, left so unexpectedly. The Miniatures, too, are gone. Not even *your shad-ow* remains to cheer poor Searls in his pilgrimage. Just like my luck.

Well, I shall come home the sooner. Do you believe I will ever come back? I suppose not by this time. Yet I shall surely come within the next year, if alive.

I can't afford to write of anything but the ordinary topics of the day, as I have had but one letter from *you* for more than six months and do not believe in being *sentimental* where there is no *reciprocity*. The plain English of it *is* I can't see why you have suddenly ceased to correspond. If your letters have miscarried, I beg *ten-thousand* pardons. If not I beg to say that I am wholly unchanged, therefore as contrary as usual.

Yours &c. N. Searls

Tuesday morning. Forgive some of the expressions in the last of this note. I wrote when out of humor.

Only days before Niles's arrival in Sacramento, Charley set out for the States carrying the letter which Billy Williams had prepared for Cornelia and the reading group. In it Billy had some words to say about his courier:

I cannot let this occasion pass without saying a word about Charley. As you are probably aware, Charley and myself were burnt out in Nevada. Charley's loss was very severe, between 3 and 4000 dollars, my own not near so much.

Charley had been thinking about going home before the fire. The fire afforded an opportunity to go, as he had lost most of his stock. He carries quite a pretty little "pile," and he also carries with him many unperjured regrets at his departure.

He has made very many friends in this country, and I *can* confidently say he has not an enemy in all Cal. He carries with him the pleasing consolation and the unanimous testimony of all his friends here that while in Cal he was true to all those characteristics that mark an "honest man"—neither by sword or deed has he deviated from the strict path of rectitude and virtue.

I had hoped that we should go back together—return to Rensselaerville to greet kind friends and embrace dear relatives. This regret is enhanced when I recollect that to *me* he has been a *kind* and *constant friend* ever since we have been in the country. . . . I shall feel his loss severely, for he was the only friend (in its true sense) that I had in California. In him I could confide—to him, pour out my whole heart without guile or fear. But now, from this time forward, "I must finish my journey alone" . . .

EQUESTRIAN CIRCUS

CHAPTER 30

NEVADA JOURNAL

February–April 1851

I

I DON'T UNDERSTAND," declared Niles Searls, who had returned to the burned-out mining camp and discovered it in the throes of a political campaign, the fire notwithstanding.

"What don't you understand?" asked John McConnell, a young attorney.

"I guess I can understand why you decided to stay and rebuild the town, but why is it none of the twenty or so lawyers appears to be the least bit interested in running for office in the new city government?"

Tom Caswell answered for the others, saying, "Would you want to be one of ten city aldermen if you could be a county judge or district attorney instead?"

"Does that mean the legislature has passed Field's bill to create a new county?" asked Niles.

"Not yet, but it looks to be a sure thing. With the county seat here at Nevada City, we'll have a chance at offices that amount to something!"

"What I'd like to see," said Niles, "is a system of law and order that will put an end to miners' courts. Lynch trials are a disgrace, even though I understand why they happen. But if we can make swift and sure justice possible here in the mountains, maybe we can restore order."

"Exactly," replied "Mac" McConnell, "and that's why we're saving our best effort for the county election, whenever it comes along. We know the gamblers and blacklegs will do everything in their power to take control. If we work together, we'll have a chance to beat them."

"By taking part in the city election all we'd do is make a few enemies, for no good purpose. We need every vote we can get later," added Tom Caswell.

Thomas Hubbard Caswell, at twenty-six, was two years older than Niles and Mac. A native of Otsego County, New York, he had gone with his family to Arkansas, where he began to read law in 1843. He studied law for eighteen months at St. Mary's College in Bardstown, Kentucky, then returned to Arkansas for further study. He was admitted to the state bar in the fall of 1848, six months before crossing the plains to California. He and a watchmaker, W. Noel, had been operating a Main Street store until the fire destroyed the building and their goods, valued at $12,000. Now their "Arkansas Store" was being rebuilt, this time on Broad Street, with the new Masonic Hall in the second story. Tom had joined the Lafayette Lodge in December.

John Randolph McConnell, twelfth of thirteen children, was born in Kentucky. At the age of seven he was taken by his family to a farm near Jacksonville, Illinois; his father died a year later. McConnell's mother was dead by the time he was ten, and he was raised by brothers and sisters. While living with a married sister in Kentucky he read law for a short time with a local attorney. He returned to Illinois, went for awhile to Mississippi, and eventually crossed the plains in 1849. While mining near the camp of Placerville he met up with another young miner and they shared their dreams of the future. Each was interested in the law, and both were politically ambitious. When his friend, Frank Pixley, went to Sacramento City to begin practicing law, Mac McConnell headed for Nevada City to do the same. He, too, was active in the Lafayette Lodge.

Much had happened in the state while Niles was in Oregon. The California Legislature ironically chose the day after the fire to pass an act to incorporate the city of Nevada. One day later, it repealed the monthly tax on foreign miners. Thomas Burdue, still believed to be James Stuart, was referred to as "English Jim" by the San Francisco papers when they reported on his conviction for the assault and robbery of Charles Jansen.

He was sentenced to fourteen years in prison, then transferred to the Yuba County authorities. Burdue was taken to Foster's Bar for examination by Justice of the Peace Oliver P. Stidger on the charge of having murdered Winslow Bar storekeeper Charles E. Moore in December. Stidger swore that the prisoner was not Stuart, whom he knew. Nevertheless, enough other witnesses were prepared to swear the opposite, so Stidger remanded Burdue to the Marysville jail to await trial in June.

The debris was nearly all gone from Main, Pine, and Coyota streets; Pine Street had been rerouted farther north and a new thoroughfare, Commercial Street, was being laid out to parallel Broad, which had not been harmed by the fire, thanks to Oregon Ravine, which crossed Pine and lay between Broad and Main streets. Business was booming on Broad Street, where some of the merchants had relocated, although many were in the process of rebuilding on the old burned-over sites, confident that Main Street again would be the dominant thoroughfare.

The principal obstacle to reconstruction was weather, for it rained and even snowed a good deal during March, particularly toward the end of the month. Money was a lesser problem, for despite their uninsured losses, most merchants possessed excellent credit in San Francisco and Sacramento and were able to persuade suppliers to furnish goods as needed.

A welcome relief to the traumatic and sobering events was provided when Pell's Circus came to town, bad weather and fire notwithstanding. Circuses differed from caravans (such as that which had visited Rensselaerville in 1848) in consisting mainly of acrobatic and equestrian acts. The only animals in the circus were the horses and ponies with which the performers worked. The circus was a great success, but when it left town, one of its employees stayed behind to create diversion of a more serious sort. His name was Miller, and he wished later he had gone earlier.

Miller and a veteran of the Mexican War who went by the name of Allen were in the temporary quarters of one of the gambling saloons one evening when a local youth, whose name was Ridgely, sought them out. Recognizing that Miller and Allen were down on their luck and not too particular how they regained it, Ridgely offered them a proposition: If they would break and enter his employer's store, Ridgely would tell them where the gold dust was secreted and share the loot with them.

Ridgely's boss was Stephen T. Napper, whose original market had been destroyed in the fire, but already Napper was operating a new meat market and bakery on Broad Street, just a few doors below Hamlet Davis's store at the corner of Broad and Pine. Ridgely knew that Napper had more than $2500 in gold hidden away, for he had observed him in the act of concealment. Miller and Allen carried out the robbery, divided the gold, and returned to the gambling house to break the bank.

In the morning the loss was discovered and Napper immediately accused Ridgely. Although his employee denied it and offered a careful alibi for his whereabouts during the burglary, Napper was unconvinced and called for the constable. Under duress, the employee gave some hints which led to the arrest of Miller and Allen. All three were turned over to the local deputy sheriff, who proceeded to transport them to Marysville for trial.

Before he could get there, however, Gus Hall and a posse of miners overtook the sheriff and demanded his prisoners. Since he was outnumbered and outgunned, he shrugged his shoulders and turned them over to Hall, and the three accused men were brought back to Nevada City to be tried by "Judge Lynch." A jury of six was selected and lawyers were chosen to prosecute and defend—the miners raised $200 to pay their fees.

The trial was held in back of the Placer Hotel. It began on April 2 and continued for two days. At the end, the jury pronounced them guilty and a sentence of thirty-nine lashes was given to each man. Miller and Allen confessed then and offered to return what was left of the money—about half—if the sentence would be reduced. The money was returned and the pair was given only twenty strokes. Ridgely, however, continued to maintain his innocence, and he was given the full count.

The whipping was administered by Charley Williams, better known about town as "Butcher Bill." Napper had offered to pay anyone $500 who would do the job, and Butcher Bill was quick to volunteer. Gus Hall led the prisoners out through the rain, across Deer Creek and up to the top of Prospect Hill, overlooking the city. Here they were stripped to the waist and tied round the base of a giant conifer. When all was ready, Butcher Bill stepped forward and laid on the strokes with a vengeance, determined to earn his pay.

When he had finished, and the men were untied, they collapsed and lay at the foot of the tree, writhing in pain. The cold wind bit into their torn and bleeding backs. The men were told to leave the town by nightfall and never come back. Long before the deadline, all three had disappeared. Ridgely died later from his wounds, according to reports which reached the mountain community, and Butcher Bill was shunned from that day forth. Some said it was because he had accepted pay, but for whatever reason, he was treated almost as if he, too, had been adjudged guilty. Some even blamed Napper, saying he should have done the whipping himself, not hired another to do it.

Because he was still on the steamer, coming back from Oregon, Niles was not present for the trial or the punishment. When he did arrive, a few days later, the city already was busy discussing the upcoming municipal election, but Niles paid it little attention. Having decided to rebuild Charley's bookstore and run it himself for awhile, he had plenty to do. In the end, he did not even vote. On election day, Monday, April 14, 1851, Niles Searls was in San Francisco.

II

IT ALL BEGAN when Nick Turner of the Nevada Hotel came down to Sacramento City two days after the fire to order furnishings and hardware for the new and better hotel he was going to erect. He stopped in at the office of the Sacramento *Placer Times* to fill them in on details of the conflagration. One of those with whom he talked was Warren B. Ewer, a newspaperman and son of a New England Baptist minister.

Ewer had worked on papers for fifteen years, mostly back in Massachusetts, but since coming to California he had been employed at San Francisco and Sacramento. For awhile he worked on the *Pacific News* with a cousin, Ferdinand C. Ewer. When Nick Turner first talked to him in mid-March 1851, Warren was one month short of celebrating his thirty-seventh birthday. The news of the fire gave him a queer idea.

"You know," said Ewer, "the crazy way things happen out here in California, it would be just like someone to go up there to Nevada and start a newspaper!"

"Sure wouldn't surprise me any," agreed Pickering, of the *Placer Times.*

"That would be just the ticket! We need a paper at Nevada!" replied Nick.

"I can see that you've probably got enough business to support it—at least, you did before the fire. What about now?" asked Pickering.

"I expect the town to be bigger than ever by summer. If the legislature votes to make a new county, then Nevada will be the county seat. Marysville won't be anything after that!"

"Well, there you are, Warren—just what you've been waiting for!"

"Me? Why me?"

"You've always talked about running your own paper. Here's your chance. Why don't you go up there and take a look at the situation?"

Eventually, Turner and Pickering convinced Ewer they were serious and he left for Nevada City the next day, armed with letters of introduction furnished by Turner. Once in the mountains, Ewer found the citizens and merchants enthusiastic.

Pickering offered him an old Ramage wooden press and several fonts of type. "It's the one on which the first California newspaper was printed," he declared.

"The *Californian?* How did you come by it?"

"When Ed Kemble bought out the *Californian* and combined it with the old *Star* to produce the *Alta California,* the press and type went with the deal. Of course, he had no use for it then, so he stored it. When he started the *Placer Times,* he brought the press to Sacramento. Afterwards he sold the paper and the press—it went through several hands after that. The new owners purchased a better press and materials and this one got pushed to one side till last year, when Jim McClatchy and Doc Robinson wanted to start the *Settlers and Miners Tribune* shortly after the squatters' riots. They used the press and type until they went broke and when the *Index* started up, last December, they put it to use."

From its earliest days, the *Index* had been an unprofitable enterprise. Sacramento had too many papers already, most just eking out a livelihood. Furthermore, the *Index* was a Whig paper in a Democratic city, and was the first daily to try to publish in the afternoon. As if this were not enough, the enterprise was launched two days before Christmas, during a dull business season. Scarcely a month had elapsed before the paper was in serious trouble.

The three printers who were its new owners tried to save the *Index* by switching to morning publication. Joseph W. Winans and H. B. Livingstone continued to edit the paper for six more weeks, until it collapsed under the combined weight of unpaid bills and uncollected debts.

One of the three publisher-printers was Tallman H. Rolfe. Tallman resigned his offices as Justice of the Peace for Yuba City and Associate Justice of the Court of Sessions at Sutter County to become involved with the *Index.* It was his first newspaper job since he, Kemble, and Yates had walked away from the *California Star.* More than once in the interim he had longed to smell printers' ink again, especially when the boom fizzled early in Sutter County. His judicial titles sounded impressive, but "Judge" Rolfe earned very little in fees where the population was so small.

When the *Index* went out of business in March, Tallman and the old Ramage press moved over to the *Placer Times* plant. When Pickering brought Warren Ewer back to look at the press, which had been purchased in 1833 by Mexican Governor José María Echeandía, Tallman jestingly remarked:

"Maybe I'll come up to Nevada and set type for you one of these days, Mr. Ewer!"

"Are you serious? Would you like to? I've already engaged a fellow, but if you'd like to come, I'll tell him I've changed my mind."

"No, no, don't do that! Jobs are hard to find these days, and I wouldn't want to take one away from the man. I was only joking, but I may come up to see how you're doing this summer. I've always been curious about Nevada City, but never got around to visiting."

Ewer was able to get the press installed in a Broad Street building in time to print the results of the Nevada City election. On April 19, 1851, Volume One, Number One of the *Nevada Journal* announced that the miners' candidate, Moses F. Hoit, had been elected mayor, receiving more votes than the combined totals of Hamlet Davis and a third candidate, a man named Young. More than 1800 men had voted.

Most of the ten aldermen were miners, although James O. Barker was owner of Barker's Exchange, the gambling saloon being rebuilt on Main Street, and Doctors E. E. Gardiner and John R. Crandall were medical men as well as miners. Gardiner had pulled a tooth for Peter Decker while working on the Yuba River, splitting off a piece of his jawbone in the process.

Another of the new aldermen was N. Henry Shepherd, who was Dick Oglesby's partner in the "Nevada Store" on Main Street, across from Mulford and Searls. Their building had gone up in flames, but they were erecting a new one. Shepherd, a man in his late thirties, had operated a daguerreotype studio in Springfield, Illinois. In 1846 the newly elected Whig congressman, Abe Lincoln, had come in to sit for his portrait. It was the first time Lincoln had observed his likeness anywhere but reflected in a piece of glass or pool of water.

III

SAM BRANNAN'S COMPLAINT that the legal system in California never hanged a man could not be made against the state of New York. Although Orville Chittenden did his best to defend Reuben Dunbar against the charge of slaying his orphaned cousins, Rensselaerville's newest young attorney, Perry Pierce, succeeded in convicting the youth. The sentence was death by hanging.

Although she approved of the verdict, Cornelia was appalled to learn that Pierce planned to witness the execution. In a letter to Addison, she made the comment that Pierce had "refined taste. Like the butcher who married the milliner" in Longfellow's *Kavanagh* and went to a neighboring town for his wedding tour, "to see a man hung."

Cornelia had seen and thought a good deal of Will Allen, principal at the Academy. There had been a sleighride to Greenville on February 4, but Cornelia had not been invited. She told Addison:

Mary went, but Ma had company to tea, and I thought I ought to stay and help entertain them—beside, I had no invitation to go. All the young people went but Allen, Cliff, and I—and why *they* did not go, and why I was not asked, I am sure I don't know. They had a fine time. Lucius Wickes invited them down to a private house to meet the rest of the Greenville young people. They had a dance, and did not get home until after 4 o'clock. Fine entertainment, too.

But I am sorry the older gentlemen, Cliff, Pierce, and Allen, were not there to give our company a little better appearance. Think they missed it, too, in not taking me.

You remember John Titus' exhibitions—well, it came off on Thursday, after you left—gloriously. How I wish I could describe the scene to you, but I won't try. It was in the Academy, and Pa, Mr. Allen, and Dr. Lay went "to see the boys didn't make disturbance." He had quite a house, and was more than paid. Allen, and I only staid a while, but he acted until ½ past 9. His sword was the poker, and shield an old Atlas. They said he covered himself with glory in Richard III.

Friday evening I read a paper which was pronounced the *best* we had had—and no wonder, with such a capital piece from Allen to give it character. Subject: "Philosophy of Dress, or an Apology for the Dandy." Capital piece from George Cornell, too. I shall expect, a fortnight from this time, another letter from you, and in it something I can put in the "Garland;" an old composition or something. . . .

Thursday eve Lucia had a grand party, which was pronounced most delightful. It certainly was lively. Beautiful cake, nuts, ice cream, parched corn, &c, added materially to the enjoyment. Allen and Cliff were not there, because they went into Albany early that morning and did not get home until 9. Cliff came up a little while, but Mr. Allen was not in the mood for visiting.

I did not mean to say one word about him, but somehow his name has slipped in once or twice, so I'll tell you that he has had the worst fit of "blues" since you left I ever saw him attacked with. . . . His blues are caused by a want of society of taste and education equal to his own, I am confident, but it cannot be remedied here. . . . Shall be looking for Allen's lecture before long.

Addison wrote Mary on February 16 and described campus life, especially extracurricular activities:

The only excitement we have had for some time past was last Friday (Valentine's day). This created some commotion among that portion of the students susceptible to the tender passion. The external evidences of the excitement were: a great rush to the post office about half an hour before mail time, and a great quarrelling for places near the receiving door; a sudden absence of all the poetry from the libraries, except [Young's] "Night thoughts," Gollop's "Course of time," and "Paradise lost;" lights glimmering in every window until two or three o'clock; and an individual and collective "flunk" at the morning recitation.

Rhyming dictionaries are in great demand, and I presume there was more execrable wit and distorted rhyme sent out from Williams the last week than during all the term beside, which is saying considerable, since we have quite a number of poets (!!!) in College. Those who have been favored with a quantity of these little missives are as happy as clams, while the non-receiving party (here's one of 'em) look with lofty contempt upon such school-boy follies. . . .

The Faculty have been requested and have consented to build a Gymnasium on college grounds, which will be a capital place for exercise when completed. In order to prepare myself to enjoy the benefits of it, I have formed a class of about 15 to take boxing lessons. We have hired an experienced teacher and commence Wednesday. Who say nothing profitable is to be learned at College? . . .

By the way, I am sporting a gold watch and chain. I lent Sophomore Hunt my poker 2 or 3 nights ago to fasten the Tutor in his room, so as to get rid of Morning Recitation, and [I] took his watch for security. The Tutor, finding his door fastened, broke it down, whereupon he very naturally captured the poker. Therefore, the watch remains in my possession. I'll teach him not to play tricks on the Tutor. Praiseworthy, ain't it?

When William Allen, the Academy's erudite young principal, gave his long-awaited lecture at the Presbyterian Church, Cornelia rose early on the next morning to record her reactions:

The most prominent subject of contemplation in my mind this morning is a vague idea that I enjoyed something rich, beautiful last night—that my taste was gratified, my expectations fulfilled, that I sat, immovable, in a crowd last night, listening with wrapt attention for an hour to fine thoughts, beautiful language, stray gems of poetry &c, which have all night long been lingering in my brain, weaving themselves into most fantastic shapes, until this morning I am too languid with over excitement to separate the true from the dim vision.

But, if I am not mistaken, your friend, Mr. Allen, stood behind the desk in the Pres. Church last night and, amid a blaze of *light* (true), before a large and as select an audience as Rens Ville affords (*all* "her beauty and her chivalry"), addressed the "Young Ladies of Renss'ville Reading Society" in a style and manner that does credit to his Alma Mater at old

Williams, if not to the mind and talents of the man himself.

His subject was one, he said, actually suggested by the occasion. After a few delicate and appropriate remarks to the "Circle," he announced as his subject, "Reading and its effect upon the formation of character." His style was very chaste and clear, and his cool, dignified look, and pleasant, easy delivery gave good effect to his sentiments.

I know I may not act the part of critic from want of ability, but I know what speaks to my taste and fancy and do not attempt to criticize. The public were generally pleased, I believe, at least they looked so.

Mary echoed her sister's sentiments in a subsequent letter to her brother, but indicated that not all "the public" was pleased:

I suppose Cornelia gave you a brief description of Mr. Allen's address to the young ladies of the Reading Society. It was the best lecture I have heard in a very long time. The girls were all carried away with it. We expected a good deal from him, but he far exceeded our highest anticipations.

Yet Mr. Ransom, Cornell, &c, saw fit to find a great deal of fault and talk very hard because he said something in favor of novel reading. We think Mr. Ransom might better have said very little about others' lectures. I expect the climax will be put upon lectures next Tuesday evening. It was announced today that Perry D. Pierce would address the Young Men's Association in the Methodist church on that evening. It will doubtless be a chef d'ouvre.

I am sure no one will think of succeeding him, and so will close the series. I think the ladies society has rather borne the palm, unless counsellor Perry D. retrieves it.

If the palm were to be handed over, Cornelia was not the one to bestow it. Her report to Addison was written after church, and she complained of feeling so dull that "nothing I have attempted . . . has awakened interest enough to keep me awake." But her lethargy disappeared as she wrote:

Oh dear, how Mr. Pierce would suffer if he knew I had neglected so long to speak of his address before the Young Men's Association, when I made a certain other young gentleman's [lecture] the theme of nearly three pages, a few weeks since. I fear he would speak more bitterly than ever of that "certain other's" fortunate applicative for favor, and his own unhappy failures. He informed Pa, gravely, not long since, that Mr. Allen's agreeable and entertaining manner in conversation was "all put on." He "understood him perfectly, there was nothing of him."

But a lecture he really did deliver in the Meth. Church, in all the pride of a high collar, new cravat, abundant whiskers, and majestic stature, combined with dignity and grace. And the critics were not down upon it. It was well spoken of in high places, being altogether a well-written, moral affair. No bad principles inculcated by him, in happy contrast with another "small affair" [which had endorsed the reading of novels].

His subject was "Enthusiasm," which he carefully avoided alluding to after its first mention. The address was written in a highly eloquent, even awfully grand style in many places, and by the mass of community was pronounced "most excellent," not one half of it being remembered or even understood at the time, I presume.

Now, I meant to praise this lecture when I commenced; have I, or not? The eloquent speaker has had a "slight misunderstanding" with his host at the hotel and has taken his bed and board in another place. Has also discontinued his visits, morning and evening both, almost entirely, at our house, and, I have discovered, he has been giving the light of his presence to the young ladies at the Dr's, in lieu of your unworthy sisters, probably attracted by the charms of the youngest daughter, with whom he is a great favorite.

Pray don't think jealousy has prompted me to dilate thus extensively at the mention of this young man, though I acknowledge my drowsy humor has quite passed away as I have rapidly driven my pen along upon this fruitful theme.

The terms at the schools taught by Mary and Deborah came to a close at the beginning of March, and once more they were free to do as they pleased with their time. Mary wrote to Addison:

For several weeks past I have postponed all business and a great many amusements until the happy day should arrive when I should be free from school. That day has come at last, and having spent one week in running about to "try my wings" and assure myself that I am free, I am once more ready to settle down into private life. I find the contrast very great between being shut up in a gloomy room with twenty little noisy, restless children, and being free to go where and when I choose, and to do what I choose, without thinking, either, that it will only last a week or two.

I do not expect to teach any more at present. Deborah has closed her school, too. We all went down yesterday through the snow to see the closing up of her labors there. We had rare sport. We have been visiting almost constantly for a week, and the effects of it, together with reading "[David] Copperfield," has not been very beneficial to me. . . .

There is a sailor boy in town—an Irish workman who is a most beautiful singer. The boys get him to sing for them whole evenings, and then coax him to go with them and give serenades. They have been here twice, once in the midst of a cold, dreary rainstorm. It was the best serenade we ever had ...

At the same time that your letter from Niles came, there was one received from Charles saying he was engaged in selling books, which was most profitable of any business he had tried. He thought he should perhaps come home next fall; if not, he should stay one year more. He made no mention of Niles' return. We hope to hear again this week. . . .

Cornelia says I must tell you that your reasons for taking boxing lessons were satisfactory to Pa, particularly where you referred to Allen and Pomeroy as authority.

Polly Niles stepped into Cornelia's room one day while she was penning a letter to Addison. Too busy to write her son, she communicated with him by way of her daughters:

Ma has just been in and says, "tell Addison it worries me to think of his being without rubbers at this wet season, when we are so liable to bad colds," and that "he had better get him a pair right away, to use in the mud and wet." "Do take care of yourself, my dear," for in sober earnest, your loving mother and squeamish sisters often feel anxious about you in your absence. . . .

Prospects for examination [at the Academy] are good. Allen is cool, steady, and though some few think "it won't be much" because Mr. Pomeroy, great self (speaking reverently), is not at the head of it, yet *I* am assured no man could do better with the materials he has than this same little friend of Dr. Duncan's, or rather, I meant to say, of yours, but was just about to inquire, how was the Dr? Make him promise to come to R Ville to see his friends next summer.

As Cornelia predicted, the examinations went off in fine manner.

Mr. Allen did himself high credit, and the school examinations were highly extolled. We were *almost* as proud of Mr. Allen this year as of our Pomeroy of last winter, only, of course, he could not be seen at a distance, on account of his diminutive size (our little man, Mr. Brewerton calls him, and every inch of a man he is, in every thing but stature).

From California came word of trouble, but even this was not enough to claim Cornelia's attention for long. There had been so many calamities during the long years the boys had been away, yet neither Charley nor Niles seemed in any hurry to return. Life went on at home, and at present it was very interesting, indeed. Cornelia told Addison:

. . . News from Charles last mail, and as you may see by the papers, Nevada City has nearly perished by fire and he is burnt out, loss stated $4,000. Niles has gone to Oregon.

Mary had an invitation to a wedding at Durham next week today, and *report* says mine is coming soon, when Mr. *Allen* comes home. Mr. Porter marries Priscilla Pratt (instead of Cornelia Niles, as has been currently reported). Were you home a little sooner, you would be of the party—it is next Thursday Eve. [May 1, 1851].

REV. WARREN'S CHURCH, MAIN STREET, NEVADA CITY (1851)

CHAPTER 31

SECOND TREATY

May–July 1851

I

NILES SEARLS WENT TO San Francisco a few days after that city suffered its most disastrous fire: the damage was estimated at from ten to twelve million dollars and was thought to be the work of arsonists. On May 11, 1851, after returning to Nevada City, Niles wrote Cornelia:

I was in San Francisco a few days since and witnessed the dire effects of the conflagration which has completely destroyed the whole business part of the City. I should not be surprised if we were to burn up again before the summer is out, in this town. Well, if the city burns again, I think I shall follow Charley's example and come home. . . .

Charley is, I hope, safe home and perhaps with you tonight recounting the scenes through which he has passed his sojourns in the land of Ophir. . . . Whether I shall ever return or not is something problematical. I begin to like California very well and should never think of coming back to live, were it not for one or two reasons. . . .

As to you and Mary, I don't know what to think of you. Why don't you get married or do something equally desperate? I am certain that with all your attractions somebody must be very smitten and am surprised that you can be so hard hearted as to refuse the boon of your love . . .

In fact, Mary's marital status was a matter of great concern to Niles. Any news which might have suggested a change in her affairs at this time would have plunged him into despair, for one of his two principal ambitions was that Mary should become his partner for life. But he could not accomplish this until his second ambition was achieved, which was the establishment of a respectable and rewarding career.

Mary was well aware of Niles's feelings for her, and guessed at his reason for not discussing marriage. However, as time passed she was more and more troubled by his strange reluctance to come home. How could he expect to realize his ambitions unless he stopped adventuring and returned to the east, where he could attend to the business of life? Neither he nor Charley had gained their fortunes in California, and the fire in Nevada City had seemingly destroyed whatever chances still remained. So why did Niles hang behind?

On that subject his letters never were clear. Always he was ambivalent about returning east, and also about remaining in California. Much later, looking back, Niles confessed to Cornelia how troubled he had been:

You and I, Cornelia, have no right to find fault with our lot. Of course, we have our troubles, many of them perhaps at the time seemingly large, but they are soon gone and are succeeded by bright and happy hours. . . . One thing has for several years afforded me more happiness and more uneasiness than all others combined. It is that of my love for Mary—not that the least dissension between us has ever given rise to a moment's pang, for we have had no quarrels or misunderstandings.

The truth is just this: my attachment for her knew no bounds and could only rest satisfied with an equal return. All this was accomplished without premeditation on either side. But then I was by nature wayward and impulsive and without experience and the fixed habits which it brings; [I] feared that instead of promoting her final happiness, Mary was only laying the foundation of future trouble [by linking her fate with mine].

One thing was with me reduced to a certainty: unless I could demonstrate to my own satisfaction my ability to secure a competence in the world, no consideration would ever induce me to consent to a union of our destinies for life. Distrusting my power to accomplish anything among those of superior advantages in my native state, I went to Missouri—had concluded to settle in Harrisonville and was pretty certain of a seat in the next Legislature when I discovered that the location was too unhealthy for a residence.

I need not tell you that Cal[ifornia] was the next Theatre of my operations—that sickness was for a year my constant companion—that Death stared me in the face and that for over a year nothing was accomplished. That was the saddest year of my life, and now when I look back, I only wonder that despair and death did not seize me as lawful prey. With the first return of prosperity came the desire to make Mary my own. With that object in view, I have since labored . . .

Excuse me, dear Cornelia, for this long story without either point or moral. I have chanced to be in a communicative mood and have told what had never been uttered to any but Mary before, and in part perhaps not even to her.

But at present, in the summer of 1851, Niles could describe his dilemma to neither cousin. Mary, who ached to understand, often wondered if she had mistaken his intentions—or his resolution to succeed in achieving them.

Niles could talk about many other things, however, and on June 8, 1851, he described life in the new county seat to Cornelia:

I have since the date of my last communication been pursuing the same monotonous course as of old. A little pettifogging, a little trade—a little fun, a little sickness—plenty of *good* friends with whom to spend the leisure hours and plenty of *bad* places to consume them.

Let me see, how have I passed the day thus far; got up before breakfast (wonderful), busied myself about the sublime mysteries of trade till 8 am, then went before the City Recorder to defend a much injured client who was sought to be fined, simply for getting inebriated and raising a *muss*. Of course my afflicted client was enraged at the little respect shown him by the minions of the Law, and like a sensible fellow made an assault upon the police officer.

In attempting to pacify him I received a tap on the nose, and, to show my love of reciprocity, floored my very respected friend, where by the assistance of the Marshal he was held till the Recorder had clapped a fine on the oppressed victim and thus the matter ended.

No, it did not end there, for, refusing to pay the fine, the prisoner was incarcerated in jail, but soon tore half the roof off of the old edifice, crawled out, went to the Office, paid his fine and then offered to repair the jail for twice the amount of the fine, and that *is* the end of the matter.

Now I am in the shop sitting behind the counter; beside me is that new *fur-hat* that I purchased the other day in Sac City—always keep it in a bandbox nights and wear the old one when the dust flies. Across the shop stands Dr. [Jesse] Moore holding some labels for bottles at arm's length before his face, trying to read them through his glasses. Fine old man, that Dr. Cured me of the chills not long since.

I left here one week ago this morning for San Francisco. Embarked on the *New-World* Steamer at Sac City Tuesday, and had the misfortune to be blowed up when about half way down. I was fortunate enough to escape without any serious injury, face slightly burned, but nothing to harm. You will see the particulars by the papers.

Of *course* no one was to blame for the accident—there never *is* in such cases. All I know is this: when we left Sac City it was said the [*Wilson*] *G. Hunt* was going to pass us before we reached Benicia.

The *New-World* had the lead by about 100 yds and maintained just about that position till we entered what is called the "slough"—in passing through that narrow crooked channel the *Hunt,* being the shorter boat, had the advantage and was soon close on to us, but had no room to pass. On approaching the lower end of the Slough the passage became straight—and in running three or four miles we had gained a full quarter and were evidently running very fast.

On coming to shoal water at the mouth of Cache Creek the steam was partially shut off, and in three minutes the connecting pipe from boiler to cylinder exploded, killing one man instantly and scalding fifteen others, several of whom have died since. There were but few passengers on board at the time, else the destruction of life must have been far greater. Three jumped overboard—two of them drowned.

Every part of the boat was filled with steam almost instantly, but being well back in the upper saloon, I did not get the benefit of it till the current of air had pretty well cooled it. I think I never saw a worse sight than that of the scalded. All night long their cries resounded from one end of the vessel to the other.

On June 21 Niles told Mary more about his living arrangements after first complaining that he had not heard from either of his cousins in a long time:

That French bedstead is one that the Dr. bought at auction in Sac City and is upon the whole rather aristocratic—the stove in that corner which stands on a box as tho it had climbed up to look out of the window is merely used for heating certain preparations only understood by the faculty. That India Rubber bag which stands in the corner so nearly empty contains a few valuables that I brought from home and has stood the shock of time and escaped the devouring element in a miraculous manner. How I love to rummage the contents of that old bag.

My wardrobe is nearly all in that Champaign Basket at the foot of the bed—items not numerous. The grey coat hanging on the bed is mine and would be pretty good, were it not for the hole that burned in it while sleeping by a campfire on the [Siskiyou] Mountains.

If you knew how much trouble it cost us to get those clean pillowcases, you would look at them more attentively—You see, Mary, we had but one pair, and do the best we could, they needed washing every *month* or *two*—Well, this morning I got some cloth and undertook to make a new pair; do the best I could, when I sewed a seam, one side would come out about three inches ahead of the other. At last, I nailed one end to a shelf and the other to the counter, but even that wouldn't work, and after breaking threads and pricking my finger for a spell, the job was abandoned in despair.

For a short time I felt a disposition to commit matrimony, but the idea was soon dispelled by the little Jew next door, who undertook the task I had given up, and soon completed it. That accounts for the new pillow cases. . . .

Sunday Evening June 22nd. The day of *rest* is passed, but how differently spent *here* from the manner at home. Instead of quiet and repose, we have nothing but tumult and confusion. Get Charley to give you a description . . . I can hardly realize that Charley, who but a few weeks ago was here with us and one of us, is now actually at home, perhaps while I write he is sitting in the parlor talking with you, just as he and I used to years ago—then perhaps Deb is there, too, and Lucia and the rest of the girls. . . .

I scarcely expected any letters by the last mail, but next time I shall look to receive some without fail—if not, I'll wait *once* more, and *then* if nothing comes, my word for it, Mary, I will never write another letter to Rens Ville while I remain in the country, but I hope and think it will be otherwise.

II

THE FIRE IN MARCH seemed to catalyze rather than retard the rapid growth of Nevada City. Each passing day saw more people arrive. Some came on foot or on the backs of animals, but an increasing number traveled on the stages from Sacramento and Marysville.

Ianthus Rolfe arrived on May 13, 1851, having traveled from Salt Lake City with one of the first groups to cross the mountains that year. The winter had been mild and snow was disappearing rapidly from the trail, even at the summit. Although Ianthus was headed for Sacramento to find his brother Tallman, he could not resist the temptation to spend a few days inspecting the first California gold camp he came to. Nevada City was not like anything he had seen or imagined; it delighted him. Already he was well satisfied with the decision not to travel with his family to southern California. The Rolfes had left Salt Lake City in March to assist in the establishment of a new Mormon colony near Los Angeles. Only Benjamin and his new wife Prudence stayed behind in Utah.

Three days after Ianthus reached Nevada City, a brash young capitalist from Europe came to town to inspect the mines. Heinrich Schliemann wanted to evaluate the risks involved in loaning grubstakes at the rate of 12% per month. He was impressed by the gold production but not by the camp. Used to the venerable and substantial cities of Europe and the Atlantic seaboard, he found Nevada City

a small and extremely nasty place in the midst of a pine-forest, and took up my lodgings at the french Restaurant of Gaudin, where I made the acquaintance of the professor of languages P. Kowalewski, who spoke marvellously well the russian language.

Peter Kowalewski, who had been giving Spanish lessons at Davis and Hirst's reading room since April, was just as delighted with Schliemann, for the latter was expert in several languages himself, including Russian, which had enabled him to make a small fortune in the import-export business by the age of twenty-nine. The restaurant and hotel, which advertised itself variously as French Hotel or Hotel de France, was run by Charles Gaudin and Pierre Dreydemie. Pierre was one of the French miners whose rich claim had been protected by the legal efforts of Niles Searls and Edward Ellis.

Board and room at the French Hotel cost eleven dollars a week with two meals a day, fourteen dollars for three a day. Mr. Kowalewski came to Nevada recommended by John Frémont and his father-in-law, Senator Thomas Benton, among others. He was a Pole by birth, but had been compelled to flee Warsaw when it fell in 1830.

After visiting Gold Run, where "even in the mud which hung to my boots I saw many particles of this precious metal," Schliemann went on to Grass Valley. Here he was shown the three operating quartz-mills and three others under construction. It was claimed that a mill could produce a clear profit of $1000 a week.

Between the Quartz mills I found a frenchman at work with the gaity so characteristic in his countrymen; he was working in a small creek and made, according to his assertion, 6 to 7 $ a day. Close to him stood some seven indian women and children, who were beseeching the frenchman to put into the pans, which they were stretching out to him, some of the dirt which he dug out; he granted their request and they eagerly ran then to the canal to wash the gold out from it.

The first election of Nevada County officers took place on May 26, 1851. In the morning an elderly miner named Cassin quarreled over a pile of wash-dirt with Bill Hayden, a thirty-year-old boot- and shoe-maker from Tennessee. Hayden, who was mean tempered, threatened to shoot Cassin if he set eyes on him again. With Hayden's reputation, the threat was one to be taken seriously, so Cassin's eighteen-year-old son bought a Colt's revolver at Bowers Brothers' Express Office, and headed up Main Street. At the intersection with Coyote Street, he turned right, found the shoemaker and killed him. Because of Hayden's unpopularity, the result of the county's first legally constituted trial for a killing resulted in a verdict of justifiable homicide.

In June, Hamlet Davis and Israel Hirst refurbished their reading room into "Dramatic Hall," so that Dr. Robinson's company could begin per-forming. A Congregational minister, James H. Warren, came with his wife from the east coast and began making plans for a new church to replace the old community structure that had burned in March. He contracted with Mr. Hall to erect a new building patterned after those presently being put up in the most up-to-date New England neighbor-hoods. Mr. Hall hired Garret Low, a newly-arrived carpenter, who in his first three weeks in California had seen little cause for enthusiasm. He was happy to receive six dollars a day from Mr. Hall in preference to what mining paid, and as for California construction methods, his first experience in San Francisco led him to write:

The way they build here is a caution. In most cases there are two sticks laid down which answer for sills. On these lay the sleepers or joists. Next they lay the floor, then set up the studding and nail the foot to the floor; side it up and put on a shingle or canvas roof. Line the inside with cloth, paper it, and the house is done. Other buildings are made by mortising holes right down in the ground for their posts and studding. Whether they are draw-bored or not I did not see.

Low worked on the church until July 5th. The temperature reached 94 degrees in the shade, but the work progressed. Meanwhile, Reverend Warren preached his sermons at Dramatic Hall by day and Dr. Robinson mounted his productions at night. When the church job was finished, Low went to work for Mr. Barr on the Odd Fellow's Lodge Hall, making seats, desks, and stands to furnish the interior after he had erected the walls and roof.

A member of Mr. Warren's congregation, widow Mary Sampson, opened a school at Nevada City, and Rosa Farrington started another over in Grass Valley. A move was taken to charter a city government at that place, but did not survive the first meeting. From the postal authorities came news that beginning July 1 all prepaid letters to and from the Atlantic States would cost six cents, while unpaid letters would be twice that amount. Prepaid letters to any part of California or Oregon would go for three cents, or six cents if unpaid.

A murder trial began in Marysville: Thomas Burdue, still protesting that he was not "English Jim" Stuart, was being tried for the murder of Charles Moore in Yuba County. Although several witnesses from Foster's Bar swore he was the man, others disagreed. Stuart was described as being the same height, having the same curly hair, slightly bald on top, same voice and accent, same color eyes. Judge Oliver P. Stidger of Foster's Bar insisted that the prisoner, though similar in appearance, was not the same; he was shorter, had different eyes, and was not as agile in his movements.

Stuart was said to have a stiff middle finger on the right hand, a ring of India ink round one finger, and ink marks between each thumb and forefinger. He had a scar on the right cheek. The prisoner's middle finger was not stiff, but a felon beneath the nail gave it a short and stubby look, and the nail itself was broad and thick and curled over the end of the finger. When the court ordered the prisoner's beard shaved, a scar was seen to extend from the right side of the jaw down his neck.

The jury found the prisoner guilty and he was sentenced to death. As Thomas Burdue sat in the Marysville jail, waiting for the day of his hanging for another man's crime, a robbery suspect was caught by the San Francisco Vigilance Committee. He called himself Stephens, but John Sullivan, who once worked for Jim Stuart at Foster's Bar, knew better. Others who knew Stuart were brought in. All said the prisoner was "English Jim." On July 12, 1851, despite several unsuccessful attempts by Stuart's former attorney, Frank M. Pixley, now San Francisco's city attorney, to have Stuart released to the sheriff, he was hanged by the Committee of Vigilance. Burdue then was retried and acquitted, both in San Francisco and Marysville.

A special election was held in Nevada City in July for the purpose of replacing two aldermen who had resigned and left the city. When the votes had been tallied, a new council member was being escorted by friends and well-wishers to Frisbie's saloon to celebrate when they were met by Tallman Rolfe and Warren Ewer. In mid-June the *Sacramento Transcript* and the *Placer Times,* facing imminent financial collapse, chose to merge rather than compete for losses. To save money, many employees were given notice, including Tallman. Having been encouraged by his brother Ianthus and his former co-worker, Warren Ewer, to come to Nevada, Tallman was now associated with the *Nevada Journal.*

The *Journal*'s publisher called out, "Who's the winner?"

"Searls is!" came the answer.

"Fine, fine!" replied Ewer. "Congratulations, Niles." He extended his hand to the young lawyer, then turned slightly to the printer at his side, saying, "I'd like to introduce you to my new assistant, Mr. Tallman Rolfe. I expect that you and he will be seeing a good deal of one another from now on."

Niles and Tallman shook hands and appraised one another. Niles spoke first: "Are you new to California as well as Nevada City, Mr. Rolfe?"

"No, I'm not. I came down from Oregon in '47."

"That *was* early. If you were in Oregon at that time, you must have traveled the Oregon Trail soon after Francis Parkman came across."

"If I recall correctly, he only came as far as Fort Laramie. We both crossed the plains in '45."

"I've always wanted to talk to someone who made the trip before '49—especially to Oregon. I was up there myself a few months ago. I was considering it for a future home, but I think it's not going to prosper like California."

"That's about what I decided four years ago!" replied Tallman with a smile.

"I only wish that my partner Charley Mulford were here so he could ask you questions, too. But never mind, if you're going to stay around here for a time, I expect he'll be back. This is where the future lies. California's economy depends on gold, and this is the heart of the gold country."

"Right you are, Niles!" laughed Warren Ewer. "Come on—let's drink to the everlasting success of Nevada County—and ourselves!"

III

TO THE WHITE INVADERS, Wema and his people were a continuing source of amusement, conjecture, and concern. On January 25, 1851, Nevada shopkeeper Peter Decker recorded these impressions in his journal:

Indians—the root diggers pass through the streets in gangs with bows and well filled quivers with best of arrows. These Indians though but mere animals are mostly of good physical development, rather less in stature than whites, of a brownish black—bushy heads, rather flat noses broad faces and low foreheads.

Walk erect and have an extraordinary expansion of the chest—much better chest than any people I had seen before. This they develop doubtless by much swimming and diving while young. Can hold breath—that is remain under water as long as I can hold my breath with several efforts. They dive and swim like a duck and then come out and roll and billow around in the deep sand and dust of the river roads for the pleasure of washing off again.

Then sit around each other and pick lice from one anothers heads and eat them. Thus are performed their ablutions.

Five days after Decker made these observations, Luther Schaeffer and some of his Grass Valley friends took a notion to walk out of town on Mill Street until they reached Wema's village. The excursion was "interesting and highly gratifying," he noted, and described the village as follows:

Their encampment was located in a lovely valley, through which ran a neverfailing stream. Their council house was in the centre of the camp; around it were the wigwams, constructed of bark, each having a hole in the centre of the roof, through which issued the smoke from the fire beneath.

The entrance to their *palatial mansions* was an aperture just large enough to admit one person at a time in a stooping posture. On a large rock I noticed several squaws—quite pretty and of fine figure, nearly nude, pounding acorns, out of which they make soup and *bread.*

The ladies were courteous and affable, and were pleased with our visit, but apparently surprised at receiving so much attention from us. When the acorns are fully ripe, the squaws saunter forth, collect immense quantities, place them in their storehouse, and when needed, pound them to a coarse powder, which they prepare in a proper manner for the lazy chiefs.

The chiefs and braves never work, but spend their time in hunting and manufacturing ornaments. Whenever the squaws go out after roots and vegetables they are always accompanied by a brave, as a "guard of honor."

Schaeffer was active in local political affairs. When the county Whig convention was held in Grass Valley on June 18, 1851, he and his fellow delegates were surprised and amused when Chief Wema appeared as an observer. Wrote Schaeffer:

During the morning *Captain* Wemah, head chief of the Indian tribe in our valley, came into the room, and as he took a seat alongside of me, I watched his countenance, feeling curious to know how the proceedings would interest him. The old chief understood about as much of the English language as a Japanese. He sat silent awhile, gazed all around the room, rose, straightened himself, turned around, exclaimed "ugh," and off he marched.

In July Schaeffer again went to Wema's camp to observe a large gathering of Indians from various parts of the county. The miners grew excited as word of the grand "pow wow" or "fandango" was passed around the camps. Schaeffer was anxious to be present when the dancing started, but he was delayed by friends whose business took longer than expected. Said he:

. . . we arrived at the camp *just in time to be too late* for the grand war—dance, in which participated the entire assemblage of chiefs, braves and warriors, many of whom were representatives from distant tribes who had come to attend the all-important "big talk" in relation to the "pale faces."

The squaws were not allowed to indulge in any of the sports, neither were they permitted to come within speaking distance of the council house. Some of the warriors were profusely decorated with fancy colored feathers, beads, shells and trinkets, and liberally daubed with paint.

After resting a short time, the gaily-decked Indians made for the council chamber, which was dimly lighted by a fire in the centre, around which the various delegations squatted in a circle.

"Captain" Wemah, who held the important position of chief over all the Digger Indians, stood in the centre of the party, and when all were quiet—not a whisper to be heard—he commenced his opening and welcome speech, delivering it with wonderful fluency, great vehemence, and wild and violent gesticulations. During his *powerful* address, he was frequently applauded by his well behaved and respectful auditory.

The old chief was dressed in his best suit: his coat, which had been given him by an American soldier, fitted him about as well as the garments that are put on a stick to frighten off the crows from a corn field; in one pocket he had a couple of empty bottles, in the other a huge

CHIEF WEMA

horse pistol, which once might have been a formidable weapon, but now lacked a trigger!

When he had concluded his speech, he called out: "Ven Wol-lupie"—"Si, si, signor." Two stout, well-developed braves seized a tub of *daintily* prepared acorn gruel, and placed it before their delegation; others were called, who followed their example, until every squad was supplied with a tub of gruel; then, at the signal of the "Captain," each Indian dipped his unwashed hands into the delectable food, and gulped down the gruel like a half-starved pig.

After the liberal entertainment was finished, the *Convention* or *Pow Wow* was called to order, and Wemah again addressed the motley crowd, with even more earnestness than before. There were unmistak-able evidences of discontent. The fire in the centre of the council house was fast dying out; the discussion waxed warm; those of the Indians who could not get inside of the chamber clambered on the roof and peeped down the hole in the middle, heedless of the smoke and the vile stench which issued forth in murky clouds.

Wemah danced, frothed and expostulated, but all to no purpose. The "Pow Wow" lost all sense of propriety, and the clever old chief stalked out in apparent disgust. No sooner had his "highness" retired than every "pale face" inside the council was unceremoniously ordered out. . . .

I passed around the camp and stopped in front of Wemah's wigwam. There the old chief lay flat upon his face, his military coat buttoned up to his chin, around him the numerous ladies of his household. Just then a friend called to me; I looked around and found I was the only "pale face" within the camp—the small hours of another day had come around. I hastened to join my companions, when we returned to our wigwams, and sought and found refreshing sleep.

The "big talk" with the pale faces to which Schaeffer made reference was an allusion to the treaties then being negotiated with the tribes of California by the federal government. President Millard Fillmore had appointed three commissioners for this purpose: George W. Barbour, Redick McKee, and O. M. Wozencraft, the latter a former Louisiana physician who was a delegate to California's Constitutional Convention in 1849.

Two treaties had been signed in March and April of 1851, but the slowness of the proceedings and the size of the task which lay ahead caused the commissioners to divide the remaining areas by drawing lots. McKee was to concentrate on the tribes along the northern coast and Oregon border, while Barbour would deal with those in the southern part of the state, except San Diego. Wozencraft was to negotiate treaties with the Indians of the Sierra Nevada and the Sacramento Valley, then go to San Diego.

On July 14, 1851, Wozencraft left Sacramento City in the company of Major McKinstry, Jesse Hambleton, Lieutenant George Stoneman and a troop of United States Army dragoons. Four days later, near Rose's Bar on the Union Ranch, a treaty was accepted by ten chiefs who represented various tribes in the counties of Nevada, Yuba, and Placer, among them being Wema and Walupa.

Under the agreement, in exchange for tools (plows, hoes, spades, picks, axes, hatchets, grindstones, scissors, needles and thimbles), supplies (flour, iron, steel, calico cloth, brown sheeting, thread, yokes, harnesses, and seeds), livestock (oxen, cattle, horses, and mules), and clothing (pantaloons and red flannel shirts for the men and boys, linsey gowns for the women and girls, and a one-and-a-half point Mackinaw blanket for everyone over the age of fifteen), the *nisenan* people were to relinquish all but about 200 square miles of the land which they had occupied for thousands of years.

A line drawn between Long's Bar and Camp Far West would mark the western boundary of the new reservation. It would take in most of the land west of Grass Valley and between the Yuba River on the north and the Bear River on the south, but would exclude the town of Rough and Ready, thanks to an addendum to the agreement. However, the government reserved to itself the right to cross over any portion of the property at any time, plus the right to:

... establish and maintain any military post or posts, public building, school houses, houses for agents, teachers, and such others as they may deem necessary for their use or the protection of the Indians. The said tribes or bands, and each of them, hereby engage that they will never claim any other lands within the boundaries of the United States, nor ever disturb the people of the United States in the free use and enjoyment thereof.

BIBLIOGRAPHY

FOR THOSE PERSONS who wish to read more about Nevada County's early residents the most useful volume (when used in combination with Comstock's *Index*) is *History of Nevada County, California*, edited by Harry L. Wells and first published in 1880 by Thompson and West. Although it was reprinted in a facsimile edition in 1970 by Howell-North Books, copies are now available only from rare book dealers. Nevertheless, many California libraries have copies to which other libraries have access. Bean's 1867 *History and Directory of Nevada County* is useful to researchers and genealogists because of its directory of persons, but most of its historical content is repeated in the 1880 work. A small amount of earlier material is contained in *History of Yuba County, California* (also published by Thompson and West), edited by Chamberlain and Wells.

Among the many published diaries and gold rush memoirs, only a few offer useful descriptions of geography, people, mines, and towns in the Nevada County area. Best are those of Peter Decker, Garrett Low, Luther Schaeffer, John Steele, Luzena Wilson, and Isaac Wistar.

Books about the Overland Trail are plentiful, but I think the finest single source is *The Plains Across*, by John D. Unruh Jr. One can avoid much tedious repetition by first reading this and Holliday's *The World Rushed In* (both were published after my research was ended, unfortunately). However, one should not overlook Alonzo Delano's classic, *Life on the Plains and at the Diggins*, published in 1854.

Not many worthwhile books have been published about the native tribes of the Sierra Nevada. Those authors I recommend (listed in alphabetical order) are Ralph Beals, Heizer and Almquist, Heizer and Whipple, Alfred Kroeber, Theodora Kroeber, Stephen Powers, and the team of Uldall and Shipley. After reading these authors one is better prepared to examine nineteenth century newspapers and diaries, most of which contain information that is misleading at best.

To study Mormon history one should examine Mormon documents, of course, but to achieve a balanced view of the larger context of those events, I suggest also reading such works as Fawn Brodie's *No Man Knows My History*, and De Voto's *The Year of Decision*, Wallace Stegner's *The Gathering of Zion*, and Stanley Vestal's *The Missouri*. While I found Reva Scott's biography of Samuel Brannan enjoyable and useful, her lively style does not always do justice to the events she describes. Only one out-and-out anti-Mormon work is listed here: *Fruits of Mormonism*, written by Nelson Slater and published in Coloma, California, in 1851. Because it describes certain alleged acts of bad treatment of goldseekers by Salt Lake City Mormons, it falls chronologically into the 1845–1851 period. However, I have chosen not to discuss it in this book, but will bring it up later. It is offered here only because of the light it casts on contemporary attitudes. (In the winter of 1851–1852 two otherwise reputable Protestant ministers distributed and promoted the book in Nevada City, a typical example of western Mormon-baiting).

Henry Christman's *Tin Horns and Calico,* and *People Made it Happen Here,* edited by Henrietta Riter, are fine sources of information about life in Albany County, New York, and in the township of Rensselaerville. For a more general look at victorian era life in America I like *The Americans, A Social History of the United States,* by J. C. Furnas, and *The Lady of Godey's,* by Ruth Finley.

Among my favorite books about life in California are *Conquer and Colonize,* by Donald Biggs; Peter Burnett's *Recollections;* Louise Clappe's *The Shirley Letters;* Christiane Fischer's *Let Them Speak for Themselves: Women in the American West;* Lienhard's *A Pioneer at Sutter's Fort;* Sarah Royce's *A Frontier Lady;* Margaret Sanborn's *The American River;* William T. Sherman's *Memoirs;* and a trio by George Stewart: *The California Trail, Ordeal by Hunger,* and *Committee of Vigilance.*

The history of printing and frontier journalism can be explored in *Newspapering in the Old West,* by Karolevitz; Kemble's *A History of California Newspapers;* in Bancroft's histories of California and Oregon; Baird's *California's Pictorial Letter Sheets;* and "Newspapers of the California Northern Mines, 1850–1860," an unpublished Stanford doctoral dissertation by Chester Kennedy. For more detailed information about old handpresses one should read Lewis Allen's *Printing with the Handpress* and James Moran's *Printing Presses.*

The remaining books in this list, each of which contributed in some small or large way to the whole, are works that should be read by anyone interested in becoming well versed in California's beginnings. The fact that I have not mentioned them in this note merely indicates that they are less specific about the subjects named.

BOOKS, MONOGRAPHS AND ARTICLES:

ABELL, ELIZABETH, comp. *Westward, Westward, Westward: The Long Trail West and the Men Who Followed It.* New York: Franklin Watts, Inc., 1958.
ADAMS, JAMES D., ed. *Old Marin with Love: A Collection of Historical Essays.* San Rafael: Marin County American Revolution Bicentennial Commission, 1976.

ADLER, MORTIMER J., CHARLES VAN DOREN and other editors. *The Annals of America.* 18 vols. Chicago: Encyclopaedia Britannica, 1968.

ALLEN, LEWIS M. *Printing with the Handpress.* New York: Van Nostrand Reinhold, 1969.

ALTROCCHI, JULIA COOLEY. *The Old California Trail.* Caldwell, Idaho: The Caxton Printers, 1945.

ANDRIST, RALPH K., and ARCHIBALD, HANN. *The California Gold Rush.* New York: American Heritage Publishing Co., 1961.

ANGEL, MYRON. *History of Placer County, California.* Oakland: Thompson and West, 1882.

ASHTON, WILLIAM F. *Survival in the American Desert: The Mormons' Contribution to Western History.* Buena Park, Calif.: William F. Ashton, ca 1967.

BAIRD, JOSEPH ARMSTRONG, JR. *California's Pictorial letter Sheets 1849–1869.* San Francisco: David Magee, 1967.

BANCROFT, HUBERT HOWE. *History of California.* 7 vols. San Francisco: The History Company, 1884–1890.

BANCROFT, HUBERT HOWE. *History of Oregon.* 2 vols. San Francisco: The History Co., 1886–1888.

BANCROFT, HUBERT HOWE. *Popular Tribunals.* 2 vols. San Francisco. The History Co., 1887.

BARI, VALESKA, comp. *The Course of Empire: First Hand Accounts of California in the Days of the Gold Rush of '49.* New York: Coward-McCann, 1931.

BAUER, HELEN. *California Gold Days.* Garden City: Doubleday, 1954.

BEALS, RALPH L. "Ethnology of the Nisenan," *University of California Publications in American Archaeology and Ethnology,* 31 (1933), 335–413.

BEAN, EDWIN F. *History and Directory of Nevada County, California.* Nevada City: Daily Gazette, 1867.

BENTON, JOSEPH A. *The California Pilgrim: A Series of Lectures.* Sacramento: Solomon Alter, 1853.

BIDLACK, RUSSELL EUGENE. *Letters Home: The Story of Ann Arbor's Forty-Niners.* Ann Arbor: Ann Arbor Publishers, 1960.

BIGGS, DONALD D. *Conquer and Colonize: Stevenson's Regiment and California.* San Rafael: Presidio Press, 1977.

BILLINGTON, RAY ALLEN. *The Far Western Frontier 1830–1860.* New York: Harper and Row, 1956.

BOGGS, MAE HELENE BACON. *My Playhouse Was a Concord Coach.* Oakland: Mae Helene Bacon Boggs, 1942.

BOHAKEL, CHARLES A. *A History of the Empire Mine at Grass Valley.* Nevada City: Nevada County Historical Society, 1968.

BOWMAN, ALAN P. *Index to the 1850 Census of the State of California.* Baltimore: Genealogical Publishing Co. 1972.

BRODIE, FAWN M. *No Man Knows My History.* New York: Alfred A. Knopf, 1945.

BROWN, JOHN EVANS. "Memoirs of an American Gold Seeker in 'Forty-nine': Experiences of a Forty-niner during his Journey across the Continent on Horseback and in Mule and Ox Trains," *The Journal of American History,* II: 1 (1908), 129–154.

BROWNE, LINA FERGUSSON, ed. *J. Ross Browne: His Letters, Journals and Writings.* Albuquerque: University of New Mexico Press, 1969.

BRYANT, EDWIN. *What I Saw in California*. Minneapolis: Ross Haines, 1967 (reprint).

BUCK, FRANKLIN A. *A Yankee Trader in the Gold Rush. The Letters of Franklin A. Buck*, comp. by Katherine A. White. Boston: Houghton Mifflin, 1930.

BURNETT, PETER H. *Recollections and Opinions of an Old Pioneer*. New York: D. Appleton, 1880 (reprinted New York: Da Capo Press, 1969).

CANFIELD, CHAUNCEY L. *The Diary of a Forty-Niner*. Boston: Houghton Mifflin, 1920.

CANFIELD, CHAUNCEY L. *The City of Six*. New York: A.C. McClurg, 1910.

CARTER, KATE B. comp. *Our Pioneer Heritage*. Vol. 6. Salt Lake: Daughters of Utah Pioneers, 1963.

CARTER, KATE B. comp. *Treasurers of Pioneer History*. Vol III. Salt Lake: Daughters of Utah Pioneers, 1954.

CAUGHEY, JOHN WALTON. *California*. New York: Prentice-Hall, 1940.

CAUGHEY, JOHN WALTON. *The California Gold Rush (Gold Is the Cornerstone)*. Berkeley: University of California Press, 1948, 1975.

CENDRARS, BLAISE. *Sutter's Gold*. Trans. from the French by Henry Longan Stuart. New York: Harper and Bros., 1926.

CHAMBERLAIN, WILLIAM H., and HARRY L. WELLS. *History Of Yuba County, California*. Oakland: Thompson and West, 1879.

CHEVER, EDWARD E. "The First Settlement of Yuba City," *Quarterly of The Society of California Pioneers*, IX:4, 227–230.

CHITTENDEN, HIRAM MARTIN. *The American Fur Trade of the Far West*. 2 vols. Stanford: Academic Reprints, 1954 (orig. pub. 1902).

CHRISTMAN, HENRY. *Tin Horns and Calico: A Decisive Episode in the Emergence of Democracy*. New York: Henry Holt, 1945.

CHURCHILL, CHARLES WILLIAM. *Fortunes Are for the Few: Letters of a Forty-niner*. Edited by Duane A. Smith and David J. Weber. San Diego: San Diego Historical Society, 1977.

CLAPPE, LOUISE A. K. S. *The Shirley Letters: Being Letters Written in 1851–1852 from the California Mines*. Santa Barbara: Peregrine Smith, 1970.

CLARK, FRANCIS D. *The First Regiment of New York Volunteers*. New York: George S. Evans, 1882.

CLELAND, ROBERT GLASS. *From Wilderness to Empire: A History of California, 1542–1900*. New York: Alfred A. Knopf, 1944.

CLELAND, ROBERT GLASS. *This Reckless Breed of Men: The Trappers and Fur Traders of the Southwest*. New York: Alfred A. Knopf, 1950.

COMSTOCK, DAVID A., and ARDIS H. COMSTOCK, comp. *Index to 1880 History of Nevada County, California, published by Thompson and West*. Grass Valley: Comstock Bonanza Press, 1979.

COMSTOCK, ESTHER J. *Vallejo and the Four Flags*. Grass Valley: Comstock Bonanza Press, 1979.

CROSS, OSBORNE, and GEORGE GIBBS. *The March of the Mounted Riflemen: First United States Military Expedition to Travel the Full Length of the Oregon Trail* . . . . Edited by Raymond W. Settle. Glendale: The Arthur H. Clark Company, 1940.

DAVIDSON, MARSHALL B. *Life in America*. 2 vols. Boston: Houghton Mifflin and the Metropolitan Museum of Art, 1951.

DAVIS, H. P. *Gold Rush Days in Nevada City.* Nevada City: Berliner and McGinnis, 1948.

DECKER, PETER. *The Diaries of Peter Decker: Overland to California in 1849 and Life in the Mines, 1850–1851.* Edited by Helen S. Giffen. Georgetown: The Talisman Press, 1966.

DELANO, ALONZO. *Life on the Plains and Among the Diggings.* Auburn: Miller, Orton and Mulligan, 1854.

DELAVAN, JAMES. *Notes on California and the Placers, How to Get There, and What to Do Afterwards.* Oakland: Biobooks, 1956 (orig. pub. New York: H. Long & Bro., 1850).

DE VOTO, BERNARD. *Across the Wide Missouri.* Boston: Houghton Mifflin, 1947.

DE VOTO, BERNARD. *The Year of Decision: 1846.* Boston: Little, Brown, 1943.

DICK, EVERETT. *Tales of the Frontier: From Lewis and Clark to the Last Roundup.* Lincoln: University of Nebraska Press, 1963.

DOWNS, JAMES F. *The Two Worlds of the Washo. An Indian Tribe of California and Nevada.* New York: Holt, Rinehart and Winston, 1966.

DUNLOP, RICHARD. *Doctors of the American Frontier.* Garden City: Doubleday, 1965.

DURRENBERGER, ROBERT W. *Patterns on the Land: Geographical, Historical and Political Maps of California.* Palo Alto: National Press Books, Aegeus Publishing, 1965.

EGAN, FEROL. *Frémont: Explorer for a Restless Nation.* Garden City: Doubleday, 1977.

ELDREDGE, ZOETH SKINNER. *The Beginnings of San Francisco.* 2 vols. San Francisco: Zoeth S. Eldredge, 1912.

ESSHOM, FRANK. *Pioneers and Prominent Men of Utah.* Salt Lake: Western Epics, 1966.

FARNHAM, ELIZA W. *California, In-Doors and Out.* New York: Dix, Edwards and Co., 1856.

FERGUSON, CHARLES D. *The Experiences of a Forty-Niner in California (The Experiences of a Forty-niner During 34 Years' Residence in California and Australia).* Edited by Frederick T. Wallace. New York: Arno Press, 1973 (reprint of ed. pub. in Cleveland, Ohio, 1888).

FIELD, STEPHEN J. *California Alcalde: Personal Reminiscences of Early Days in California.* Oakland: Biobooks, 1950 (orig. pub. 1893).

FINLEY, RUTH E. *The Lady of Godey's: Sarah Josepha Hale.* Philadelphia: J. B. Lippincott, 1931.

FISCHER, CHRISTIANE, ed. *Let Them Speak for Themselves: Women in the American West, 1849–1900.* Hamden: The Shoe String Press, 1977.

FRENCH, JOSEPH LEWIS, ed. *The Pioneer West: Narratives of the Westward March of Empire.* Garden City: Garden City Publishing Co., 1937 (Boston: Little, Brown, 1923).

FROST, JOHN. *History of the State of California.* Auburn: Derby and Miller, 185?.

FURNAS, J. C. *The Americans: A Social History of the United States, 1587–1914.* New York: G. P. Putnam's Sons, 1969.

GARNER, WILLIAM ROBERT. *Letters from California 1846–1847.* Edited, with a sketch of the life and times of their author, by Donald Munro Craig. Berkeley: University of California Press, 1970.

GILBERT, FRANK T., HARRY L. WELLS, et al. *Illustrated History of Plumas, Lassen and Sierra Counties, with California from 1513 to 1850.* San Francisco: Fariss and Smith, 1882.

GILMORE, N. RAY, and GLADYS GILMORE. *Readings in California History.* New York: Thomas Y. Crowell, 1966.

GLASSCOCK, C. B. *A Golden Highway.* New York: Bobbs Merrill, 1934.

GREY, WILLIAM (WILLIAM FRANCIS WHITE). *A Picture of Pioneer Times in California.* San Francisco: W. M. Hinton, 1881.

GRINNELL, GEORGE BIRD. *Trails of the Pathfinders.* New York, Charles Scribner's Sons, 1911.

GROH, GEORGE W. *Gold Fever: Being a True Account, Both Horrifying and Hilarious, of the Art of Healing (so-called) During the California Gold Rush.* New York: William Morrow, 1966.

GUDDE, ERWIN G. *California Gold Camps.* Berkeley: University of California Press, 1975.

HANDLIN, OSCAR. *This Was America.* Cambridge: Harvard University Press, 1949.

HART, HERBERT M. *Old Forts of the Far West.* Seattle: Superior Publishing Co., 1965.

HAVEN, CHARLES T., and FRANK A. BELDEN. *A History of the Colt Revolver and the Other Arms Made by Colt's Patent Fire Arms Manufacturing Company from 1836 to 1940.* New York: William Morrow, 1940.

HEIZER, ROBERT F., and ALAN J. ALMQUIST. *The Other Californians: Prejudice and Discrimination under Spain, Mexico, and the United States to 1920.* Berkeley: University of California Press, 1971.

HEIZER, ROBERT F., and MARY ANNE WHIPPLE. *The California Indians: A Source Book.* Second Edition. Berkeley: University of California Press, 1971.

HELPER, HINTON. *Dreadful California (The Land of Gold).* Edited by Lucius Beebe and Charles M. Clegg. Indianapolis: Bobbs-Merrill, 1948 (orig. pub. 1855).

HINES, GUSTAVAS. *Wild Life in Oregon.* New York: Hurst, 1881.

HOLBROOK, STEWART H. *The Columbia.* Rivers of America Series. New York: Rinehart, 1956.

HOLLIDAY, J. S. *The World Rushed In.* New York: Simon and Schuster, 1981.

HORN, HUSTON. *The Pioneers.* The Old West Series. New York: Time-Life Books, 1974.

HOWARD, ROBERT WEST. *This Is the West.* New York: Rand McNally, 1957.

HULBERT, ARCHER BUTLER. *Forty-Niners: The Chronicle of the California Trail.* Boston: Little, Brown, 1931.

HULSE, JAMES W. *The Nevada Adventure: A History.* Reno: University of Nevada Press, 1965.

HUNT, ROCKWELL D. *California's Stately Hall of Fame.* Stockton: College of the Pacific, 1950.

HUNT, ROCKWELL D. *John Bidwell: Prince of California Pioneers.* Caldwell, Idaho: The Caxton Printers, 1942.

JOHNSON, WILLIAM WEBER. *The Forty-Niners.* New York: The Old West Series. New York: Time-Life Books, 1974.

JOHNSTON, WILLIAM G. *Experiences of a Forty-Niner.* New York: Arno Press, 1973 (orig. pub. in Pittsburgh, 1892).

KAROLEVITZ, ROBERT F. *Newspapering in the Old West.* Seattle: The Superior Publishing Co., 1965.

KELLY, CHARLES, and DALE MORGAN. *Old Greenwood: The Story of Caleb Greenwood, Trapper, Pathfinder, and Early Pioneer* (revised edition). Georgetown: The Talisman Press, 1965.

KEMBLE, EDWARD D. *A History of California Newspapers 1846–1858.* Edited by Helen Harding Bretnor. Los Gatos: The Talisman Press, 1962 (reprinted from supplement to the *Sacramento Union* of December 25, 1858).

KINYON, EDMUND. *The Northern Mines.* Grass Valley: The Union Publishing Co., 1949.

KROEBER, ALFRED L. *Handbook of the Indians of California.* New York: Dover, 1976 (orig. pub. by the United States Government Printing Office, Washington, D.C., 1925).

KROEBER, THEODORA. *Ishi in Two Worlds: A Biography of the Last Wild Indian in North America.* Berkeley: University of California Press, 1961, 1976.

LAVENDER, DAVID. *Land of Giants: The Drive to the Pacific Northwest, 1750–1950.* Garden City: Doubleday, 1958.

LAVENDER, DAVID. *Westward Vision: The Story of the Oregon Trail.* New York: McGraw-Hill, 1963.

LAXALT, ROBERT. "The California Trail: To the Rainbow's End," *Trails West.* Washington: National Geographic Society, 1979, pp. 108–143.

LETTS, JOHN M. *California Illustrated.* New York: Wm. Holdredge, 1852.

LIENHARD, HEINRICH. *A Pioneer at Sutter's Fort, 1846–1850.* Translated, edited and annotated by Marguerite Eyer Wilbur. Los Angeles: The Calafia Society, 1941.

LOCKLEY, FRED. *Across the Plains by Prairie Schooner: Personal Narrative of B(enjamin) F(ranklin) Bonney.* Seattle: The Shorey Book Store, 1968 (reprint of 1929 ed.).

LOTCHIN, ROGER W. *San Francisco, 1846–1856: From Hamlet to City.* New York: Oxford University Press, 1974.

LOW, GARRETT W. *Gold Rush by Sea.* Edited by Kenneth Haney. Philadelphia: University of Pennsylvania Press, 1941.

LYNCH, JAMES. *With Stevenson to California 1846–1848.* N. P. 1896. (Reprinted with Francis Clark's "Stevenson's Regiment in California," under the title "The New York Volunteers in California," Glorieta, N.M.: Rio Grande Press, 1970.)

LYNES, RUSSELL. *The Tastemakers.* New York: Harper & Bros., 1955.

MACMULLEN, JERRY. *Paddle-Wheel Days in California.* Stanford: Stanford University Press, 1944.

MARCY, RANDOLPH B. *The Prairie Traveller: A Handbook for Overland Expeditions.* New York: Harper & Bros. 1859 (reprinted Williamstown: Corner House Publishers, 1968).

MARRYAT, FRANK. *Mountains and Molehills, or Recollections of a Burnt Journal.* New York: Harper & Bros., 1855 (reprinted Stanford: Stanford University Press, 1952, with intro. and notes by Marguerite Eyer Wilbur).

McCARRY, CHARLES. "The Mormon Trail: Marching to Zion," in *Trails West.* Washington: National Geographic Society, 1979, pp. 76–107.

M'COLLUM, WILLIAM. *California As I Saw It.* Buffalo: George H. Derby, 1850 (reprinted Los Gatos: The Talisman Press, 1960, edited by Dale L. Morgan).

MCGLASHAN, CHARLES FAYETTE. *History of the Donner Party.* N.P. 1880. (Reprinted Stanford: Stanford University Press, 1940; revised in 1947. Bibliog. and notes by George H. Hinkle and Bliss McGlashan Hinkle. An illustrated edition was published in San Francisco: T. C. Wohlbruck, 1931).

MCKITTRICK, MYRTLE M. *Vallejo, Son of California.* Portland, Oregon: Binfords and Mort, 1944.

MELENDY, H. BRETT, and BENJAMIN F. GILBERT. *The Governors of California.* Georgetown: Talisman Press, 1965.

MORAN, JAMES. *Printing Presses.* Berkeley: University of California Press, 1973.

NORTON, HENRY K. *The Story of California from the Earliest Days to the Present.* Sixth Edition. Chicago: A. C. McClurg, 1923.

OGLESBY, RICHARD J. "Richard J. Oglesby: Forty-Niner—His Own Narrative," in *Papers in Illinois History and Transactions for the Year 1938,* Mildred Eversole, ed. Springfield: The Illinois State Historical Society, 1939. , pp. 158–171.

O'MEARA, WALTER. *Daughters of the Country: The Women of the Fur Traders and Mountain Men.* New York: Harcourt, Brace and World, 1968.

PADEN, IRENE D. *Prairie Schooner Detours.* New York: The MacMillan Co., 1949.

PADEN, IRENE D. *The Wake of the Prairie Schooner.* New York: The MacMillan Co., 1945.

PANCOAST, CHARLES EDWARD. *A Quaker Forty-Niner.* Edited by Anna Paschall Hannum. Philadelphia: University of Pennsylvania Press, 1930.

PARKMAN, FRANCIS JR. *The Oregon Trail: Sketches of Prairie and Rocky Mountain Life.* New York: Educational Publishing Co., 1912 (orig. pub. 1846–47 in serial form and 1849 in book).

PAUL, RODMAN W. *California Gold.* 2nd edition. Lincoln: University of Nebraska Press, 1967 (orig. pub. 1947).

PETER, KATHERINE, and JAMES J. JONES. *Voices of the Californians.* Sacramento: State Dept. of Education, 1971.

PERKINS, ELISHA DOUGLASS. *Gold Rush Diary.* Edited by Thomas D. Clark. Lexington: University of Kentucky Press, 1967.

POWERS, STEPHEN. *Tribes of California.* Berkeley: University of California Press, 1976 (reprint of 1877 ed. by The United States Government Printing Office).

RASMUSSEN, LOUIS J. *San Francisco Ship Passenger Lists.* 4 vols. Colma: San Francisco Historic Record & Genealogy Bulletin, 1965–1970.

RITER, HENRIETTA, ed. *People Made It Happen Here: History of the Town of Rensselaerville ca. 1788–1950.* Rensselaerville, N. Y.: The Rensselaerville Historical Society, 1977.

ROBERTSON, FRANK C. *Fort Hall: Gateway to the Oregon Country.* New York: Hastings House, 1963.

ROBINSON, FAYETTE. *California and Its Gold Regions.* New York: Stringer and Townsend, 1849 (reprinted New York: Promontory Press, 1974).

ROWE, JOSEPH ANDREW. *California's Pioneer Circus: Memoirs and Personal Correspondence Relative to the Circus Business Through the Gold Country in the Fifties.* Edited by Albert Dressler. San Francisco: Albert Dressler, 1926.

ROYCE, JOSIAH. *California from the Conquest in 1846 to the Second Vigilance Committee in San Francisco.* New York: Alfred A. Knopf, 1948 (orig. pub. Boston: Houghton Mifflin, 1886).

ROYCE, SARAH. *A Frontier Lady: Recollections of the Gold Rush and Early California.* Edited by Ralph Henry Gabriel. New Haven: Yale University Press, 1932 (reprinted Lincoln: University of Nebraska Press, 1977).

SANBORN, MARGARET. *The American: River of El Dorado.* Rivers of America Series. New York: Holt, Rinehart and Winston, 1974.

SAWYER, LORENZO. *Way Sketches.* New York: Edward Eberstadt, 1926.

SCAMEHORN, HOWARD L., ed. *The Buckeye Rovers in the Gold Rush: An Edition of Two Diaries.* Athens: Ohio University Press, 1965.

SCHAEFFER, LUTHER MELANCHTON. *Sketches of Travels in South America, Mexico and California.* New York: James Egbert, 1860.

SCOTT, REVA. *Samuel Brannan and the Golden Fleece: San Francisco's Forgotten Jason.* New York: The MacMillan Co., 1944.

SEARLS, NILES. *Diary of a Pioneer and Other Papers.* San Francisco: Robert Searls, 1940.

SENGSTACKEN, AGNES RUTH. *Destination West.* Portland, Oregon: Binfords and Mort, 1942.

SEVERSON, THOR. *Sacramento: An Illustrated History 1839–1874.* San Francisco: California Historical Society, 1973.

SHERMAN, WILLIAM TECUMSEH. *Memoirs.* 2 vols. New York: D. Appleton, 1875.

SHINN, CHARLES HOWARD. *Mining Camps: A Study in American Frontier Government.* New York: Alfred A. Knopf, 1948 (orig. pub. New York: Scribners, 1885).

SHUCK, OSCAR T., ed. *Representative and Leading Men of the Pacific.* San Francisco: Bacon and Co., 1870.

SINGLETARY, OTIS A. *The Mexican War.* Chicago: The University of Chicago Press, 1960.

SLATER, NELSON. *Fruits of Mormonism.* Coloma: Harmon and Springer, 1851.

SOULE, FRANK, JOHN H. GIHON, and JAMES NISBET. *The Annals of San Francisco and History of California.* Together with the continuation through 1855, compiled by Dorothy H. Huggins, and index by Charles H. Goehring. Palo Alto: Lewis Osborne, 1966.

STEELE, JOHN. *In Camp and Cabin: Mining Life and Adventure in California During 1850 and Later.* Lodi, Wisconsin: John Steele, 1901 (reprinted New York: Citadel Press, 1962).

STEGNER, WALLACE. *The Gathering of Zion: The Story of the Mormon Trail.* New York: McGraw-Hill, 1964.

STEGNER, WALLACE. "The Oregon Trail: Road to Destiny," in *Trails West.* Washington: National Geographic Society, 1979. pp. 40–75.

STEWART, GEORGE R. *The California Trail: An Epic with Many Heroes.* New York: McGraw-Hill, 1962.

STEWART, GEORGE R. *Committee of Vigilance.* Boston: Houghton Mifflin, 1964.

STEWART, GEORGE R. *Donner Pass and Those Who Crossed It.* San Francisco: California Historical Society, 1964.

STEWART, GEORGE R. *Good Lives.* Boston: Houghton Mifflin, 1967.

STEWART, GEORGE R. *Ordeal by Hunger* (with Supplement). Boston: Houghton Mifflin, 1960.

STONE, IRVING. *Men to Match My Mountains: The Opening of the Far West 1840–1900.* Garden City: Doubleday, 1956.

STREET, FRANKLIN. *California in 1850.* Cincinnati: R. E. Edwards, 1851 (reprinted New York: Promontory Press, 1974).

STREETER, FLOYD BENJAMIN. *The Kaw: The Heart of a Nation.* The Rivers of America Series. New York: Farrar & Rinehart, 1941.

SWASEY, WILLIAM F. *The Early Days and Men of California.* Oakland: Pacific Press, 1891.

SWISHER, CARL BRENT. *Stephen J. Field: Craftsman of the Law.* Washington: The Brookings Institution, 1930.

TAYLOR, BAYARD. *Eldorado, or Adventures in the Path of Empire.* New York: George P. Putnam, 1850.

TEMPLETON, SARDIS. *The Lame Captain: The Life and Adventures of Pegleg Smith.* Los Angeles: Westernlore Press, 1965.

ULDALL, HANS JORGEN, and WILLIAM SHIPLEY. *Nisenan Texts and Dictionary.* Berkeley: University of California Press, 1966.

UNRUH, JOHN D. JR. *The Plains Across: The Overland Emigrants and the Trans-Mississippi West 1840–60.* Urbana: University of Illinois Press, 1979.

VAN EVERY, DALE. *The Final Challenge: The American Frontier 1804–1845.* New York: William Morrow, 1964.

VESTAL, STANLEY. *Joe Meek: The Merry Mountain Man.* Caldwell, Idaho: The Caxton Printers, 1952.

VESTAL, STANLEY. *The Missouri.* The Rivers of America Series. New York: Farrar and Rinehart, 1945.

VIOLETTE, EUGENE MORROW. *A History of Missouri.* Cape Girardeau, Missouri: Ramfre Press, 1957 (reprint of 1918 ed.).

WALLACE, IRVING. *The Twenty-seventh Wife.* New York: Simon and Schuster, 1961.

WATSON, JAMES TOMPKINS. "Across the American Continent in a Caravan— Reminiscences of Captain Joseph Aram," *The Journal of American History,* I:4 (1907), 623–632.

WEBB, CATHERINE J. *A Family History of California.* Berkeley: Catherine Webb, 1975.

WEBB, CATHERINE J. *History Reconstructed: Stories of Tallman, Ianthus, Horace and Samuel (Rolfe).* Berkeley: Catherine Webb, 1978.

WEBER, SHIRLEY H. *Schliemann's First Visit to America, 1850–51.* Cambridge: Harvard University Press, 1942.

WELLS, HARRY L., J. ALBERT WILSON, H. B. RICE, and ALLEN M. FREEMAN. *History of Nevada County, California.* Oakland: Thompson and West, 1880.

WHITSELL, LEON O. *One Hundred Years of Freemasonry in California.* 3 vols. San Francisco: Grand Lodge F & AM of California, 1950.

WILKINS, JAMES F. *An Artist on the Overland Trail: The 1849 Diary and Sketches of James F. Wilkins.* Edited by John Francis McDermott. San Marino: The Huntington Library, 1968.

WILSON, LUZENA STANLEY. *Luzena Stanley Wilson '49er: Memories Recalled Years Later for Her Daughter Correnah Wilson Wright.* Oakland: The Eucalyptus Press, Mills College, 1937.

WISTAR, ISAAC JONES. *Autobiography.* New York: Harper and Bros., 1937 (orig. pub. 1914).

Woods, Daniel B. *Sixteen Months at the Gold Diggings*. New York: Harper and Bros., 1851 (reprinted New York: Arno Press, 1973).

Woodward, W. E. *The Way Our People Lived*. New York: E. P. Dutton, 1944.

Wray, Ken, ed. *100 Years of Nevada County*. Nevada City: Nevada City Nugget, 1951.

DOCUMENTARY SOURCES

Newspapers:
The Californian, 1846–1848.
California Star, 1847–1848.
Alta California, 1849–1851.
Placer Times, 1849–1851.
Marysville Herald, 1850–1851.
Sacramento Transcript, 1850–1851.
Nevada Journal, 1851.
The Salt Lake Tribune, April–July 1934. ("Day by Day with the Utah Pioneers," by Andrew Jenson.)

Legal Documents:

California Constitution of 1849.

Private Correspondence:

Letters from Niles Searls to Polly Niles, Cornelia Niles, Mary Niles, and Addison Niles, October 22, 1844 to November 30, 1852.

Letter from Polly Niles to John Niles, December 22, 1839.

Letter from Polly Niles to Cornelia Niles, ca November 1848.

Letters from Charles Mulford to Cornelia Niles, Mary Niles, and Addison Niles, April 14, 1844, to February 23, 1851.

Letters from Addison Niles to Cornelia Niles and Mary Niles, July 2, 1846, to June 26, 1851.

Letters from Cornelia Niles to Addison Niles, Mary Niles, Guly Titus, Niles Searls, and Polly Niles, August 1, 1846, to July 20, 1851.

Letters from Mary Niles to Cornelia Niles and Addison Niles, May 11, 1848, to March 9, 1851.

Letter from Nancy Niles to Mary Niles, September 11, 1848.

Letter from Nancy Niles to Polly Niles, October 22, 1847.

Letters from Deborah Wickes to Harriet Rider, Mary Niles, and Cornelia Niles, ca June 1, 1848, to August 31, 1851.

Letter from Alice Searls to Cornelia Niles, February 18, 1849.

Letter from John Niles to Cornelia Niles, June 15, 1848.

Letter from John Niles to Addison Niles, November 24, 1850.

Letter from Abram Searls to John Niles, April 5, 1850.

Letter from William D. Williams to Cornelia Niles, February 24, 1851.

Unpublished Manuscripts:

Kennedy, Chester Barrett. "Newspapers of the California Northern Mines, 1850–1860; A Record of Life, Letters and Culture." Ph.D. dissertation. Stanford University, 1949.

Lopes, Frank Albert. "A History of Grass Valley, California." M. A. thesis. Sacramento State College, 1956.

INDEX

THIS BOOK WAS DESIGNED
AND ILLUSTRATED BY THE AUTHOR.
COMPOSITION BY DWAN TYPOGRAPHY.
TEXT SET IN SABON EXTRACTS IN
ITC CHELTENHAM BOOK, TITLES AND SUBHEADS IN
POSTER BODONI ITALIC, INITIALS IN BANK SCRIPT.
PRINTED ON GLATFELTER B-16 NATURAL TEXT,
BASIS 50, BY THOMSON-SHORE, INC.

ABOUT THE AUTHOR

David Allan Comstock is a writer, painter, and designer of books who lives in a remote corner of California's Sierra Nevada forest, miles from the nearest utility lines. He and his wife Ardis built their six-sided, pole-supported house in the early 1970s; they cook and heat with wood, read by oil lamps, and in many respects share the lifestyle of pioneers described in his books. The Comstocks jointly compiled *Index to the 1880 History of Nevada County* and *Nevada County Vital Statistics, 1850–1859,* while researching his books.

BRIDES OF THE GOLD RUSH

This sequel to *Gold Diggers and Camp Followers* is a true account of life in the 1850s, when California's three largest cities were San Francisco, Sacramento and Nevada City. It continues the stories of Tallman Rolfe, Niles Searls, Charley Mulford, and their eastern cousins and friends. Niles and Charley marry hometown sweethearts and bring them to Nevada City. Simmon Storms and David Bovyer, novice Indian traders from New England, befriend Chief Wema and try with mixed success to shield the nisenan tribes from invading whites and their diseases.

As in *Gold Diggers and Camp Followers* Comstock relies heavily on a rare collection of letters written by residents of Rensselaerville and Nevada City in the 19th century. In addition, three lively newspapers prospered in Nevada County in this period, and microfilm records are in plentiful supply.

The 1850s were exciting and formative years for an amazing parade of ambitious young men and women, and many, like William M. Stewart, Aaron Sargent, George Hearst, and Edward D. Baker, became important figures in American history. The leading talents of the time regularly performed in local theaters, and the notorious dancer Lola Montez, once the intimate friend of Franz Liszt and the King of Bavaria, for a time lived at Grass Valley, Nevada City's neighboring town.

Brides of the Gold Rush is available from Comstock Bonanza Press, 18919 William Quirk Memorial Drive, Grass Valley, CA 95945.